To Roger

With Warm Good Wishes

and Happy memories of earlier days

of enjoyment together

[signature]

Flight Path

Flight Path

the autobiography of
Sir Peter Masefield

with
Bill Gunston

Airlife
England

Copyright © 2002 Sir Peter Masefield & Bill Gunston

First published in the UK in 2002
by Airlife Publishing Ltd

British Library Cataloguing-in-Publication Data
A catalogue record for this book
is available from the British Library

ISBN 1 84037 283 4

Typeset by Phoenix Typesetting, Ilkley, West Yorkshire.
Printed in England by Biddles Ltd., www.biddles.co.uk

Airlife Publishing Ltd
101 Longden Road, Shrewsbury, SY3 9EB England
E-mail: airlife@airlifebooks.com
Website: www.airlifebooks.com

Foreword by Bill Gunston,
OBE, FRAeS

This book is the result of collaboration. Sir Peter had several times begun to write his life story. Eventually he asked me to assist. Most of the earlier chapters are based on his own draft notes compiled over many years. The rest are based on conversations I have had with him, on notes contributed by Lady Masefield and members of his family, and on many other sources. For the sake of continuity, and because I believe it reads better, the entire work is written in the first person.

I would like to thank Sir Peter for his generous trust and close co-operation; Lady Masefield and Sir Charles for their helpful comments; and especially Richard Masefield for going beyond the line of duty in helping in every way possible.

Preface

This book is really a collection of memories over a period of more than 80 years. For example, in 1917, when I was three, I remember walking along the beach at Lytham St Annes in Lancashire and coming upon a magic thing. From my precious rag book of pictures of aeroplanes I recognised it as a biplane which had crash-landed. From that moment I was interested in aeroplanes, but what really made me determined to make aviation my life was finding a Siskin fighter of RAF No 12 Squadron rolled into a ball in one of my father's hospital fields in 1926 (the pilot had parachuted to safety). Or perhaps it was the breathtaking beauty of a Bristol Bulldog fighter at the 1929 Olympia Aero Show in London.

Since then I have been fortunate beyond belief. Unlike most people I have had not one career in aviation but a succession of totally different ones. At school I organised an aviation club and built and flew model aircraft. I then took a degree in Engineering and became an aircraft designer. I have worked at the bench, helping to build aircraft and also to maintain them in service. I have been a journalist, an editor and a war correspondent, both in the front line in France in 1939 and in B-17 Flying Fortresses of the US Army Air Force in 1943 and 1944. I played a central role in developing the crucial wartime subject of aircraft recognition. I have been a Civil Servant, an Air Attaché and Secretary of a War Cabinet Committee. I have run airlines (British European Airways and British Caledonian) and aircraft manufacturing companies (Bristol Aircraft and the Beagle Group). I have run airports (the British Airports Authority) and the monolithic London Transport.

Additionally I have been President of the Royal Aeronautical Society, the Royal Society of Arts, the Royal Aero Club, and involved with so many other organisations I have collected them into the final chapter. This still left time for me to fly 126 types of aircraft – all of them interesting, and some much better than others – and to fly as passenger in approximately 350. I also wrote a book, about great airships and their tragic problems.

My friend, Bill Gunston OBE has written more than that, and has been a most expert and kindly help in drawing together all the disparate threads to produce this biography. Without him it could not have been done.

I am reminded that about 650 years ago Geoffrey Chaucer wrote:

> 'The lyf so short, the craft so long to lerne,
> Th' assay so hard, so sharp the conquerynge.'

And about a century ago George Santayana wrote:

> 'There is no cure for birth and death, save to enjoy the interval.'

The formative years

I was born at 2.15 a.m. on Thursday 19 March 1914. I was strictly non-airworthy, but some strenuous semi-aerobatic swinging around – performed by Dr Hilda Northcroft, a family friend from New Zealand – caused me to take a surprised breath and see what the world had to offer. I was given the Christian names Peter Gordon. One of my earliest memories is of helping my nursemaid, Jessie Oldacre, to polish the big brass plate on the gatepost of our home, Tolima, No 10 Albert Road, Trentham, in North Staffordshire, in England's Midlands. The plate said DR W. G. MASEFIELD MRCS LRCP, DPM.

There were a lot of Masefields, the most famous having been my cousin John, who from 1930 to 1967 was Poet Laureate. One family tradition has it that the name originated at the Battle of Maserfield, fought in May 641 near Oswestry in Shropshire, at which the Pagan Penda defeated and killed the Christian King Oswald, to establish Mercia as the dominant Anglo-Saxon kingdom.

In our family it was easy to make history come very much alive. My paternal grandfather, John Richard Beech Masefield, owned a large house, Rosehill, standing in 30 acres of grounds at Cheadle, ten miles from Trentham. He told me that in 1851, at the age of 14 months, he travelled with his parents by train to London, to visit the Great Exhibition at the Crystal Palace in Hyde Park.

He went on to say that news of Wellington's victory at Waterloo had been brought to his own father by the mail coach. An earlier coach had taken his great-grandfather, William Masefield, to London in 1745. Returning home in December of that year, William had been prevented from celebrating his 18th birthday on 6 December 1745, because the Duke of Cumberland's troops were billeted in all the local inns. They were there to repel a horde of wild highlanders, who were rampaging south, led by Prince Charles Stuart, whom my ancestor certainly did not think of as *Bonnie* Prince Charlie! Fortunately, Derby was as far as the feared clansmen got, or I might never have existed.

My grandfather was a local Justice of the Peace, and head of Blagg, Son & Masefield, solicitors, of Cheadle. With his wife Susan (née Blagg) he raised two boys and three girls. His eldest son, Charles, was expected to inherit the business. The second son, William Gordon, chose to be a doctor, and from autumn 1904 trained at the Middlesex Hospital in London. He found comfortable lodgings in a house run by the Misses Mary Ann and Louie Price. Visiting there in 1904 was a family named Lloyd-Owen.

They had recently returned from 11 years in Australia, where as a consultant mining engineer Edmund Lloyd-Owen had contracts to develop two large coal mines near Ipswich, in Queensland. It so happened that Lloyd-Owen's second daughter, Marian, took a shine to the young medical student, and the feeling was soon reciprocated.

Flight Path

My grandparents' house in Staffordshire – Rosehill.

Lloyd-Owen's next assignment was in Colombia, and in 1909 the intrepid family left Bogota and crossed the Plain of Tolima to a mercury mine high in the Andes. In early 1912 the newly qualified Dr Masefield followed them, and returned with his fiancée, who like him was aged 27. On 13 August 1912 they embarked on a marriage which was to last almost 62 years.

My father was able to purchase a general practice at Trentham. Like most young men, his brother Charles joined up soon after the outbreak of war in August 1914. My father was needed in England as a doctor, and in May 1915 I was followed into the world by my brother David. Unlike most doctors at that time, my father did his rounds in a car, a Model T Ford. However, by mid-1916 he decided that his duty lay in the Army (my mother had always insisted 'Your country may need you, but your family needs you *more*!').

PGM with his parents, 1914.

He naturally joined the Royal Army Medical Corps, and was soon attached to the King's Royal Rifle Corps (KRRC). With his departure, my mother took her two boys to stay in a house just one field away from my grandparents at Rosehill.

Life in those days was at a slow pace. Each morning my grandfather would get up at 5 o'clock – a practice I find I have continued – and do a few household tasks, bathe and dress. He would then walk the mile or so to Cheadle town. Here he would buy *The Times* and a local paper, and then visit the barber's to be shaved with a great cut-throat razor, and occasionally have his hair trimmed. He was then ready for the day. After walking back to Rosehill he would take his dog for a turn round the house, and then at about 7.30 come in for breakfast. His routine was the same all through the year.

In August 1917 my father was at a training camp at Blackpool. He was given embarkation leave before sailing from Folkestone for France, and I went with my mother and grandmother to join him. We stayed at the Queen's Hotel at Lytham St Annes. I was excited to see aeroplanes, lots of them, flying from nearby Squire's Gate aerodrome.

One particular day is as vivid in my memory as if it were yesterday. Thursday, 19 August was bright and sunny, the sea was blue, and the air crystal clear. We would

Peter and David on the beach at Lytham St Annes, with their father about to go to War.

have enjoyed it, but my parents received a War Office telegram saying that my Uncle Charlie was 'missing, severely wounded and a prisoner of war'. Deeply distressed, we went for a stroll along the sand dunes. Suddenly I found that, right in front of us, was an aeroplane. Painted yellow, it had smashed its undercarriage. It might have been an Avro 504, but the image that sticks in my mind is more like a B.E.2c. Such aircraft were easily splintered. This encounter had a profound effect on directing the course of my life.

Uncle Charles had joined the 5th North Staffords. At the Battle of Loos he had led an audacious and successful assault on a German front-line position, and won an immediate Military Cross. Only a few weeks later he and his platoon were surrounded, and we later learned that, on 2 July 1917, he had died in a German field hospital.

My father also had a distinguished career, and, unlike most of his fellow-officers, he survived. He was demobilised from the Army of Occupation in Germany in March 1919, the Colonel of the 20th KRRC writing 'He is all that a regimental doctor should be and has always set a splendid example to the younger officers.'

In May 1919 my father was appointed Junior Assistant Medical Officer at Severalls Mental Hospital, north of Colchester, Essex. The family, which by now included 2-year-old Stephen, moved there from Cheadle. The furniture went by van, while we began the journey in a horse-drawn cab. I vividly remember how the cab's velvet-lined interior smelled of mothballs, and as it had rubber tyres I could clearly hear the clip-clop of the hooves. Next, we boarded a train, pulled by a Midland Railway 4-4-0 Compound locomotive in gleaming crimson livery.

Until proper quarters could be found at Severalls we moved into rented accommodation at Daniel's Farm, Great Horkesley. In 1919 it was still common for a house to have no electricity, but that farm had hardly changed in the previous 100 years, and it had no gas or running water either. Life revolved around chamber pots, and hip baths filled with jugs of water heated on the kitchen range. Each day David and I would walk a mile to receive lessons from a Miss Lena Stagg. Though I was only five, I noticed that she was not only good at her job but also decorative.

In August 1920 we were able to move into a flat above the main entrance in the

Centre House at the hospital. At least we had electricity, gas, and a proper bathroom with hot water. On 1 February 1921 father was appointed Deputy Medical Superintendent. David and I used to play with many other small boys, and in an old notebook of David's I found the roll-call of THE GRAND ARMY. I headed the list, as 'General Peter Gordon Masefield'. Next came 'Colonel Tommy Hammond', and some way down was 'Captain David Masefield', followed by various privates.

Sadly, in September 1922 THE GRAND ARMY was disbanded when I went as a weekly boarder to a Prep school, Holmwood House, near Lexden. I was homesick, especially for David's company. Whenever I could, I went to the end of the school's approach drive, to gaze mournfully at Severalls' brick water tower four miles away.

Holmwood House was run by a couple named Duggan, but the most respected member of staff was Assistant Master N.O.R. Sergeant. Recently demobilised from the Army, he typified the enthusiastic Boy Scout leader. He could bring history to life, and held my rapt attention, as, with coloured chalks, he explained in detail what happened at Waterloo in 1815 and on the Somme 101 years later. On Saturday mornings we would all gather round the piano and do our best with 'Land of Hope and

Peter (right) and David at Severalls in 1921.

Glory', 'Rule Britannia', 'Annie Laurie', 'The Old Folks at Home' and 'Little Grey Home in the West'.

On 7 May 1925 David was cycling when he was struck by a car. The car's door handle caused a terrible injury from which my brother died two days later. He had been my constant companion throughout childhood. His death left me bereft and lonely, and for my final Summer Term at Holmwood my parents allowed me to be a Day Boy.

Each morning I would cycle to Colchester railway station, where I would catch a tram and go to the terminus just beyond Lexden. From there I would walk a mile and a half to the school. In the evening I would buy a halfpenny bar of chocolate to consume on the open upper deck of the tram, and then retrieve my bike for the ride home.

Three months after David's death our depleted family spent ten days on holiday at Rosehill. While my mother and Stephen went by train, I accompanied my father in his new open-top four-seat Rover 10, taking two days in each direction. We stayed at a hotel in Baldock, and happened to have dinner with an American couple touring England. They kept us enraptured with glowing accounts of 'God's Own Country', which I made an early resolution to visit as soon as possible.

We returned to a new address: Centre House, Brentwood Mental Hospital, at which my father had been appointed Medical Superintendent. The BMH was again in Essex, but Brentwood was 30 miles nearer London, and rapidly growing into a suburb. Our

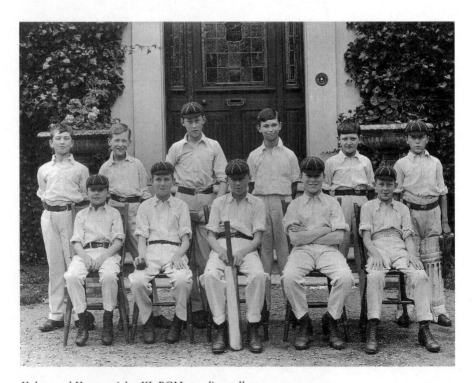

Holmwood House cricket XI, PGM standing tallest.

family also included Cinders, a little grey pony who often pulled my mother in a four-seat trap, a little Cairn terrier named Bran, and a beautiful and affectionate cat named Teddy.

The BMH was enormous, with over 2,000 patients. My father had the courage to do something without precedent: insist that those patients who were judged to be harmless should be allowed almost complete freedom. They were absorbed into the households of the doctors, taught how to help in the house and grounds, service machinery on the hospital farm, and generally prepare themselves to be useful citizens when they were ready to leave. This work eventually brought my father a CBE, and Presidency of the Royal Psychological Society.

In September 1925, I started as a Day Boy in form Upper II at Brentwood School, under Headmaster Jimmy Hough. Whereas Holmwood House had barely 30 boys in all, Brentwood's large, cold and remote classrooms housed up to 40 each, and the total was about 700.

For my 12th birthday my grandmother at Rosehill gave me an appropriately sized longbow, a quiver of arrows and a straw target, which gave me many hours of enjoyment. I also spent hours listening to that newer invention, the wireless (radio). In 1925 the family started with a cat's-whisker receiver, but progressed to a proper set with valves and a loudspeaker. Before long I tuned in to 900 metres and listened enthralled to Croydon Tower in two-way conversation with Handley Page W.8 and W.10 airliners.

I spent my pocket money constructing a Gauge-0 railway in our dimly-lit attic. At Christmas 1928 I was given a Meccano set, and I also began making a wooden Blériot XI monoplane. At the BMH there was a full-scale monoplane which had been made many years earlier for a New Year's Eve dance. With the help of a cousin and my brother Stephen I modified it into a fair representation of a Blériot. It was built around my bicycle, but I could never pedal quite hard enough to get airborne!

In 1926 the BMH was building a new house for the Medical Superintendent, in hospital grounds alongside the road to Warley. With four bedrooms and a kitchen fitted with what then were innovations, it even had electric light throughout. We moved in early in 1927, and named our new home Greenwoods.

Soon afterwards, on my 13th birthday, I was given a kit from which one could construct a balsa-wood and card model of a Blackburn Velos torpedo-bomber seaplane. Little did I think that in my first full-time job I would help to design a Velos successor, the Swordfish.

In October 1926 I passed the entrance examination to Westminster School (its proper name is the Royal College of St Peter). In July 1927 I was taken to the school, in Dean's Yard, beside the Abbey. There I joined an apprehensive group of aspiring new boys, who one by one were led away from a room where we were all doing a stiff written examination, and conducted to the awesome presence of the Headmaster.

Capped and gowned, Dr Costly White examined each boy's background, his hobbies and knowledge of the Scriptures, and finally asked each to repeat 'How now, brown cow?' and 'The Warm baby on a cold slab had hiccups; he was covered with handfuls of white handkerchiefs'. It was evident that, though dulcet tones north of Berwick, west of Fishguard or south of Dover might be admissable, the *only* English accents expected were those of Oxford or Cambridge.

On the grey afternoon of 16 January 1928 I found myself one of 13 new boys, all wearing a stiff wing collar and black tie, black waistcoat, striped trousers, tailcoat and black top hat. I was accompanied by a trunk and regulation tuck-box. I found myself assigned to Rigaud's House, in Little Dean's Yard, under form-master Basil Hardy.

I discovered that each new boy became the 'Shadow' of an older boy, called his 'Substance'. My Substance was Charles Boggis-Rolf, whose task it was to instil into me all the quirks and practices peculiar to the School and each House, including the nicknames of the many masters. Of course, the most junior boys could be summoned to serve as fags (servants) to seniors.

As fag for Max Aitken, son of Lord Beaverbrook and four years my senior, I foolishly cooked a can of baked beans on his study fire without first opening it. When it exploded, it plastered the walls and ceiling with not only the contents but also live coals. I might even have got away with this, but the beans utterly ruined a prized letter sent to Max by the famous racing driver who was soon to become Sir Malcolm Campbell.

This was serious, and I was lucky to be awarded the mild sentence of 'three of the best'. With my posterior draped over an armchair, before a full assembly of House Prefects, I first received a 'sighting shot' from Graham, the Head of House. Of course this was deadly accurate. As the injured party, Max was allowed the other two. His first stroke missed my posterior, and instead swept the House cups off the mantlepiece with a shattering crash – to the delight of the serried ranks of the Junior Common Room, whose ears were applied to the door. His next swipe was painfully accurate, but I got away with two out of three because Westminster's rules allowed no substitute for an abortive swing.

I was then sent, sorely smarting, to Victoria Street Post Office to dispatch a telegram of good wishes to Mr Campbell for his Land Speed Record attempt at Daytona Beach, Florida. In fact, he had already set a new record, at 206.06 mph, on the previous day, 20 February 1928. Years later I was to know well the father of Max and the son of Sir Malcolm.

On 6 October 1927 I took my first step along the road leading to a life of aviation. I was taken by my father to the Royal Aeronautical Society in Albemarle Street. In their conference room, wide-eyed at the back, I listened to Frederick Handley Page hold forth on 'Aviation's future'. Then the meeting's Chairman rose to his feet to open the discussion. Tall, urbane Lord Thomson of Cardington, the former Secretary of State for Air, said 'Not long ago, all we have heard this evening would have sounded like a fairy story . . . aeroplanes and airships plying the air routes of the world, turning lands throughout the Empire into realms of gold.'

It made a great impression on a boy of 13. Little did I think that the noble Lord would die in one of his airships, and that I would write a book explaining what happened.

I naturally became an enthusiastic member of the School OTC (Officers' Training Corps). On 3 February 1928 we cadets were privileged to line the final 100 yards of the route into the Abbey of Earl Haig's funeral procession. We had no difficulty holding back the sombre crowd, while a single Abbey bell tolled mournfully. I vividly recall the long blue coat and huge white moustaches of *Maréchal* Foch, and of the late Field Marshal's horse being led up to the Abbey with its master's boots reversed in the stirrups.

On a happier occasion, we marched out of Dean's Yard to enjoy a Field Day. Trailing a line of traffic behind us, we marched to Victoria Station and went by private train to Amberley, in Sussex. Here we marched with sloped arms for two miles, in a biting wind, before engaging in battle from copse to copse against Lancing College, firing off hundreds of rounds from our SMLE rifles. Nothing could have been less like real war, but it did bear a resemblance to the 1870 Zulu War in which our Colonel's father had served.

Even a brief spell at Westminster left an indelible impression. Morning prayers in the choir stalls of the Abbey, with the Lord's Prayer in Latin. Roll-call at the two great stones at the entrance to 'up school'. Cricket on Vincent Square, and soccer in Dean's Yard. The OTC armoury in the Cloisters, and drill in Little Dean's Yard. The spartan wooden benches, bare boards and lockers of the Junior Common Room. The frantic rush to answer a fagging call. Always, each quarter of an hour, the boom of Big Ben.

I had at last become acclimatised to the famous clock, so that I could sleep at night in the 20-bed Junior Dormitory of Rigaud's House, when I was laid low by a severe attack of measles. This was followed by a chronic ear infection. So severe was this that, in summer 1929, my parents decided to remove me from the Thames marshes after a mere three terms, totalling 36 weeks. After a period being tutored at home, I was sent in September 1929 to the bracing English school in Switzerland.

Despite my sufferings, 1929 was for me an *annus mirabilis*. When the year started, I imagined I would gain my Certificate A in the Westminster OTC and proceed to the Royal Military Academy at Woolwich to begin my career as a gunner. It was not to be like that. All through that glorious summer of 1929 my life revolved around aviation.

The last great British indoor Aero Show was held in London's Olympia, and I was there. I was captivated by the speedy fighters: the Bristol Bulldog, Hawker Hornet (predecessor of the Fury) and Fairey Firefly. As, a little earlier, Sir Sefton Brancker said of the young Alan Cobham, 'Ever since he was exposed to this environment, there is no doing anything with him where aeroplanes are concerned.'

It set me on a new course in life. The RAF Pageant was held at Hendon, and my father took me there. A new airport, called an Air Park, was opened at Heston by Nigel Norman and Alan Muntz, and I was there. Over the new airport a Siskin fighter of the RAF performed a brilliant display. It landed, taxied close to me and stopped. The pilot got out and, seeing my admiring look, said 'A good 'plane, but a wee bit draughty.' Later I was to run a great airline, and that pilot was to be my Chairman.

The Schneider Trophy air race was competed for at Cowes, and my father took me to watch from the end of Southsea Pier. The giant new airship R.100 flew over Greenwoods only about 200 feet above the ground. Each week I devoured *The Aeroplane*, and each month *The Meccano Magazine*. I scored a couple of 50s playing grown-up cricket for my father's hospital. Events crowded one upon the other. The grass aerodromes were alive with the sound of colourful new aeroplanes, and their clubhouses with popular tunes of the day, some of them from 'the talkies' (motion pictures with a sound-track).

In September 1929 I went to Chillon College, at Villeneuve, in the Swiss Canton

Flight Path

Chillon College, 1931, PGM at the rear in line with the centre of the doors.

PGM about to win CCAC rise-off-ground contest with a flight of 30.4 seconds.

of Vaud, near Montreux on Lake Geneva. This time I was not apprehensive but intensely interested. There was plenty of academic work, but it was leavened by rowing, swimming, skiing and luge racing down the college's steep approach drive. We went by tram to Vevey for science lessons, in French, at a well-equipped laboratory. I played plenty of cricket, often against local British residents, and football against Rosé near Geneva. In Villeneuve, alongside our sports fields, was an unofficial tuckshop where we munched chocolates whilst listening to Paul Whiteman's 'I can't give you anything but love, Baby' on a wind-up gramophone. I started a Chillon College Aviation Club, organised model-aeroplane contests on the soccer field, and produced the *CCAC Magazine*.

Coming home for the 1930 summer holidays, I went by overnight train to Paris, and at Le Bourget boarded G-EBLF *City of Glasgow*, an Armstrong Whitworth Argosy of Imperial Airways. The three-engined biplane deafeningly and bumpily lurched its way to Croydon.

I took three of my CCAC friends on a wonderful four-day trip. This was sparked off by an invitation from Sqn Ldr J.H.O. Jones, CO of RAF No 209 Squadron, to visit

Argosy City of Glasgow *about to leave misty Croydon in March 1929 with the first Air Mail for India. This was the first aircraft I ever flew in.*

their base at Mount Batten, Plymouth. We set off in my father's Rover 10, driven by his chauffeur, Sayers. After picking up my friend Stuart Lyon, from near Newbury, we visited RAF Andover, where we were excited to see the speedy Fairey Fox bombers of No 12 Sqn.

We went on to Mount Batten, where we boarded one of the RAF's largest aircraft, a Blackburn Iris III flying boat, with three 825-hp Rolls-Royce Buzzard engines. From the open gun cockpit in the bow I had a wonderful view as we sedately proceeded to the Solent and back, on the way passing low over three J-class yachts. Motoring back from Plymouth, we called at Westland Aircraft at Yeovil. We were welcomed by Mr Robert Bruce, the Managing Director, and were most agreeably shown round by the Chief Test Pilot, Harald Penrose. On the assembly line were the last of 565 Wapitis for the RAF. We rounded off a memorable tour with a visit to Handley Page at Cricklewood, where Mr G.C.D. Russell escorted us round the shop in which the impressive H.P.42 airliners were being built for Imperial Airways.

On 3 May 1932 I sent my parents a letter from Chillon, part of which read:

'We have rigged up a telephone between our room and Sidebottom's, and are going to extend it to Leather and Plunkett's room after tea today. It is worked by wireless headphones and some old bell wire and is very successful. We are going to rig up bells, so that we can ring each other up. I am going to get a couple of torch batteries

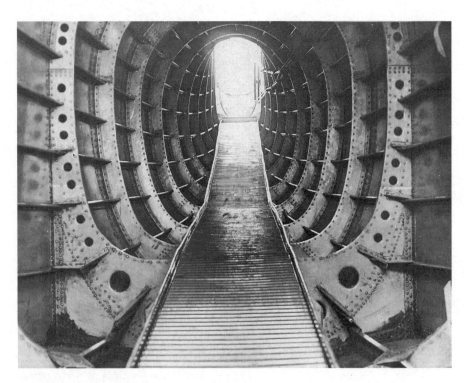

Inside the Iris III, looking towards to the tail cockpit.

The Faltboote*: Paddles had to be synchronised!*

Inseparable friends in their final term at Chillon: from the left, Richard Leather, PGM, John Lewis (who in 1936 was my Best Man) and Oliver Plunkett.

to work the bells, in Villeneuve after tea, when I shall post this (as I shall be going down there to superintend rolling the pitch).'

My happy years at Chillon ended in July 1932. I pooled my slim resources with Richard Leather and we bought a secondhand *Faltboote*, a folding canoe. We collected maps, rucksacks and thermos flasks, took the train to Basle, unfolded our boat, and put it on the River Rhine. Initially shocked by the speed of the current, which fortunately was in our favour, we paddled to Cologne, a distance of some 300 miles. On 27 July I arrived back at Greenwoods.

Three weeks later I went with the family to the Mount Argos Hotel, at Barmouth on the Welsh coast. On 18 August, just across the Irish Sea from Barmouth, James Mollison took off in his Puss Moth *The Heart's Content* to attempt the first solo flight across the North Atlantic westbound, against the prevailing wind. On Saturday the 20th he succeeded, but by then something had happened to put even that out of my mind. At 4.30 on that afternoon – as I noted in my diary – I met a stunning blonde aged 19. Her name was Patricia Rooney. She has been the most important thing in my life ever since.

2

Up at Cambridge

To say that Pat bowled me over is an understatement. Once or twice I managed to hear her voice on the telephone, and I bombarded her with letters almost daily, until my mother eventually wrote to ask her to discourage me from doing this . . . 'since it is clearly interfering with his work.' Pat and I were not to meet again until her 20th birthday, 3 October 1932, when we had tea together at the Trocadero restaurant in London's Shaftesbury Avenue. A few days later I went up to Jesus College, Cambridge, to start my degree course in Engineering, while she returned to the Polytechnic School of Art in London's Regent Street.

At Jesus College, Cambridge, 1932. (Not so studious as I looked!)

Up at Jesus College.

Though I realised that this imposed a strain on the family finances, my father was determined that I should follow in the footsteps of his own father, who had studied law at Jesus College, and rowed in the Jesus First Boat. This eased the way for me to be accepted by the college. The most difficult part was to sit for the University's Little Go entrance examination, which included a Latin element. I struggled with Livy Book 9, and eventually knew this by heart in both Latin and English. I was greatly relieved that my father accepted the fact that I chose to study Engineering rather than Law.

For my first year I had to be 'In College', and was allocated rooms on the first floor of 10 Chapel Court, overlooking both Chapel Court and Jesus Lane. I made many friends who broadened my horizons in college, on the river and at the University Engineering Laboratories. One, who appears in Chapter 23, was Frank Whittle.

I was also doing my best with limited resources to learn to fly. My first lesson – or more accurately 'familiarisation flight' – was on 23 October 1932. It took place from the new de Havilland aerodrome beside the Great North Road at Hatfield. This was still being constructed, but the company's Reserve Flying School had already moved there from Stag Lane, and it was the intention to move the aircraft factory to Hatfield as well (the first Hatfield-built aircraft flew in 1934). I could get there in 30 minutes in an MG Midget which I co-owned with Dick Wrightson of Trinity.

Accompanied by Chief Instructor C.A. Pike, who later was to be the Hatfield Aerodrome Manager, I climbed into an aircraft which was much more significant than I realised at the time. Registered G-ABRC, it had started life with the Experimental Registration E.6 as the very first of more than 8,500 Tiger Moths.

I subsequently had dual instruction at both Marshall's aerodrome at Fen Ditton, Cambridge, and at Heston, a western suburb of London, on such machines as the Avro Club Cadet, D.H. Cirrus Moth and B.A. Swallow. In November 1932 I flew with Sammy Morton of Hillman's Airways in a Gipsy Moth to meet Pat at Croydon. We then flew on to the little grass aerodrome which had just been opened at Gatwick, to introduce her to the world of aeroplanes.

On 20 December 1932, while 'down' for the Christmas vacation, I flew from Maylands, a small grass aerodrome near my parents' home, in a Puss Moth of Hillman's Airways. At Croydon I picked up Pat, and an amazing amount of luggage, and we flew back above cloud to stay at Greenwoods.

Pat later wrote:

> 'You can imagine with what fear and trepidation I went, knowing how his mother resented the fact that Peter had fallen in love with me just as he was starting at Cambridge. Soon after we arrived at the house his mother came stomping up the drive, dressed in *a gym tunic* and slashing angrily at the grass verges with a hockey stick. A most unnerving sight!'

On 20 December 1932 Pat accompanied me to a local house-party dance, and on that evening she agreed to become my wife. However, in those days young people were far more circumspect, and we did not become officially engaged for almost two more years. During this period she began earning small sums with beautiful Indian-ink illustrations for children's books and advertisements.

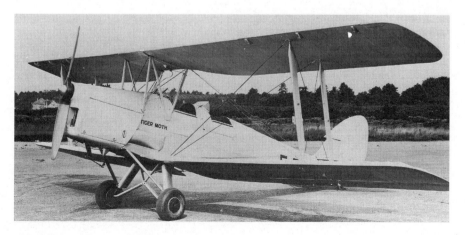

E.6, the first prototype Tiger Moth.

This was a 'golden age' of aviation, and London was surrounded by aerodromes. The main airport was in the south at Croydon. To the south-west was Brooklands, centre of so many things aeronautical as well as of motoring. Just a few miles apart were the 'air parks' and company aerodromes of Hanworth (Feltham), Heston, Hounslow, Heath Row (two words), Hatfield, Stag Lane, Hendon, Radlett, Broxbourne, Maylands, Fairlop, Redhill, Gatwick, Gravesend and several others. From here swarmed brightly coloured aeroplanes made in British factories, by such famous companies as Avro, de Havilland, Spartan, Blackburn, Percival and Miles. British factories also produced the lustier machines of the RAF, which droned and snarled from Northolt, Kenley, Biggin Hill, North Weald and Hornchurch. There was not one foreign-made aeroplane in the Royal Air Force, nor in any British airline or flying club.

It was a marvellous time to be an air-minded teenager. I was especially fortunate to count among my friends Whitney Straight. Two years older than me, he was now up at Trinity. In our first year at Cambridge we were not permitted to have cars, so we added to the city's vast communal population of bicycles. But nothing was said about aeroplanes, and Whitney had two, a Gipsy Moth and a Moth Major. After all, his immediate family included both the Whitneys and the Waldorfs.

On Whit Sunday, 17 April 1933, Whitney and I took off from Fen Ditton aero-drome in his smart D.H.60G Moth Major G-ABYV. We flew across central London, and then set course for Brooklands. On arrival, Whitney rushed off to inspect his beautiful new Maserati, jet-black, which he had entered in two races round the Mountain Course. He won one of these, in record time, from the scratch position.

While he was thus engaged I took the Moth over to the fuel pumps and refuelled it. Parked nearby was the elegant High-Speed Fury, fresh out of the Hawker assembly

Jesus First Boat (PGM at No 6) closing on the one in front at Grassy Corner.

Croydon Airport in 1932.

hangar and about to receive serial K3586. I was no less delighted to chat with its designer, Sydney Camm, and the Chief Test Pilot about to take it on its maiden flight, P.W.S. (but known to everyone as 'George') Bulman. Another thrill was inspecting Malcolm (later Sir Malcolm) Campbell's latest *Bluebird*, which had just pushed up the World Land Speed Record to 272.1 mph. Whitney and I then flew back to Cambridge, passing over Heston, Hendon, Hatfield and Duxford in 42 minutes. Then we mounted our bicycles and pedalled to our respective colleges.

During the 1933 Summer Term I worked hard for my First Year examinations. I rowed in the Jesus eight in the May Races on the River Cam (which in Cambridge is called the Granta), having the satisfaction of two bumps on boats ahead without being caught from behind. I played a little cricket, and planned a 'work experience' course for the Long Vacation from July to late September. My sights were set on Croydon Airport, because Pat lived nearby at Wallington. Eventually I had two vacation jobs there, the first at Imperial Airways and the second with General Aircraft Ltd (GAL).

Once the Henley Regatta was over in June, I got down to arranging my vacation courses. An advertisement in a Croydon newspaper led me to a 'bed-sit' at 4 Blenheim Gardens, Wallington, a stone's throw from Pat's home. Number 4 was the home of Frank Plant and his wife – two of the nicest people I ever met – and their small baby. They charged me a very reasonable 30 shillings (£1.50) per week, inclusive of breakfast and high tea, which was a more substantial meal than the traditional British 'tea'. Only a few years earlier, the death of Frank's father had compelled him to leave Dulwich College and earn a living, and this he was doing as a skilled fitter at GAL.

My parents generously allowed me to borrow my mother's little Morris 8 car. Each morning at 07.20 I would drive with Frank along Stafford Road to the GAL workshops. These were in No 1 hangar at Croydon Airport, which had been built in 1917 as the National Aircraft Factory. I would then park by Imperial's hangars.

Imperial Airways was Britain's international airline. I was excited to start work there in July 1933 as an apprentice maintenance engineer on their Armstrong Whitworth Argosy and Handley Page H.P.42 airliners. These great galleons of the sky reflected the airline's philosophy of safety and reliability being more important than speed. Neither of these many-strutted biplanes could cruise faster than 100 mph. Imperial was beginning to lose customers to the much speedier monoplanes of rival airlines.

I had already flown as a fare-paying passenger in both the Argosy and H.P.42. The cabin of an Argosy was a mere 50 in (1.27 m) wide. It contained 18 wicker seats, and as these were not fastened to the floor there was no point in having seat harnesses. One could slide open the celluloid windows, and some passengers found this a useful alternative to a sickbag when they were overcome by turbulence. On one occasion turbulence was so violent that a passenger sitting in front of me pierced the fabric ceiling with his head. He said the view was striking 'but it was a little draughty'.

At the front of the cabin were an airspeed indicator and an altimeter, and on the side of each engine nacelle was a 'rev counter' indicating the rotational speed of the adjacent engine. Even on the short flight between London and Paris one had over three hours to fill in, and I used to jot down the readings. Altitude never exceeded

Handley Page H.P.42 G-AAGK Hannibal.

2,000 feet, and a typical airspeed was 92 mph (148 km/h) at 1,300 rpm. But my abiding impression of the Argosy was its noise. With three Armstrong Siddeley Jaguar 14-cylinder air-cooled radial engines roaring a few feet away, with nothing but fabric in between, the only way to communicate was by writing notes. Imperial handed out cotton wool before boarding, but one was quite deaf for a good half-hour after landing.

Working on the Argosies I picked up odd snippets of knowledge. For example, I quickly discovered that, on starting up, the three engines used to spray split pins from their rocker arms. An apprentice, on occasion me, was always detailed to collect up all the split pins as they showered down, in order to avoid possible damage to expensive tyres. Why the loss of split pins did not allow the rocker shafts to work loose, causing engine failure, was never explained, nor was the fact that such pins (presumably properly installed) should repeatedly fall out.

Imperial's eight giant Handley Page H.P.42 airliners came in two versions. The H.P.42W (Western) had four 600-hp Bristol Jupiter XFBM engines and seated 38. The H.P.42E (Eastern), later called H.P.45, had fully supercharged 550-hp Jupiter XIF engines and seated 18 or 24. An unusual feature was that two engines were on the lower wing and the other two on the upper.

Compared with the Argosies, the Handley Pages were much larger and somewhat faster, and their block speed between London and Paris was a dizzy 97 mph (156 km/h). If a departure from Croydon was into a stiff headwind on a clear day I could still see the distinctive machine 20 minutes after take-off. Imperial tried to make up for the long time spent in the air by snappy turnrounds on the ground. The aim was one hour between arrival and departure. One of the many tasks to be done in that time was to top up the oil tank behind each engine, and I have memories of being at a frightening altitude on the upper wing hoisting up cans of oil on a rope.

Once a year each Handley Page was given a complete overhaul. Among other things, the engines were changed, and all the fabric was stripped off and replaced. While I was working in the maintenance hangar in the summer of 1933, G-AAXC *Heracles* was on overhaul. I crawled all over her as we put everything back together. Then, to my delight, Capt. Arthur S. Wilcockson let me sit with him in the enclosed cockpit (all Imperial's previous cockpits had been completely open) on the test flight following the overhaul. He let me fly, and, though the control wheel was enormous, I found it really hard work. I gained a new respect for the Imperial pilots, who spent their lives putting out all their strength in making such aircraft go where they were directed.

My second vacation course was with GAL, at a nominal wage of one shilling (5p) a week. Though a small firm, my time with them was particularly valuable, for I was passed from one department to another, learning from each. Four men ran GAL. The Chief Engineer, H.J. Stieger, was a Swiss. After working on the enormous Beardmore Inflexible (which had been that *rara avis* in Britain, a cantilever monoplane) he had patented a form of metal-girder cantilever wing construction which he called Monospar. Always immaculate, he resembled an advertisement for hair cream.

He had recently appointed as Chief Designer Frederick Crocombe, who was 32 and seemed to model himself on Stieger. One evening each week he gave a lecture to the half-dozen apprentices. I became friendly with one of them, K.G. Seth-Smith, who in

1942 was killed testing a Hawker Typhoon. The General Manager was the friendly and helpful Major M.S. Marsden, who at 39 already had 22 years of aviation experience.

Flight Lieutenant H.M. Schofield was GAL's only test pilot. He had survived a horrific crash at the 1927 Schneider Trophy contest at Venice when he took off to test the Short Crusader racing seaplane with the aileron wires crossed! He had gone on to instruct at the Oxford University Air Squadron, but he eventually overcame the knowledge that I was an undergraduate from 'the other place'. On several occasions I flew with him as flight observer, and after one flight he invited me to join him at lunch at the Aerodrome Hotel with Capt. W.E. Johns. Johns was the author of the famous 'Biggles' books, and the Editor of the monthly *Popular Flying*. He became a firm friend.

Most of our test flying concerned the Monospar ST.6. This was one of GAL's attractive series of light twin-engined monoplanes powered by Pobjoy Niagara radials of 85 hp each. Registered G-ACGI, in recognition of Crocombe's graduation from the City and Guilds Institute, it was unusual in having a manually retractable under-carriage. While Schofield cruised around such places as Gatwick and Kenley I would have the floorboards up and my head down, trying to make the cable system either get the wheels up or get them down again. As this troublesome landing gear increased the cruising speed over that achieved with a clean spatted fixed gear by only about 5 mph it was eventually abandoned, though two further ST.6s were built and sold.

However, what was not then appreciated was the dramatic improvement it made possible in engine-out performance. When I returned to Cambridge I wrote a memo-randum in favour of the retractable undercarriage. This brought down on my head much scorn from the Senior Lecturer in Aeronautics, Bill Farren. Later he became Sir

G-ACGI, the Monospar ST.6, was beaten by two weeks by the Airspeed Courier as the first British aircraft with retractable landing gear.

William Farren, and preceded me as President of the Royal Aeronautical Society, but I have always remembered his contemptuous rejection of such complications as retractable undercarriages and variable-pitch propellers. He insisted that 'There is no need for cruising speeds ever to exceed about 130 mph . . . about twice the speed of an express train, and that should be enough for anybody.' He thought such a cruising speed would 'take a long time and much ingenuity to achieve.'

While I was with GAL a batch of 24 four-seat ST.4s were on the production line. Though reasonably priced at £1,725, only 14 were sold, and the rest stood in the hangar until they were converted into improved versions. At the end of 1933 GAL was forced to shut down, but managed to arrange refinancing. Restarted at Hanworth under George Handasyde, GAL eventually completed a total of 86 of the light twins, the final ST.25 Universals being five-seaters with twin fins and rudders.

In my second year at Cambridge the academic work was harder, and directed by Farren and Melvill Jones increasingly towards aeronautics. Despite this, Pat and I have delightful memories of the 24-hour Jesus College May Week Ball, where music was provided by Charlie Kunz (pronounced 'coons') and his famous orchestra. We danced until dawn, and finished up on 'the Backs' of the river in a well-upholstered punt.

As far as funds allowed, I continued with my flying, and in the summer of 1934 I had a number of flights on Avro Club Cadets with the Airwork School at Heston. On 5 July, in G-ACHO, I flew with my instructor Brian Davy in murky weather, which made it impossible to see far ahead. I landed at Brooklands. Among the swarm of lightplanes were two Vickers Victoria troop carriers and the Hawker P.V.3 fighter which had just made its maiden flight.

My friend Dick Wrightson, who had gone halves with me on my first car, was not only an aircraft enthusiast but had enough money to think of buying aeroplanes. Together we worked out how to break the world long-distance record. Though hare-brained, such a project was not beyond the bounds of possibility. Bill Farren went over our arithmetic, and eventually Dick purchased G-ACHX, the 21st D.H.84 Dragon to come off the line at Hatfield.

Dick needed a tail wind, so he named the Dragon *Aeolus*, after the Greek god who commanded the winds. It was fitted with extra tanks, while Dick laid plans to take off down a newly laid straight stretch of the A1 highway (the Great North Road) south of Hatfield. At that time there was not one aerodrome runway in the United Kingdom.

Probably fortunately, in August 1933 two Frenchmen, Codos and Rossi, pushed the record to 5,657 miles, which was beyond what we calculated the Dragon could achieve. However, having got G-ACHX, Dick set up a small charter company at Heston called Wrightson & Pearce. It moved to Croydon, as Wrightways. It was run by Dick with G.P. MacGillivray (accounts), Major Hereward de Havilland and James Pelly Fry (pilot).

They removed the long-range tanks from the Dragon, and used it to operate a contract to fly 1,400-lb loads of newspapers from Croydon to Le Bourget, the Paris airport. During the long vacation of 1934 I joined Wrightways, not least because it promised to give me an insight into sales and accountancy. I enjoyed accompanying Chief Pilot Jack W. Duggon on some of the Le Bourget flights, taking off at 05.00. We would have a cup of real French coffee and then, armed with a bundle of long baguettes, would fly back to land at Croydon at 9.30, ready for the day's real work.

The Dragon never let us down. In 1950 I acquired the 40th to be built, G-ACIT, and flew it for a number of years as the BEA communications aircraft. In 1960 I re-purchased it for Beagle, and as a family conveyance, and when it was finally withdrawn from use in 1981 it was almost the oldest active machine on the UK register. Today it is in the Imperial War Museum at Wroughton.

During that 'Long Vac' on 30 August 1934, Pat and I announced our engagement. It was *de rigeur* to do this by placing a notice in *The Times*.

I received my Batchelor of Arts degree in Engineering on Saturday 22 June 1935, and 'went down' from Cambridge. What next? For the only time in my life I was looking for a job. I wrote letters to some of Britain's many aircraft companies.

3

At Fairey Aviation

I had no idea what response my letters might elicit. The first reply came from the reconstituted General Aircraft, now at London Air Park, Hanworth. I went to see them, and was interviewed by the new Chief Designer, George H. Handasyde, who in 1913 had formed the Martinsyde company to produce aeroplanes. He offered me a job in the design office at £3 per week. I would work not only on the Monospar ST.25 but also on the BA Swallow, Eagle and Double Eagle. I said that I would let them know.

The second reply came from the Fairey Aviation Company. I went to their much bigger factory at Hayes, Middlesex, where I was interviewed by Chief Designer Marcel Lobelle. He offered £3.10s (£3.50). Until then I had not appreciated that 1935 was an excellent time to be looking for work in the previously struggling aircraft industry. Soon encouraging responses also came from Vickers-Armstrongs, de Havilland, Handley Page and Hawker, all near London (by which I meant near Wallington). However, Fairey, with their stable of elegant aircraft, seemed particularly attractive.

Accordingly, on 11 August 1935 – my father's 50th birthday – I joined Fairey Aviation as a junior draughtsman. For the first eight months I lived 'in digs', initially in miserable 'bed-sitters'. Eventually I found a comfortable front room, with high tea thrown in, for 28 shillings (£1.40) a week with the very Scottish Mr and Mrs Ramsey at Tayside, 24 Keith Road, Hayes, an easy bicycle ride from the factory.

Back in 1910 Richard Fairey had been a young electrical engineer, but he made such good rubber-powered flying models that he had to put them into production for sale by Gamage's huge toy shop. Poached by Short Brothers as Chief Engineer, he then set up his own firm in 1915. Some of his first products were seaplanes, so he built up a second big establishment on the Hamble River near Southampton. By the 1930s he had many aircraft in production, some coming from Avions Fairey in Belgium.

Fairey was a formidable individual, fully 6 ft 6 in (2 m) tall, and rarely seen to smile. He was the Commodore of the Royal Thames Yacht Club, and owner of *Shamrock V*, which he had bought from Sir Thomas Lipton. His Main Board directors were Major Tom M. Barlow, previously a Senior Technical Officer at the Aeroplane & Armament Experimental Establishment at Martlesham Heath; Squadron Leader Maurice E.A. Wright, who had joined the Royal Naval Air Service from Cambridge, and in 1914 had received Aviator's Certificate No 938; F.G.T. Dawson; Works Manager Wilfred Broadbent; and Company Secretary A.G. Hazell.

Fairey's chief designer, Lobelle, had come to Britain in 1914 as a refugee from Belgium, when it was being overrun by the Germans. He played a major role in creating the Belgian connection. Chief Test Pilot was Flt Lt Chris Staniland, who was every boy's idol because he was also a brilliant exponent on racing cars and motor cycles.

In the past Fairey had tested seaplanes at Hamble, and landplanes at Northolt, Heston and White Waltham. By 1935 the main flight-test establishment was the Great West Aerodrome (also known as Heath Row after a tiny village) on the Great West Road in Middlesex. In 1934 I had landed there in an Avro Avian of Airwork from Heston.

Fairey had bought the 150-acre site for £15,000. He got C.P. Hunter, famous for his 'Hunterised' airfields with a surface like a bowling green, to lay out a fine aerodrome. Had Fairey had a crystal ball, he might not have done so, because in 1944 his aerodrome was requisitioned for use by strategic bombers. Having got their hands on it, the officials changed their minds about its use, and two years later Fairey's Great West Aerodrome had been submerged by London's Heathrow (spelt as one word) Airport. Not a penny in compensation was paid until 1964, by which time Fairey was dead and Fairey Aviation had ceased to exist. The centre of the old field, laid out with such care by Hunter, was roughly in the centre of the concrete apron in front of Terminal 2.

In 1916 the Fairey drawing office had been in London's Piccadilly, and the factory in Clayton Road in Hayes, in the bleak flat clay of Middlesex. In 1917 a factory was started on a virgin site at nearby North Hyde Road, beside the Great Western Railway (GWR). When I started there in 1935 it was already huge. In front was an attractive white administration block, in the foyer of which was displayed one of the company's coarse-pitch propellers from a Schneider-winning S.6B racing seaplane.

In 1935 the principal product was the IIIF – almost uniquely, the III family (Roman 3) never received names – multi-role biplane, of which 379 went to the Fleet Air Arm and 243 to the RAF. From these had been derived the Gordon for the RAF and Seal

Heath Row: the billiard-table aerodrome and Fairey's hangar.

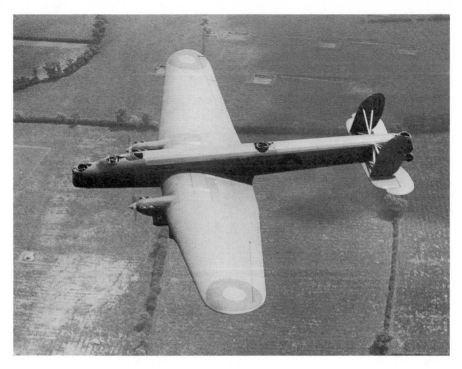

K1695, the Hendon prototype, re-engined with Rolls-Royce Kestrels.

for the FAA, and both achieved further large export sales. They were produced in land and seaplane versions, as was the speedy Fox, made at Hayes and in Belgium in fighter and bomber versions. In contrast, the Hendon heavy bomber stood out against the silver biplanes in being an olive-drab monoplane with a span of almost 102 feet.

Thus, it was a thriving and rapidly growing firm that I joined in August 1935. Already the recently built drawing office housed more than 100 draughtsmen, under John Charnley. My drawing board was behind that of Jack Finnimore, who later went to GAL and then held senior posts in BOAC. The stress office was headed by an affable ex-Cambridge man, Geoffrey Brewer. Two years later Geoffrey was about to get married when he sadly became the only fatal casualty in a train smash at Swanley Junction.

Though Fairey were about to create a new generation of aircraft, there were still to be three more fabric-covered biplanes. These were the Fantôme single-seat fighter for Belgium, the Seafox (unrelated to the Fox, and powered by a 395-hp Napier Rapier air-cooled engine) to be carried on warship catapults, and the TSR.II, TSR signifying Torpedo Spotter Reconnaissance. On the drawing boards, and taking shape in the Experimental Shop, were a new tactical bomber to Specification P.27/32, and the P.4/34 two-seat naval fighter, both streamlined stressed-skin monoplanes.

My first job was on the Hendon. There had been much argument over whether the pilot's cockpit should be open, or enclosed by a transparent canopy. In the end it was decided that production machines should be enclosed, and I was assigned the task of designing a tandem dual-control cockpit. This was duly achieved, and tested on K1695, the prototype. This had overshot the airfield and been badly damaged. It was rebuilt, and eventually fitted with 695-hp Rolls-Royce Kestrel engines.

My abiding memory of flying in the Hendon was the flexibility of its fabric-skinned fuselage, made of welded steel tubing. If Chris flung the monster into a steep turn, the wings would rotate while the tail carried straight on. Then, with a 'click', it would hasten to follow.

My next job was one of the oddest in the entire aircraft industry. It was to design an installation for a brass handbell and an ultrasonic whistle for the observer's cockpit in the seaplane versions of the Seal and the new TSR.II. The handbell was to be rung after alighting in fog. The whistle was to frighten off flamingoes and similar hazards before taking off from (for example) the Nile at Khartoum. I tested the whistle. I heard nothing, and birds ignored it, though I was told that it upset dogs a mile away.

The installation was to be stressed to 9g. I applied my Cambridge stressing technique to such effect that on the first 'test to destruction' the bell's handle and clapper were pulled out, leaving the bell in place. The bell was then strengthened, and a repeat test pulled the cockpit decking clean off the fuselage.

This must have impressed Lobelle, because he transferred me to redesign the TSR.II's landing gear. This had to be made stronger, to survive hitting carrier decks

K4190, the Swordfish prototype.

in stormy seas even when the aircraft was carrying heavy loads such as a 21-inch torpedo, bombs or rockets. The design gross weight had risen from 6,800 lb to 9,500.

The company had already received an order for a pre-production batch of three aircraft, to specification S.38/34. The first of these, K5660, was taking shape in the Heath Row assembly shops, with whom my relations were close and cordial. Each morning and afternoon I cycled to and fro measuring up, redesigning, check-stressing and confirming that my drawings agreed with the hand-made parts. In early December the last Hayes-built parts were sent down the Harlington Road, and on the frosty last day of 1935, Chris Staniland flew K5660 from Heath Row. He was delighted with it.

By this time the aircraft had been named the Swordfish. Though outwardly obsolescent even in 1935, it was to prove one of the great aircraft of World War 2. Fairey delivered 692, and another 1,699 were made by Blackburn. The exploits of these seemingly ancient machines, cruising at a mere 100 mph, included destruction of an Italian fleet at Taranto and the crippling of the mighty German battleship *Bismarck*.

On 8 May 1936 I applied the finishing touches to the first production Swordfish. On the following day, a Saturday, I lunched on the balcony of the Croydon Aerodrome Hotel, and watched a procession of H.P.42s taking off and landing all through the meal. It was difficult to tear myself away, but I felt I ought to, as that afternoon Pat and I were married at Wallington parish church.

We spent our honeymoon at the King Arthur's Castle Hotel at Tintagel, on the rugged north coast of Cornwall, and then briefly at a hotel at Clovelly, further north on the same coast, in Devon. The two weeks cost £31 10s (£31.50) – ten weeks' wages! We came back to live in a three-room first-floor flat at 18B North Common Road, Ealing. I commuted to the Fairey works by GWR train, buying a weekly season ticket.

Our weekly expenditures were:

	£	s	d
Rent	1	7	0
Rates		10	0
Ealing-Hayes train		4	4
Gas		4	0
Electricity		4	0
Telephone		3	6
Lunch at Fairey (five days only)		5	6
Housekeeping for Pat	2	0	0
Week-end		5	0
Papers, etc			8
Miscellaneous		6	0
	5	10	0

After deductions my weekly wage was £3 8s, so there was the considerable shortfall of £2 2s. My father generously gave me an allowance of £9 per month, enabling us to do better than break even. In fact we found that careful household management could even be fun. Pat carried on selling her beautiful ink drawings through her agents, Baynes & Arris, and that helped a lot. I gave up my pipe, which I had smoked at Cambridge. Gradually I too began to earn small extra amounts from freelance articles, starting with 10 shillings (50 pence) for a report of a Royal Aeronautical Society discussion for the weekly magazine *The Aeroplane* of 2 October 1936.

Mr and Mrs Peter Masefield, 8 May 1936.

On 25 September 1936 I accepted £2 in exchange for my car. Each day I would walk from Hayes station to the factory. As one of three Experimental Shop liaison designers, I often cycled through three miles of lanes to the aerodrome. Today the area once called Middlesex is a sea of houses, the villages having become suburbs of London. However, in 1936 my route went past vegetable gardens, apple orchards and the fields of Heath Row Manor Farm. The aerodrome was just beyond 'The Magpie', a public house said to have been a haunt of the highwayman Dick Turpin.

On my way to Heath Row one sunny day in June 1936 I met a small herd of cows being driven by a tiny girl. I dismounted, to walk past. A silver-haired lady cycling from the opposite direction did the same. I then heard the following conversation:

'Oh Mary, what are you doing here? Why aren't you in school?'

'Well, ma'am, I've got to take these cows to the bull.'

'But surely your father could do that?'

'Oh no, ma'am, it's got to be a bull.'

By this time aircraft were making the journey from the factory to the aerodrome in increasing numbers. On several occasions I flew with Chris Staniland in the Swordfish, standing in the roomy aft cockpit tethered to the floor by harness and cable. Flying over the endless market gardens which surrounded Heath Row, in the strong breeze behind the 775-hp Bristol Pegasus engine, was a delightful way to spend a warm afternoon. One day we took the Swordfish at full throttle round the Brooklands race track very accurately, at an extremely low level, trying to break John Cobb's lap record of 143 mph. We failed.

The Hendon II was obsolete before any were built, so 60 of the order for 74 were cancelled. The rest were made at a new factory at Heaton Chapel, in Cheshire, and the first flew in September 1936. Its bomb load of 1,400 lb carried for 1,250 miles at 130 mph compared poorly with the sleek new bomber built to P.27/32. It was to be powered by an engine with twice the combined power of the Kestrels of the Hendon.

On 10 March 1936 Chris had made the first flight of K4303, the prototype of this speedy new bomber, of stressed-skin construction. By this time the British Government was at least coming to believe that it ought to start placing large orders for weapons, and Fairey received an initial order for 655 of these aircraft 'off the drawing board'. About to be named Battle, they were potentially formidable, with a bomb load of 1,000 lb carried in an internal bay for 1,000 miles at a cruising speed of 300 mph.

This presupposed that the engine would be that for which the aircraft was designed, the Fairey P.24 Prince. Designed at Hayes by Capt. Graham Forsythe, this was a remarkable powerplant, with 24 liquid-cooled cylinders arranged in H formation. The 12 left-hand cylinders drove one half of a coaxial propeller unit, and the right-hand cylinders drove the other propeller. Take-off power was 2,200 hp, but in cruising flight either half-engine could be shut down and its propeller feathered.

The problem was that G.P. Bulman (no relation to the Hawker test pilot) at the Air Ministry was determined that Fairey should stay out of powerplants. In 1924 the

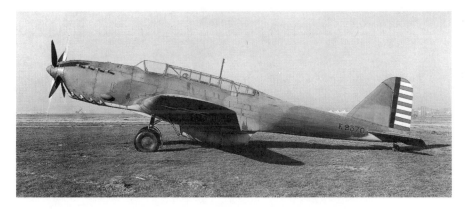

As the Battle should have been, with the P.24 engine (at Wright Field in 1942).

Ministry had refused to buy the Fairey Fox until its Fairey (licence-made Curtiss D-12) engine was replaced by a Rolls-Royce Kestrel. Now it refused to support the P.24 Prince, even though it was running well on test and its promise was enormous.

Accordingly, the Battle had to go into production with a Rolls-Royce Merlin engine of less than half the Prince's power. Cruising speed fell to barely 200 mph. The tragedy was that this was so much faster than the biplanes the Battle replaced that nobody (outside Fairey, that is) could see that it would be woefully inadequate. In France in 1940 the Battles were seen to be death traps, shot down with ease.

At weekends I usually found events I could cover for *The Aeroplane*. On 5 June 1936 I covered the opening – by Viscount Swinton, Secretary of State for Air – of the new airport at Gatwick. The centre of attention was the radical terminal building, at the time called 'the Martello Tower', after the circular towers that once defended England, but later known as 'the Beehive'. It was designed by Morris Jackman, a prominent private owner. Before the opening ceremony we all had a slap-up lunch in one of the two British Airways hangars. I shared a table with Harry Broadhurst and his pilots of the RAF Aerobatic Team. I was astonished at the way they knocked back the 'liquid refreshment'. Then they went out and put on a brilliant show in their Gloster Gauntlet fighters, which were tied together with elastic ropes. Someone said they had to be tied together, or they would have fallen over.

By the autumn of 1936 I was beginning to get on in the company. Indeed, I was selected by Lobelle, and then by Richard (later Sir Richard) Fairey himself, to lay out the design of a special hangar for the D.H.87B Hornet Moth and Stinson SR-8B Reliant used by Richard Fairey Jr and by Geoffrey Hall, Fairey's brother-in-law.

This work led me to become familiar with the inner sanctum up the stairs at the western end of the first-floor corridor of the administration block. Here was Fairey's office, with an enormous desk. One door led into a one-man lift. Another led, through

Gatwick Airport 'Beehive' in 1936.

a bedroom, into the sumptuous Board Room. Everything was panelled in walnut. Later I discovered that another door, which led into a bathroom was, in fact, an escape route from unwanted guests, via what looked like a walnut-faced cupboard.

Each week the work became increasingly interesting, as well as increasingly demanding and responsible. My gross weekly wage rose to £4, but Pat and I were still 'as poor as church mice'. Accordingly, having acquired some works experience, in the autumn of 1936 I wrote around to various aircraft companies, including some on the US West Coast. I was delighted and impressed to receive offers of employment from Consolidated at San Diego, Douglas at Santa Monica, Northrop at Hawthorne, Lockheed at Burbank, North American at Inglewood and Vultee at Downey. All offered about $100 (then equivalent to £20) per week, five times what I was getting at Fairey!

Of course, I was sorely tempted but, in the end, after long discussion, we decided to remain in England. What tipped the scales was that I had been offered a wide-roving insight into the whole aviation scene. By this time I had contributed several short items to *The Aeroplane*. Out of the blue, a letter arrived from CGG, Charles Grey Grey, the magazine's famous Editor. He enquired whether I would accept the post of Assistant Technical Editor, and write on the whole field of aviation from the design, manufacturing and operational aspects.

If I stayed at Fairey Aviation I would advance on the design side with such new aircraft as the Battle, Fulmar, Albacore, Firefly and the exciting new FC.1 airliner. This would have meant 'learning a lot about little'. Had I stayed, my salary would have gone up, but only in small increments. Moreover, though nobody knew it then, after the war I would have been distressed to see the entire Fairey factory demolished, like almost all Britain's aircraft factories, and replaced by a gigantic spare-parts store for the German Mercedes car company. Or I could take my pick in California. Or I could join *The Aeroplane* in the heart of London and write. This would mean 'learning a little about a lot'. I chose to write.

4

At The Aeroplane

Reporting and commenting on Royal Aeronautical Society lectures for both the Society and *The Aeroplane* had just provided welcome extra pocket-money. Now, suddenly, I had the chance to join the editorial staff of this famous weekly. Not only did CGG offer me a higher salary, but I was sure that becoming the magazine's Assistant Technical Editor would broaden my horizons. I would have virtual *carte blanche* to visit any factory, airline, Air Force squadron or flying club in Britain and, to a growing degree, throughout Europe.

When I joined the editorial staff on 28 December 1937 the magazine was published by a small company owned by the Sassoon family. The financial arrangements had been fixed up by CGG, then 62, who presided over his team with benevolence, as was the editorial policy, based on his own skilled but dogmatic ideas. Central to his attitude was an unshakeable belief in British tradition, and a dismissal of modern American aircraft as 'things which often crash and burn up'. Unfortunately, he also had a weakness to be influenced by flattery. He was flattered by the Italians and Germans, as related later. He was an extraordinary character, and his own worst enemy.

Our offices, a Mecca for visiting enthusiasts, were at No 175 Piccadilly. We had four small rooms on the first floor (in US parlance, the second), up two flights of stairs. Our Piccadilly address was cramped and inconvenient, but it had that indefinable thing called class. Once a week I would go late at night with CGG and Leonard Bridgman to a printers near London Bridge to put the next issue to bed.

We were disappointed and dismayed when, in February 1939, everything changed. We were taken over by Temple Press Ltd, a soulless company run by Roland E. Dangerfield, who thought he knew a lot about aviation. We became just one of many magazines, most dealing with transport subjects, which all had to move into a big purpose-built complex of offices and printing works at Bowling Green Lane, in Clerkenwell, in the old City of London.

A similar thing happened to our respected rival weekly, *Flight*. Like them, we were now a small team in a big company. Even with secretaries, we did not number a dozen. My main colleagues were Leonard Bridgman (joint Editor), Thurstan James (Technical Editor and post-war Editor), F.D. Bradbrooke, our dedicated photographer Charles Sims and, not least, Cecily McAlery, who knew more about the RAF than anyone except possibly Lord Trenchard. 'Mrs Mac' had enjoyed a blissful marriage until Flt Lt McAlery was killed in a Sopwith Snipe of No 1 Sqn in 1924. She was the only person CGG feared. As soon as World War 2 broke out she joined and helped form the WAAF (Women's Auxiliary Air Force), eventually retiring as a Group Officer.

Of course, let loose on the world's aviation scene I was glad to work even longer

Technical Editor, The Aeroplane, *early in World War 2.*

hours than I had at Fairey Aviation, but I enjoyed every minute. It was a time when the British aircraft industry was made up of hundreds of companies, more than 30 of which designed and manufactured complete aircraft. For some, times had been hard, but by 1938 the floodgates were at last (belatedly) opening, to try to counter the growing might of Hitler's *Luftwaffe*.

Just at this time I was visited at *The Aeroplane* by two eminent Americans. One was General Henry H. 'Hap' Arnold, Commanding General of the US Army Air Corps. The other was Wellwood E. Beall, Vice-President Engineering and Sales of the Boeing Airplane Co. I was astonished that they visited our offices, and even more surprised that they had picked me to show them around our industry. In some places I learned as much as they did, because, unlike me, they had Security clearance.

What I did not then appreciate was the importance of those friendships. (During the coming war Hap sent me on combat missions with the US 8th Air Force and on a tour of the US aircraft industry.) We first visited the huge new Fairey factory at Heaton Chapel, near Stockport. Inside were seemingly endless production lines for

The Whitley I at RAF Finningley.

Battles, to equip the light bomber squadrons of the now rapidly expanding RAF. Even then, I had a twinge of uneasiness about their ability to survive in a war.

We visited the Armstrong Whitworth factory at Baginton, Coventry, which was still building a few Ensign airliners but was mainly full of Whitley bombers. They were switching over from the Mk III with Armstrong Siddeley Tiger engines to the Mk IV with Merlins. Moreover, the rear turret of the Mk IV had four Browning guns, a far cry from the single drum-fed Lewis of earlier Whitleys. A little later I flew in a Whitley I at RAF Finningley. On the same occasion I flew in a Vickers-Armstrong Wellesley, the first type of aeroplane to be constructed along the geodetic principles of Barnes Wallis.

We visited Short Brothers at Rochester. Here the S.23 'Empire' flying boats were in production, and far larger numbers were about to be built of the outstanding Sunderland, the RAF's maritime-reconnaissance derivative. The company had also designed the first of the new breed of four-engined heavy bombers, the S.29 Stirling. Without my American companions I would not have known this.

Short's Chief Designer Arthur Gouge was livid. He had been instructed to keep the span of the Stirling below 100 feet so that it could enter RAF hangars. This meant a high wing loading, which in turn meant long take-offs and landings and, even more undesirable, predictable inability to climb above the reach of anti-aircraft guns. He said 'You don't design aircraft according to hangars.' In contrast, the Hendon, a bomber of an earlier generation, had a span of over 100 feet yet it weighed much less than one-third of the weight of a Stirling! I was unable to report such nonsenses.

We also visited Hawker Aircraft at Kingston, the huge and growing Avro plant at Chadderton (Manchester), and the Supermarine works at Southampton, which was just starting to build Spitfires.

In contrast to such weighty matters, the 1930s were a marvellous time for private flying. As already noted, Britain was packed with light aircraft made in British factories. They flew from ordinary grass fields. One just got in and took off. There was no need to get permission, no flight planning, and no need for radio. If one wished, one could simply fly to a major airport, such as Croydon, and land there. I often flew to Croydon, and could not help noticing the delightful sign just outside on Purley Way which proclaimed: ROSEMOUNT SCHOOL FOR GIRLS, PREPARATORY FOR BOYS.

Once a month we published a column contributed by 'Spry' Leverton, the representative at Croydon of KLM, the famous Dutch airline. Always humorous, it was also often penetrating. He arranged for me to make an extended tour of the Netherlands, the reports of which ran to many pages in successive issues. It was a particular pleasure to meet Dr Albert Plesman, who had formed KLM in 1919 and had been its Chairman ever since.

Plesman was one of the truly great men who created and directed aviation in the first half of the 20th century. Every aircraft manufacturer, airline or air force was led by such a man. All were not only towering characters, but at heart were enthusiasts dedicated to aviation. Now that we are in a new century I cannot help regretting that such people appear to be an almost extinct species.

Another contributor was the delightful Constance Babington-Smith, who to us all was 'Babs'. From early 1937, when she was an elegant 24, her brilliantly written satires 'For Aeroplanes Only', always lampooning something or someone with gentle subtlety, was often the first thing readers looked for. On the outbreak of war she was as quick as Mrs Mac in joining the WAAF, and she became famous as a photo interpreter. She appears in Chapters 16 and 26.

In November 1937 I bought the de Bruyne (pronounced brooney) Snark. Dr Norman de Bruyne had designed this neat four-seat monoplane in 1934. It was built by his company, Aero Research Ltd, at Duxford, and made its first flight at Fen Ditton in December of that year. Aero Research specialised in adhesives and composite construction, pioneering the Redux bonding method used in countless aircraft after 1939. In 1936 the Air Ministry bought the Snark, allocated the Service serial number L6103 and tested it at Farnborough. They were interested not only in the structure but also in the thick cantilever wing. When they had done with it they removed the Gipsy Major engine and offered the rest at £50.

I scraped together the required amount – I think Pat knew that any protest would be futile – and through a long winter night towed what had once more become the civil G-ADDL tail-first, with wings folded, to my parents' home at Brentwood. From there it went to the Rollason hangar at Croydon, where, with the assistance of Fred Griffiths, I set about restoring it to airworthiness. In August 1940, the task was still not finished when the Snark received a direct hit from a German bomb.

In July 1938 Sir Kingsley Wood, the Air Minister, announced the formation of a Civil Air Guard (CAG). We on *The Aeroplane* had campaigned for such a body, whose members would be able to train at flying clubs at greatly reduced rates (the difference being met by the Air Ministry) on the condition that they signed an undertaking that, in any national emergency, they would offer their services to the RAF, or in some other flying capacity. For impecunious people like me this was wonderful, and I joined like a shot. Flying with the CAG enabled me to extend my flying experience in a way that Temple Press would never have considered paying for.

A Snark wing hardly fitted into my parents' summer house. In the background is my little Flying Standard car.

Every few days there came an opportunity to fly, or fly in, something interesting. In May 1939 I was invited by D.L. Hollis Williams to sample G-AEMA. This had begun life in May 1937 as the C.W. Cygnet, a side-by-side two-seater with a 90-hp Cirrus Minor. In 1938, as the General Aircraft Cygnet, it was rebuilt with a 150-hp Cirrus Major, a new windscreen and canopy, twin fins and, not least, nosewheel landing gear. The first British 'tricycle undercarriage' had been a clumsy affair tested on a Monospar S.T.26. In contrast, the Cygnet was neat, and it is sad that only nine, of a planned 100-plus, could be completed before the war stopped such activity.

From the start, it was obvious that Temple Press was totally unlike the little family firm I had known in Piccadilly. From Managing Director Dangerfield down, the company was interested only in making money. Its attitude gradually eroded the loyalty I had felt for the little firm I had joined. It also had no qualms about firing CGG after he had written a succession of articles in qualified adulation of Hitler and Mussolini and their air forces. His Achilles' heel was his susceptibility to flattery, and the Germans and Italians knew only too well how to use him.

All through 1939 I flew with the CAG whenever I could, though spare time was almost non-existent. A big moment came right at the start of the year when I was cleared to go solo. The aircraft was Gipsy Moth G-AAET. Later I flew mainly B.A. Swallow monoplanes, and I received my A-licence later that year.

I have the keenest memories of the International Air Show held at Brussels-Evère in July 1939 to celebrate the 25th anniversary of the Belgian Air Force. I flew there in a Lockheed Electra of British Airways. The occasion was the last time for about fifty years that the Chiefs of Staff of the air forces of Belgium, France, Germany,

On 26 July 1938 Dick Asjes, test pilot of NV Koolhoven, flew to Heston with his wife to demonstrate the improved F.K.52 to the British Air Ministry. He gave me an exciting ride.

Heston from the F.K.52, in a very tight turn.

In October 1938 I went up to the roof at Bowling Green Lane to photograph the first barrage balloon to rise over London.

Great Britain, Italy, the Netherlands and Poland all shook hands. I couldn't help noticing how hot and uncomfortable our own Sir Cyril Newall looked in full-dress uniform, complete with a sword, and a plumed shako on his head. I also felt the tension, and the contrast between the expansive bonhomie of General Milch of the mighty *Luftwaffe* and the gloom of General Pyski of Poland.

As I flew back to Croydon – all the way at about 700 feet – in a three-engined Savoia-Marchetti S.M.73 of Sabena I could sense that we were coming to the end of a marvellous and happy era. I had many memories of garden parties at various aero clubs and the Royal Aeronautical Society, with the sky full of brightly painted light aircraft and of RAF squadrons performing air drill in silver biplanes with colourful unit markings. I felt an impending sense of doom, and realised that the bright paint might soon give way to dull camouflage.

It all came to a head at the end of August, when a mass exodus of children began from London. It was widely assumed that the city would be bombed within days of war breaking out. So, on Saturday 2 September 1939 Pat and I loaded our own little girl, 17-months-old Vicky, into a clip-on chair in our little Flying Standard car, and drove to Lee Cottage, Charlbury, in deepest Oxfordshire. We were welcomed by Aunt Muriel, widow of my father's brother Charles, killed in 1917. It was all happening again.

At 11 a.m. next day, together with almost everyone in Britain, we heard Prime Minister Chamberlain say that we were at war with Germany. At dawn on the following day I said goodbye – for how long? – and returned to London past busy

Northolt, where Hurricanes of No 111 Sqn and Blenheim fighters of 604 Sqn were taking off.

And so back to Bowling Green Lane, amidst blackout paint and sandbags. I typed a letter to the Air Ministry, volunteering for aircrew duties on the strength of my A Licence, 31 hours' flying, and membership of the CAG. I took it round to Adastral House in Kingsway. Then I went home to a strangely empty 24 The Ridge, Surbiton.

Soon I flew to France (next chapter). Three weeks later, I was summoned to the Air Ministry recruiting office in Kingsway, joining a queue of eager young men. After a Medical Board came the Interview Board. The Chairman was Air Vice-Marshal Frederick C. Halahan, whose 'gongs' were possibly unique: CMG, CBE, DSO and MVO. His probing questions showed that he was a regular reader of *The Aeroplane*:

'So you want to join the GD (General Duties) Branch as a pilot? So do countless other men of your age, but you already have your A Licence. Unfortunately, your eyesight isn't up to RAF pilot standards . . . bad luck. But how is *The Aeroplane* doing, now that CGG has retired? How would they manage without you?'

I tried to sell him the idea of my wearing the newly available contact lenses, but to my astonishment he said

'I really think that, at least for the present, you are better employed on *The Aeroplane*. Our shortage is aeroplanes, rather than aircrew. It's vitally important that your paper keeps everyone informed . . . you know it's in every Station Library and Mess. And your articles on German aircraft and aircraft recognition are just the stuff . . . We'll put you on our call-up list and see you in three months.'

Three months came and went. Each time I enquired, I was told to 'keep at it'. My revered colleague 'Brad' had joined the ATA (Air Transport Auxiliary) as a ferry pilot. Tragically, he was soon to die as co-pilot of a Liberator taking other ferry pilots back to the USA. I quickly followed his example, and got myself accepted as an ATA pilot. Then I was thwarted again, by Lord Beaverbrook, as explained later.

In the meantime I worked around the clock. With CGG gone, I indoctrinated E. Colston Shepherd into the Editorial Chair, arranged War Correspondents' passes, assembled all we knew about German aircraft, and set up a foundation for nationwide instruction in aircraft recognition, as explained in Chapter 6. This meant a full-time day on top of my normal full-time job as the magazine's Technical Editor, in succession to Thurstan, who had taken a post at the Air Ministry. The amount of aeronautical news was growing daily.

Looking back, I think the good-natured Halahan was the first of a number of people who, all unsuspecting, took successive decisions over the course of the war which meant that I survived (and could write about them!).

5

The 'Phoney War'

Selected news media could nominate staff members to be War Correspondents. Thus, early on the morning of Monday 6 November 1939 I put on an unfamiliar uniform for the first time. It comprised a khaki battledress with scarlet shoulder flashes saying WAR CORRESPONDENT, plus a peaked cap. I then took the Southern Electric train to Waterloo and presented myself at Adastral House in Kingsway, home of the Air Ministry.

There I met six others wearing the same strange garb: my opposite number H.F. 'Rex' King of *Flight* (who later became a Squadron Leader in RAF Intelligence), Lord Donegal of *The Sunday Dispatch*, Oliver Stewart (he had won a Military Cross in the Royal Flying Corps and an Air Force Cross in the RAF) of the *Morning Post*, Edwin Shepherd of *The Times* and *The Observer* (later he was the Editor of *Aeronautics*), Ronnie Walker of *The News Chronicle*, Peter Lawless of *The Daily Telegraph*, and James Wentworth Day of Illustrated Newspapers. We piled into two cars and headed down the Great West Road to Heston.

Here, as in Kingsway, there was an urgent sense of war. The white central buildings were now painted in green and black camouflage. On the apron was D.H.86B G-ACZO, formerly of Jersey Airways but now commandeered for National Air Communications. It too was camouflaged, even over the windows. As a result the interior was dim and eerie – one of many examples in early wartime days of bureacracy gone mad. We got in, accompanied by three RAF ground crew, and at 10 o'clock took off for France.

After a miserably bumpy flight in the almost blacked-out cabin we landed at Reims-Champagne, the airport for the Marne-Ardennes region of eastern France, Here we were close to the frontier with Germany, yet camouflage was conspicuously absent. The white terminal buildings stood out clearly, as did the large hangars of the *Armée de l'Air*, while the breeze fluttered through a prominent yellow windsock. In front of the hangars paraded a squadron of sleek Potez 637s and six lumbering Potez 540s, all lined up in perfect rows. By contrast, round the edge of the field 16 Fairey Battles of the RAF's No 226 Sqn were dispersed as far as possible under trees and hedges. I viewed the Battles with paternal interest, and regretted that they still lacked the intended – and available – propeller spinners which would have added 5 mph to their dangerously inadequate speed.

We boarded a decrepit bus which managed to convey us three miles to the centre of Reims, past enormous cemeteries from World War 1 which reminded us what might lie in the future. We alighted at the best hotel in the city, the *Lion d'Or*. This appeared to have been taken over by the RAF and the corps of War Correspondents. Round the bar (where else?) we found six old friends, C.P. Robertson's Air Ministry Press Officers. All ex-Fleet Street, but now in uniform, we greeted Stanley Bishop,

L.V. Dodds, Arthur Narracott (later of *The Times*), Freddie Gillman (later of BOAC), René McColl and David Grant.

With them were the first War Correspondents: Sid Bonnett of Gaumont-British News, Walter Duranty of the *New York Times*, Bill Henry of CBS, Charles Gardner of the BBC (later publicity manager of Vickers), Robert Walling of Reuters, B.J. Hurren of the Society of British Aircraft Constructors, Noel Monks of the *Daily Mail*, and Mary Welsh of *Time* and *Life*, who was then Mrs Noel Monks but later became Mrs Ernest Hemingway.

Immediately, all the talk was about the RAF in France, and what was likely to happen. It was evident that Stewart, King, Grant, Hurren and myself were the only ones present who had the slightest knowledge of aviation. When the War began on 3 September everyone had expected fighting to start at once, so the RAF was already in France. We overlooked the fact that Hitler was busy subduing Poland, and not a single *Panzer* tank crossed over from the German Siegfried Line to the French Maginot Line. It appeared to be taken for granted that this fresh conflict would be dominated by 'lines' of trenches and blockhouses. So, as the exceptionally bitter winter set in, the next few months became known as the Phoney War, and our worst enemy was boredom.

To support the British Expeditionary Force (BEF) the RAF had sent two separate contingents to France. The Advanced Air Striking Force (AASF) comprised ten squadrons of Battles, all from Bomber Command's No 1 Group, supported by two squadrons of Hurricanes. The AASF was commanded by Air Vice-Marshal Patrick H.L. Playfair, whose HQ (code name Panther) was just south of Reims at the *Château Polignac*. This was the property of the Pommery champagne company, for which the Nazi diplomat von Ribbentrop had once been a salesman.

Some 80 miles to the north was the Air Component of the BEF. This was made up of four squadrons of Lysanders, four of Blenheim Is, two of Hurricanes and two Auxiliary (AAF) squadrons of Gladiator biplane fighters. This force was under the command of Air Vice-Marshal G.H.B. Blount, whose HQ (code name Violet) was in a mill near Arras. It was next door to a malodorous sewage farm. Of course, all such details were not to be reported.

At the *Lion d'Or* the atmosphere was wholly unreal. Uniforms were everywhere, so we War Correspondents did not feel out of place. On entering the hotel through revolving doors we handed our greatcoats and caps to a dark-haired girl who, at 10 francs a time, hung them in an adjacent boiler room to thaw out.

Months later I learned that, during the German offensive, she had been discovered transmitting information by short-wave radio to the Germans, and at the end of May she was shot at dawn by the French at Troyes. In retrospect it was remarkable to find a real spy in our midst – and female, at that – because in November 1939, as we knocked back *coupes* of champagne at ninepence a glass, the talk revolved endlessly around rumours of every kind of spy imaginable, without any evidence whatsoever.

On the other side of the city the dispersal at St Léonard was much better than at Champagne. At one end of this small grass field were Curtiss Hawk 75s hidden among trees. We found a Potez 63 under two leafy branches and a net, whilst Morane-Saulnier M.S.406 and Dewoitine D.510 fighters (with fixed landing gear) were hidden

Battles of 88 Sqn, escorted by 'les merveilleux Curtiss'.

in rustic lean-tos made in the same way. In a cow byre was a four-seat Caudron Simoun. Most *Armée de l'Air* pilots far preferred the imported Hawk 75 to their Moranes and Dewoitines, and even the chambermaid at the hotel asked if I had seen *les merveilleux* Curtiss which would drive the *Luftwaffe* from the sky. Every French person I met was totally relaxed about the war. How could anything go wrong, was not the Maginot Line impregnable?

We had spirited debates on the subject, egged on by Oliver Stewart, who had had long experience of fighting over the Western Front in Sopwith Pups and Camels. The French pilots agreed that the Curtiss could outmanoeuvre the French fighters, but found that, in a mock dogfight 'ze 'urricane' could outclimb, outdive and turn inside 'ze Curtiss', so it was *'Ah, c'est formidable!'*

On the bright and frosty morning of 7 November we paid our respects to Air Vice-Marshal Playfair. Over coffee he outlined his forces and objectives, assisted by an old friend, Sqn Ldr (later Gp Capt.) Tim Morice, DSO, MC, who after a distinguished career in the Royal Flying Corps had been Dunlop's Aviation Manager. Tim was Chief Field Censor, a job which, he told us, was not to his taste at all.

From AASF HQ we drove to 75 Wing at St Hilaire-le-Grand, where Gp Capt. A.H. Warner was in charge of three Battle squadrons, Nos 88, 103 and 218. He came with us to Baconnes, near Mourmelon, where the 16 Battles of 88 Sqn were parked in the open round a stubble field. Wg Cdr Riversdale-Elliot, clearly very popular with his 18 crews, showed us with some pride how the 360-odd men of the squadron were settling in. The leaky upper rooms of a *château* ruined in 1915 were fast being converted into reasonably comfortable living quarters, while outside the various messes were superb inn-signs copied by a squadron artist from those of favourite pubs around Salisbury and Andover (88 Sqn had come from Boscombe Down). They had even transformed Baconnes into 'the English village', a showpiece visited by King George VI.

Nearby, at Aubérive, were the Fairey Battles of 218 Sqn. Here, Wg Cdr L.B. Duggon made us welcome, and it was at once obvious that most of the pilots were Australians. We learned that their Guest Nights were rather special events, much appreciated by the French pilots flying Curtisses and Moranes from an aerodrome a mile away.

However, the showpiece of the AASF was Berry-au-Bac, north of Reims. Here 71 Wing under Gp Capt. R.M. Field administered two Battle squadrons, Nos 12 (Wg Cdr A.G. Thackery) and 142 (Wg Cdr A.L. Falconer). The airfield was firm and level grass, surrounded by silver-birch trees. The Wing HQ was the *Château Fagnières*, the envy of all other units, not least because of its nine bathrooms.

The noses of Battles were poking out from almost every hedgerow and copse in that part of France. They were kept busy making low-level reconnaissance flights along the Siegfried Line. Instead of a crew of two and 1,000 lb of bombs they carried a crew of three and 500 lb of cameras. Instead of the expected 200 mph at 20,000 ft, where several had already fallen victim to *flak* and Messerschmitts, they were now hedgehopping at full throttle at 220 mph (I could not help reflecting that with the intended Fairey engine they would have been 100 mph faster). Their low-level oblique photographic coverage had proved most useful, in addition to the high-level vertical mosaic which was virtually complete.

That evening we downed scores of *coupes* entertaining Playfair and his staff. Despite this, we managed to be on the road at 08.30 next day to visit one of the AASF's

A Battle of No. 150 Sqn in 1940.

two fighter squadrons. We drove in four cars 70 miles towards the front line, passing through Verdun. Eventually we came to the village of Rouvres-en-Woëvre. Outside a girls' school (later we found it was the Squadron Mess) was an RAF truck. Further on was a muddy field. We had reached 73 Sqn.

All round the edge of the field were Hurricanes, each at the end of a long oozy track showing where it had taxied. I was shocked to find that they were of the original Mk I type with fabric-covered wings, a 1,030-hp Merlin II driving a fixed-pitch two-blade propeller, and even with kidney-type non-ejector exhausts. Some were airborne, one had its engine swinging from a hand derrick, and another had its rudder removed for re-covering with fabric. At several aircraft the 'erks' (ground crew) were busy with stencils applying the new code letters TP, and red/white/blue stripes were being doped on the rudders. The bold rudder stripes, a sudden return to pre-war marking, were because several of 73's aircraft had been intercepted (for real) by French Curtiss pilots whose aircraft recognition left something to be desired.

We were welcomed by Sqn Ldr Brian 'Red' Knox. He hailed from Dublin, and personified the burly thrusting fighter pilot, with a shock of bright red hair. I commented upon the propellers, and he said:

> 'We should have had variable-pitch props weeks ago. They would help at all altitudes. Sometimes it's a job even to get airborne. In fact, we've had to work out a special technique: full power with the stick back in your stomach, don't let the tail come up until you've almost reached flying speed and then see-saw off the mud. Try a normal take-off and you just nose over.'

He went on:

> 'There's not much doing down here at Rouvres. There are only 200 inhabitants, but a lot of them remember the German occupation in 1914–18 when 27 villagers were shot for 'non-cooperation'. They seem to prefer us to the Germans . . . but when we need a bath – and I really mean need, not just want – we fly in to Reims-Champagne and beg a tub at the *Lion d'Or* or at the HQ *château*. But I'm not quite myself at the moment. We scrambled nine an hour ago, and my youngest pilot, 'Dicky' Martin, is missing. From the radio call it looks as if he was hit by French AA fire, and he was seen to go down with smoke pouring out.'

At that very moment a French army truck drew up with a squeal of brakes. Out came a bedraggled figure, covered in oil, scorched, and with a bandaged hand. He was the missing pilot, Flg Off. J.C. Martin. He poured out his story. He was climbing up to intercept a flight of Dornier Do 17s when his propeller and reduction gear suddenly disappeared, hit by a French AA shell. Oil gushed over the windscreen and canopy, and the only way to see out was through a gash in the side of the fuselage. Relieved of weight on the nose, the Hurricane went into a flat spin, but the hood was jammed and Martin could not get out. Near the ground he managed to recover from the spin and, squinting through the hole, made a belly landing in a field. As the aircraft came to a stop it burst into flames, but he kicked his way out through the top of the canopy.

As the young pilot finished his story there suddenly came the sound, high up and far away, of three short bursts of machine-gun fire. About half a minute later there was a longer burst. Then came an eerie sound, rising in pitch to the wailing crescendo of an aeroplane diving vertically. Suddenly we saw it, trailing smoke, until it vanished behind trees. A plume of black smoke rose slowly into the sky. Was it a Hurricane or a Dornier? Then someone said they had caught a glimpse of a light-blue underside; it was a Hun.

Minutes later a Hurricane, L1827, swept over the field, pulled up in a stall turn, put its wheels down and landed, bucking in the mud. Fabric was flapping loosely over the gun ports. The hood slid back and tousled black hair emerged. Knox said 'It's "Cobber" Kain, the boy from Auckland.' Wearing an RAF jacket over pyjamas, and with a black scarf round his neck, 'Cobber' (New Zealand for a friend) told us how the nine fighters had failed to make contact with the reported Dorniers. Suddenly he spotted a single Do 17, much higher and going flat out for Germany. At full throttle for 15 minutes, he caught it at 27,000 feet.

We had heard his bursts of fire. Eventually the EA (enemy aircraft) fell over on its port wing and went down in a dive which became vertical. He followed it down, his airspeed going 'off the clock' at 450 mph, with fabric beginning to rip off the fuselage, but the Dornier was diving even faster. It went in near the village of Lubey.

Two other Hurricanes intercepted Dorniers, claiming one as a 'possible'. One of 73's pilots was hit a glancing blow on the head by return fire, but landed safely. Having heard all this, we set off for Lubey. We found a procession of French soldiers and peasants, some going towards the plume of smoke and others coming away with souvenirs. The Dornier had hit the centre of the village's main street, gouging a long trench about 12 feet deep. The wings had brought down telephone wires and grazed the side of a house. The pit still flamed and spluttered black smoke, two propeller blades stuck out from the metalled road surface, and on top of the heap in the pit was a battered oleo leg. Nearby were the tailcone, an undamaged oxygen bottle, a piece of elevator and some loaded 7.92-mm MG.15 magazines. Then we found a label which read:

> Do 17P Werke Nr. D.17.1056.
> Flugzeugwerke Halle GmbH. 23 März 1938.

I will not dwell on the scraps of humans we found, which the French were prodding with sticks, excitedly exclaiming *'Les Boches, les Boches'*. Even 'Cobber' was subdued.

Back at Rouvres 73's carpenters had constructed a bar, and here the pilots and seven scribes toasted the first Ace (five confirmed victories) of the new war. Then, the long drive back to the plush comfort of the *Lion d'Or*, where we felt humbled to think of 73 out in their bleak and spartan surroundings.

On the 9th, from a lofty eminence, we watched Battles put bombs on a white cross in a field far below. On the left the river Aisne wound through a wooded valley, backed by the steep dark slopes of the Argonne forest. No more sombre or lonely site could be imagined, around the remains of villages which had been destroyed nearly

*PGM in War
Correspondent's
uniform.*

a quarter of a century previously and never rebuilt. Their names were a mockery: Hurlus, Le Mesnil-les-Hurlus, Perthes-les-Hurlus, Riport and Tahure. Against each name on the map was *village détruit*.

The Battles came in over our heads. I was not then too familiar with Merlins, and noticed how they made a deep reverberating sound, rather than the familiar crackle of the Kestrel. As each Battle passed overhead I saw it lift in the sudden violent 'bump' from the wind blowing up the steep slope. Each dropped a 250-pounder. Except for a dud – which was one of several bombs to hit the exact centre of the cross – each raised a 100-foot cloud of grey-white smoke. The sound took several seconds to reach us.

As we turned to leave that desolate and lonely place the Sun set. The sky turned blood-red, and mountainous purple clouds built up in the east where, on the far horizon, we could peer into the darkness of Germany. All around were trenches, dugouts and overlapping craters in a land where poison gas had ensured that nothing would grow. The dead soil was littered with countless rifles, damaged helmets, water bottles, boots, even pieces of bone, for as far as the eye could see. Some 300,000 had died here.

I began to understand why the French had built their Maginot Line. What I could not understand was why they had stopped building it right where I was standing, leaving it to peter out in the dark forest of the Ardennes.

Four months later, on 10 May, the mighty German war machine came through that very spot, and through Belgium. The French and British armies were routed, and the Battle squadrons were almost wiped out. It is being wise after the event to point out that, had they had the originally planned Fairey engines, far more would have survived. Even so, the gallant AASF would have been totally unable to stem the over-whelming onslaught.

6

Friend or foe?

In 1914 any pilot who flew over friendly troops was likely to attract a hail of bullets. Belatedly, aircraft of the Royal Flying Corps were hastily painted with enormous Union Jacks, while the French adopted target-like roundels of red, white and blue. The Germans painted on various forms of bold black cross.

Despite this, 'own goals' continued. At even quite a modest distance, painted markings are invariably difficult to see, especially when looking up from the ground or a ship against a sky background. The fact remains, that throughout that bloody conflict we now call World War 1, countless unfortunate airmen were killed by fire from their own side. It was belatedly recognised that in a modern war the subject of aircraft recognition is a matter of life or death.

Unfortunately, while a few types of aircraft stood out like the proverbial sore thumbs, most looked (to untrained eyes) just like their opposite numbers on the enemy side, though boy enthusiasts might spot the differences instantly.

In fact, after the 1918 Armistice the subject of aircraft recognition hardly mattered. Throughout Western Europe selecting a horse's fodder or learning naval history was considered to be far more important than being told how to tell one aeroplane from another. Some air forces (but almost no armies or navies) did promulgate official books of silhouettes of aircraft. In Britain the RAF had *Air Publication 1480*, which was a loose-leaf album of such illustrations. However, keeping AP.1480 up to date was considered a menial and almost childish task, often ignored or given to someone with no interest in the subject as a routine chore. The need to consult the publication hardly ever arose, and the silhouettes themselves were of an unbelievably poor standard. The fact that aircraft recognition could be a matter of life or death was completely forgotten.

At *The Aeroplane* we had a fine drawing office with talented artists. They were experienced in producing drawings of aircraft which were accurate in every detail. Some were complex 'cutaways' showing how the aircraft were made, and how they worked. Others were of the traditional 'three-view' type: head-on, side elevation and plan.

When World War 2 began, we were appalled to see the silhouettes in AP.1480. It seemed self-evident that our ability to produce accurate drawings should be mobilised like everything else to assist what had become known as 'the War Effort'. Overnight, we started drawing accurate silhouettes of the types of aircraft which were likely to play a role in the coming conflict.

Just how to draw such images requires some thought. A solid black shape is rather boring. Too much detail is confusing, and can put off someone who is already thinking 'I'll never be able to learn all this'. Many official silhouettes, apart from being grossly inaccurate, had representations of whirling propellers. As they cannot be seen, I

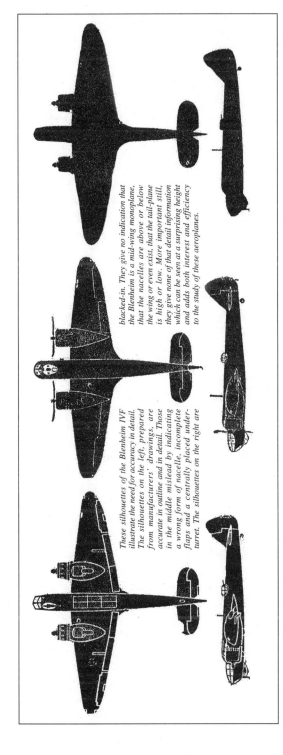

These silhouettes of the Blenheim IVF illustrate the need for accuracy in detail. The silhouettes on the left, prepared from manufacturers' drawings, are accurate in outline and in detail. Those in the middle mislead by indicating a wrong form of nacelle, incomplete flaps and a centrally placed under-turret. The silhouettes on the right are blacked-in. They give no indication that the Blenheim is a mid-wing monoplane, that the nacelles are above or below the wing or even exist, that the tail-plane is high or low. More important still, they give none of that detail information which can be seen at a surprising height and adds both interest and efficiency to the study of these aeroplanes.

The great silhouette debate: an illustration from The Aeroplane Spotter for 3 April 1941.

decided that 'revolving blades' should be omitted. We soon established criteria for the production of accurate silhouettes with just enough detail to give a sense of character and add interest, though 'the great white line controversy' simmered for months. After all, said some, aircraft don't actually have white lines pointing out their details.

Quite quickly, from the middle of October 1939 a growing flood of aircraft-recognition material emanated from Bowling Green Lane. It was gratefully welcomed by the Services and by the Observer Corps, and the circulation of *The Aeroplane* rocketed. What I had not considered was that our efforts would arouse hostility among 'official quarters', whose ineptitude and unforgivable lassitude in the production and distribution of such material was plain for all to see.

The urgent need for attention to be paid to this neglected subject was evident from the very start of the war. Only 15 minutes after the Prime Minister's fateful broadcast, a Bloch 220 airliner of Air France, plotted on radar, was for some reason *assumed to be an enemy aircraft*. Plying its lawful route from Ramsgate to Croydon, flying quite low in broad daylight, it caused the air-raid sirens to wail throughout London. The public had expected this to happen. When no bombs fell, there were feeble explanations.

Three days later, on the morning of 6 September, a jittery searchlight battery on the Essex coast reported 'a high-altitude formation of aircraft heading towards the Thames estuary'. No such formation existed, but from this seemingly trivial beginning there swiftly grew an incredible shambles. It involved seven famous front-line Hurricane and Spitfire squadrons of RAF Fighter Command, and all the AA (anti-aircraft) batteries in the region.

Dogfights followed in which a Hurricane was shot down and its pilot killed, while another managed to make a crash-landing after suffering severe damage. Sirens wailed throughout London and South-East England, and some of the hundreds of rounds fired by AA guns damaged aircraft from 54, 65 and 74 Sqns.

This disgraceful episode has gone down in RAF history as 'The Battle of Barking Creek'. At the time, it showed the overriding need for training in aircraft recognition. Instead, in its embarrassment the Air Ministry took refuge in court-martialling three unfortunate officers, and in blaming deficiencies in the control and reporting system. As far as possible, nothing was allowed to get into the newspapers, and the whole thing was swept under the official carpet.

Even after this shocking episode there were countless instances of mistaken identity. Very few of these were allowed to come to the notice of the public, even when the people tragically killed were famous, or when the aircraft involved was in some way special. Always, one wished a boy enthusiast could have been in the fighter's cockpit, or at the AA gun site, to shout 'Stop! It's one of ours!' At Bowling Green Lane all the staff of *The Aeroplane* could do was to ignore the jealous anger we were arousing among the inept officials, and try to meet the huge and growing demand.

Back in 1925 a part-time civilian body, called the Observer Corps, had been formed to report on the movements of aircraft taking part in RAF exercises. This was found to be so useful that it was continued, but with no official training and virtually no funding. Observers were unpaid, and the corps was one of many organisations which relied upon the enthusiasm of its members.

From September 1939 the corps expanded dramatically. Observers now manned hundreds of posts throughout Britain 24 hours a day. They plotted the track, height and speed of every aircraft they detected. What they found more difficult was to report its identity, and they deluged us with requests for information. Can you believe that they had no instruction in aircraft recognition?

On Saturday 18 November 1939 H. James Lowings, a member of Post V.1/19 at Guildford, Surrey, called a meeting of as many observers as he could reach in 'The Abbot's Kitchen', a restaurant in the local High Street. The result was that Lowings sent out a further invitation:

> 'It has been suggested that a study circle, or club, should be formed in Guildford to provide facilities for members of the Corps to make themselves proficient in the practice of detecting, plotting and identifying aircraft. It is further suggested that the Club should meet at regular intervals, and that its activities should include: the collection of large-scale photographs; the collection of scale models of aircraft; the collection of gramophone records of engine sounds; and papers and addresses.
>
> In order to discuss the suggestions more fully, a meeting will be held on Saturday the 9th of December 1939, at The Corona Cafe, Guildford, at 2.30 pm. Tea will be served at 4 pm. The speaker on this occasion will be Peter Masefield, of "The Aeroplane". His subject will be "The Recognition of Aircraft". Enquiries should be addressed to H. James Lowings, 34 High St., Guildford, Telephone 150.'

The result was that there was formed at Guildford 'The Hearkers' Club'. The strange name arose because some rural member said Observers had to be 'out there an' 'earkin' (listening). The club sprang directly from official neglect, and from the recognition of an urgent need for training, which was otherwise totally lacking.

From this tiny beginning, the idea of a voluntary study and social club took off. From the start, it established a framework for the transmission of knowledge, and for the essential competitive atmosphere which inspired a will to do better throughout the corps. By the time the crucial summer of 1940 was upon us, strenuous unofficial work had brought the corps to an unimagined level of proficiency in telling friend from foe. Later the Air Officer Commanding Fighter Command, Air Chief Marshal Sir Sholto Douglas, was to write 'The Observer Corps and radiolocation are equal partners in the raid-reporting system of this country.'

Though later IFF (identification friend or foe) devices were developed, during the Battle of Britain the newly built British radiolocation (later called radar) stations could not provide any information on the types of aircraft which were being detected. Throughout this period I spent almost every Sunday lecturing on the subject to RAF stations, Army headquarters and AA batteries, and to the Observer Corps, from Tangmere to Turnhouse, and from Gatwick to Glasgow. There was no machinery whereby I could receive any payment for this work, but occasionally I did qualify for a supplementary ration of petrol.

By the end of 1940 there were 15 Hearkers' Clubs in England, Scotland and Wales, and more than 100 were being formed. The need had become obvious, so that at the beginning of 1941 the clubs were voluntarily reconstituted as a proper nationwide organisation called the Observer Corps Club (OCC). By then it had received some spasmodic official support from both the Corps HQ at Bentley Priory, alongside that of RAF Fighter Command, and also from the Air Ministry and the newly formed Ministry of Home Security.

For the first time, the need to tell one aircraft from another had spawned a nation-wide organisation, with a constitution that was democratic and legally sound. Also for the first time, there was official encouragement for what had grown to be thousands of Observer posts to form a study circle, and for every three or four posts to form a branch of the OCC. Not least, there was now a formal basis for proficiency assessment and testing. The task facing spotters was considerable, as some 250 of the 400-odd types of aircraft flying over Europe were armed and dangerous. Of these, 62 were selected as being the most important, to be learned for the Third Class qualification, which was the acknowledged minimum requirement for aircraft spotters throughout the country.

This completely new term 'spotter' had come to have real meaning. Throughout the land there had grown up a vast body of individuals, not connected with the Observer Corps, whose task was to watch out for enemy aircraft. At virtually every major factory in Britain someone would be found on the roof, day and night. If the air-raid sirens wailed, the factory just carried on working. It was the duty of the watcher on the roof to warn of *imminent* danger. He would press a 'panic button', whereupon everyone would instantly get into a prearranged safest – or rather least-dangerous – location, probably lying on the floor (for example, underneath a machine tool). The same procedure was followed at thousands of other establishments, such as hospitals, where disruption had to be kept to a minimum.

The need to avoid disruption led to the formation of teams of 'spotters'. Soon they were urged to follow the example of the Observers in forming clubs, for their better efficiency and capability. In January 1941 the first Spotters' Club was formed, at Southend-on-Sea, in Essex. By this time massive daylight attacks by the *Luftwaffe* had ceased, but coastal towns such as Southend were frequently attacked by fast and solitary hit-and-run raiders, such as an Fw 190 with a single heavy bomb. For this reason, aircraft identification had to be both accurate and immediate.

The number of spotters soon far exceeded even the number of members of the Observer Corps. When the first club was formed at Southend it was called No 1, in the certain knowledge that it would be followed by others. It was indeed. By the end of 1941, while the number of OCCs had reached 155, the number of Spotters' Clubs had passed 220. Ultimately the total reached 808.

In 1944 South-East England was under flying-bomb attack (See Chapter 16). This was novel, in that the missiles flew in straight lines (with a few errant exceptions!). Accordingly, spotters on the roof were advised to give a warning only if they could see a bomb coming absolutely head-on. In this totally new kind of attack, workers of all kinds, and children in schools engrossed in important examinations, could ignore bombs (or at least try to), even if their noise was deafening and they fell close by.

One factor which had a major effect on the progress of telling friend from foe, and also in managing the burgeoning OCC and Spotters' Clubs, was that in December 1940 I gained the permission of the Directors of Temple Press Ltd to launch a weekly magazine, to be called *The Aeroplane Spotter*. It was designed solely to meet the needs of the Observers and the spotters. Temple Press agreed to price it at 3d (1.2 of today's

Vol. 1. No. 1

JANUARY 2, 1941

FOR THE ALERT

The **AEROPLANE SPOTTER**

Proprietors:
TEMPLE PRESS LTD.

Managing Director:
ROLAND E. DANGERFIELD

Head Office:
BOWLING GREEN LANE
LONDON, E.C.I

Telephone: TERminus 3636

Incorporating
THE HEARKERS' CLUB BULLETIN

Edited by PETER G. MASEFIELD
M.A. (Eng.) Cantab; A.F.R.Ae.S.
Technical Editor of "THE AEROPLANE."

3D

WEEKLY

EVERY THURSDAY

HAWKER HURRICANES OF THE R.A.F. FIGHTER COMMAND

THIS NEW PUBLICATION, for those concerned in aircraft identification, is both supplementary and complementary to the information on aircraft recognition published each week in THE AEROPLANE. The need for such a news sheet has been expressed partly in the vastly increased sales of THE AEROPLANE, arising from its special services in identification matters, and partly in the demand by those in the R.A.F., in the Anti-Aircraft batteries, in searchlight crews, as well as in the Navy, the Mercantile Marine, the Army and the Home Guard, the Observer Corps, the Balloon Barrage and among the "Jim Crows" or roof watchers, for full, regular and accurate information in words, photographs and silhouettes on the recognition of aircraft.

Since the War began THE AEROPLANE has devoted much attention to aircraft recognition in the course of its normal service on aeronautical matters. The subject has grown so much that THE AEROPLANE has not the space available to deal with it in the way called for by its national importance. Hence the founding, with official support and recognition, of THE AEROPLANE SPOTTER. In it we hope to supply in compact and useful form just that which is required by aircraft spotters without making it essential for

them to buy THE AEROPLANE at three times the price.

THE AEROPLANE SPOTTER will also contain exclusive features of its own and will provide each week a real news service on the latest developments in aircraft recognition and its problems—so far as censorship permits.

Accuracy is the first essential in work of the type which this new publication sets out to perform. The demand for material on aircraft recognition has become so great within recent months that a flood of hastily prepared and dismally inaccurate information has been sent out from many quarters not closely in touch with aeronautical matters. These pitfalls we hope to avoid and we are confident that the exceptional facilities enjoyed by THE AEROPLANE, now also available for THE AEROPLANE SPOTTER, will make possible the dissemination of the most up-to-date and precise information obtainable officially or unofficially. We have set ourselves the highest standards. We shall welcome constructive criticism in maintaining those standards. We present this first issue of THE AEROPLANE SPOTTER in the knowledge that it answers an urgent need, in the desire to perform a national service, and in the hope of gaining both the co-operation and good will of its readers in the discussion of an absorbing subject.

The first page of something that far exceeded my wildest expectations.

pence), one-third the price of the parent journal. It was to appear every Thursday.

Predictably, the management had doubts. Paper was severely rationed, and the only way a new periodical could be launched was for it to carry no advertising, virtually guaranteeing that it would be unprofitable. The staff at Bowling Green Lane were already fully extended, and – and this was seen as potentially a most serious consideration – would thousands of readers switch from the big weekly, which was a proven success, to the unprofitable cheaper product?

After much argument, the Directors agreed to use a small part of their paper ration for the proposed new weekly, as a contribution to the War Effort. The first issue was dated 2 January 1941. Its paper was of much poorer quality than that used for *The Aeroplane*, but it was adequate for the purpose. I told the Directors that the circulation might exceed that of *The Aeroplane*, which was then in the region of 15,000. In fact, it went 'through the roof', and stabilised at about 200,000 copies a week. To the relief of the management, almost all of this was to readers who either did not buy *The Aeroplane*, or who subscribed to *The Aeroplane Spotter* as well. So popular was it that it was continued after the war, and the last issue appeared on 10 July 1948!

Then on 3 May 1941, at a conference held at the Royal Aeronautical Society in London, the organisation of the new Spotters' Club was thrashed out. It was attended by delegates from all over Great Britain. Among other things the country was divided into 12 parts, each with a Regional Council. Our deliberations were supported by officials from the Ministry of Home Security, the Observer Corps, the Air League of the British Empire and the Air Training Corps (ATC).

By August 1941 these clubs had all come under the umbrella of what, after prolonged discussion, was called the National Association of Spotters' Clubs (NASC). Each club was urged to indicate in its title if it was made up mainly of members of the ATC, or Raid Spotters (on factory roofs), or a school or other kind of group.

By this time aircraft recognition, and its instruction, had become a fine art. While the number of aircraft in the sky, and the number of AA guns, never ceased to grow, the number of 'own goals' fell encouragingly. By 1944, with over 30,000 aircraft flying over Britain, losses from friendly fire were rare. (Over the sea things were different, and Allied pilots learned in the hardest way to avoid going near any Allied ship.)

Problems remained, however. On 18 March 1941 Mr G.M. Garro Jones MP (later the first Lord Trefgarne) complained to the House of Commons that 'The training of the Observer Corps has been left almost entirely to the technical journals. It is well known that this large body of men . . . are practically run and organised by a private journal . . .'

In the next *The Aeroplane Spotter* I wrote a long piece which began 'Mr Jones, who is well aware of the exaggeration in this statement, paid too high a tribute to *The Aeroplane Spotter* . . . it was doubtless intended to call attention to Government neglect of the Observer Corps . . .' I learned later that Jones's speech, and my tongue-in-cheek editorial, had caused an almighty row in the Corridors of Power. The immediate result was that on 9 April the previously neglected corps had the prefix Royal conferred upon it by HM The King. Moreover, while the new ROC would remain a civilian body, it was henceforth to be issued with a uniform, and be given official recognition and some financial support. It seemed a strange way to get things done.

At the same time, recognition was given to a new private-enterprise journal by allocating paper for *The Journal of the Royal Observer Corps Club*. This was put together at Fair Oaks aerodrome in Surrey, by a small group of enthusiastic friends of *The Aeroplane Spotter* and a keen observer, Charles Tapp, of the publishing house Tapp & Toothill Ltd of Leeds. The 'Journal' was circulated privately throughout the ROC.

Unlike the 'Spotter', the ROC paper was not viewed with displeasure by officials fearing some new evidence of ineptitude. In October 1941 someone in the paper-allocation department of the Government had the bright idea of killing two birds with one stone by transferring to the ROC journal the entire paper ration we had previously used for *The Aeroplane Spotter*. To their credit, the Directors did not hesitate, but transferred paper from a Temple Press magazine which, though much bigger and more profitable, had little relevance to the war. This enabled the 'Spotter' to keep going, but only on alternate Thursdays. Increasingly packing in information like the proverbial quart in a pint pot, the 'Spotter' never missed an issue, and never failed to appear on time.

Apart from the matter of paper, the ROC Journal did not really compete with *The Aeroplane Spotter*, and I gave it all possible assistance. In doing this I found myself at variance with the Directors of Temple Press, who, in contrast to their assistance to the 'Spotter', appeared to see the ROC publication as unfairly sponsored competition. They were also increasingly irritated by my many spare-time activities.

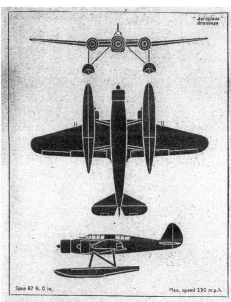

A page from the identification handbook of Japanese aircraft which we hastily produced in early 1942. Later this seaplane was reported to be the AI-104, and it received the Allied code name Ione. It was one of many 'Japanese aircraft' which were pure fiction.

In the course of 1941 the problems of aircraft recognition were multiplied. Though many of the refugee aircraft from countries overrun by Germany were no longer able to fly, hundreds of new types had to be learned when, in June 1941, the USSR became Britain's ally, followed in December by the USA, and by Japan as an enemy. Astonishingly, nothing had been done by British Intelligence to learn about the aircraft of the Soviet Union and Japan. Our ignorance of modern aircraft of these countries was almost total. We would have been in dire straits had it not been for the enthusiastic ferreting of John H. Stroud, of BOAC. He was also a talented artist able to portray aircraft of which we had no adequate photograph.

The ROC paper ran for 16 issues, ending in December 1942. The chief reason for its demise was that on 1 September 1942 there appeared the first issue of *Aircraft Recognition*, with the sub-title *The Inter-Services Journal* (ISJ). This new monthly at last recognised what had for years been obvious: the need for an official periodical devoted to a matter which made possible the unhesitating engagement of the enemy whilst avoiding needless tragedies. Because it was official, it was able to include information on the many secret types of British aircraft, of which all mention was forbidden to *The Aeroplane Spotter*. I never understood why this prohibition even extended to types of aircraft that were known to have been captured by the enemy.

The ISJ was produced within the Ministry of Aircraft Production by an Inter-Services Recognition Committee which I was invited to chair by the Minister, Col J.J. Llewellen. The Members were old friends: G. Geoffrey Smith of *Flight*, Leonard Bridgman of Jane's, Sqn Ldr C.H. Blyth of the Air Ministry, Charles Tapp of the ROC, Douglas Jenkins and H.L. Gaunt. Though the Committee met each week, I wrote virtually the entire contents of the first three issues myself, from Room 3003, in Cook's Building, in Stratton Street, off Piccadilly, where we were allocated office space.

The ISJ appeared monthly. It was allocated a massive ration of high-quality art paper, and was distributed free to all of His Majesty's Service units throughout the world, all ROC and spotter posts, and various Government departments. In stark contrast to officialdom's previous total neglect of the subject, I was able to obtain for the first issue of the 'Journal' messages of goodwill not only from the Minister of Aircraft Production, but also from the First Sea Lord, the Chief of the Imperial General Staff, the Chief of the Air Staff, the Commandant of the ROC and the Inspector-General of Civil Defence. Quite encouraging!

Of course, the 'Journal' could take its pick of available contributors. One who was rapidly making a name for himself was a young RAF Flying Officer, E.A. 'Chris' Wren. He had a brilliant knack of drawing 'oddentification' cartoons which exaggerated the characteristics of each aircraft. His originals were often in colour, though in *The Aeroplane Spotter* we could barely manage black-and-white! The official 'Journal', however, even progressed to colour, and by 1943 its scope had been widened to include armoured fighting vehicles and ships. It therefore changed its title to *The Inter-Services Recognition Journal*.

As related in the next chapter, in June 1943 I was invited to join the Combat Course of the US Army 8th Air Force, following which I made an extended tour of the United States. I was therefore forced to hand over the reins at *The Aeroplane Spotter* to Peter F. Murray (who was himself called up in October 1944, handing over to Charles W.

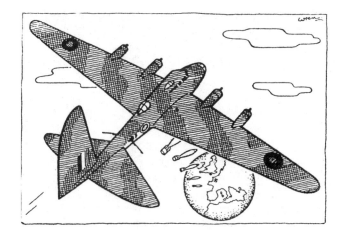

*One of 'Chris' Wren's
Oddentifications: the
RAF Fortress I
(B-17C) of 1941.*

*'Whistle, whistle, little bomb,
How I wonder where you're from.'
'Up above the World so high,
There's a Fortress in the sky.'*

Cain). In the issue dated 3 June 1943 I thanked numerous people, including Colston Shepherd, Mrs Joan Bradbrooke, Sydney Veale, Charles W. Cain, Peter F. Murray, R.G. Moulton, Charles F. Andrews and Peter Brooks. However, because it was a monthly, able to call on considerable resources, I was able to stay at the helm of the 'Journal' for 32 issues until, in June 1945, I was sent to the USA as British Civil Air Attaché.

All this extra work, from the beginning of 1942, had made my relations with the Directors of Temple Press increasingly strained. It would have been much simpler just to have gone to Bowling Green Lane each day. I would have collected the same pay packet, and been far less harrassed, and I would not have had to resign in June 1943.

As it was, in the turmoil of the end of the war in Europe, I wrote my last contributions to *The Inter-Services Journal*, and in July 1945 sailed with my family for America. Thus ended, without thanks and certainly not for any pay, an extremely strenuous episode in my life which was virtually the story of aircraft recognition.

7

Flying with 'The Mighty 8th'

Amonth after Pearl Harbor, at the beginning of that momentous year 1942, 'Hap' Arnold, the Commanding General of the US Army Air Force, issued an order establishing a new formation, the 8th Air Force. Its mission was to proceed to England and carry out strategic bombing operations against Germany. In the course of time, and despite grievous losses, it was to grow into the mightiest single strategic-bombing force in the world, even bigger than the RAF's Bomber Command.

Of course, we in Britain welcomed our American allies as warmly as our beleaguered state allowed, and did all we could to help them in coming to our aid. At the same time, our own bitter experiences made us warn them that trying to bomb 'Fortress Europe' in daylight, especially beyond the range of fighter escort, would inevitably lead to unacceptable losses.

The RAF had tried it, suffered terrible losses and soon turned to bombing at night. Even the previously all-conquering *Luftwaffe* had decided that England was an excellent place for bombers to avoid in daylight, even with a strong fighter escort. We also had a suspicion that Americans were somewhat prone to boast, and that (for example) the Norden bombsight could not, as was claimed, 'put a bomb into a pickle-barrel from 25,000 feet'.

I had written in *The Aeroplane* and the *Sunday Times* that precision bombing in daylight of German-occupied territory, at least in north-west Europe, would invite unsupportable casualties. Yet this method of attack remained the planned operating procedure of the US Army 8th Air Force.

Therefore, to me especially, the first combat mission by the 8th was big news. It came on 17 August 1942. I was invited as a War Correspondent to Bovingdon, in Hertfordshire, where I was welcomed aboard B-17E 41-9023 *Yankee Doodle* by the aircraft captain, Lt Sanford T. Smith. Assigned to the 414th Bombardment Squadron (BS) of the 97th Bombardment Group (BG), this aircraft had just led the second flight of bombers in the first raid of the war by the 8th Bomber Command (BC), against a marshalling yard at Rouen. All the B-17s had returned safely.

Thus, *Yankee Doodle* was not 'the first American ship to poke her nose over Nazi-occupied Europe,' as many papers proclaimed, but it got all the publicity, because on board had been the 8th BC Commanding General, Ira C. Eaker, with whom I had had the pleasure of discussing air war problems in some detail a year earlier.

After I settled into the comfortable cockpit we took off and did steep turns and circuits for 1 hr 15 min. There was plenty to write about, from the careful way the engines were idled after landing to cool down gently, to the way that, with aromatic fuel, smoking was permitted anywhere on board.

On my return I commented on my belief that daylight missions by B-17s over Nazi-held Europe would be very dangerous. General Arnold knew that, though I doubted the ability of heavy bombers to survive determined opposition in daylight, I was at least a passionate believer in the Allied cause, and in particular in the necessity for the closest co-operation between our two countries. I owe him a great debt, because he sent me not only on a tour of the US aircraft industry but also on the combat training course of the 8th Air Force in order for me to fly a real combat mission (or, if I chose, more than one).

This was a unique privilege which, so far as I know, was accorded to no other British civilian. It was not viewed with equal enthusiasm by either the British Air Ministry or my working colleagues, though it did enable me to forge a close link with Air Marshal 'Bert' (Sir Arthur) Harris, Commander of RAF Bomber Command.

For me, this was a parting of the ways. I had had so many commitments for so long that, with reluctance, I resigned from Temple Press, as related in the previous chapter. For the immediate future I had *carte blanche* from General Arnold to fly with the 8th AF, both as a War Correspondent and as a liaison officer with RAF Bomber Command. When this particular task was over, I looked forward to fulfilling various roles both at home and in the USA.

Unlike my first visit to Bovingdon, when I had the status of a journalist, at the end of June 1943 I reported back there 'for real'. Bovingdon was now the home of No 11 CCRC (Combat Crew Replacement and Training Center). Here, for the first time, I worked alongside 'the Yanks'. The officers were immaculate in their dark olive jackets and sharply creased trousers of a sandy pink colour. In contrast, the ground crews wore oil-stained overalls, and, to my astonishment, spoke to the officers as equals, and in the most casual manner. On the other hand, I quickly realised that in the things that mattered our Allies were absolutely on the ball. With every day I spent amongst them, as my understanding deepened, so did my respect.

I went through their two-week Combat Course, which aimed to put a final polish on operational bomber aircrew. I found myself the only Briton among some 250 men from all over the United States. They welcomed me as an interesting phenomenon, in most cases the only Englishman these 20-year-olds had ever met. Throughout the 14 days I hardly drew breath from answering their questions about the island in which they found themselves, and the strange people alongside whom they had come to fight.

In between answering their questions I learned about the Boeing B-17F Fortress, its 1,200-hp Wright Cyclone R-1820-97 engines, their General Electric B22 turbo-superchargers and Hamilton Standard propellers, and all the many systems that brought the aircraft to life. I also completed the gunnery course, with the powerful 'fifty-calibre' (0.5-in) Browning, a far more effective weapon than the RAF's puny 0.303-in version. From the start, I was impressed by the sheer quality of everything. In the RAF, everything had to be done to a parsimonious budget.

On 17 June 1943 I made my first flight as a crew member in an American military aircraft. It was Ship No 41-9119, one of the B-17Es, which by this time had been replaced in the Combat Groups by the B-17F, with a frameless Plexiglas nose which increased interior room and gave a better view ahead (which was where the enemy fighters mostly came from). I flew with Lt J.K. McLaughlin and his crew from the 326th BS, 92nd BG. With code letters JW-G, but without a name on the nose (this was a training aircraft), we flew from Bovingdon to the Wash, where we circled at low level a safe distance from shore blasting a surface target with 'fifty-calibre' fire.

Next came numerous circuits at Bovingdon, and then, on a beautiful clear evening, we climbed to 34,900 feet over Great Orme's Head. Below, Anglesey looked the size of a postage stamp, and I could see across Wales and England to the North Sea. I reflected on the fact that not many RAF aircrew had flown so high. With no pressurisation, we breathed oxygen in long gulps.

The course covered everything from how to abandon ship, using the British 24-foot chest-type parachute, to prisoner-of-war escape procedures and survival techniques. Morale was sky-high. Losses had been moderate, and claims for German fighters shot down enormous (and implicitly believed). Then came a shock: on 13 June 26 B-17s were lost over Kiel, with 260 crew-members.

Six days later, on the 19th, I qualified as co-pilot on the B-17E and F, with a further Certificate of Proficiency in air gunnery. After the paperwork had been completed, I was cleared for combat flying. I first reported to High Wycombe for a day of briefing by Gen. Eaker and Brig-Gen. Fred Anderson. I then spent a day with Colonels Curtis LeMay and Norcross at the 4th Wing HQ at Elvedon Hall, near Thetford. On 6 July I boarded 42-2429, General Eaker's Beech AT-7 Navigator VIP liaison aircraft. We flew to Honington, a P-38 fighter station in Suffolk, and on to the 96th Bomb Group, at Snetterton Heath, in Norfolk.

The 96th was made up of the 337th, 338th, 339th and 413th Bomb Squadrons. Its Commander was Col Archie J. Old Jr, who as a general 14 years later was to fly round the world non-stop in a flight-refuelled B-52. The Group had seen much action, and ultimately was to suffer the second-heaviest losses in the entire 8th AF. Previously based at Andrews Field (Great Saling) in Essex, it was still settling down at Snetterton in the Nissen huts and large T-2 hangars which had been erected only a few weeks previously. Around the perimeter were the dispersals of the four squadrons. Painted olive-drab, their B-17Fs were unusual in the colourful 8th AF in that they were devoid of any special unit markings, apart from the Group's white C in a black square at the top of their prominent fins.

Hap had picked the 96th as the Bombardment Group with which I would serve as a crew member on combat missions. They got down to it straight away. On the day I arrived I boarded B-17F 42-30160, *Dallas Rebel*, commanded by Capt. W.B. Nance. We acted as lead ship on a 1 hr 40 min practice mission.

That night was my first at Snetterton in an eight-bunk Nissen hut. The huts all appeared to be continuously infused with the dulcet tones of Dinah Shore, usually rendering 'Paper Doll'.

On the following day, 7 July, I joined the Group's Commander aboard Capt. Carrol Bender's 42-29941 *Tarfu*, on a mission giving Col Old an opportunity to observe problems for himself. On Sunday the 11th I flew with Maj. Tiller and his crew aboard 42-30183 *Dry Run III*. I moved into the 1st-pilot seat and flew the aircraft, and finally practised landings. On the following day I boarded the same aircraft, but this time commanded by Capt. J.R. Irish. We dropped bombs very accurately on the Bradwell range. On the 13th I joined Capt. MacLachy and his crew aboard 42-30130 *Klap Trap II*, for a 4 hr 50 min simulated mission.

By this time I was considered combat-ready. One's apprehension is probably greatest on one's first combat mission, and I remember it as if it had all happened yesterday.

At 00.45 (quarter to one in the morning) on 14 July 1943 about 600 Snetterton folk (more than the population of the nearby village) were awakened, and the base came to life. It was a bright starlit night, and from far overhead came the heavy drone of Lancasters returning from Aachen. I had cocoa in the Nissen hut bunk room, and at 01.30 breakfast of eggs (real, not powdered, as I was used to) and peaches and molasses. Then all the crews climbed into trucks, cigarettes glowing like fireflies, and headed for the 02.00 briefing.

I blinked on entering the brilliantly lit briefing room. On the huge map of Europe was a thin black ribbon pinned to show our track. It went to Paris, so the Group's Mission No 14 was expected to be easier than most. The suavely capable Briefing Officer, Maj. Reynolds Benson of New York, announced that the target would be the hangars, workshops and aircraft park at Le Bourget. I knew Le Bourget well, as it was the airport for Paris, where – as Benson reminded us – Lindbergh had arrived 16 years before. Since 1940 it had become a major *Luftwaffe* base, and also a production factory. Other Groups were going to support us, while yet others were to bomb the airbases at Villacoublay, on the south side of Paris, and Glisy near Amiens.

I was assigned to Capt. Gary Lambert, of the 338th Sqn. Like almost every 'ship' in the 8th, his B-17F-80-BO, No 42-29945, was proudly named, in this case *Daisy June III* after Lambert's girl friend. In almost pitch darkness, the 11 of us gathered beneath it, and dressed for the fray. First, fleece-lined trousers, jackets and boots. Then the yellow 'Mae West' lifejacket. Then the experimental British-made flak suit, with steel strips sewn into canvas, and the harness for the clip-on chest-type parachute. Next, the throat-type microphone, goggles and earphones, and finally the oxygen mask. Carrying our parachute packs, steel helmets and one-man K-type dinghy, we climbed on board through the small door on the starboard side just ahead of the tail.

Gary Lambert took the left seat in the cockpit, with Capt. Alfred Drabnis and myself to alternate on the right. Navigator Lt Dean Howell and bombardier Lt Dan Markowitz, friends from earlier trips, settled into the nose, while Tech. Sgt Ed Loscot manned the radio compartment behind the bomb bay. Our crew of 11 was completed by left waist gunner S/Sgt James A. McDermit, right waist gunner S/Sgt Lewis P. Pruden, top-turret gunner Tech. Sgt Thomas E. Musgrove, ball-turret gunner S/Sgt Hugh W. Russel, and tail gunner S/Sgt Charles C. Diffendoll.

We had on board a modest fuel load of 1,698 US gallons (6,428 litres, 1,414 imp. gal.) of 100-octane, weighing 10,188 lb. We also had 16 bombs of 300 lb, 5,970 rounds of .50-calibre weighing 1,791 lb, plus 969 lb for the 12 guns. This gave a take-off weight of 57,730 lb (26,186 kg), which with a 10-mph wind along the Snetterton runway gave a take-off run of 2,950 feet, to unstick at 110 mph and reach 50 feet at the 3,950-ft mark.

The Group started engines at 04.50, beginning with No 3 with its fuel booster pump. There was a glimpse of pink dawn in the eastern sky as we slowly taxied round the newly laid concrete perimeter track between twinkling gooseneck lights. Behind us was a moving forest of red and green wingtip lights. The B-17s ahead of us thundered off at 30-second intervals, and at 05.15 it was our turn, to lead off the High Squadron.

One-third flap, all generators on, booster pumps on, tabs zero, tailwheel locked, cowl flaps all open, manifold selector at 8, fuel pressure 16 lb, oil 75 lb, oil temperature 70 °C, cylinder heads 205 °C; then throttles were inched forward to 2,500 rpm at 46 inches, all on auto-rich. Lambert called 'Release brakes', and Drabnis briefly pressed his toes on the pedals. No longer straining at the leash, *Daisy June III* surged forward. As we passed the tower I saw four control officers silhouetted against the lightening sky. One was Archie Old, and he waved.

Drabnis called out the speeds; at 100 Lambert hauled us off, and at 125 Drabnis snapped up the wheels. There was just enough light to see the boundary sweep past as we climbed away at 140 mph. Lambert turned the manifold-pressure selector to open the exhaust waste gates, and set 38 in on all engines on the two dials, each with two needles. Throttles still wide open, he pulled back on the pitch to give 2,300 rpm. With flaps now up and booster pumps off, we climbed steadily at 350 ft/min, with a fuel flow of 435 US gal/hr.

From behind Lambert's seat I turned and opened the door into the brightly lit bomb bay. We were carrying sixteen white-painted 300-lb bombs in four vertical rows, their sides reflected in the bay walls. I shut the door and went forward into the nose. Here I was to man the starboard cheek gun. Necklaces of ammunition filled most of the limited space.

At 05.35 we began to formate. Ahead I could just see the dim shapes of the lead squadron picking up formation. Behind us our own squadron was forming up. At 8,000 ft we came out above the cloud tops into a sky just beginning to lighten. Every moment more aircraft were arriving and manoeuvring into place, great black shapes with gold flames licking from their turbosuperchargers. Climbing through the 14,000-ft level, the main Group elements joined up between 06.10 and 06.20.

Orbiting in a giant circle, we crossed the Suffolk coast at Orford Ness. I heard Gary's voice in my earphones, 'Last chance for a cigarette, boys. By the way, do you know it's Bastille Day? Guess that's France's Independence Day.'

Up ahead was the lead ship, Capt. Vernon Iverson's *Mischief Maker*, with lead navigator Richard Davisson and lead bombardier Michael Arpair. I heard Iverson call out 'Put on oxygen masks.' Lambert called each of us in turn to check that we heard the order. At 06.35 we crossed Mersea Island. German radar operators were already plotting our progress. At 06.45 I saw the Thames estuary, crossed by plumes of smoke from London, where I could see hundreds of barrage balloons.

I listened to Dean Howell running through the main points of the mission. We are to be on oxygen for just over three hours. RAF Spitfires will escort us on the outward journey, but, with their short range, we will be on our own for more than an hour, and it will be by far the most dangerous hour at that.

At 07.12 the whole Battle Wing was over Selsey Bay at 23,000 feet. Settled into our cruise regime, we had 2 100 rpm at 31 in Hg, to give 155 mph indicated. A quick scan of the operating chart showed this to be about 228 mph true. Fuel burn had fallen to 265 US gal/hr. We majestically headed out towards France in a vast armada of V-shapes all following the lead ship. All around, turrets were swivelling and elevating their guns to keep the oil circulating. The B-17 was an almost all-electric aircraft, but a small hydraulic system was provided to power the turrets, as well as the engine cowl flaps and wheel brakes. I found by foolishly touching it with an ungloved hand that the skin of the nose was painfully cold. At 07.15 guns were tested, and I fired a short burst into the cloud over the Channel.

Gradually the entire formation became brightly lit by the rising sun. We fished out blue glasses, standard issue. Far below, the earth was still in deep shadow. Suddenly, vapour trails began to stream out behind the engines of the lead squadron. Soon the entire formation was leaving behind a carpet of brilliant white condensation, trailing for as far as the eye could see behind us. Then, equally suddenly, the contrails ceased as we ran into a new stratum of air.

All around were my friends. On the left was *Georgia Peach*. It tucked in close, and I could see the oxygen-masked faces of the crew. Our wing man was Capt. Carrol Bender's *Tarfu*, and to port was Capt. W.B. Nance's *Dallas Rebel*. Everywhere I looked there were familiar B-17s, with the formations now tightening up noticeably. Every crew was ready for action, with helmets on heads and safety pins removed from the bombs. Snug in fleece-lined suits and gulping down oxygen, 2,000 men were going into battle five miles above the cloud-covered land of France. Black *flak* bursts appeared off our port wing, and I adjusted my helmet.

To me our great formation was a beautiful sight, and at 07.58 another beautiful sight appeared: two squadrons of RAF Spitfire IXs climbing past us. In an ominous quiet, as we passed Rouen the Spits turned back to England. We ploughed on, making a ground speed of 244 mph with a small tail wind. Within minutes Lambert's excited voice cried 'Here they come! 11 o'clock! Give 'em Hell!'

Dean, Dan and I all opened up with the three nose guns, firing at four Fw 190s coming in from dead ahead. They were closing rapidly, with bright flame winking from the cannon in their wings. They seemed to swell enormously in the final moment as they flashed past under us. I learned later that at some point a 190 collided with a B-17 from the 381st Group at Ridgewell. Amazingly, the stricken Fort made it back to a belly landing at Manston in Kent.

The next half-hour kept us busy. The intercom never stopped: '2 o'clock . . . 12 o'clock very low . . . look out there . . . 11 o'clock high . . .' The Bf 109s and Fw 190s darted around us like a swarm of bees, pressing home their attacks with determination. Always, as they reached us they half-rolled inverted, to present their armoured undersides. I noticed that many had extra cannon added on under the wings. We could not hear them above the thunder of our engines, and the constant chatter of our guns.

Soon the nose was filled with cordite smoke, and it became difficult to wade through the mass of hot empty cartridge cases. Suddenly 'Got him, got him, the son of a bitch!!' The left waist gunner had heavily hit a 109F which pulled up close; he saw pieces flying off.

At 08.25 I saw *Dallas Rebel*'s bomb doors opening. Seconds later the sticks of bombs began to go down. From the astrodome above the nose I could see sticks falling all around us, the B-17s rising and falling like carousel horses. Accuracy depended on the bombardiers' thumbs, but the cloud had cleared and the Wing had got it spot-on. Later I peered down at Le Bourget to see the bombs bursting in a tight pattern across the workshops and hangars.

Suddenly, terrifyingly, a B-17 blew up on our port beam. I counted only five parachutes. Now enemy fighters were coming in from the beam as well as from head-on. An Fw 190 came in from 1 o'clock. It swelled bigger, and I felt I simply couldn't miss. Then there was a crash, and a whirling draught. One of the 190's cannon shells had hit the end of our Plexiglas nose, blowing the upper part clean off. Dan, his main

I took this photo on 20 July 1943 on one of my later missions with the 96th Bombardment Wing. The bombs are falling on a Messerschmitt repair factory.

work as bombardier done, was firing the nose gun. At the last instant his aim made him turn away; if he hadn't, the shell would have hit him in the face. As it was, he had a minor neck wound.

Suddenly the fighters disappeared, except for a 190 which formated with us out of range. He was giving our height, course and speed to the *flak* batteries. Within seconds came 'Crump . . . crump . . . crump!' from three bursts right in front of us. One had a vivid red centre, and acrid-smelling black smoke came in through our broken nose. Another shell burst immediately ahead of our port wing tip. A distant B-17 reared up on end, and with painful inevitability spiralled majestically out of formation. Minutes later we were out of range of that *flak* battery, and the agile Messerschmitts and Focke-Wulfs returned.

Lambert said that his oxygen supply had been hit (afterwards we considered that his oxygen regulator had been damaged by blast from the top turret). All the time, the intercom was alive with warnings and comments, mostly unprintable. As we left Paris behind, the fighter attacks diminished, but the *flak* continued. Over Evreux I clearly saw red flashes from a battery of guns in a wood. About 15 seconds later the black bursts arrived all around us. We already had much local damage from shell splinters, and this made holding formation more difficult.

At 08.50 I could see the city of Caen ahead, and more fighters appeared. Dan shouted to me, 'Hey, quit firing, they're Spits!' (and I had been giving the 96th

After my first combat mission, on 14 July 1943; from the left: S/Sgt Diffendoll, T/Sgt Loscot, Lt Howell, S/Sgt McDermit, S/Sgt Musgrove, Flt/Off (Capt.) Drabnis, PGM, T/Sgt Pruden, Col Old, Capt. Lambert, Lt Markowitz, and S/Sgt Russel.

Col Archie J. Old Jr helps me on with my beautiful leather jacket. Pity the 96th censor obliterated the insignia on the photo.

instruction in aircraft recognition!). This time our escorts were mostly Mk Vs, some with clipped wings. They stayed with us all the way back. Enemy fighters kept away, but over Le Havre we suddenly ran into yet another *flak* barrage.

We left the enemy coast behind at Trouville, heading 017° for Beachy Head. Lambert let me relieve Drabnis and help bring *Daisy June* back. Once the bombs had gone, at exactly 08.00, IAS had been pulled back to 140 mph (208 true) to let stragglers keep up. At 2,000 rpm, consumption was down to 194 US gal/hr.

Over the Channel we were able to take stock. A shell splinter had ripped apart Dan's fluorescent printed bombing tables, and his C-2 plastic bombing computer had slammed into the shoulder of his leather jacket. As the adrenalin rush faded we realised that the air coming in the shattered nose at 27,000 feet was well below freezing.

We then discovered hits on the wings and near the bomb bay, and as *Daisy June* was becoming difficult to fly Drabnis came back to apply hands more expert than mine. Then the oxygen finally gave out, but by this time we were letting down through the 15,000-foot level and could manage without it. We joined the long queue of B-17s coming in to land at Snetterton Heath, and touched down at 10.46.

We had been airborne for 5 hr 31 min, and had flown some 982 miles whilst burning 1,370 US gallons of fuel. Our block speed had been 178 mph, and mean fuel burn 248 US gallons per hour. We gathered everything up, our combat films went off to be processed, and we headed for debriefing. I learned that the 96th had lost four B-17s.

Three days later I was presented with a USAAF flight jacket, autographed by the crew. In the USAAF there was usually a photographer around to record any event, but the photos of the presentation were passed to the censor, who obliterated the insignia of the 96th BG from the prints. Ever since, this jacket has been one of my most treasured possessions.

Over the following week I flew further missions aboard 42-30160 *Dallas Rebel* (Capt. Nance), 42-29941 *Tarfu* (Group Leader Col Archie Old), 42-30183 *Dry Run III* (Maj. Tiller), then *Dry Run III* again (Capt. J.R. Irish) and finally 42-30130 *Klap Trap II* (Capt. MacLachy).

As related later, in September 1944, when the 8th Air Force had become even larger, I went back to the 96th and flew a further two missions. I was proud to have flown with the 8th. As 'Hap' Arnold had intended, it did change my opinion of daylight precision bombing, but the cost was severe. On several future occasions the 8th was to suffer grievous losses, and the total casualties of the 8th Air Force were to reach 47,000, of whom over 28,000 were killed.

Today Snetterton (the 'Heath' has been dropped) has for many years been an important circuit for motor-racing. I am glad that it has not been wiped off the map as have most other wartime airfields. Perhaps the crowds who attend the races may occasionally stop and reflect on the fact that they can enjoy doing so thanks to the gallant young Americans who were there, so far from home, before them.

8

To the USA

S unday 8 August 1943 was special. From the moment I awoke I was filled with anticipation and excitement. I am sure that I was the only British civilian, and certainly the only one under the age of 30, to be invited to leave our war-torn island and fly on a comprehensive tour of the United States aircraft industry and Army Air Force. Now the day of departure had arrived! It had all been arranged by an eminent man I could now claim to call my friend, 'Hap' Arnold, Commanding General of what since 20 June 1941 had been the US Army Air Force. He had suggested that I should follow my flights on operations with the 8th Air Force in England with an extensive tour of the United States.

It was to be a two-way process. I was to see for myself what was going on in the aircraft factories and Army bases, and report back to my own country. I was also to tell the Americans what we British were doing in the various theatres of war in the air, and especially about the exploits of RAF Bomber Command. Hap's staff opened doors normally closed, and organised everything in detail so meticulous that I found it truly astonishing. Every part of my trip seemed to be planned at length, and then printed to the tune of about 32 copies, each stapled to form a major book!

Wearing my War Correspondent's uniform, and carrying a modest suitcase, I reported to what had become RAF Heston. Here I was directed to the desk of the 27th Air Transport Group, USAAF. From the start it was obvious that the magic name 'Arnold' gave me a VIP status, and I was quickly ushered on board a C-47 (USAAF DC-3). In 2 hr 25 min we were landing at Prestwick, on the coast of Ayrshire, Scotland. Here I was fed and watered, and shown to a room for the night.

Next morning I met the crew of 42-32948, a shining new Douglas C-54 Skymaster. Ordered by American Airlines as a civil DC-4, but commandeered by the AAF, it had a mere 26 comfortable airline-type seats. With four Pratt & Whitney Twin Wasp R-2000 engines driving Hydromatic propellers, big flaps and twin-wheel tricycle landing gears, it was a far cry from the fabric-covered biplanes I had been used to, just as the DC-2 had opened British eyes back in 1934. Our first leg of 5 hr 12 min took us to what was then called Meeks Field, but later became Iceland's Keflavik Airport. We stopped there for the night. Next morning, with full tanks, including long-range tanks in the front of the former passenger cabin, we took off for the 11 hr 46 min leg to Presque Isle, in the state of Maine. At last I was in the United States.

On the next day, 10 August, I was shown round the base, and made copious notes at interviews with USAAF staff. At nightfall I boarded 41-90095, a Douglas C-53 Skytrooper, for the 3 hr 27 min flight to New York La Guardia. Though the C-53 was the passenger version of the C-47, its cabin was full of partly inflated aircraft-tyre inner tubes, urgently needed down south. There were six of us who had just flown the Atlantic, and we were glad to lie down on the soft inner tubes and sleep.

What we had not expected was that, while we slumbered, thunderstorms ahead had caused the pilot to elect to climb to over 12,000 feet. After a while I awoke to find myself pressed gently but extremely firmly against the roof of the cabin by the expanding inner tubes. As far as I knew, the other passengers were in the same state. It was impossible to move an arm or a leg, though breathing was not affected. In a way, it was not unpleasant.

As we let down towards New York, the tyres gradually subsided. As I sank, soon I could look out of the windows. Having lived in a blacked-out Britain, it was amazing to see the brilliant lights of the huge city. We refuelled and went straight on to Washington National.

I was kindly met by a Royal Navy Captain, Caspar John, the son of the painter Augustus John. He introduced me to many members of the British Air Commission. This was fulfilling an enormous task principally concerned with liaising with our great ally and, in particular, testing and evaluating American aircraft and equipment for the RAF and RN. I finally got to bed in the small hours.

On the following day I met Col Stan Chester, USAAF, of 'Hap' Arnold's staff. He had been sent to collect me, and he drove me to the Pentagon. I believe this was at that time the world's largest inhabited building. I certainly did not dispute the fact that finding one's way around the five floors of the five wings on each of the five sides could pose a major problem. Each of the outer faces was 283 m (well over 300 yards) long! The building was not quite completed, but the 30,000 staff were hard at work running the USA's war.

On arrival at the Pentagon I was greeted most warmly by the top man himself, Secretary of Defense Cordell Hull. I was frankly amazed at how much time he gave me, and the interest he showed in all the details of my mission. He then took me to meet 'Hap'. (I could not help but contrast this with the way I, or any American aviation journalist, would be treated in Britain. Instead of being regarded as someone doing important work, I would be most unlikely to get past the public relations manager, or his assistant.)

Most of the following day was taken up by a meeting with top staff, cordially headed by Robert A. Lovett. He was Assistant Secretary of War for Air, and under President Roosevelt was the man who ran all the air power of the Army, Navy and Marine Corps. We thrashed out the details of the planned fact-packed tour, intended to last for more than two months. Among other things, I undertook to write dispatches for *The Sunday Times*, and whenever possible to give talks to my host establishments, and local and national broadcasts. Colonel Chester and two pilots were assigned to accompany me throughout.

Chester had been assigned a Beech AT-7 Navigator, one of the prolific family of Beech 18 derivatives. Powered by two 450-hp Wasp Juniors, this neat aircraft cruised at about 185 mph, and had a range of nearly 600 miles. With serial number 42-2449, it was practically new, like almost all the Army and Navy aircraft throughout the United States. With Maj. J.T. Fitzwalter in command, we took off from Washington National, and headed first for New York La Guardia. We refuelled, and went on to Cleveland, and then on to Willow Run.

About thirty miles west of downtown Detroit, and built and run by the Ford Motor Company, this impressive mile-long plant was reputed to be turning out one of the

With Majors Hudson and Fitzwalter in front of the AT-7 on 13 August 1943.

most complex aircraft in the world, the Consolidated B-24 Liberator heavy bomber, at the rate of one aircraft every hour. Unfortunately, by this time night had fallen. I was relieved when everyone in my party agreed that the USA was a big place, and that we needed a faster aircraft in order to cover the ground.

On the next day we retraced our steps through Detroit airport and Cleveland to La Guardia. Here we happily climbed into 42-57223. This had been built as NC36603, a Lockheed Lodestar airliner, impressed into the AAF as a C-56D. Powered by R-1690-25 Hornet engines, it could cruise at 200 mph. Once again we staged through Cleveland, but now we went on through Chicago Midway, Minneapolis, Bismarck, Billings and Spokane, to Boeing Field at Seattle. Here my old acquaintance Wellwood Beall greeted me most kindly. He took endless pains to ensure that I saw everything, not only the massive output of the B-17 (in which I had a strong personal interest) but also the fantastic manufacturing programme for the new B-29 Superfortress. Dozens of plants were feeding the B-29 assembly lines at Boeing Renton, Boeing Wichita, Bell Marietta and Martin Omaha. This was an eye-opener to me, as at that time the very existence of the B-29 was secret. My briefing was, of course, off the record.

It was almost too much to take in, especially as I had to write my dispatches for *The Sunday Times*, and make frequent broadcasts on local radio stations or give interviews to local journalists. Throughout, I was impressed by the obvious meticulous planning that had been done to open doors, brief my hosts in the greatest detail, and arrange things for me to do. Whenever appropriate, Hap had instructed that I was to fly in newly built aircraft, and if possible fly them myself. Everything went like clockwork, and I kept wryly contrasting this wonderful tour with how a young American journalist would have fared in England.

From Seattle I naturally went south to California. The climate may have had something to do with the fact that this big State had become virtually the aircraft-production capital of the Allies. Employment in the Californian aircraft plants was in the region of half a million, and in 1943 almost every plant was on a three-shift basis, running at full stretch 24 hours a day.

Accordingly, after saying goodbye to my new friends at Boeing I boarded the faithful Lodestar. Again with Maj. Fitzwalter in command, we flew by way of Portland and Mills Field (San Francisco) to Burbank, part of the vast sprawl of Los Angeles. Burbank was the home of Lockheed Aircraft.

In the mid-1930s Lockheed had been near to collapse. When the new twin-engined Model 10 Electra had a wheel jam in the retracted position on its maiden flight there was doubt that money could be found to repair it. A few dollars were scraped together, and customers began to appear. In April 1938 a small team worked day and night to build a mock-up (full-scale model) of the fuselage of a proposed reconnaissance bomber for Britain's RAF. A British team inspected it, and asked for changes. These were all done *in 24 hours*. The British team were so impressed that they ordered 200 of the proposed aircraft. It was named Hudson, and the RAF eventually bought more than 2,000. The British orders suddenly made Lockheed big and prosperous.

I was met by the President, Robert E. Gross. Bob was diminutive in stature, but

By 1943 I had broadcast many times on the BBC and NBC, so being faced with American microphones held no terrors.

impressive in everything other way. A lawyer, he had personally rescued the ailing company, and built it up in partnership with a dedicated team which included his brother Courtland S. Gross, as General Manager. The VP and Chief Engineer was Hall L. Hibbard, under whom was the mercurial Clarence L. 'Kelly' Johnson, the brilliant head of design. I was to know them particularly well in years to come. Even on this first visit Bob invited me to stay at his beautiful Bel Air home, where at dinner we were joined by his wife Mary and their beautiful 17-year-old daughter Palmer.

Again, there was too much to see in a short time. Lockheed's employment exceeded 91,000, mostly in 18 plants in southern California. One of them, run by a subsidiary, Vega Aircraft, was busy delivering 2,750 Boeing B-17s. Lockheed's own products included the Hudson, PV-1 Ventura and PV-2 Harpoon reconnaissance bombers. Coming into production was the mighty Constellation airliner, which had first flown at the beginning of the year. After testing by the Army Air Force, this prototype was now back at Lockheed, re-engined with 2,000-hp Double Wasps. (It might have been a good idea to stay with that engine, because the engine chosen for production, the Wright R-3350 Duplex Cyclone, was to give a great deal of trouble.)

Apart from 113 made by Vultee, Burbank was also the sole source of the unique P-38 Lightning twin-engined long-range fighter. People who could not tell one aircraft from another could identify the P-38 with its short central nacelle and a tail carried on two booms extending aft from the engines. Uncannily quiet, because it had no normal exhaust pipes (the hot gas escaped through a system of valves which could

With a B-17F – one of the last to be painted olive-drab – at Douglas Long Beach. From the left: PGM, Majors Hudson and Fitzwalter and Colonel Stith.

At Douglas Long Beach on 24 August 1943. My shoulders proclaimed BRITISH WAR CORRESPONDENT.

duct it through a turbo-supercharger), it was finished off like a Cadillac. On my visit I was delighted to squeeze into one of the few with a second seat behind the pilot. It was an obsolete RP-322 version, originally intended for the RAF. The Lockheed pilot really wrung it out, affording me a feel for how far the technology had progressed since my ride in the F.K.52.

Though Bob Gross was 'Mr Lockheed', and the man whose face might appear on the cover of *Time* or *Life* – again I could not help thinking how British mass-market magazines ignored Bob's British counterparts. He took me to all the key people, and also handed me one of his suits when he heard how we in Britain were issued with coupons permitting us to buy clothing (later Pat unpicked the trousers and turned them into a skirt for herself). After the war I was shocked when Bob's brother Courtland and his wife were murdered in their home by an intruder, who was never caught.

On the opposite side of LA from Burbank is Santa Monica, the home of Douglas

Aircraft. Again, I was greeted by the top man. Donald Wills Douglas had started his company in the back of a barber shop on Pico Boulevard. Now he had 157,200 employees (the total peaked at that figure almost on the day of my visit). As in the other big plants, half of this enormous total were women, whom the American media characterised as 'Rosie the riveter'.

The list of Douglas aircraft in large-scale production was without parallel. Santa Monica was concentrating on the A-20 Havoc/Boston family, and on the C-54A, and various secret new types. On 23 August I boarded a brand-new C-54A, gleaming in its unpainted finish, and sat in the co-pilot's seat alongside AAF acceptance pilot, Col Stith. He let me fly on the 22-minute initial workout, landing at the enormous Douglas plant at Long Beach. Just south of LA, Long Beach had finished delivering 999 A-20s, and was now in production with the C-47, the new A-26 Invader and 3,000 Boeing B-17Fs and Gs. We then worked through the rest of the C-54A's acceptance test on our 30-minute return flight to Santa Monica.

A new plant leased by Douglas at Oklahoma City was at full blast turning out 5,409 C-47s and variants, while an even newer leased factory at Chicago was making 655 C-54s. The vast Navy plant at El Segundo, directed by its brilliant Chief Engineer Ed Heinemann, was producing 5,323 SDB/A-24 Dauntless dive bombers. He had been responsible for the design and initial production of the A-20 and A-26, and was working on several new designs. At Tulsa, Oklahoma, a leased plant was churning out the A-24, A-26 and Consolidated B-24! Who would have thought that in 1997 the proud name of Douglas would pass into history?

On one of my few afternoons off I visited the California Aero Flight Academy, at Ontario (not to be confused with the Canadian province). They briefly looked at my US Pilot License (which I had obtained automatically on production of my British A Licence) and let me loose on USAAF 40-1716, a Boeing PT-13B Kaydet. Resembling a much bigger Tiger Moth, with more than double the power (280-hp Lycoming R-680), I found it pleasant to fly, and tried my hand at aerobatics.

Roughly between Santa Monica and Long Beach, the enormous plant of North American Aviation at Inglewood had finished making AT-6 Texan/Harvard trainers, which were now coming off the line at Dallas, Texas. Instead, Inglewood was in mass-production with the P-51 Mustang, with the Allison engine, and was working on a version with the Packard-built Rolls-Royce Merlin. Also at Inglewood was a further seemingly endless assembly line of B-25 Mitchell attack bombers. The B-25 was also in production in a leased plant at Kansas City, while the new company-owned plant at Dallas was building not only the trainers but also the P-51 Mustang and the Consolidated B-24 Liberator. Discounting various experimental prototypes, during World War 2 NAA made 41,479 aircraft, more than any other company in the world.

The faithful Lodestar took me to many other aircraft companies, as well as to training bases from Florida to Canada. My first visit to a training base was to one of the sprawling sites of Williams Field, outside Phoenix, Arizona. My intensive visit ended with squeezing in beside Capt. F.H. Scott in a Curtiss AT-9 Jeep. This diminutive twin-engined trainer was deliberately designed to reproduce the 'hot' characteristics of fighters and attack bombers. In other words, it was not for novices.

Some of my transportation (as Americans say) was in a Lockheed C-60, another version of the Lodestar built on USAAF contract and powered by 1,200-hp Wright

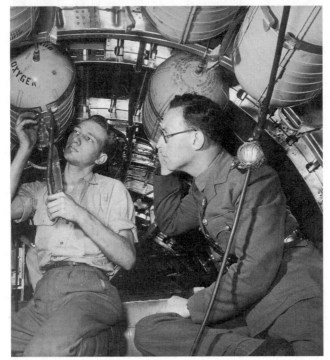

My last plant visit, on 2 September 1943, was to Consolidated-Vultee at Fort Worth, Texas. From the left: AAF Plant Rep. Lt-Col Roy E. Ludick; PGM; Cdr Roland G. Mayer, Assistant Division Manager; and my pilots Maj. J.T. Fitzwalter and Maj. Roland L. Hudson.

Watching the installation of oxygen bottles in a B-24J at Fort Worth.

R-1820 Cyclone engines broadly similar to those of the B-17. On two C-60 flights I flew as co-pilot to aircraft commander Capt. Al Carl.

I liaised with the Canadian Government in Ottawa, all the time being called upon to give broadcasts. I then returned to visit plants in the eastern United States.

By Friday 17 September I was used to the scale of American aeronautical establishments, but nevertheless I found the Wright Field and Patterson Air Force Base complex (later simply called Wright-Patterson) breathtaking. This was the centre of AAF experimental flying, and one of the newer arrivals was a Sikorsky YR-4 helicopter. It was the first helicopter – as distinct from autogiro – that I had seen. I was intrigued to do 15 minutes' dual with Col Cooper, one of the exclusive band of pilots already qualified on such machines.

On Sunday 25 September I visited the impressive plant of Republic Aviation at Farmingdale, on New York's Long Island. It had essentially one product, the big, powerful and pugnacious P-47D Thunderbolt fighter-bomber. Together with a second assembly line at Evansville, Illinois, and a few made by Curtiss at Buffalo, total P-47 production was 15,586, fractionally more than the total for any other US fighter in history.

From Farmingdale I took the Long Island railroad back to Manhattan, and on the following day, among other things, I went in the evening to the CBS studio to do a

With my pilots at one of the largest P-38 training bases, at Tucson, Arizona.

broadcast interview on my impressions of American fighter production. Moments after the broadcast was finished I was handed a cablegram, addressed to me 'care of the British Consul-General, New York'. It read: 'REQUIRE URGENT TALK STOP ADVISE DATE RETURN LONDON SOONEST STOP BEAVERBROOK'

I wondered wherein I might have erred? During the previous six weeks I had cabled numerous comments to London, and almost anything might have incurred the famous Beaverbrook wrath. Dropping everything, I made arrangements to return to London immediately, and telephoned Hap in the Pentagon to explain the situation. I cabled back: 'PLAN REACH LONDON 30 SEPTEMBER STOP WILL TELEPHONE ON ARRIVAL STOP MASEFIELD.'

9

The British answer: form a committee

This chapter digresses from the narrative to describe how Britain handled the revolution in aircraft design which began in the early 1930s. Fabric-covered, wire-braced biplanes gave way to stressed-skin cantilever monoplanes with retractable undercarriages, flaps, and efficiently cowled engines driving variable-pitch propellers. With increased flight performance came the ability to reduce fuel consumption by flying at increased heights, leading to the introduction of pressurised cabins.

Britain's national airline, Imperial Airways, concentrated on safety rather than speed, overlooking the fact that it could have both, while the RAF was so parsimoniously funded that new technology took a back seat. By 1937 it was obvious that Britain was falling behind, and under Lord Cadman a committee was formed to 'inquire into Civil Aviation'. It 'expressed concern', and recommended that the newly formed British Airways should have exclusive rights throughout Europe, while Imperial Airways continued to link the Empire. On aircraft design it said nothing.

On 14 May 1941 the Prime Minister appointed Lord Brabazon (holder of the British Pilot's Licence No 1) to succeed Lord Beaverbrook as Minister of Aircraft Production. In turn, 'Brab' asked Sir Henry Tizard to serve as a Special Technical Adviser. The upshot was the formation of a secret Special Advisory Committee, chaired by Sir Roy Fedden. Its meetings were in the beautiful home of the Royal Aeronautical Society in Hamilton Place, near Hyde Park Corner. Its task was to study whatever was new and important in aviation technology, and report direct to the Minister of Aircraft Production. By the end of the war it had met for more than 500 hours, and had submitted 40 detailed Memoranda to four successive Ministers. Today these documents make interesting and impressive reading.

Three months later, in August 1941 Government officials formed a somewhat ineffective 'Departmental Committee on Post-war Policy for Civil Aviation'. It was chaired by Lt-Col Sir Francis Shelmerdine, who had just been appointed as Director-General of Civil Aviation (DGCA). By this time the national airline BOAC had lost three of its Short C-Class flying boats through accidents, and three Armstrong Whitworth Ensign landplanes which had been destroyed on the ground during the retreat from France. Moreover, the elegant D.H.91 Albatross had shown that its wooden structure rapidly became dangerously unsafe.

Soon after the war began, and with no recorded discussion, the momentous decision was taken to concentrate all the efforts of the British aircraft industry on combat aircraft. The projected next-generation airliners, the Fairey F.C.1 and Short S.32, were both cancelled. In the same vein, when the sadly unimpressive report of the

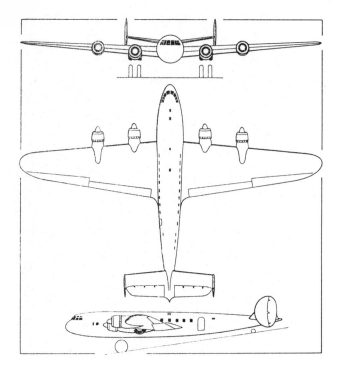

*Had the Short S.32
been built, passengers
would not have liked
the way the wing spars
divided the interior
into three
compartments.*

Shelmerdine Committee appeared in January 1942 it was hastily buried inside the Air Ministry, lest it should distract attention from the primary objective of winning the war.

Realising that everything possible must be done to maintain a reliable air link with the USA, the Under-Secretary of State for Air, Capt. Harold Balfour, took it upon himself in late 1940 to commit the Air Ministry to purchase three new Boeing 314A flying boats at £259,250 each from Pan American, which had originally ordered them (the American airline had ordered six, and retained three). These great aircraft were delivered to BOAC between May and July 1941. I was to know them well, as related later.

This marked the start of a long period in which, because of Government policy, or rather lack of it, we had no British airliners other than the Short Empire 'boats with either high speed or long range. Even before the war British Airways had had to import Lockheed 10 Electra and Lockheed 14 airliners because nothing with similar performance was available in Britain. Prime Minister Chamberlain had to use both these American types on his missions to appease Hitler.

Such a situation was disquieting, but it was pushed into the background. The nation's efforts were directed wholly to winning the war. In August 1942 this task looked terribly difficult, and Prime Minister Churchill flew to Moscow to tell Stalin that there was no chance of Britain opening a 'Second Front' in Western Europe in that year.

To get to Moscow he had to fly via Gibraltar, Cairo and Tehran. In 1942 such a mission posed the United Kingdom a serious challenge. The only way Mr Churchill could be carried was well wrapped in blankets in the freezing converted bomb bay of a Consolidated Liberator II, AL578 named *Marco Polo*, much of the time wearing an oxygen mask!

Lack of suitable aircraft was now deeply worrying. Following private and unofficial discussions, in September 1942 a group of well-informed people who had no direct connection with air transport (this was deliberate) formed an Independent Committee on the Future of Civil Aviation. It was in no sense an instrument of the Government. Its Chairman was Capt. Arthur G. Lamplugh, the Chairman of Lloyds underwriters. The members were A.J.A. Wallace Barr, Chairman of the KLG sparking-plug firm; Walter C. Devereux, Chairman of High Duty Alloys; George H. Dowty, Chairman of the Dowty Group; Leslie L. Irvin, Chairman of the Irvin Air Chute parachute company; Alonso Limb, Managing Director of the Castrol oil company; H.E. Nicholls, of Handley Page and the Intava oil company; Oliver Simmonds MP, Chairman of Simmonds Aerocessories; and myself as Secretary.

We held 32 weekly meetings, took evidence from 40 carefully chosen people, and produced a report published on 20 May 1943. Its main recommendations were that, after the war:

1   British air transport should be removed from the control of the Air Ministry.
2   It should be placed under a new Ministry of Civil Aviation, with a Minister of Cabinet rank.
3   A British Airports Authority should be formed, to develop and operate the nation's major airports.
4   British air transport should be operated by six strong airlines, each with a geographical sphere of interest.
5   There should be a plan for a comprehensive range of new civil aircraft.
6   There should be a national programme for air education and training, and of support for flying clubs.

By the time that these forward-looking recommendations were published, the official machine had begun to act. Churchill had had no time to think about the absence of modern British airliners until he had to make his gruelling flights in the converted Liberator. These voyages brought home to him the need for action. (Incidentally, as soon as Churchill returned from Moscow, another Liberator II, AL504, was demilitarised and returned to San Diego, where it was stripped of camouflage and fitted out as a relatively comfortable VIP transport. The opportunity was taken to stretch the fuselage, and fit a tall single fin of the type designed for the US Navy RY-3 version. Named *Commando*, AL504 became the Government's principal long-range VIP aircraft. In May 1945 it disappeared between the Azores and Canada with the loss of its crew and a number of important passengers.)

Accordingly, in December 1942 the Prime Minister called in the new Minister of Aircraft Production, Sir Stafford Cripps, and his predecessor, Lord Brabazon, and told them that he was concerned that nothing was being done to provide for the future of British transport aircraft. In fact, five months previously, the A.V. Roe (Avro) company had – as a rather daring private effort, which could even have been considered a misuse of scarce alloys – flown a noisy and primitive transport development of the Lancaster bomber, called the York. Though useful, this was hardly an aircraft for the post-war era.

The reaction was to form yet another committee. Though two of the committees previously mentioned were still active, Brab consulted Sir Henry Tizard and, with Stafford Cripps, proposed to Churchill the formation of a small committee of senior officials charged with making specific recommendations for post-war civil transport aircraft. Churchill invited Lord Brabazon to be Chairman, and on 23 December 1942 the Brabazon Committee (later called the First Brabazon Committee) held its first meeting. Nothing was announced.

In addition to the Chairman, the members of this committee were: Sir Henry Self, Permanent Secretary, Ministry of Supply; Sir Francis Shelmerdine, whose own committee had been disbanded; William P. Hildred, who had replaced Sir Francis as DGCA; and N.E. 'Nero' Rowe, Director of Technical Development, Ministry of Aircraft Production (MAP). The Secretary was Kelvin T. Spencer, First Secretary, Operational Requirements, at the MAP. Special Technical Adviser was John H. Riddoch, Private Secretary to the DGCA.

This committee held ten meetings over the course of seven weeks, and reported on 9 February 1943. It recommended the development of five completely new types of aircraft, as well as civil adaptations of the Avro Lancaster and York landplanes, and of the Short Sunderland III and Shetland flying boats.

Some weeks later the decision was taken to form a Second Brabazon Committee, with more comprehensive and detailed terms of reference. It was made up of eight members. Apart from Lord Brabazon, the only one who had served on the original committee was William (from 1944 Sir William) Hildred. The only aircraft constructor was the doyen of that species, Capt. Geoffrey (from 1944 Sir Geoffrey) de Havilland. There were three representatives of the national airline BOAC. Major Ronald McCrindle and Alan Campbell-Orde were pioneers of British air transport, the former as CO of the RAF Communications Squadron in 1919, and Campbell-Orde as one of its pilots. In the 1930s they had helped set up British Airways. The third BOAC Board member was Major Roland H. Thornton, a private pilot who was also a member of the Air Registration Board and a partner in a Liverpool ship-owners. Gp Capt. William Helmore was an adviser to the MAP, a director of Wakefield oil, Member of Parliament for Watford, inventor of the Turbinlite for night interceptions and an aviation broadcaster. Air Commodore Alfred R. Wardle had flown in the RFC in 1915–18, and became Director of Operational Requirements at the Air Ministry.

John Riddoch became the new Committee's Secretary, in place of K.T. Spencer, who became one of three Technical Advisers. The other two advisers were 'Nero' Rowe and a newcomer, Cyril B. Collins, an Air Ministry Technical Officer.

Brab summed them up as 'a useful mixed bag'. They were to hold discussions with many companies, and with representatives of Commonwealth countries. The committee met on 62 occasions from 25 May 1943, and produced 151 papers. It remained formally in existence until 12 November 1945, and brought its recommendations up to date with a revised report in December 1945.

It recommended the construction of seven prototypes in five categories. It ignored all conversions of existing aircraft. As the world's greatest conflict reached its climax, this committee occupied a substantial slice of the attention of several Cabinet Ministers, including Churchill, and senior civil servants in five Government departments.

Sadly, the implementation of the resulting Recommendations fell far short of the committee's hopes and ambitions. More than half the proposals fell by the wayside, and of the largest types that entered service one suffered a series of catastrophic accidents, and the other was four years late, which crippled its impact on the market.

I should comment that the biggest British aircraft ever built, the Saunders-Roe SR.45 Princess flying boat, was never considered by any committee at all, but was simply proposed by the manufacturer and accepted by the Minister of Supply, who ordered three. It was never ordered by BOAC or the RAF. It was built with ten Bristol Proteus turboprops (eight of them in coupled pairs) after rejecting the Armstrong Siddeley Cobra and Python and the Rolls-Royce Eagle, Clyde and Tweed. It was responsible for the fact that the Proteus had a reverse-flow layout. This had serious consequences (see Chapter 36).

In the course of time the simple Brabazon Committee plan became convoluted:

Brabazon I   This was to have been a large (150-ton) aircraft for the North Atlantic. Specification 2/44 was to be met by the Bristol 167 Brabazon, and an initial four were ordered. One was built (G-AGPW) and flown on 4 September 1949. The other three were to be of a considerably modified Mk II type, with four pairs of Proteus turboprops. As noted above, this engine was specially designed to be fed by wing-root intakes, and thus had to have a reverse-flow compressor. Eventually both the Mk I and Mk II were scrapped.

Brabazon II   This was to be a replacement for the hundreds of DC-3/C-47 aircraft on European and other short-haul routes. It was to be met by the Airspeed A.S.57 Ambassador (Specification C.25/43). The prototype (G-AGUA) was flown on 10 July 1947. Though 20 were produced as the BEA 'Elizabethan' class, the parent firm de Havilland ignored promising further sales and filled the Airspeed factories with lucrative jet-fighter contracts. In 1945 **Brabazon IIB** turboprop aircraft were added: the Armstrong Whitworth A.W.55 Apollo and Vickers-Armstrongs VC.2 Viceroy. Two Apollos were flown, but, partly because its Mamba engine was thought less promising than the RR Dart of the Vickers aircraft, they were abandoned. The VC.2 became the V.630 Viscount (Specification 8/46). The prototype (G-AHRF) was flown on 16 September 1948. Thanks to the leadership of designer George Edwards, it was successfully developed in weight and power, and 445 were built.

Brabazon III   This was called the MRE (Medium-Range Empire) aircraft, and was regarded as possibly the most important type of all. It was to be met by the Avro 693, successively with four Bristol Hercules piston engines, then six Bristol Centaurus, and finally four Rolls-Royce Clyde turboprops. Faced with apparently greater priorities, Rolls-Royce abandoned this potentially important engine, which was doing outstandingly well in flight tests. Avro recast the 693 around four Rolls-Royce Avon turbojets, and finally decided that they had too much other work to continue. The Avro 693 was at once replaced by the broadly similar Bristol 175 (Specification 2/47) with four Centaurus engines. This in turn was developed into the Britannia, with Proteus turboprops. The prototype (G-ALBO) was flown on 16 August 1952. Partly because of the reverse-flow layout of the engine, which resulted from its original use in giant aircraft that were later cancelled, Britannia development took years longer than planned. Eventually 85 Britannias were built, almost all for BOAC or the RAF.

Brabazon IV   This was a bold proposal for a jet-propelled mail carrier, possibly with North Atlantic capability. It was to be met by the D.H.106 (Specification 20/44). Wisely, the de Havilland Aircraft Company developed this as a passenger aircraft, named Comet. The prototype (G-ALVG) was flown on 27 July 1949. The Comet 1 entered BOAC service on 1 May 1952, but by 1954 had suffered catastrophic fatigue failures of the fuselage skin. The programme was almost abandoned, but eventually the completely redesigned Comet 4 entered BOAC service in 1958. Total production was 112.

Brabazon V   This was to be a local-service aircraft. In 1945 the group was divided into two sub-types. The Brabazon VA feeder liner was to be the Miles M.60 Marathon (Specification 18/44). The prototype (G-AGPD) was flown on 19 May 1946, but Miles was taken over by Handley Page and the Marathon was tried but rejected by BEA. Eventually 20 were foisted on the RAF as crew trainers. Brabazon VB described a Rapide replacement for air taxi services, to be met by the D.H.104 Dove (Specification 26/43). The prototype (G-AGPJ) was flown on 25 September 1945, and 542 were built.

As related in later chapters, I was asked by Lord Beaverbrook to see if anything could be done more quickly, and it was decided that the thing to do was to form yet another committee. This, the Civil Air Transport Committee, was the most powerful of the lot. It comprised 11 'Right Honourables', with Lord Beaverbrook as Chairman and myself as Secretary.

10

Meeting the Beaver

I t all began on the sunny morning of 18 July 1940. I was in *The Aeroplane* offices in Bowling Green Lane when my telephone rang. It was always ringing, but this call was unusual: 'The name is Frank Owen . . . Lord Beaverbrook has asked me to invite you to come and see him and have a talk. Can you manage 3 o'clock . . . ?'

Accordingly, ten minutes before that time I found myself with Frank Owen in the waiting room outside the bustling office of the Minister of Aircraft Production in Thames House, on Millbank. Frank, very Welsh, had been Liberal MP for Hereford. Now, at 35 and prematurely grey, he was Editor of the *Evening Standard*, and he stood high in the favour of the man who, feared by many, was 'the Beaver' to the media, but 'Max' to his friends. I had just contributed an article on 'The Air War' to his newspaper. Perhaps the Beaver did not like it? Frank had no idea.

We went in. The second most powerful man in the War Cabinet was sitting at an enormous desk, with six telephones (at the time considered extraordinary). He jumped up, wearing a blue suit and a broad grin. 'Ah, Mr Masefield. You are making yourself quite a reputation. That article you wrote for the *Standard* – good stuff. And you write for my old friend Gomer Kemsley. Great paper, *The Sunday Times*. Fine piece last Sunday about the Hurricane and Spitfire. But you keep anonymous . . . your name should be blazoned in the headlines.'

I suggested that what was written was more important than who wrote it, but he cried 'You're wrong (his distinctive Canadian voice made it "wraaang"). Make your name. Never hide your light under a bushel. Doesn't do the bushel any good!'

After about twenty minutes I decided that he must want me to boost his Ministry, the MAP, in *The Sunday Times*. A week later, on 24 July, he made a stirring and indeed brilliant speech, about toilers in workshops and young fighter pilots – one of whom was his son, Max Aitken, whose wrath I had incurred at school but who was now CO of 601 Sqn flying Hurricanes up to 18 hours a day in the front line from Tangmere.

During the next few months I received frequent notes from the Beaver, variously praising me, and exhorting me to write on particular topics. My working days involved writing for *The Aeroplane*, for Eric Bowater at the MAP and for *The Sunday Times*, all the while expecting and hoping to be called up for RAF aircrew duties.

There were also many intelligence tasks. In mid-August I was at the RAE (Royal Aircraft Establishment) at Farnborough studying and reporting on *Luftwaffe* aircraft. These were displayed in a large hangar in varying states of disrepair after crash-landing following the attentions of RAF fighters, which in most cases had been Hurricanes. They had already been studied in detail by RAE and RAF experts. They included a Bf 109E and Bf 110C-5 (both of which at the time we in Britain called 'Me' aircraft, despite the evidence of their factory plates), a Do 17Z-2, two He 111Hs and a Ju 88A-1.

I probably knew as much about these aircraft as anyone in the country, and set out on a tour of RAF fighter stations to talk about the enemy, and point out any weaknesses.

On a beautiful 12 August I went to RAF North Weald, commanded by the great Irish rugby cap Victor Beamish. He was an impressive and charming man, with an attractive Irish brogue. He took me round in the station Humber to see Nos 56 and 151 Squadrons. Both had been fighting non-stop for three months. Their pilots were at readiness, but relaxed in deck chairs outside their Nissen huts. All were confident and boyish aircraft enthusiasts, and we were soon deep in discussion.

At No 56 I met Geoffrey Page. He was shot down on that very afternoon, but despite serious burns survived to become one of my colleagues in Washington and a top Vickers-Armstrongs man at Weybridge. Taffy Higginson was to go on to design missiles at Bristol, and Michael Constable Maxwell was, much later, to join me in flying Chipmunks. Sadly, super-enthusiast 'Jumbo' Gracie, who went on to command No 601 Sqn, and give 'thumbs-down' to the Bell Airacobra, was killed in 1944 flying a Tempest. Beamish himself was to locate the *Scharnhorst* and *Gneisenau* steaming up the Channel on 12 February 1942, only to be killed two months later.

At that time there was a widespread belief that the Ju 88 had a gun firing down and to the rear. I told them that, perhaps astonishingly, they did not. Suddenly Nos 56 and 151 were scrambled. About an hour later Gracie and Page came back and delightedly told me they had studied several Ju 88s from close quarters and confirmed what I had said. (Later Ju 88s were, in fact, equipped with a rear ventral gun.)

At North Weald we lunched in the Mess, which a month later was completely destroyed by Dorniers and Heinkels. After lunch I went up to 151 Sqn, where a prominent participant was their young handlebar-moustached CO, Teddy Donaldson, who shortly after the war set two World Speed Records in a Gloster Meteor IV. Soon the squadrons were again scrambled. Just as they returned, a telephone rang in one of the Nissen huts:

DAMAGED IN TRANSIT. – A Junkers Ju 88K shot down by anti-aircraft fire during a raid on Portland on August 11 – the first day of the massed attacks against Great Britain. The radial cowlings of the liquid cooled motors have been removed for inspection purposes. One of the dive brakes can be seen extended under the wing.

Our first intact Ju 88 was shot down on the Dorset coast on 11 August 1940. I wrote the caption before inspecting it.

'Peter!' said the now familiar Canadian voice, 'I'm told that you have been studying German aircraft. You have written a report? Will you send it to me this evening? Goodbye to you.'

Before putting *The Aeroplane* to bed I made a copy of my report and took it round to Thames House. I never heard why he wanted it so urgently, but that was his style.

On that day RAF Fighter Command shot down 48, but lost 31 fighters, with 13 of the pilots saved. The following day, 13 August, was called by Goering *Adlerangriff* (assault of the eagles). The *Luftwaffe* launched some 1,500 aircraft against RAF No 11 Group, and lost 73 aircraft shot down over southern England. The RAF lost 13 fighters, and a further 47 assorted aircraft were destroyed on the ground.

So I plugged on. In September 1943 Francis Williams, dean of journalists, told me that to have written Air War articles which appeared on the front page of *The Sunday Times* for 172 consecutive weeks was 'a Fleet Street record'. I told him that Lord Kemsley, W.W. Hadley and Valentine Heyward of that paper could not have been more tolerant and considerate, and utterly unlike the popular image of newspaper barons.

On Wednesday 30 April 1941 the Beaver invited me to lunch at Claridges. I found myself seated opposite him, among 15 editors and Fleet Street writers on air affairs. Over coffee Max treated us to a stirring review of his first year's work at the MAP. He threw in a few titbits, such as the first news of the Hawker Tornado and Westland Whirlwind fighters and the four-engined Short Stirling bomber. Of course, this was off the record.

What he did not tell us was that on the previous day he had asked Churchill to be allowed to resign and leave the Government. When I knew him better I realised that, though he was certainly exhausted, his main reason for the request was that he tended to lose interest once a crisis was over. The Prime Minister asked him to stay in the War Cabinet, with a newly invented role: 'Minister of State'. Previously he had been the first Minister of Information (in 1917) and the first Minister of Aircraft Production (in 1940).

He moved from Millbank to 12 Downing Street, and then at the end of May 1941 to Shell-Mex House as Minister of Supply. When I next saw him, he was in an office overlooking the Thames which I myself was to occupy in 1965.

Our paths did not cross again until 8 March 1943. I was in Warleywoods Hospital at Brentwood, recovering from an emergency appendicitis operation, and was surprised to receive a sympathetic letter from him. Obviously dictated, it went on to say 'I thought of quoting you in the Lords next Wednesday the 10th on an estimate of production in Great Britain . . .' Unfortunately I could not help him, as I had no papers with me. By the time I was out of hospital he had disappeared with Churchill to Washington, to plan the Second Front.

Two months later I sent Max a copy of the Lamplugh Report (see Chapter 9). I learned later that it had been précised for him by George Malcolm Thompson. Then other matters intervened, but on the evening of Monday 26 September 1943 a cablegram was handed to me in a CBS studio in Manhattan. As related in Chapter 8, it read: REQUIRE URGENT TALK STOP ADVISE DATE RETURN LONDON SOONEST STOP BEAVERBROOK.

Of course, I had to cut my visit short. On the 28th I boarded a C-54 of USAAF Air

Transport Command at La Guardia and, by way of Stephenville (Newfoundland) and Prestwick, I landed on the following day at Northolt. I went straight home to West Hill Court at Highgate, in North London. Sleepily, I telephoned Max's Fleet Street office, and told the faithful George Miller that I was back. He said 'I will tell the Master.'

I heard nothing until, two days later, I was again in a broadcasting studio, this time with the BBC at Broadcasting House. I had just come off the air when Vincent Alford's secretary put her head round the door and said, with tones of awe, 'Lord Beaverbrook on the line for Mr Masefield.'

'Peter! I have just been hearing you speak. You do well. Now will you come and work for me? The Prime Minister wants me to look into British and Empire aviation, for when the war is over . . . Come and see me at Gwydyr House. Miss Hogg will fix a time. Good bye to you.' I had said just one word, 'Hello'.

So began three years of very active and interesting life in 'the Corridors of Power'. My particular corridors were in Gwydyr House (pronounced 'Gwiddear') in Whitehall.

11

Beavering

O n 21 September 1943 the Chancellor of the Exchequer died suddenly. He was Sir Kingsley Wood, whom I had known well as Air Minister before the war. Three days later the Prime Minister, Winston Churchill, reshuffled his Government. Among other things he persuaded Max (Lord Beaverbrook) to come back into the Government as Lord Privy Seal. In practice, this title meant that he was Mr Churchill's Jack of all Trades.

He at once asked me to work for him. I cut short my tour of the USA and at 10.30 on the morning of Wednesday 6 October 1943, I presented myself at stately Gwydyr House. Completed in 1773, it had once been the home of the Reform Club. Later it had housed the Directorate of Civil Aviation, and then the office of the Air Minister. Its address is No 2 Whitehall, opposite the Horse Guards and next to the Banqueting Hall, through a window of which Charles I had stepped onto the scaffold to lose his head.

As I entered, it seemed that losing one's head was still a distinct possibility. As I ascended the beautiful staircase I was almost thrown down it by a dark-coated, white-haired figure who dashed past muttering 'That man, my God, that man . . .' and hurried down Whitehall like the White Rabbit in *Alice in Wonderland*.

I later learned that the flying figure was C.A.C. Hendriks, CBE, the Lord Privy Seal's official PPS (Personal Private Secretary). After 11 days of the Beaver, he was indulging in a nervous breakdown. He never returned.

On the first-floor landing I was met by a sturdier character, Elizabeth Hogg, the APS (A for Assistant). A Scot, she was very blonde, very precise, and very much in complete command. She had already coped effortlessly with two previous LPSs, Lord Salisbury and Arthur Greenwood, and clearly intended to do the same with Max.

She welcomed me kindly. She vanished behind an oak door, and in a flash was back, saying in her cultured Edinburgh accents 'The Lord awaits'.

The room I entered was perhaps the finest in the Government. It stretched across the house from Whitehall to the gardens behind. It had a wondrously moulded ceiling, and floor-to-ceiling windows at each end. The sole occupant was seated at a desk half-way along the western wall. As so often, he was wearing a blue suit and blue tie. His broad face was surrounded by wisps of white hair, the white eyebrows beetling, and his wide mouth creased in a broad grin.

Rising from his desk, he said 'Peter, how are you? The Lord God (pronounced Gaad) moves in mysterious ways . . . Now you must come to work for me here? Steer us along the forward path. You've shown me you have imagination and vigour. You know about air transport – but we have to move it fast, along the high road.'

I said that I would be privileged to work for him, but that I would need about four weeks to complete my present commitments. Even though I had ceased to work for

Temple Press in June 1943, my life was still somewhat complicated. I was committed to *The Sunday Times*, to writing for various other papers and journals, and frequently to broadcasting on the BBC. Now I was the centre of a wrangle.

I had, at last, received instructions from the Air Minister to proceed to Lords Cricket Ground on 1 November *en route* to join the ATA as a ferry pilot. But Lord Sherwood, the Under-Secretary of State for Air, had decreed that I was not to join the ATA, and had instructed the BBC that they were to get me seconded to them as a War Correspondent. I told the ATA that I felt like a pawn, and that my purpose was to serve where best I could.

I was delighted at Max's invitation. Though I had hoped to join the ATA, I assured him that I would be ready to throw up all other commitments to work for him on post-war aviation, but that he would have to fix it. He replied, 'Is that so? I want you to start tomorrow. I've got an Empire Conference. It starts on Monday. I'd like you there.'

He rang for Miss Hogg. 'How soon can we get Mr Masefield on my staff?' She replied, 'It will take two or three weeks. The Treasury has to be brought in.'

'Ah, dammit! I guess I'll have to wait. But I can't give you a month. Come in three weeks. Miss Hogg, get me Archie Sinclair [Air Minister], I'll fix it with him. Goodbye to you.'

I left the beautiful house and lunched with Lord Kemsley, to tell him of my American trip. I also told him of my talk with the Beaver. He said, 'Of course, you'll have to go. We want you back on *The Sunday Times*. But it looks as if we'll have to lose you for a bit, unless he'd let you write anonymously?' I said I thought not, sad as I was to leave the great paper where I had enjoyed high favour.

Eventually it was all sorted out, and on 25 October 1943 I reported for full-time work at Gwydyr House. My title was to be Personal Adviser on Civil Aviation to the Lord Privy Seal, and Secretary of the War Cabinet Committee on Post-War Civil Air Transport.

Max could not have had a better office. Quite apart from its magnificence, it was opposite the Admiralty, a few doors from the War Office, and within shouting distance of the Air Ministry in King Charles Street. Shouting was unnecessary – though sometimes practised – because, to assist London in its almost impossible task of running the war, all the Government offices were linked by an efficient scrambler telephone network.

When I joined Max's staff it numbered just three, though backed by efficient short-hand-typists and messengers. Betty Hogg reigned supreme. She was aided by two Personal Secretaries, George Malcolm Thompson and David Farrar. Erudite, cynical and hard-working, they were Max's eyes and ears. Both had been with him from Stornoway House, through the MAP (Ministry of Aircraft Production), at 12 Downing Street, at Shell-Mex House and in the political wilderness in Fleet Street. Now they inhabited a top-floor room where they drafted his letters and papers, and summarised for him long and often confused official documents.

Surprisingly, Farrar had even collaborated with his boss in writing *The Sky's the Limit*. Published in late 1942, it was a penetrating and double-edged account of the first days of the MAP. Inevitably, it caused a stir.

These old campaigners charitably admitted me at once into their 'closed shop'. We soon also admitted the slight, elegant figure of Evelyn Bingham Baring (not Sir Evelyn, but likewise a member of the banking dynasty). He came to help us in financial negotiations with various shipping and transport companies. Aged 50, he was very much an unruffled gentleman, who regarded life as leisurely fun, though he had an adroit and penetrating business sense. I found him a delightful and amusing colleague.

On my first day I sat down to read the files. They were bulky, complex, confusing and irresolute in their policy, but among them were the Minutes of the so-called Three-day Commonwealth Conference which had been held at Gwydyr House a week earlier. In addition to Max, who chaired the conference, the Ministers who attended were Viscount Cranborne, Sir Archibald Sinclair, Lord Leathers, Sir William Jowett, Lord Cherwell, Mr Richard Law, Captain Harold Balfour, Mr Ralph Assheton and the Duke of Devonshire.

Nothing was announced publicly, but a week later Max reported to the House of Lords. He said 'Every issue was dealt with in 2½ days. If that displeases your Lordships I must apologise. There are ways of making conferences last longer.' Not if Max was running them!

Piled high on my desk, I found files on a previous conference, set up by Sir Francis Shelmerdine. As related in Chapter 9, this report had been ignored. I found that it asked many questions, but offered no answers. Other files showed that, in addition to having been triggered by the discomfort of Churchill's flight to Moscow, the Brabazon Committee was the result of pressure from two MPs, Robert D. Perkins and Group Captain J.A.C. Wright.

I then found a long and detailed Minute dated 10 June 1943 from Churchill to Lord Cherwell (previously 'the Prof', Professor F.A. Lindemann), his Personal Scientific Adviser. It proposed a global plan for civil air transport, with 'all airports open to through traffic of all nations (except the guilty)', if possible without subsidies. Three days later he said in the Commons, 'The first thing is a family talk [i.e. with the Commonwealth] which will . . . have no aim prejudicial to the United States. Thereafter we shall discuss with them, and also with Soviet Russia.'

The conference had debated two main subjects: post-war civil aircraft, and what became known as 'The Howe-Beaverbrook Agreement'. This called for an Empire-wide route network, 'each Dominion, the UK and India operating sections of the route adjacent to its territories'. This idea had been tried before the war with 'the Kangaroo route' between the UK and Australia, operated by Imperial to Karachi, by Indian Transcontinental to Singapore, and by QANTAS on to Sydney.

On the evening of 11 October Balfour had suggested that a civil version of the Lancaster IV (a bomber which was soon renamed the Lincoln) might be able to operate non-stop on the North Atlantic. This bomber was intended to be produced in Canada as well as in England, and the idea was supported by C.D. Howe, Canadian Minister of Munitions and Supply. The Howe-Balfour proposal was referred to the Second Brabazon Committee, which on 25 October reported favourably. Ronald McCrindle and Alan Campbell-Orde of BOAC, both of whom I knew well, thought that a Lancaster IV with a pressurised passenger fuselage could be 'effective but not very economical'. Thus began the programme for the Tudor, which was never recommended by a Brabazon Committee.

On the following evening Max invited me to dine at 95 Arlington House. He held forth on his 353 days at the MAP, and told me that since then he had read all my pieces in *The Sunday Times*. He asked me to give him a report on my recent US visit. He sent copies of this to Cripps and Sinclair, after he had added marginal notes on such important aircraft as the Mustang, B-29 and Constellation.

Around midnight we got to the main talk. We agreed that we were on the brink of a great new era of global air transport. The Americans would have powerful long-range pressurised aircraft. We would have design capacity, lots of experienced people, and airfields and flying-boat bases throughout the Empire, and little else. He said, 'It'll be like when the horse-and-buggy gave way to the automobile. We've got to do some horse-trading for Britain . . . Perhaps we can sew it up by the end of the year.' That was on 26 October 1943. Two years later we were still at it.

In October 1943 Max had yet to be exposed to the interminable complexities of international civil aviation. I had studied the problems for some three years, and nothing crystallises a positive viewpoint so much as having to write about it in depth over a long period. Just before joining his staff I had written a major article for the January 1944 issue of *The Atlantic Monthly*, published in Boston, in which I set out my views.

These were that there should be a vigorous British effort by a number of strong British airlines flying British aircraft in a competitive world as free as possible from pettifogging restrictions. This came to be embraced by Max as his formal line. It was totally at variance with that adopted by the Air Ministry – developed chiefly by that prodigious worker but rigid thinker, Sir Arthur Street, the Permanent Under-Secretary. He insisted that there should be a single 'chosen instrument' (presumably BOAC) and a tight protectionist control of traffic rights.

There were thus the seeds of a major internal confrontation before the UK could bring any unified policy to the international table. The position was complicated by the suggestion, initiated by Canada and Australia, that there should be a Commonwealth airline in which each country would operate specific sectors.

Undoubtedly, this would have been impractical, and it was not pursued. What did emerge clearly was that Max was looking towards his role in civil aviation in the same mood as he had when he built up the MAP at Stornoway House, and preparing to do battle with the Air Ministry.

He said he wanted a detailed survey over the whole field of post-war air transport. He wanted to know about existing and future types of aircraft, the proposed structure of British airlines and Government administration, and international agreements, first with the Commonwealth, then with the USA and finally with the Soviet Union. Finally, there should be a Ministry of Civil Aviation.

Well into the next day, Max yawned. He said 'How fine to be back among the seats of power. Never forget that there is only one real "inside" and that's in the Government machine.' Then he sent me home to Highgate in his official car.

12

Planning Utopia

After I had digested the voluminous files at Gwydyr House, most of which covered a mass of ineffective debate on future civil aviation, my first task was to ask Lord Brabazon to come and recount to Lord Beaverbrook the work of his new Committee. Brab came, lit a cigarette in a long holder, and launched into a tirade against 'the Air Marshals'. He still had much to do to try to refine the specifications for future aircraft, but repeated requests to the Air Ministry had brought no response. He wanted some action. Max sat back and smiled. He said 'I'm much obliged to you.' Action came swiftly.

As I assimilated the background, I went around Whitehall and got to know the powers behind the Ministerial thrones. At the Air Ministry Sir Archibald Sinclair was served by his PS Ronnie H. Melville. He soon became Sir Ronald Melville, Permanent Secretary to the Minister of what was called, successively, Aviation, Technology and Aviation Supply. His successor at the Air Ministry was Richard C. Chilver. He was likewise infinitely patient and helpful.

Sir Archibald's APS was Reggie Maudling, who in 1955 became Minister of Supply (responsible for ordering, and then for cancelling, many important new aircraft). Later he was Chancellor of the Exchequer, and finally Home Secretary.

The Permanent Under-Secretary, the dour and inflexible Sir Arthur Street, was well served by his harassed PS Ned Dunnett, who as Sir James Dunnet became Permanent Secretary at the Ministry of Defence. Under Sir Arthur was the DGCA (Director-General of Civil Aviation), W.P. (later, at Max's instigation, Sir William) Hildred. His Deputy, George (from 1948 Sir George) Cribbett, had been brought over from the Treasury. He was full of robust but doctrinaire ideas for the strict regulation of civil aviation.

Two frequent visitors were the Minister of Information, Brendan Bracken, and his PPS (Parliamentary PS), Ronald Tree. We also often saw the Postmaster-General, Capt. Harold F.C. Crookshank, and his PPS, S.D. (later Sir Donald) Sergeant, who (astonishingly, in such company) was an aircraft-recognition enthusiast. At the Foreign Office, civil aviation centred around John H. Le Rougetel (who became Ambassador to Persia and then to Belgium) and John Cheetham (later Ambassador to Mexico). At the Colonial Office was the meticulous Wilfred J. Bigg, CMG. All good men and true, but with little knowledge of, or interest in, the complexities of post-war aviation.

As Max began to get a feel for the problems, Gwydyr House started to hum, and at 11.00 on the 11th day of the 11th month (Armistice Day) of 1943 we held the first meeting of the War Cabinet Committee on post-War Air Transport. Max sat at one end of the long table at the Whitehall Gardens end of his room. I, the only non-Minister, sat at the other. As the Ministers trooped in, greeting each other,

I thought they must be as interesting a collection as had ever gathered in that historic house.

On the Beaver's right was the Secretary of State for Air. Archie Sinclair was tall and lean, of course wearing a black coat and dark striped trousers, his wing collar and black bow tie emphasising the thinness of his neck.

Opposite Sinclair was Stafford Cripps, the Minister of Aircraft Production. As thin as Sinclair, he wore a grey suit and steel-rimmed glasses. He lacked Sinclair's mellowness, but was always precise and ascetic – almost a Western Gandhi. Next sat the Prime Minister's 'familiar', Lord Cherwell. Still known as 'the Prof.', the former F.A. Lindemann had the appearance of a rather drooping hawk. Opposite him, next to Sinclair, was the Viscount Cranborne. He was shortly to become the Marquess of Salisbury, and Leader of the House of Lords. In 1943 he was Secretary of State for the Dominions. In contrast to the stocky figure of the Chairman, he was another tall and gangling figure. However, he had a warm and vivid personality, and was 'Bobbety' to his friends. He spoke only to make a solid point, and with good humour.

Next to Cherwell was the totally different Lord Leathers, the Minister of War Transport. This cheerful and unflappable businessman had little interest in the world of aviation, but Max always showed a great regard for him. Beside him, jovial and hearty, was the President of the Board of Trade, Hugh Dalton. As soon as he learned my name he showered me with quotations from the verses of my kinsman John Masefield, delivered in his booming voice. Opposite again, next to 'Bobbety', was Richard Law (later to become Lord Coleraine), the Minister of State at the Foreign Office. Short and thickset, he was one of Max's favourites, as the son of Bonar Law, a former Prime Minister whom Max's machinations had brought to office.

At later meetings four other members attended. They were the bluff and kindly Oliver Stanley, Secretary of State for the Colonies; red-headed Brendan (later Sir Brendan) Bracken, always high in Max's favour; Ralph (pronounced 'Rayfe') Assheton, the Financial Secretary to the Treasury, slight, neat, quick and 'on the ball'; and Geoffrey Lloyd, the PUS (Parliamentary Under-Secretary) for Petroleum, and eminent in post-war administrations. Fortunately for the superstitious, we never had all 12 members present, because I would have made it 13. On one occasion I casually produced a slide-rule to provide quick answers. This apparently extraordinary act stopped the discussion completely!

For a year we met on alternate Thursdays, and sometimes more often. I was astonished to find that, as Chairman, Max was not only firm and effective but also patient. On the Thursday preceding each meeting he and I would draft the agenda. I would then take the draft to the Cabinet Office, where it would be printed on the light blue Cabinet paper. On my second week we hatched a *Memo on Future Policy*, pursued with Max's characteristic energy.

> 'We must draw up a firm and resolute policy in our own interest. Otherwise we shall be faced with the accomplished fact that America alone is dominating the Air Transport services of the World. Such a programme must be vigorous and lively, developing our own resources to the limit of our powers, so long as the War Effort is not damaged thereby.

'Projects for airlines are useless without aircraft. We would be most unwise to develop routes with American aircraft, or to continue to use them for overseas operations. The Avro York is not suitable for trans-ocean routes which require long range. A civil version of the 120ft-span Lancaster IV is required at the earliest possible moment.

'This must be flying in prototype form a year hence, and in 18 months from now (by May 1945) should be in service in numbers. If properly developed, it should be the equal of anything the Americans can set alongside it.

'A difficulty may be foreseen between ourselves and the United States because of the energetic spirit in which we may be seen to enter the field. But it is of vital importance to the total War effort of the United Nations that Britain, as a main participant in the struggle, should develop as swiftly as possible those strategic routes upon which her full military efficiency depends. This is a duty laid upon us, irrespective of longer-term considerations. We are bound to provide for the essential transport of personnel and supplies across the North and South Atlantic and to the Far East.'

This was powerful stuff!

In his committee Max forcefully advanced this policy from the Chair. It certainly struck a responsive chord from the members. One of the more immediate results was that I was detailed to examine all possibilities for interim aircraft, while the Second Brabazon Committee continued to address the long-term needs. Special emphasis was to be given to the 'civil Lancaster IV', later named the Tudor. Alas, this was to be dogged by shortcomings and was eventually abandoned, as related later.

Meanwhile, the Top Secret 'Operation Overlord' – the long-awaited invasion of northern France – was being planned. Churchill had left aboard the battle-cruiser HMS *Renown* for the Cairo conference with President Roosevelt, and went on to the Tehran conference at which they met Stalin. On the PM's way back he fell ill with pneumonia at Tunis (which he insisted on calling 'Carthage'). Max asked me how Mrs Churchill could be conveyed to his bedside. RAF Transport Command offered a Dakota. I said that a Liberator, or even a noisy York, would be much quicker and less hazardous. A York was produced.

Over Christmas 1943 Max was constantly on the telephone to me from his estate, Cherkley, near Dorking. Pat and I were invited to dine with him, and conveyed there and back in Max's Rolls-Royce. On 27 December Churchill got up from his sick bed and flew to convalesce at the US Army's 'Villa Taylor' at Marrakesh, in Morocco. From there he summoned Max, who left on the same day. He was accompanied by his son Max Aitken, who was taking up an RAF command in Cairo, David Farrar, and his faithful valet Nockols. That left Thompson and me minding the shop, with stern admonitions to keep him constantly informed by Foreign Office bag.

I sent him frequent assessments of the aviation situation. I also ploughed on with my analysis of existing and potential transport aircraft in order to have a complete Paper ready for Max's return. He arrived back on 18 January 1944, having travelled from Gibraltar with the fully restored Churchill aboard HMS *King George V*. We immediately plunged into political turmoil. This began with an ineffective House of

Lords debate on the 19th on one of the innumerable 'moves for papers' raised by the Marquess of Londonderry 'to ask His Majesty's Government what progress they had made with their policy for post-War aviation.' There was much talk, but virtually no action. Everyone was preoccupied with 'Overlord', and with the vague threat of German rockets.

13

Planning future airliners

W hile Max was in Africa I spent much of my time trying to ensure that I knew what was in the Gwydyr House files, and that I understood the meaning of every sentence, which was sometimes even more of a challenge. The size of the task was daunting. I never piled all the buff-covered files on top of one another, but had I done so they would have been about as tall as I was.

I tried not to be awed by the sheer bulk of paper. I felt bound to try to extract from it some firm policy issues which I could put before the Beaver on his return. Gradually, four courses of action emerged:

> The United Kingdom would have to engage in discussions with other countries, notably the United States, with the objective of harmonious agreement on future routes for commercial air traffic, together with bilateral agreement on each country's rights on those routes.

> His Majesty's Government (HMG) would have to formulate a policy on the future structure of British airlines – in American parlance, commercial carriers – which would carry our flag on the world's air routes.

> HMG would also have to decide upon the post-war departmental responsibility for civil aviation.

> Most important of all, decisions had to be taken on future British transport aircraft.

Of these four matters, I thought the last might prove the longest to resolve. Whereas I fondly thought that the others could be settled by a few round-table meetings, the bringing into service of a complete range of post-war civil transport aircraft might take more than a year. In fact, the talks alone were to take more than a year, and producing the actual aircraft (with a few exceptions) much longer.

After the war, arguments were to rage over the supposed British decision at the start of the war to ignore the development of new transport aircraft, and to leave such aircraft to the Americans. In fact, I was never able to discover any document suggesting (still less implementing) such a policy. All that happened was that no orders were placed for new British transport aircraft, and the few already in hand were abandoned. The Fairey FC.1 was terminated by the Air Minister soon after the war began, while Short Brothers simply stopped making the three S.32s (14/38) in May 1940.

Nothing then happened until, goaded by questions in the House of Commons, Lord Brabazon was asked to form a committee to examine what was needed. The members of this committee are listed in Chapter 9. Nothing was said in public until a very brief statement was made on 10 February 1943, followed by a much longer statement by Viscount Cranborne on 11 March. In part, he said:

> 'His Majesty's Government are fully alive to the importance of post-War civil air transport . . . The War has acted as a forcing house for technical development . . . We must not fail to play our full part in the development of civil aviation after the War.
>
> 'Since the outbreak of war the resources of the British aircraft industry have been concentrated on the production of combat and training types. When we look back at the urgent need of 1940 and 1941 . . . no one could question the wisdom of this policy. Nevertheless, the time has now arrived when His Majesty's Government should consider what can be done – without impairing our War Effort – to prepare for the return of peace. That is why the Government . . . set up a Committee under Lord Brabazon to consider broadly the types of civil aircraft likely to be required. Their Report, which is a secret document, was received three days ago. It recommends that work should start immediately on the design of civil aircraft . . . and on preparing for the conversion of military aircraft . . . for civil work.
>
> 'Whatever form of collaboration may be devised for post-war civil air transport, it will clearly be the duty of this country . . . to play a prominent part in the production and operation of civil aircraft. The aircraft-manufacturing industry is today our largest industry. We possess great technical skill and experience in . . . design and construction . . . The War Cabinet have decided that the design of a limited number of types of civil aircraft shall proceed . . . without impairing the War Effort . . .'

The noble lord went on to outline at some length the plans of HMG for post-war civil air transport. Not surprisingly, he made no mention of the United States in this context, but he had much to say about the British Empire, and a little about the United Nations.

He did not disclose the fact that there would be a Second Brabazon Committee. As explained in Chapter 9, this had wider terms of reference. This Second Brabazon Committee did not report until long after the war was over, when it was far too late to launch any completely new designs capable of competing with the established American types for the immediate post-war period. Fortunately, back in November 1943 Max, Lord Brabazon and I had held discussions at Gwydyr House to try to ensure that at least some British civil aircraft would be available at the end of the war, even though they would be of an interim nature.

To me it was self-evident that, in the immediate post-war era, the United States would have civil transport aircraft superior to any others. Two already existed, the Douglas DC-4 and, especially, the Lockheed Constellation. What was equally obvious was that post-war Britain would be impoverished, in a way that had never before happened. In particular, we would be desperately short of dollars. Could we avoid having to buy American aircraft?

It was clear that, to do this, we would have to work fast to produce the best possible aircraft derived from designs which already existed. One such aircraft had already appeared. First flown on 5 July 1942, the Avro York was essentially a Lancaster bomber with a new fuselage. It was the simplest possible derivative, without pressurisation. Chief designer Roy Chadwick had convinced his boss Roy Dobson that one York could be produced as a company venture, consuming relatively few man-hours or scarce raw material.

Finding materials and parts for a production run was harder, but by 1944 Yorks were in production. Nobody pretended they were more than a stop-gap. One example was fitted with Bristol Hercules engines, which did at least make it less deafeningly noisy, but the basic design was not in the same class as even a C-54 (DC-4). When planning post-war airports, the ultimate 'worst-case' take-off was taken to be a York on a hot day with an elephant on board and one engine out. In fact, a York actually managed to get into precisely this situation. According to calculations, it needed every inch of a 10,000-foot runway, and as it did not have such a run available its ability to clamber into the air remains a mystery.

Avro was also the company charged with producing the only other firm project for a new aircraft resulting from Max's Commonwealth Conference of October 1943. Originally called 'the Howe-Balfour aeroplane', it went ahead in early 1944 as the Avro 688.

Lacking the knowledge to pontificate on the design of anything technical, be it an aeroplane, warship or ocean liner, the leaders of our country were prone to spending a great deal of time and energy deciding on what each new creation should be called. Often the name selected, such as Viceroy, Viscount and Britannia, proved to be a handicap in international marketing. Boeing has shown that a consistent series of numbers is a much better marketing ploy, but in the first weeks of 1944 the Cabinet Committee spent many hours deciding that the Howe-Balfour should be named the Tudor. This was thought to be a natural follow-on to 'Lancaster'. It was announced, as a piece of important hot news, by Max in the Lords Debate on 19 January 1944.

This aircraft was given the Air Ministry Specification number 29/43 (I can't help commenting that that is approximately 29 more specifications than the British industry receives each year today). Apart from the fact that it should be essentially a Lancaster IV with a pressurised fuselage, not much else was decided except that, as strongly recommended by Beverley Shenstone, to save time it would retain the Lancaster IV landing gear with a tailwheel. Despite the extra design effort, I had advocated a tricycle undercarriage.

A.V. Roe were authorised to start work in March 1944. As the Tudor could not be ready until about the end of 1945, it was evident that some stop-gap aircraft were needed to tide us over. In fact, the First Brabazon Committee had considered which military types might usefully be modified for civil use. Its Report, on 9 February 1943, not only recommended five completely new designs but also said that useful civil transports could, or should, be developed from the Lancaster and York, and the Sunderland III and Shetland flying boats.

The Second Brabazon Committee became so bogged down in the final detail of its proposed new types that it did not pursue the possibility of converting existing military types. Probably rightly, it saw its task as planning 'clean sheet of paper' aircraft for the post-war era.

Accordingly, at Max's request, in early November 1943 I went to Lord Brabazon's London apartment in Eaton Square to discuss the need for interim civil transports. I talked with 'Brab' himself, with the competent Secretary of his Second Committee

Ian Riddoch, and with its three technical advisers, C.B. Collins, 'Nero' Rowe and K.T. Spencer. We came to the obvious conclusion that, if Britain did not produce interim types, the only alternative would be to buy American. We examined such British transport aircraft as were actually flying (ignoring those built before 1939). The miserable total came to 12 Sunderland IIIs, three Yorks and a demilitarised Lancaster.

A week later, on the 11th, and again on 15 November, Max's Civil Air Transport Committee endorsed his belief that interim types had to be produced, and produced quickly, and that the only way this could be done would be to develop them from current military aircraft.

Max was marvellous at cutting through proverbial Red Tape and getting things done quickly. He straight away said 'This job can be done most quickly by one man going round the industry.' As the Brabazon Committee was totally immersed in specifications for new types, the task was foisted on to me. I discussed with Max how we should go about it. We agreed that the first thing to do was for me to find out BOAC's opinion of what aircraft might be required, and then see what might be done quickly to meet the need, even if incompletely.

Accordingly, my first visit was to Airways House, close to Victoria Station. I had long discussions with Aubrey Burke and Maj. R.H. 'Bob' Mayo. I then went to the Air Ministry's Department of Civil Aviation at the corner of Parliament Square, for a talk with George Cribbett.

It could hardly have been more discouraging. Nothing whatsoever was being done. Even the York – an obviously inadequate bomber conversion – was not yet in production for RAF Transport Command, let alone for civil use. Almost all BOAC's fleet was American, and rapidly becoming out of date – principally Dakotas, Liberators and Lodestars. Obviously, war production had to have priority, but there was now no shortage of military aircraft, whereas there were no new British civil aircraft at all.

It was clear that interim types could be produced in two ways. The quickest method was simply to take bombers or reconnaissance flying boats off the production line, fit them with seats and rudimentary furnishings and paint civil registration. A preferable method would be to design new fuselages.

I was busy throughout the winter of 1943/4 analysing the requirements and trying to match them against existing aircraft, or minimum modifications thereof. While Max was with the PM in sunny Marrakesh I travelled, by road and rail, through the cold and dark wartime winter to visit design offices and factories.

I went by train to Manchester and thence to Chadderton and Woodford to see A.V. Roe Ltd. I talked with Managing Director Roy (soon to be Sir Roy) Dobson and Chief Designer Roy Chadwick about the Type 691, then called the Lancaster Transport and later, the Lancastrian. Totally uneconomic, this still seemed a useful aircraft for long-range transport of VIP passengers and mail (which was really the only kind of payload considered). We also discussed the Type 688 Howe-Balfour project, later called the Tudor.

I drove up London's Edgware Road to Cricklewood. The vast Handley Page factory was stuffed with Halifax heavy bombers, taken by road to the assembly plant at Radlett, but my discussions with Sir Frederick, and with Chief Designer Reg Stafford, centred on the H.P.64 Halifax Transport and on the completely new H.P.68 Hermes, which was then being designed as a company private venture.

I went down to Rochester in Kent to see Arthur Gouge, who had lately resigned as Chief Designer of Short Brothers, and with his successor C.P.T. Lipscomb. Though it was 'the first aircraft company in the world', having built balloons since 1900 and aircraft since 1908, it had been taken over by the Government. Minister Cripps had deliberately snubbed the management by visiting Rochester and calling a meeting of the workforce – whom he addressed as 'Comrades' – and inviting nobody to join him on the platform except the Convener of the Shop Stewards' Committee! I discussed the Stirling V transport and glider tug, which was then about to go into production at the Belfast plant of Short & Harland. We ranged over Sunderland developments, and the huge Shetland flying boat, which was then taking shape at Rochester and about to receive its wings from Saunders-Roe in the Isle of Wight.

I travelled to Coventry to see the giant Armstrong Whitworth factory at Baginton. My old friend the Managing Director H.K. Jones, and Chief Designer Jim Lloyd, briefed me on their A.W.55 high-speed local-service airliner, to be powered by two Merlins. Later this design was to be enlarged and planned with four Merlin 35 engines, and finally with four Armstrong Siddeley Mamba turboprops, in which form it flew as the Apollo in April 1949.

One of the most straightforward and interesting talks was held with Rex Pierson, who had been Chief Designer of Vickers, and later Vickers-Armstrongs, since 1914. Their large factory was at Weybridge, alongside the famous motor-race track of Brooklands. Assisted by George Edwards, Pierson was already well advanced with a civil airliner derived from the Wellington bomber.

Finally, on 13 January 1944, I went by GWR train past my old haunts at Hayes to Bristol. Here I talked for two days with Chief Engineer (Aircraft) Leslie Frise, Chief Designer (Aircraft) 'Doc' Russell and Sales Director Ken Bartlett about their gigantic Type 167, for which the unintended name 'Brabazon' appeared to have stuck. They were also well advanced with the design of the Type 170, a completely new and simple twin-engined aircraft primarily to carry freight.

My visits appeared to have stirred a largely sleeping giant which, while churning out aircraft for the war, had not been enlivened by having anyone come to talk about civil aircraft. Brochures began to arrive at Gwydyr House, and Chief Designers came to see me with rolled-up drawings.

Out of all the talk, by the time Max arrived back from Marrakesh I had put together a list, illustrated by three-view drawings, of eight types of interim civil aircraft which the manufacturers knew could be built in the short term. We divided them into four categories:

Landplanes:

Long-range: Avro 691 Lancaster Transport (later named the Lancastrian).
Medium-range: Handley Page Halifax VIII, later named the Halton, followed by the Handley Page H.P.68 Hermes.
Short-range: Bristol 170 Freighter, from which was derived the Wayfarer passenger aircraft.

Vickers-Armstrongs V.491 Wellington Transport (later named the Viking).
Armstrong Whitworth A.W.55 (2 Merlins), developed into the Apollo.

Flying Boats:

Long-range: Short/Saro S.35 Shetland.

Medium-range: Short S.25 Sunderland III conversion. This led to the *Hythe* class and S.25/V Sandringham family.

The de Havilland Aircraft Company was fully preoccupied with the D.H.98 Mosquito, the D.H.100 Spider Crab (later called Vampire) jet fighter and the D.H.103 Hornet. Thus, it did not figure in the list of interim types, though when it came to completely new designs it was another matter entirely!

There were various other possibilities. Short Brothers had plans for a properly engineered civil derivative of the Stirling to specification C.18/43. This project, the S.37, would have had a much-needed increase in span and a pressurised fuselage with a nosewheel, but it remained on the drawing board. Even the little Miles company had for many years had an ambitious plan for a very advanced transatlantic airliner called the Miles X. Featuring a blended wing/body shape, it never received any official support.

At the start of 1944 Roy Dobson arrived at Gwydyr House carrying a complete set of general arrangement drawings for a civil transport derived directly from the Lancaster, each labelled AVRO 691 LANCONIAN. We talked, and about two weeks later, when Max had returned, he came back again to show us a modified design.

In fact, the first Lancaster transport had been produced in Canada. Avro-built R5727, an early B. Mk I which had served with No 44 (the first) Lancaster Squadron, had been supplied as a pattern aircraft to Victory Aircraft, Avro's subsidiary at Malton, Toronto (later renamed Avro Canada). Once Victory was in production with the B. Mk X it had no further need of R5727, so they removed the turrets, faired over the nose and tail, put extra tanks in the bomb bay, and ten seats in the constricted aft fuselage, which was provided with three new windows. Registered CF-CMS, it was handed to Trans-Canada Airlines and used to inaugurate the Canadian Government's service between Montreal and Prestwick. Carrying 9,000 lb of mail, it made the first eastbound crossing in 12 hr 26 min on 22 July 1943.

By the time I was planning new transports, Victory had converted two of their own Lancaster Mk X bombers. Together with the sole British-made York, these were the only new landplane transports constructed in the British Empire since the start of the war. By early 1944 Avro had built two more Yorks, and converted a Lancaster for BOAC.

The first York was a military aircraft. The first new British civil transport to appear since 1939 was Avro Lancaster I DV379. Built by Metropolitan-Vickers, it had a varied non-operational career before being declared surplus and struck off charge in the autumn of 1943. Registered as civil aircraft G-AGJI, it was stripped of armament and on 20 January 1944 handed to the BOAC Development Flight at Hurn. There it was used as a testbed, especially for the highly supercharged Merlin 102 engines with semi-annular radiators and the four-blade reversible-pitch propellers intended for the Avro Tudor.

After studying the revised Avro 691 plans 'Dobbie' showed us, we did little except to change the name to Lancastrian and organise a contract for production aircraft for BOAC under Specification C.16/44. The rear fuselage was equipped with three large settees, each arranged to seat three passengers. These faced transversely, to the right. Each settee could be converted into a bunk, while three more could hinge down from above. Thus, as a sleeper, the Lancastrian could carry only six passengers.

Today such an aircraft appears ludicrously uneconomic, but – except in the USA – things were different in 1944. The only airline passengers were diplomats, senior officers and other VIPs. (Even when the all-new Tudor flew, it was planned for just 12 passengers.) Though it was uncomfortable and noisy, the Lancastrian could at least fly a 4 000-mile sector at 230 mph, and did go some way to meeting the immediate need. Avro delivered 82 to the RAF, BOAC, British South American Airways, Skyways, Silver City, Flight Refuelling and the Italian airline Alitalia.

An obvious question is why a six-seater should have been preferred to the York, which could seat 50. The answer is that the Lancastrian had the range to operate across the North Atlantic. So the next question is, 'Why did BOAC use Lancastrians only on the route to Australia, which Yorks could have operated?'

Moreover, by modern standards, the safety record of these primitive airliners was appalling. Of the 23 Lancastrians operated by BOAC, eight crashed or disappeared without trace within five years, while of BSAA's 13, four were lost.

Indeed, the general safety record of air travel in the mid-1940s was terrible, not because of enemy action but because the equipment was by modern standards inadequate and unreliable, and the crews lacked modern navigational aids. To a

Avro delivered 82 Lancastrians. G-AGLS is seen taking off on 28 May 1946 to fly the first BOAC service to Australia from the muddy wastes of Heathrow.

considerable degree this even applied to American aircraft, though they had the benefit of continuity of development. Moreover, they had been designed for the job, whereas our interim machines were all to some degree flawed, and had poor operating economics.

My eight weeks of hard work between November 1943 and January 1944 could do little to bring British interim aircraft up to the class of the DC-4 and Constellation, but they did enable British airlines to continue, or to start, operations with British aircraft. They enabled five of our aircraft companies to maintain employment and keep production lines going while better aircraft were being designed. Without them, British airlines would have had to buy American aircraft with scarce dollars, and in turn this could lock them in to US-supplied aircraft for all time.

The interim types were:

Avro 691 Lancastrian: 82 built, in service 1944–52.
Bristol 170 Freighter/Wayfarer: 214 built, in service 1945–70.
Handley Page H.P.70 Halton: 140 built, in service 1946–53.
Handley Page H.P.81 Hermes 4: 29 built, in service 1947–60.
Short Hythe/Sandringham/Solent: 68 built, in service 1945–58.
Vickers-Armstrongs V.C.1 Viking: 163 built, in service 1945–60.

We also made a final examination of the prospects for airships. During the war there was no certainty that the rigid airship had gone forever. A small but enthusiastic group were convinced that, using later materials and constructional principles, modern engines (for example, turboprops burning low-volatility fuel) and inert helium instead of hydrogen, the dirigible might have a useful commercial future.

This view was not shared by any airline in Britain or the USA. It was also not shared by Lord Brabazon, whose task as assessor of the inquiry into the R.101 disaster (held in 1931, months after the airship's loss) had disillusioned him for all time. Despite this, Max agreed with me that 'lighter than air' was worth a brief look.

Between the Wars Britain had built two great airships:

R.100 – The 'private enterprise' ship. Registered G-FAAV, built by the Vickers subsidiary The Airship Guarantee Company at Howden, in Yorkshire. Duralumin with fabric skin, six 670-hp Rolls-Royce Condor engines, disposable lift (payload) 54 long tons, cost £471,000. Launched 16 December 1929, in summer 1930 flew to Montreal and back, despite serious problems. Total flying time 296 hr 49 min. Pointlessly destroyed after the loss of R.101, Vickers never being fully paid.

R.101 – The 'Government' ship. Registered G-FAAW, built by the Royal Airship Works at Cardington, in Bedfordshire. Stainless steel with fabric skin, five extremely heavy 585-hp Beardmore diesel engines, disposable lift (as built) 38 tons, cost £777,000. Launched 14 October 1929, subjected to major modification, crashed 5 October 1930. Total flying time 127 hr 11 min.

R.102, R.103 – Registrations G-FAAY/Z reserved, design studies by Royal Airship Works June 1929 to March 1930 for improved ships with disposable lift of 100 tons. Never built.

I went across Whitehall to the Admiralty, where Lt-Cdr N.S. Norway, RNVR, was working. He had been one of the R.100 team (and flew to Montreal and back in her), and later wrote novels under the pen-name Nevil Shute. We did a careful study of what I called **R.104**, with seven Merlin engines and helium to give a disposable lift of 100 tons. Assuming a cost of £2 million, a cruising speed of 87 mph and a seven-hour fuel reserve on a westbound crossing against a 27-kt headwind, we tried in every way to do justice to its possibilities and to schedule more trips per year or look for savings.

In the end, we reluctantly decided that such a ship could not compete – not even against a mighty Bristol Brabazon with seats for only 30 passengers. Max summed up R.104 as 'a pretty face, but no good in the kitchen'.

Just before Christmas 1943 four of us had toiled all day studying airship files from Air Ministry archives. At last we packed up, and walked through the blackout to the comfort and warmth of the Royal Aero Club at 119 Piccadilly. After dinner we relaxed with coffee and a superb 1927 port. One of our number was Wg Cdr Tom Cave-Brown-Cave, CBE, FRAeS. He had been a great airship man, and saw off R.101 on its fatal voyage on that wild night in October 1930.

A long discussion about what happened to that great ship lit a spark which made me determined to do what nobody had done at the time: find out exactly why the R.101 crashed. I found that I had embarked on a powerful and deeply moving human story, with unexpected facets and overtones. It was also evident that the airship 'did not have to crash', and could have turned back to England for repairs and a fresh start. Eventually I wrote the whole story in *To Ride the Storm*, a 560-page book published in 1982 by William Kimber.

Since 1944 there have been many further airship studies. In my opinion, making every possible favourable assumption, a reliable and profitable airship project has yet to appear, but the subject still attracts a devoted band of adherents.

14

Limbering up

The Beaver docked at Plymouth on Tuesday 18 January 1944, and arrived by train at Paddington that afternoon. He came straight to Gwydyr House, and bore me off to Arlington House to concoct his speech for the morrow.

The Debate in the Lords was to be one of eight, tirelessly put down by former Air Minister Lord Londonderry, in 1942, 1943 and 1944, all pressing for progress on post-war civil aviation. Lord Beaverbrook was to be principal spokesman for the Government. Though it was his second debate since he had taken office, he was quite unprepared. However, seeing this coming, I had drafted the outline of a speech, often in consultation with George Cribbett at the Department of Civil Aviation at the top of Whitehall.

Max and I went through this draft until late, and I then worked further on it through the night. Next morning I put it in front of him in the form he liked, in gigantic type on what were called 'short sheets'. We spent next morning going through it again until he was happy.

Predictably, he departed widely from the text created with such care. He ranged over the whole field of civil aviation, and even harked back to his days at the MAP. He began by thoroughly confusing their lordships by saying that 'the chosen instrument', BOAC, 'is not a monopoly at all. It has a monopoly of subsidies for overseas air traffic, but nothing else. So far as overseas air traffic by private companies, shipping companies or other concerns may be carried on without any subsidy, then there can be no objection . . . The same applies to aircraft transportation within Great Britain.'

He went on to say that, after the war, responsibility for air transport should remain with the Air Ministry. He launched into a robust statement of plans:

> 'Since I spoke on October 20th we have done a great deal . . . First of all, there is an aeroplane which is known as the Brabazon' [it wasn't until that moment]. 'The all-up weight is designed to be more than 100 tons, with a speed of 250 mph and a capacity for 50 passengers and two tons of mail . . . the most ambitious aircraft programme so far set in hand in this country.
>
> 'A long time must elapse before the Brabazon makes its maiden journey. It is for that reason that a project for another type has been launched . . . the journey over the North Atlantic in winter as well as summer with 12 passengers and baggage will be an easy flight. The aeroplane is named the Tudor' [again it hadn't been; now it was]. 'If it is ready before the end of the War, and we expect it will be, it will be suitable as a military transport.'

He then dwelt on the need for an international conference to get post-war civil aviation off to a proper start on a global basis. He switched to a song of praise for the aircraft industry, and for the inspiring role played by Prime Minister Churchill. He went on, in ringing tones, to recall the Battle of Britain: 'We must build or die. We had the pilots, but not the planes. We built and lived – and we are still building. The aircraft industry, which served us so well in our hour of greatest peril . . . will not disappoint the highest hopes of those of us who believe in the dazzling future of civil aviation throughout the Empire . . . from the snows of the North to the heat of the Equator . . .'

Totally unscripted, it was an astonishing performance. Having just spent two weeks in sunshine with Churchill, it was an opportunity to pay back in praise his own Churchillian fervour – with a dram or two obliquely to his own account. On the other hand, it did not satisfy Lord Londonderry.

With Churchill back running the war, and Max's speech out of the way, we could take stock. I presented to Max my conclusions on interim aircraft. He was delighted, and the document was approved at the Committee Meeting on 17 February. A programme for immediate civil aircraft was set up in outline, and handed to Sir Stafford Cripps at the MAP, W.P. Hildred at the Air Ministry, and on to the aircraft industry.

We then turned to the next two aspects – the second and third wheels of his air-transport coach. These were a strong airline operating industry and satisfactory international agreements. At Max's request, I wrote briefs on both. We discussed, and even argued. Then, with a few original twists of his own, Max became clear on both issues, and set the wheels in motion. We then approached a more difficult subject: the essential forthcoming talks with the Americans.

The British position was far from clear. The Air Ministry line, backed by BOAC, was hesitant and cautious, wary of American exploitation of their commercial and equipment advantage. Their view was that traffic rights should be confined to what the war-depleted and impoverished British could mount in opposition, and grant concessions gradually and as sparingly as possible.

At Gwydyr House we instead saw the world as a great place of equal opportunity. The entire planet should be opened up under a liberal policy of regulated competition. Neither 'open skies' nor a restrictive straitjacket. Probably, in the immediate post-war era, British aircraft would not be able to compete on equal terms, so selective traffic subsidies could be paid until the new British aircraft were ready for service.

These were still early days in international air transport. We British had little experience to draw on, apart from services with Empire flying boats and a few short-haul landplanes. Everything remained to be evolved. Max was excited about new aircraft, and Empire links. He hated the idea of months of boring negotiations.

We discussed all this at length, sometimes overlooking Green Park on the balcony of No 95, the top flat in Arlington House, sometimes in the more sombre apartment at 64 Brook Street, and sometimes at Cherkley where, as February departed, the buds were forming in the extensive woods.

At each establishment the door was always opened either by stocky lugubrious Albert, whose surname I never knew, or by the suave and courtly Nockols, whose first name was Albert but never used. They were poles apart: Albert the Cockney valet, in a brown suit and on occasion a green baize apron, Nockols impeccably clad in a dark suit as if for the City. I never could decide which of the two, Max or Nockols, held the other in greater esteem, though each obviously enjoyed the occasional sparring match.

By this time I knew the Beaver well, and my cautious regard had blossomed almost into affection. He was unlike any other man I ever knew. For all his foibles and tough exterior, he was at heart deeply sensitive and often lonely. Critical, thrusting, demanding, self-centred and intolerant, he could also be kind and even generous, just as he could be hasty and vindictive. He could reverse passionate feelings within hours.

He perpetually maintained a hard front, even when the man inside had softened. I often thought of the frightened little boy in Canada, whose Presbyterian father had drunk away the family's slender funds. Early troubles made him suspicious of the world, and sometimes of his friends. Some have said he was evil; he was not, though that depends on how the word is defined. Some have said he was ruthless; he was not, but he was unpredictable. He was fascinated with power and politics. He was some-times unfair, yet often magnanimous. He was mesmerised with the written word, yet impatient. His character was kaleidoscopic.

The better I came to know him, the more wary I became. When I joined his staff I had the Grade of Assistant Secretary, and my pay plummeted to £830 per annum. Max offered to make it up. I felt I had to refuse. I worked hard and conscientiously at Gwydyr House. I enjoyed all the contacts, especially with my colleagues on his staff. Most of all, I enjoyed the stimulation of Max's character.

I now regret that I kept him at a distance, since his influence could have been help-ful. Later he invited me to work on his newspapers, but I was determined not to be cajoled, nor to become his 'lackey'. He offered me a safe seat in Parliament, I turned it down. Later still he invited me to take over the Chairmanship of BOAC. I refused.

However much I kept Max at arm's length, the flood of callers at Gwydyr House did not. Of course, one of them was his son. My schoolfriend Max Aitken had had a meteoric rise as a fighter pilot. Though he was now a group captain, his father was constantly worrying about his safety, and when he visited Gwydyr House greeted him with unconcealed delight.

Apart from 'young Max' the most welcome visitors were Brendan Bracken and Michael Foot. The former, red-haired, tousled and freckled, was Minister of Information. He doted on *The Financial Times*, drinking with Beaverbrook, and convivial conversation. Foot aroused the Beaver's admiration for his command of words. It was an odd relationship, but cordial for all that. One day Max said to me 'He's a reincarnation of Dean Swift. The lampooning cloak of Swift has fallen on his shoulders.' Certainly, they both revelled in a turgid stirring of the waters of public life.

The Beaverbrook Court, at his four addresses, was graced by an extraordinary cross-section of wartime London. However much the man was obsessed with poli-tics, and the world of Beachcomber and the *Daily Express*, not the least of his enjoyments was the company of a galaxy of decorative and intelligent females. They had to be both. Not only did Max unwind and delight in the presence of a beautiful and clever woman, but he appeared to hold a fascination for the opposite sex – and not just for the presents which he invariably sent them on *his* birthday.

He was a selective picker. In the course of 20 months, I came to know – at least, well enough to pass the time of night – four extraordinarily beautiful women. For each of them Beaverbrook held the attraction of a skilled and enthusiastic connoisseur. But, enough said.

In the world of politics, in addition to Bracken and Foot, constant visitors included Dick Law, Herbert Morrison, Beverley Baxter, Ronald Tree, Alfred Beit and Oliver Simmonds. From Fleet Street came Arthur Christensen (whom I often saw at Arlington but never at Gwydyr), Tom Driberg, Herbert Gunn, William Barclay, John Gordon, Kingsley Martin and, on one occasion, Hannen Swaffer, flamboyant in an ancient cloak. At Arlington I also often came upon the grave and courtly E.J. Robinson. General Manager of Beaverbrook Newspapers, he was a strong influence, and a man to whom Max showed profound respect. As we moved towards American talks the populace included aviation officials, notably Hildred, Cribbett, Le Rougetel and John Cheetham.

If Max was at Cherkley in the evening – and he was invariably there on Sundays – he would preside over the dinner table. He would then adjourn to the cinema, where the entire household would assemble, and talk into the small hours. Then, with a 'Good-bye to you', he would retire to bed, leaving his guests to strike out for home. At such an hour, possible 03.00, my journey to Highgate, even by official car, was wearisome.

However, such evenings often had memorable moments. On one occasion one of the kitchen maids had screaming hysterics. The piercing sounds penetrated to the dining room. The imperturbable Nockols was despatched to investigate. He returned slightly flustered. 'I regret, my Lord, there seems to be no doing of anything with her. Cook has tried the sovereign remedy of putting ice cubes down her neck, but it only seems to make her worse.'

Such diversions did not deflect us from winning the war, and planning for peace. The target date for the completion of all our post-war plans was the end of 1944. I talked it over with the Old Man (as he was occasionally referred to). He agreed that such a schedule was possible. 'Do me a Memorandum. You've got all the points in your head. You see the answers. Put them down. Let's see the whole pattern.'

Here was a chance to draw together into one document the results of our four months of work. Over the weekend 11–13 March 1944, just ahead of preparing for a meeting of the Cabinet Civil Air Transport Committee at 10.15 on Thursday the 16th, I drafted 'A Plan for Civil Air Transport'. It endeavoured to state the objectives and draw all the threads together.

Reading this Memorandum today, I cannot help thinking how 'starry eyed' it was. It was full of youthful zeal to bring about a new order into the air, with the Union Jack flying high, Commonwealth solidarity, and encouragement for private enterprise. Max blessed it. We circulated it to the CAT Committee, and I sent the first 10 paragraphs to Hildred and Cribbett at the Department of Civil Aviation. We discussed draft White Papers.

In the middle of all this we learned that the top US civil-air negotiators, Dr Adolf Berle (pronounced 'Burley') and Dr Edward P. Warner, were about to arrive in London for talks. Max was to take the Chair. We quickly ran again through the draft plan of 14 March. In essence it made six main proposals:

1   An **International Air Transport Authority** to control routes, rates and charges, regulate competition, prevent over-capacity and lay down technical standards, much of it through operators' conferences.

2   A **Commonwealth Air Transport Corporation**, to operate a strategic round-the-world service calling only at British Commonwealth territory. The UK component would be BOAC, with some Dominions shareholding.

3   A British **Ministry of Civil Aviation**.

4   A British **Air Transport Licensing Authority**.

5   A number of **British airlines** to fly in parallel with the Commonwealth Corporation on international and domestic routes, including possible shipping and rail participation where licensed in the public interest.

6   A British **Civil Aviation Commission** to co-ordinate policies through the British operating companies, in which it would have a holding.

The plan proposed the operation of 12 main routes, each by a separate British company. There would also be a number of Colonial and foreign airlines with British participation. With some daring, I estimated that, by 1955 (12 years on), the British and related airlines might require a total of 6,600 aircraft, which would range in gross weight from 6,000 lb to 400,000 lb. They would employ some 630,000 people.

This was what Max described as 'a high, wide and handsome plan. Let us address ourselves to it, and see what Master Berle has to say.'

15

Americans in London

Before the war the Atlantic seemed to be so wide that to fly across it made headlines. Only in the final weeks of peace were there any transatlantic commercial services, with long-range flying boats. Nevertheless, it was clear that, once the conflict was over, still more capable transport aircraft would make services between North America and Europe increasingly important. Obviously, we British had to talk about this with the United States.

In the early years of the war we were preoccupied with survival, but on 27 February 1942 the Foreign Minister, Anthony Eden, sent a note to Washington to the effect that HMG (His Majesty's Government) would expect detailed consultations before any commercial air services were started through British territory. On 28 July of that year a formal document was drawn up called 'The Halifax Agreement'. This was an Exchange of Notes which stated that no airline of either country would seek to set up arrangements which would exclude airlines of the other until the shape of post-war civil aviation had been decided at a formal conference.

As I have related, Prime Minister Churchill's long and uncomfortable flights in 1943 had spurred him to devote some thought to future civil aviation, and among other things to the need for discussions with Commonwealth countries. It was also evident that talks must be held with the United States. The first real steps towards Anglo-American discussions on civil aviation were taken by him on 13 September 1943.

Previously, he had informally discussed the subject with President Roosevelt at the latter's home at Hyde Park, New York. He then boarded a train for Halifax, Nova Scotia, to return to London, and *en route* he set down on paper what had been said:

'Prime Minister to Mr President:

'I have told our Government that you made no objection when I said that we intended to hold a preliminary Commonwealth meeting in London or Canada, and that this would be only to focus our own British Commonwealth ideas for subsequent discussion with the United States Government.

'I said that, about the proposed International Conference, you thought it might wait till the matter had been discussed at the forthcoming tripartite Anglo-Soviet-American meetings. I mentioned that your preliminary view comprised:

i. There should be private ownership;
ii. Key points should be made available for international use on a reciprocal basis;
iii. Internal traffic should be reserved to internal companies;
iv. Government support may be required on an international basis for certain non-paying routes.'

At that time, conditioned by the DC-3, we took it for granted that short-haul domestic routes would be the money-spinners, and that long-haul services would be prestige and diplomatic links which would need a subsidy. We had no idea that what would eventually happen would be the reverse!

As noted earlier, out of the blue we at Gwydyr House learned that Drs Berle and Warner were about to arrive in London. Ed Warner was 'Mr American Aviation'. Vice-Chairman of the Civil Aeronautics Board, he had spent a varied lifetime in aviation (including working as I had for a spell on a magazine), and he had a reputation for integrity and encyclopaedic knowledge.

Berle was a bird of different plumage. Able to recite long texts in Greek and Latin at the age of five, he sailed through the entrance examination for Harvard at 12, but was not permitted to enter those hallowed portals until he was 14. Once there he 'had an academic career of such distinction he never quite recovered from it'. He helped negotiate the Treaty of Versailles, and was then a member of President Roosevelt's Brains Trust (they originated the name) which set up the New Deal. He considered the President 'an inspiring, vital man, for whom I burned to do service'. On top of other onerous duties, in 1939 Roosevelt appointed him chief US negotiator for civil aviation in the State Department.

Berle and Warner stopped off in Montreal for brief and inconclusive 'softening-up talks' with the Hon. C.D. Howe, the Canadian Minister of Civil Aviation, and H.J. Symington, the President of Trans-Canada Airlines. They then came on to London,

Dick Hildred, Director-General of Civil Aviation (left) quizzing the U.S. Civil Air Attaché, Livingston Satterthwaite, at a Royal Aeronautical Society dinner.

where they were joined by Livingston Satterthwaite, the US Civil Air Attaché.

The British team comprised Max, who took the Chair, Richard Law from the Foreign Office, accompanied by John Le Rougetel, George Cribbett from the Air Ministry's Civil Aviation Department, Evelyn Baring and myself.

No more ill-matched pair could have been found than Lord Beaverbrook and the small, intensely serious, intellectually arrogant and sarcastic Berle. The latter arrived believing that British policy might seriously handicap the attempts by US carriers (American word for airlines) to expand beyond the shores of the United States, especially if we formed 'an Empire air-transport bloc'.

He had some justification for this, and in April 1944 the two great partners were building up to extreme positions. On the one hand was the US desire for 'freedom of the air', with the right to pick up and and set down traffic without reservation. On the other was the rigid view of the British Air Ministry, led by Sir Arthur Street, that there must be 'order in the air' by restricting all competition, predetermining frequencies and protecting traffic rights.

The talks on post-war civil air transport began at Gwydyr House at 10 o'clock in the morning on Monday 3 April 1944. Max greeted Berle and Warner at the Whitehall door and led them to my ground-floor office, in which had been installed a long conference table set for nine. Max at the head had Berle, Warner and Satterthwaite on his right and the British team on his left. I sat at the end facing him and took notes, while two stenographers sat at a separate table.

Max opened by telling Berle – he appeared to speak to him personally – that Anglo-American accord on aviation was the key to future prosperity, and to the development of the world's air routes (as always, he called them 'rowtes'). Berle diplomatically echoed these views. Warner, large and comfortable, and with a dozen sharpened pencils in the top pockets of his waistcoat, reiterated his belief in post-war aviation. The conference then got under way.

There were six items on the agenda:

1   The need for agreement on technical standards.
2   The possibility of an International Civil Aviation Authority.
3   The banning of enemy nations (Germany and Japan, but not Italy or other minor Axis allies) from post-war air-transport activities.
4   The need for a policy towards leased air bases.
5   The question of air-traffic rights.
6   The fixing of fares and rates.

The agenda had been arranged in order of anticipated difficulty, starting with the easiest. On that first morning we made splendid progress. For a start, there was immediate unanimous agreement that every effort must be made to establish all technical standards, especially those affecting safety. It was also agreed that these could best be evolved by an international organisation, though Berle and Warner made it clear that they expected US standards to be adopted. This was left for later argument.

There was immediate agreement that neither Germany nor Japan should be permitted to operate civil airlines, at least for a substantial period.

Then came the first possible problem. On 2 September 1940, when Britain was literally fighting for its life, in return for 50 obsolete American World War 1 destroyers, it leased to the United States for 99 years nine areas in the Western hemisphere on which the United States constructed major air and naval bases. These were:

1   Antigua (Coolidge Field).
2   Bahamas (Oakes Field, Nassau).
3   Bermuda (Kindley Field).
4   British Guiana (Atkinson Field, Georgetown).
5   Jamaica (Palisadoes, Kingston).
6   Newfoundland (Harman Field, Stephenville).
7   Newfoundland.
8   St Lucia (Beane Field).
9   Trinidad (Piarco, Port of Spain).

Somewhat to our surprise, there turned out to be no intractable problem here. Accord was quickly reached that, provided these bases were designated as Entry Ports by the countries on whose soil they stood, they would be available equally to all nations, subject only to agreement on traffic rights. It was accordingly agreed that the legal title to the base was academic.

The agreed basic principle was that each nation would provide designated international airports in its own territory, as might be required for the development of future air transport. This completed an excellent first day's talking. It was arranged that we would all meet in the evening at Claridges for an agreeable dinner, satisfied that a good start had been made. The US team then left Gwydyr House. This left us, as usual, seated under Max at 'evening prayers', dealing with the mail and reviewing how the first day had gone.

'Ah,' said Max, 'Berle. A strange fellow.' In his characteristic way, he lowered his head and gazed up from under his bushy eyebrows at Thompson. 'What did you tell me? Berle's a Papist? And a Tractarian? Now will you go out Thompson, and see what you can find which he might look on as something to carry home from London. What d'you say?'

'Well, Sir,' said George, 'How about something a little personal, something in line with the Tractarian Movement? How about Cardinal Newman's hat? That would be personal, Papist and on top of the Tractarian Movement.' Max guffawed. 'You get it, Thompson . . . search London for it.'

Alas, no hat. But George did track down instead a beautiful vellum-bound First Edition of Newman's *Apologia Pro Vita Sua* instead. When Berle received it at the end of the conference he was delighted. He did not know that George had tapped his own forehead, saying 'He's mad, poor gentleman, quite mad.'

Over the next two days we moved into the turbid waters of traffic rights and rates. Max let George Cribbett make most of the running. Tuesday saw Cribbett and Berle holding forth, with great passion and at formidable length, expounding diametrically opposed views on air-traffic operations. Max said it was 'a display of great forensic power'.

The setting up of an international body to decide upon technical standards had presented no difficulties. In contrast, the giving to such a body of any powers over air-traffic allocations was bitterly opposed by Berle, and dismissed by Warner as 'simply not practical'.

In contrast, the subject of cabotage was dealt with in minutes. Thus, all traffic between New York and Chicago was wholly that of US domestic airlines, while all traffic between London and Glasgow was wholly British. Equally, quite brief amicable discussion led to agreement that all traffic between the United Kingdom and Bermuda (for example) would be regarded as cabotage, and so would traffic between the United States and Puerto Rico or Hawaii.

On the other hand, traffic between a home country and a self-governing dominion would be just like traffic between any other two sovereign nations. This agreement was an important clarification in thinking. After two days, the first four agenda items had been cleared.

There remained the thornier air-traffic problems. Almost a year earlier, on 27 May 1943, Ed Warner had made his own position clear in a classic Wilbur Wright Memorial Lecture to the Royal Aeronautical Society. He said,

> 'I am concerned here with economics and with engineering, and I shall say nothing of politics except to make a personal profession of faith in which I hope you can all join. My hopes for the future are rooted in the central hope that air-navigation agreements will henceforth be drawn to the prescription that air transport is a Good Thing; that the need of the whole World to share in its benefits should be a prime consideration in the planning of air routes; and that there shall be no return to the evil days when air transport was regarded with such caution and suspicion that it had to be administered in paltry and carefully measured doses, with the authorisation to operate internationally being parsimoniously doled out, schedule by schedule.'

Good words. Unfortunately they were not in line with the formula of the British Air Ministry, and we wasted the morning of Wednesday 5 April restating national positions. At noon Max bore Berle off to lunch with Winston at No 10, while Cribbett and I took Warner and Satterthwaite to lunch at the Royal Empire Society. Here Air Marshal Sir Richard Peck gave a lunchtime talk, 'The RAF and its tasks', with Lord Clarendon in the Chair.

A mellow Max and even mellower Berle returned for one final session. We achieved one more positive agreement: both the UK and USA would help to revive a post-war International Air Traffic Association, on the lines of the shipping conferences, mainly to agree fares. At Warner's suggestion this would be renamed the International Air Transport Association (IATA).

The conference wound up with an agreement that there would be no exclusive agreements between airlines to 'sew up traffic'. There was also agreement that, once both our parties had sounded out other countries – Max stressed 'the Empire', at which Berle winced visibly – there should be a World Air Conference.

Ed Warner and I spent an hour drafting a non-commital Press Statement. We then all adjourned to an official HMG dinner at Claridges. It was presided over by an ebullient Max, proposing toasts in the flamboyant manner one associates with Russians. We were still doing it at midnight.

Berle and Ed left for Poole Harbour on the 8th, and arrived back in Washington by PanAm Boeing 314A two days later.

This small conference laid the foundations for post-war civil air transport. In particular, four things emerged, which have remained clear and unequivocal ever since:

1   The way to the International Civil Aviation Organisation (ICAO) was mapped out, with Warner as the first President of the Council.
2   The long rumblings over the question of the US-leased air bases were finally cleared away.
3   Agreement was reached for the setting up by governments and airlines of a new IATA.
4   Cabotage rights were agreed as unassailable.

On 18 April the Prime Minister reported on the discussion to the House of Commons. Among other things, he said: 'Sufficient agreement was reached for both countries to support the holding of a conference in the expectation that final dispositions could then be achieved. Concessions were made by both, but they relate only to the basis on which discussions will be launched at an International Conference ... which both HMG and the United States Government hope will be held this year ...'

Thus, a large hurdle was scrambled over, to make progress along what was clearly a long trail. That led first to Chicago, and then on to the winning post at Bermuda.

16

V-weapons

When I speak to some young Britons today I am astounded at their ignorance of their country's history. Many know nothing about the Battle of Britain. Even fewer realise how close London came to being wiped off the map four years later. Had even half of the planned 1,000 tons of high explosive fallen on London every day during the first six months of 1944 the capital would have had to be evacuated, and the city as we know it would have ceased to exist.

The threat was real, and the danger immense. Since before the war German scientists and engineers had worked on two totally dissimilar weapons which were years ahead of contemporary thought by the Allies. They had the potential to destroy London and the other cities – among them, Southampton and Antwerp – against which they were aimed. They failed because they arrived too late, and this gave the Allies just time to devise countermeasures. They also failed because of inept and inefficient administration by the German staff. Moreover, even had they been fully successful, they could not have won the war for Germany. The forces marshalled against Hitler were growing in strength beyond anything that Germany could counter.

On one of my first days at Gwydyr House Max brought me into discussions of 'vengeance weapons'. Like the British public, I had never heard of them. Max relished a controversy around a mysterious threat. He was in the thick of arguments which raged inside and outside the Cabinet about the possibility of attack by these vaguely reported weapons.

Max was one of the group which took the rumours seriously, and forecast dire consequences and a need for urgent action. The other camp, forcefully led by 'the Prof.' (Lord Cherwell), pooh-poohed the whole idea and dismissed it as fiction.

Max had come into the picture on his appointment as Lord Privy Seal on 24 September 1943. By that time the reports of *Vergeltungswaffen* (retaliation weapons) were too numerous to be ignored, and Churchill had formed the War Cabinet Committee for Operational Counter-Measures against V-Weapons, more succinctly called the Crossbow Committee. Its Chairman was Duncan Sandys (pronounced sands), who had – apart from marrying one of Churchill's daughters – commanded an anti-aircraft rocket battery before being appointed Deputy Minister of Supply. He soon saw Max as an ally.

Apart from the Prof. almost everyone – notably Archie Sinclair, Stafford Cripps, Harold Balfour and Max himself – viewed the threat as potentially very serious. The Prof., however, told about giant rockets, retorted 'Wooden dummies . . . they're all baloney.' He contented himself with repeating this over and over again.

He was born Frederick Alexander Lindemann in Baden-Baden in 1886. His engineer father came from Sidmouth in Devon, but became a naturalised Alsatian. After a distinguished career at Oxford, the Prof. was brought into the war as Chief Scientific

Adviser to the Prime Minister. His awesome position made it difficult for anyone to argue with him on scientific matters. He unbent to talk to me about my writings on the subject, and in particular my flying with the 8th Air Force.

Aged 58, he was the epitome of an academic: tall and thin, with a narrow egg-shaped head on which was often a bowler slightly too big for him. He had a dome forehead, a white moustache and a thin, high-pitched voice, which went even higher when he was arguing. He relished feuds, his biggest being with my Cambridge mentor, the great Henry Tizard. He obviously disliked Sandys, and bitterly resented the fact that this young man should have been picked to chair the Crossbow Committee.

He would walk across Whitehall and glide silently up the stairs, to enter Max's room unannounced. At Gwydyr House he seemed stiff and remote, enveloped in an air of sarcastic superiority, possibly as a defensive pose in what he felt to be hostile territory. At a conference table, Max sat head-down, his eyes missing nothing despite the deep brows almost hiding them. In contrast, the Prof. threw his head back, his chin thrust out and his eyes hooded like a hawk.

Not only did he resent the Sandys Committee, but he also read into Max's interest in the subject a personal slight. Sandys himself was not a member of the Civil Air Transport Committee, which brought the others into frequent contact – though he was often with Max at Arlington House – but the other members spent much of their time listening to the vehement 'It's all rubbish' insistence of the Prof. Max would occasionally intervene with a short but devastating remark.

It was in early November 1943 that Max sent for me unusually early. I found him gazing over Whitehall with a green Cabinet paper in his hand. He turned from the window. 'Peter, this is Top Secret . . . You gave me a report on those German aircraft at Farnborough in 1940. And I saw the technical reports from Holland you wrote just before the Germans invaded.' I was astonished. I had no idea those reports had gone to the MAP, and was amazed that he should have remembered them.

He went on,

> 'Here's a new puzzle for you. Sandys and Sinclair believe the Germans are working on some kind of long-range weapon to attack London. It may be a giant gun, but Sandys thinks they are working on a long-range raaaket . . . The RAF have photographed what look like launching rails at many places in northern France. They all point at London. The Air Ministry think they may have developed both raaakets and pilotless aircraft, and the aircraft may get here first. What do you think?'

I suggested that it could be something along the lines of our own Queen Bee radio-controlled targets. 'For example, if they filled up a Focke-Wulf 190 with explosives, and launched it off a rail in the direction of London, it could pose quite a problem. On a one-way trip it could carry a 2,000-lb bomb.' Max pondered, and said, 'Huh! Let me have a note about that. But Duncan Sandys still thinks they've got raaakets.' What we did not know was that we still had 32 weeks before the first flying bomb arrived.

The first hint of such weapons had been contained in a fantastic parcel of intelligence information left anonymously at the British Naval Attaché's office in Oslo in

November 1939. So amazing and detailed was the information that it was *dismissed in London as a hoax*! This was despite the fact that, at the very start of the war, Hitler himself had boasted of 'secret weapons with which we ourselves cannot be attacked'.

In December 1942 reports began coming in from many sources of reprisal weapons, wonder weapons and other vague horrors. In fact the giant A.4 (V.2) rocket was first successfully fired on 3 October of that year. The A.4 programme was so huge that reports of its existence became more frequent and persistent.

In November 1942 one of Rommel's staff officers, General Ritter von Thoma, was captured and brought to London. On 22 March 1943 he was put in a room with another captured *Afrika Korps* commander, General Cruwell. Astonishingly, they fell for an old trick: they never suspected that the room was bugged. Von Thoma said, 'Something must have gone wrong with those rockets; I saw them on test 18 months ago, and here we are in London and there are no sudden bangs, the rockets do not seem to be arriving.'

That clinched it, and on 15 April 1943 the Chiefs of Staff Committee sent a Minute to the Prime Minister informing him of these reports, recommending that Sandys should direct an investigation into their veracity. Five days later Churchill gave his assent – emphasising that he had not suggested the appointment, because Sandys happened to be his son-in-law.

What had finally triggered this Minute was a comparison of RAF reconnaissance photographs. On 15 May 1942 Flt Lt D.W. Steventon had flown a Spitfire XI on routine coverage of Kiel, Rostock and Swinemünde. Almost a year later, in April 1943, the photographs were compared with new ones, and it was suggested that new earthworks could be rocket test sites.

Sandys asked Dr R.V. Jones, Head of Air Ministry Scientific Intelligence, to assist. On 17 May 1943 Sandys sent his first report to the War Cabinet, describing rocket development at Peenemünde and noting that air reconnaissance had 'provided further important information'. The evidence showed a 'heavy rocket capable of long-range bombardment' and 'jet-propelled aircraft and airborne rocket torpedoes'.

On 28 June he further reported that reconnaissance photographs showed large rockets, which 'might have a range of up to 130 miles'. Sites from which they could attack London were possibly being prepared in northern France.

In that month of June 1943 Peenemünde was covered by RAF photo aircraft four times. The fourth sortie, on 23 June, showed two A.4s on road vehicles within the stadium-like earthworks. At this point my glamorous young colleague from *The Aeroplane* came into the picture. Constance 'Babs' Babington-Smith had joined the WAAF in July 1940, and by 1941 was a photo interpreter at Medmenham, working under Wg Cdr Hugh Hamshaw Thomas, FRS, of Cambridge.

She was told to look out for 'anything queer' at Peenemünde. She soon found four little tailless aircraft, which were later discovered to be Me 163B rocket interceptors. However, the size of the research station clearly showed its importance, and on 17 August 1943 the RAF dropped 2,000 tons of bombs on it. It was the first attack to be directed by a Master Bomber, in this case Gp Capt. John Searby, CO of 83 Sqn.

This seriously delayed all the V-weapons, though several crucial target areas, including the V.1 test side at Peenemünde-Ost, were missed. An offer by the US 8th

Constance Babington-Smith – a delightful contributor to The Aeroplane, *and from the early days of the war an expert and inspired photo interpreter, based at Medmenham. 'Babs' was the first to identify the V.1 and V.2 missiles.*

Air Force to follow up in daylight was – in my opinion very foolishly – not accepted. On the other hand, on 27 August 1943 the 8th Air Force was allowed to bomb a concrete structure in the Forêt d'Eperlecques in northern France. This had the important effect of delaying A.4 operations while the entire weapon system was made mobile.

On 8 November 1943 the Crossbow Committee discussed what were dubbed 'ski sites' in the Pas de Calais area, so-called because the main building was long and narrow, with a curved end. At that time 19 had been found, but the number soon rose to 26, and then to 96, most aimed at London.

Each had a main building with a doorway no less than 22 feet wide. Could this be to admit small aircraft? 'Babs' searched every part of every photo taken in the Peenemünde area, and on 13 November, in a remote corner of nearby Karlshagen airfield, she found a tiny aircraft. Its span was about 20 feet, so she called it Peenemünde 20. She had discovered the V.1, or, to give it its correct designation, the Fieseler Fi 103.

On 28 November a reconnaissance Mosquito found its primary target, Berlin, covered by cloud, so instead it took photographs of Peenemünde. These did not reach 'Babs' until 1 December. Studying the prints she noticed, on a kind of ramp by the

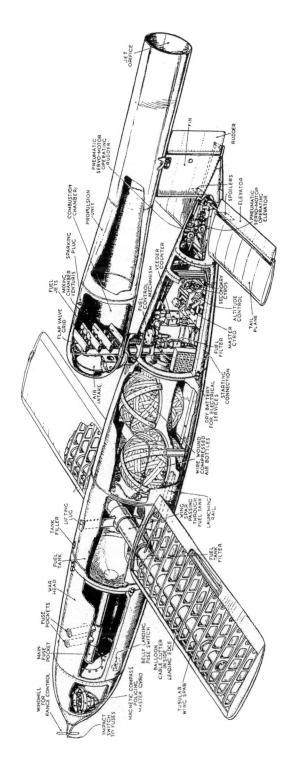

The first cutaway drawing of a V.1 flying bomb, by Max Millar of Flight.

shore of the Baltic, the same tiny aeroplane. That was another clincher, and linked 'Peenemünde 20' with the ski sites.

Churchill had invited the Prof. to chair a committee to decide action. He refused, so that task went to Cripps. With hindsight, it would have been prudent to move thousands of anti-aircraft guns from Scotland and Ulster, where their crews were bored from inactivity, to new sites in Kent, or even to hundreds of offshore ships. Instead almost nothing was done, and as no attack seemed imminent the Crossbow Committee was wound up.

On 20 December the 8th Air Force started bombing the ski sites, and every one was eventually obliterated. This saved London from a planned assault by 500 flying bombs each day. Instead, the 40,000 workers of the Todt organisation were set to work installing a simpler launch system which was much more difficult to discover. By late May 1944 at least 68 of these new installations had been identified, but it was suspected that there were far more, most of them hidden in or among farm buildings.

On 6 June 1944 the Allies invaded north-west Europe, and a week later the long-expected V.1 attack began. Thanks to Allied bombing, it was not a mighty assault. A mere seven bombs were launched on that day, only one of which caused casualties, at London's crowded Bethnal Green.

On Friday the 16th, at about 7.30 on a bright morning, I was shaving in the bath-room of our apartment at West Hill Court, off Mill Field Lane in Highgate, in north London. Suddenly I heard a strange sound, a throbbing noise like an infuriated motor-cycle. It got rapidly louder. I dashed out onto our terrace in time to see a small aeroplane with stubby untapered wings approaching at high speed from over the apartments opposite. Its streamlined body showed clearly against the early-morning sky, as did stabs of flame from what was clearly a jet-propulsion tube above the tail. It thundered overhead; then, suddenly, there was silence. Within seconds the bomb dived steeply, and plunged behind trees on Parliament Hill Fields. There was a deafening explosion, the windows shook, and a huge belch of black smoke rose high into the sky.

About 15 minutes later I heard another flying bomb coming. This one thankfully carried on into the distance, still going at full speed. Within an hour I had packed Pat and our family of, by then three, children off to my parents' house at Brentwood. I then went to Gwydyr House and gave Max a fair drawing of the bomb, which he took to the Cabinet. He asked me to prepare for him an appreciation of the situation, and if possible a note on the effectiveness of the defences.

On that day *Oberst* Wachtel's *Flakregiment 155(W)* managed to launch 244 bombs from 55 sites. Of these, 45 crashed soon after launch, 144 crossed the English coast and 72 reached London. Seven were shot down by fighters and 25 by AA fire (11 of these falling on London), but none were caught by the balloon barrage. A further 50 were launched against Southampton. During the next two weeks some 2,000 more bombs were launched.

General Sir Frederick Pile, the Commander of Anti-Aircraft (AA) Command, came to Gwydyr House. Diminutive in stature but – as Max said – 'with fire in his belly', Pile described the disposition of more than 1,000 balloons in a great arc around London's southern suburbs. South of the balloons were 785 AA guns, and between there and the coast were fighters.

'I don't think that's right,' said Max, 'if they're any good, the balloons will pull the bombs down on to the houses. Why don't you move them into open country?' A little later they were moved. Time showed that the guns were the most effective defence, with radar direction, and ammunition with a new proximity fuse supplied from the USA about which Pile talked with enormous enthusiasm. In his view, 'We could hardly ever actually hit a bomb, but the VT fuses bring them down almost every time.'

The problem with the fighters was that at low level most were not as fast as the bombs. The only one with a clear margin over the average bomb was the Hawker Tempest, which at 2,000 feet could reach about 350 knots (403 mph). Even with a dive, this was a little enough margin over the bomb, which in any case was a tiny target. Scoring against bombs was opened on that Friday, 16 June, by Sqn Ldr A.S. Dredge of 3 Sqn, who proved that it could be done. Number 3 Squadron got six more bombs on that day, five of them over the Channel, which was obviously the best place to get them. Eventually 'Bee' Beamont's Tempest Wing, based at Newchurch, of which 3 Sqn was part, shot down 638. Admittedly, the bombs didn't fight back, but pilots had to get quite close to hit them, and they then might have to fly through an almighty explosion.

Someone called the bombs Doodlebugs. Gradually Londoners began to accept them as 'all in the day's work'. By 31 July over 4,740 Londoners had been killed, and 800,000 buildings damaged or destroyed. The worst incident came on the first Sunday, 18th June, when more than 200 people were killed during a service in the Guards Chapel at Wellington Barracks, near Buckingham Palace.

On the evening of that day *F155(W)* launched its 500th bomb. Among all the devastation there were odd incidents. On more than one occasion two bombs, launched from different ramps, would be seen in tight formation, and an odd thing was that each bomb alternately pulled ahead and then fell back. One bomb thundered over Kent in a wide curve and flew back towards France. Another dived into a haystack and failed to explode, to be pounced on for analysis.

One morning in late June I was going over some papers with Max when the familiar throbbing sound approached. We were now used to it, but just as it got overhead the sound ceased. Max and I took one glance at the great expanse of glass on each side. We dived together, from opposite sides, into the knee hole under his desk. Our heads met at high speed in the middle. Max said one word, 'Goddam!'. Then came a mighty explosion, and we saw a tower of smoke just across the river.

Between 13 June and 1 September 1944 a total of 8,617 flying bombs were launched against London. Of these, 2,290 hit the city. Subsequently the attacks gradually diminished, as launch sites were captured, and the bombs finally had to be carried near to England by modified He 111 bombers. At last, on 7 September Sandys issued a Press Statement which began, 'Except possibly for a few last shots, the Battle of London is over'. Londoners breathed a huge sigh of relief. His timing could hardly have been worse. Just 24 hours later an A.4 rocket fell on London, and it was followed by 1,114 others.

The existence of a programme to develop a giant rocket had been disclosed in the ignored 'Oslo parcel', and by 1943 we began to learn many of the details. On the very day flying bombs first hit London an A.4, without a warhead, lost guidance and plunged into a cornfield in Sweden. After delicate negotiations, which involved giving the Swedes coveted mobile radars, British experts were allowed to examine the remains. Analysts then predicted a launch weight of 26,000 lb and a warhead weighing about a ton, delivered over a range of about 200 miles. These guesstimations were spot-on.

The first A.4s fired 'in anger' fell on Paris on 7 September. On the 8th two arrived in London. After some delay, radar plots showed that they had been launched from the Wassenaar Road just south of The Hague, and from the island of Walcheren. We already knew that the entire A.4 system was mobile, so the air attacks which were immediately launched against the firing sites were unlikely to have had any effect.

The first rocket to hit London fell in the middle of a road in Chiswick. It was thus possible to think of a cover story, and newspapers on 9 September reported 'a gas-main explosion'. Unfortunately, from then onwards the gas mains exploded rather frequently, and no cover story could account for the fascinating fact that, *after* the colossal bang of the warhead, anyone still alive (and for miles around) heard an awesome whooshing rumbling, which took perhaps ten seconds to die away.

This was the delayed sound of the rocket's approach, at a speed of roughly a mile a second. It had much in common with thunder. It was also evident that the rockets could leave vapour trails, both climbing up above the stratosphere, reaching altitudes exceeding 60 miles (96 km), and even on plunging back at Mach 5.5 to the point of impact.

Churchill was in Quebec, accompanied by Max and the Prof. According to Max, the latter was confounded, and 'took the news with no good grace. He just said, "A trifle; as I thought".' He meant 'As I had not thought', and the rockets were hardly 'a trifle'.

The A.4 was given the popular designation 'V.2', as the second of the reprisal weapons. The fact that anyone on the receiving end never heard it coming affected people in different ways. Most, even those who hated the flying bombs, were completely untroubled. At the same time, the big rockets were something against which there was no defence whatsoever, save to push back the enemy out of range of England.

Some of the 'incidents' were horrific, none more so than on 25 November, when a rocket fell on a shopping centre at Deptford to kill 160 and injure 135. I accompanied Max on a quick tour of some sites, and this was a macabre experience. One day a rocket killed more than 30 Presbyterian ministers attending a conference. Max asked me, 'What d'you think would be right, Peter? A memorial plaque?' I timidly suggested a pension fund for widows and children. 'Great', said Max. He pulled out a cheque book. 'Miss Hogg,' he said, 'send this to the right people.' The cheque was for £60,000, in 1944 an astronomic sum.

Between them, the two V-weapons caused 42,380 British civilian casualties, of whom 8,938 were killed. To these must be added 2,900 aircrew and 490 aircraft of the RAF and USAAF lost in the attacks against the weapons and their launch sites.

Though the Fi 103 (V.1) caused more devastation, the A.4 (V.2) was the more significant technical achievement. It was, in fact, the first stage of Man's journey to the Moon. I duly handed to Max the requested 'appreciation of the situation'. The note concluded, 'In all of this we may see the seeds of future transport possibilities.' Max scribbled across it, 'Not for me', and we turned to consider the problems of post-war airlines.

Typical specifications of the V weapons were:

Fi 103 (V.1) Span 17 ft 4¾ in (5.3 m); length 25 ft 11 in (7.9 m); launch weight 4,806 lb (2,180 kg); propelled by a pulsejet with spring flap-valves with a frequency of 47 Hz, burning low-grade petrol (gasoline); cruise speed 400 mph (644 km/h) for maximum range 150 miles (241 km); autopilot/compass guidance, flight terminated by a small nose propeller driving a 'distance-run' counter which stopped fuel feed and put the bomb into a dive.

A.4 (V.2) Length (height) 45 ft 11¾ in (14.0 m); body diameter 66 in (1.68 m); fin span 11 ft 9 in (3.57 m); launch weight 28,373 lb (12,870 kg); propelled by a rocket engine burning liquid oxygen and alcohol; cutoff speed (also impact speed) about 3,600 mph (5,795 km/h); maximum range about 200 miles (322 km); guidance by gyros and integrating accelerometer, with a timing mechanism to cut off propulsion. The rocket thereafter followed a free ballistic trajectory.

17

Washington non-stop

In July 1944 anyone able to look out across London would have seen giant pillars of smoke, each marking the place where a V.1 Doodlebug had fallen. At Gwydyr House we had additional worries to occupy us. Searching through my old note-books reminds me of the constant comings and goings, among them:

John Booth and Evelyn Baring to discuss air routes to and within South America;

Cecil Critchley, Ronnie McCrindle and Bob Mayo to discuss BOAC services;

F.W. Farey Jones to discuss new independent airlines within the United Kingdom;

Dick Hildred and George Cribbett to discuss a new Government *White Paper on Aviation Policy*;

Ernest Hives and Bill Lappin to discuss Rolls-Royce engines for future civil air transport;

Basil Kingsley-Martin to discuss articles for the journal *New Statesman*;

Alfred Lamplugh to discuss the further work of his committee;

John le Rougetel and John Cheetham to discuss Foreign Office aspects on aviation, especially those involving Washington;

David MacIntyre to discuss the future of Prestwick airport;

Dan McVey to discuss the future of civil aviation in Australia;

Harold Roxbee-Cox to discuss jet engines (which are featured in Chapter 23);

Livingston Satterthwaite, the US Civil Air Attaché, to discuss imminent talks in Washington;

K.T. Spencer and Jock Gray to discuss the further work of the Brabazon Committee;

Sir Frederick Sykes to discuss fundamental air-transport policy;

and Fred Winterbotham, Rex Pierson and Barnes Wallis of Vickers to discuss future aircraft.

Gwydyr House was central to British aviation policy. I found myself in meetings for most of each day, and drafting follow-up Papers for most of the night.

To try to winkle out statements on the main issues, Lord Londonderry initiated a two-day debate in the Lords on 10/11 May 1944. He had set down six main headings: ministerial responsibility; international regulations; domestic, Empire and inter-national airlines; 'chosen instruments' and subsidies; types of aircraft; and the scope and powers of airlines. These matters were still burning issues a quarter of a century later.

The debate gave Max a prized opportunity for verbal fireworks. He said that the recent conference with the United States had been 'satisfactory to both parties'. He made it clear that his CAT (Civil Air Transport) Committee of the War Cabinet had three main duties: to co-ordinate UK policy on civil aviation; to recommend further ministerial responsibility and departmental organisation; and to assume responsibility for an international air conference. He emphasised that his committee was not an executive body; its recommendations were subject to sanction by the War Cabinet.

He went on to describe what were then the principal British interim transport aircraft, mainly the York, Halifax, Tudor and Shetland, and then reported 'Mr Berle had assured us most generously . . . that the United States is prepared to make transport aircraft available to Britain on a non-discriminatory basis in the interim period, before British production gets going . . . Of course, we are not satisfied to rely on aircraft from the United States . . . We shall do all we can to promote our own supplies of aircraft . . . The interests of the air industry in Britain I never forget.'

He went on to discuss 'the elimination of uneconomic competition, the setting up of national quotas, equilibrium between transport capacity and traffic offering . . .' This was the pure milk of the Street/Cribbett philosophy. Max said it, but he did not for a moment believe in it.

He then turned to the first two Freedoms. 'I am authorised by the Prime Minister to say that we join with the President in subscribing to the right of innocent passage for all . . . and the right to land anywhere for refuelling and other non-traffic purposes.'

He then endeavoured to explain cabotage. Lord Addison intervened to say that this was a new word to him, and he would like a little more illumination.

Lord Beaverbrook repeated: 'Cabotage is the right of a nation to carry its own traffic within its own territory.'

Viscount Samuel: 'To the exclusion of other nations?'

LB: 'To the exclusion of all.'

Lord Barnby: 'Not over other territory?'

LB: 'No, it relates to the territory of the country concerned.'

Viscount Trenchard (confused): 'In a straight line over everybody's country?'

LB: 'The noble Viscount will know if an aeroplane goes in a straight line or not . . .'

After a further explanation, the noble Viscount repeated: 'In a straight line? That is the question we all want answered.'

LB (exasperated): 'I cannot say whether it is in a straight line or not . . .'

As the debate dragged on, it was evident that few of their lordships had the foggiest notion of the meaning of the word. Some, with aural difficulties, had apparently heard it as 'sabotage'. Little wonder that they were, as it were, 'at sea'.

On the second day, the subject of an independent British airline to South America, financed by shipping companies, was generally approved. Indeed there were suggestions that other future BOAC routes might be hived off. This spurred Max to say 'Do these companies want to take over some services, leaving a residue to BOAC? If so, it is open to shipping companies to go to the Foreign Office and state their position.'

Viscount Trenchard still did not understand cabotage: 'This matter is most serious. If there is no innocent passage, it makes cabotage senseless, as you describe it.'

LB: 'It is the noble Viscount's opinion . . . but I cannot see it myself. Take a flight from here to Jamaica. I cannot see that refusal by any country to permit innocent passage would interfere with a flight from here to Jamaica.'

At the debate's conclusion, Max claimed much progress, while Charlie Londonderry, as usual, expressed himself as dissatisfied. Clearly, it was time to go to the United States, and try to clear the air. As well as civil aviation, within Lord Beaverbrook's remit we also had to discuss future policy on oil (crude petroleum). Here, we were concerned about policy on the Middle East, and especially the ambitions in that theatre of the United States.

Max and I relaxed on the Arlington roof-top verandah. 'How shall we go?', he asked, 'flying boat . . . bomber?' I suggested 'One of the new Liberators of 45 Group. I will have a word with Brackley and see what he can lay on.'

As ever, Air Commodore H.G. Brackley, at RAF Transport Command HQ at Harrow, was ready and eager to help. I told him that there would be only eight passengers, and suggested that we might propose to make the first direct flight between our two capitals. 'It would be a nice gesture if the British Minister in charge of civil-aviation planning were to fly non-stop from London to Washington in an American-built aeroplane with a British crew.' Max warmly concurred.

Bob Mayo of the Royal Aero Club was roped in as official observer, just as he had been for the Alcock and Brown flight in 1919. Harold Perrin, the Club's Secretary-General, sent seals to Brackley to fasten to the cowlings to qualify the prospective flight as an official record.

Before boarding Marco Polo; *from the left: PGM, G.M. Thompson, Geoffrey Lloyd, Sir William Brown,* the Beaver, *Victor Butler and Ralph Assheton.*

On the afternoon of 20 July 1944, we were glad to leave the flying bombs and drive down the Western Avenue to Northolt. There, in front of one of the two North Side hangars, was parked AL578, the famous Liberator II named *Marco Polo*, which had just arrived there from Montreal. Back in 1941 it had been one of the first Liberators. It had crashed at Montreal, and had lain there derelict for more than a year until the demand for transatlantic aircraft became so great that it was rescued and rebuilt. It was fitted with ultra-long-range tanks, and had subsequently flown many epic missions.

On that July evening *Marco Polo* had been refuelled until not another drop could be squeezed in. On board were more than 2,300 gallons of 100-octane. The flight plan turned out to be one of just over 19 hours, so in theory we had a two-hour endurance margin. In practice, the calculated 3,665 miles was extremely close to AL578's limit, even ignoring the normally prevalent headwinds.

Our party comprised Max, the Lord Privy Seal complete with red dispatch box; Ralph Assheton, Financial Secretary of the Treasury; Sir William Brown, Permanent Secretary of the Air Ministry; Geoffrey Lloyd, Parliamentary Secretary of the Ministry of Fuel and Power; Victor Butler, First Secretary and oil specialist; George Malcolm Thompson; and myself. We were photographed against the Liberator's black nose on which the aircraft's name stood out in white Chinese characters. These had been inscribed during a mission to Kunming with Lord Louis Mountbatten.

Northolt's main runway was (and still is) a mere 5,525 feet (1,684 m) long. Max did not know the problem, but I did, and so did Brackley. However, there was a useful 12-knot westerly breeze, and the aircraft commander, Gp Capt. George P. Evans OBE (an American from Brooklyn, but in the RAF) said he was quite happy. So off we went at 18.20 local time, at absolutely full power. If a double-decker bus had been on its way along Western Avenue to Uxbridge at the wrong moment we could not have climbed over it. However, by the time we left the North Wales coast we were at 6,000 feet, and we continued a laboured but steady climb for the next ten hours.

The Liberator had had its bomb bay comfortingly sealed, and equipped with four seats along each side, together with seven mattresses and sleeping bags on the floor. For much of the time we played rummy, Max doing so with panache. He then read Churchill's *Great Contemporaries*, doubtless searching disconsolately for mention of himself.

Not least, with tremendous gusto, he sang a famous ditty from beginning to end, word perfect. I can still hear his rasping Canadian accents lustily overcoming the thunder of four Twin Wasps:

> 'The sons of the Prophet are brave men and bold,
> and quite unaccustomed to fear.
> But the bravest by far in the ranks of the Shah
> was Abdulla Bulbul Ameer.'

And so on through many verses. Years later, I learned that it had been written by the popular singer Percy French, who hailed from New Brunswick, the Beaver's home State. It lulled Max to sleep.

As dawn broke over Nova Scotia I went forward to discuss the situation with

George Evans and his navigator. Careful checking suggested some doubt that we would make it, but, as our weight fell, so did the fuel consumption. Eventually, as we swept over the Capitol, we still had 40 minutes' fuel left. We landed at Washington National at 09.16 local time, 19 hr 55 min from Northolt. It was the first direct flight between the capitals, and also the first non-stop Ministerial flight across the Atlantic by landplane.

On arrival, the Beaver was greeted by Secretary of State Cordell Hull and Berle. We then drove off to the Mayflower hotel with motor-cycle outriders.

The next few days were hectic. After a meeting with Lord Halifax and British Embassy staff on the afternoon on which we arrived, we plunged straight into talks with Berle on post-war traffic rights, and – on the other side of the House – with Cordell Hull and Ed Stettinius on oil. The first round of talks lasted until the 28th. We spent that night drafting cables back to the Cabinet Committee in London.

On the 29th I flew to New York to talk with C.R. Smith and Ralph S. Damon, respectively the Presidents of American Airlines and TWA. Smith had been made Deputy Commander of the USAAF Air Transport Command, with the rank of Major-General. I returned to Washington on the following day.

A formal air-transport conference was arranged for 3 August at Washington National Airport. On the British side: Max, Paul Gore-Booth and me. On the US side: Berle, Ed Warner, Welch Pogue and Stokely Morgan. One of the bones of contention was Lowell Yerex's plan for the involvement of British interests in Transportes Aéreos Centro-Americanos, as outlined in Chapter 22.

Max played for time. Berle pressed for a large international conference. Max replied, 'Yes, but it must be in London.' He confided in me that he had no intention of taking part himself: 'I prefer a "knock-down and drag out" meeting. I haven't got patience for long wrestling matches. Maybe we can get Lord Leathers to take it on; it's just his cup of tea.'

After tidying up, and more informal talks, Max, Thompson and I flew to New York on 4 August. In all, the talks lasted three weeks, and made progress on both topics, aviation and oil. For me they were especially valuable in that I came to know the principal American civil-aviation negotiators: Berle, Morgan and Garrison Norton at the State Department; Pogue, Chairman of the CAB, and Warner his deputy; and General George of Air Transport Command, and his deputy, C.R. Smith, who (as already noted) before and after the war was President of American Airlines. I was also able to make useful contacts at the Embassy, notably Gore-Booth and George Middleton.

General George saw us off to New York, in one of his C-53s (DC-3) with a VIP interior. The flight took 85 minutes, and we were met at North Beach Airport – which was rapidly becoming known as La Guardia Field – by C.R. Smith. Max at once went to the Waldorf Astoria, where we were both welcomed by the manager as long-lost friends. Max settled into the VIP suite in one of the 39-storey towers.

He went up to the roof and stripped to blue and white striped underpants, dark glasses and a Panama hat. Then he lay on one of the day beds, soaking up sunshine. 'Peter . . . how much we have missed the sun all these years. What a country we'd have, if only we had this sunshine . . .' Suddenly the energetic Beaver was indolent. Thick white hair curled on his chest, the hat tipped over his nose, enormous freckles blotched his arms and shoulders.

'That fellow Berle,' came from under his hat, 'he's only after one thing, you know.'
I ventured 'Cardinal Newman's hat?' 'Ah, Peter, you mock me . . . he's really after
PanAm flying everywhere and sweeping up all the trade. He and that fellow Trippe
want to dominate the rowtes [routes]. We've some rough stuff ahead. They'll try to
bring Middle East oil into it . . .'

After some days of meetings in New York, Max and I drafted, and then sent to
London, a long telegram:

> 'Civil aviation in the US is making rapid progress . . . 100 more transports than
> 18 months ago . . . Idlewild Airport is to cost $165 million . . . 1,173 DC-4s, 4,035
> C-46s and nine Constellations before the end of 1945 . . . the DC-6 a bigger faster
> version of DC-4 . . . 25,000 boys and girls taking aviation courses . . . post-war
> reconstruction employing more than a million in factory, field and in the air . . . our
> only chance is to equip ourselves with British aircraft at the earliest moment,
> converted bombers are not adequate . . . a policy of buying American would only
> confirm the US manufacturing position. Only the Secretary of State for Air can
> solve the puzzle . . . Unless we build British aircraft promptly civil aviation must
> pass to the control of the United States on a manufacturing and operating basis.
> Arise, O Israel.'

On 13 August we went to La Guardia and boarded Churchill's special single-fin
Liberator AL504, *Commando*. We took off at 17.06 local time, and again our flight

AL504 Commando, *the unique Liberator II with LB-30A features and an RY-3 tail.*

plan was non-stop, this time with favourable winds. In the hands of the Prime Minister's personal pilots Wg Cdr W.H. Biddell and Flt Lt F. Donaldson we again set a record in reaching Northolt in 17 hr 34 min. Seven months later this unique aircraft was to vanish over the Atlantic while taking a high-level delegation to a conference marking the end of the enormous Commonwealth Air Training Plan.

Max called a CAT Committee meeting for the 17th. He harked back to his 'Arise' theme. 'We must get out of the horse-and-buggy era. Either the British aircraft industry must be allowed to have a go, and be supported with sufficient funds, or we must give up to the Americans. That would be a disaster.' Prophetic words.

He turned to the Air Minister, and to the Minister of Aircraft Production, and, in that rasping voice of his, said 'Archie . . . Stafford . . . I say to you: piss or get off the pot.' They did neither, and in another year it was too late.

18

Preparing for Chicago

When we returned from Washington in August 1944 we could see that a major international conference on civil aviation was not likely to be long delayed. Our talks with Berle and other Americans had already laid the foundations for such a conference, and for the subsequent peacetime development of the world's airlines.

Max was determined that the big conference should be in London. He was equally determined not to have to conduct it. Accordingly, on 22 August he invited Archie Sinclair and Lord Cranborne to meet him at Gwydyr House. He asked me to be with him when they arrived.

He launched straight off into his theme. 'Archie, Bobbety . . . we must advance a plan for a new ministry to take care of this civil air business. An air conference can't be long delayed. You, Archie, have far too much on your plate at the Air Ministry. This conference needs time and effort and patience. I cannot sustain it myself, nor do I desire to do so . . . Now, what about Philip Swinton? He knows aviation well. He is wasted in West Africa. What do you say to bringing him back to take on this job?'

A long discussion followed. Should civil aviation go to Lord Leathers at the Ministry of War Transport? Or to Hugh Dalton at the Board of Trade? After the pendulum had swung this way and that, Max came back to Swinton. 'It's just the job for him.' Sinclair and Cranborne – I thought reluctantly – concurred.

On the following afternoon, following the scheduled meeting of the CAT Committee, the matter was broached informally to the other Ministers. But by this time the need for action had become urgent. We had received a cable from Berle proposing a further imminent meeting to set up an Anglo-American agreement to launch air services, and the postponement of the proposed multinational conference until after the war.

The CAT thought hard, and met again on 29 August to agree a reply from Max which I had drafted. It read:

'I have now had an opportunity of consulting my colleagues on the subject of your proposals . . . so that commercial flights can start without delay.

'We ask you for a postponement of your project of moving out on to the civil air routes of the world.

'We still feel that the next step should be to hold an international conference in either London or Washington at the earliest date convenient to us both.

'If you should find it difficult to hold a conference in Washington we shall understand your position and stand ready to call a conference ourselves in London.'

Word came from our Embassy in Washington that the President would find a conference there embarrassing, in view of the then position of the Senate and House of Representatives, and in the face of all the airline pressure groups. A more modest conference in London, with the Dominions present, did seem to be possible.

What we had not reckoned with was Berle's determination to act, and to keep the initiative. In the meantime, on Saturday 3 September – the fifth anniversary of the start of the war – I drove up to Snetterton Heath in order to fly a further mission with the 96th Bomb Group. Now the 8th Air Force was huge, but it had suffered grievous losses in its courageous daytime missions, and in the first half of 1944 the 96th BG had sustained the highest loss rate in the entire 8th AF. Sadly, all the crews were now strangers to me.

Their spirit, however, was if anything even higher than it had been a year earlier. I flew as co-pilot in the right seat with Capt. John Mickeljohn and his crew aboard B-17G 43-77603 *Suffolk Punch*.

We were one of 357 B-17Gs, escorted by 609 fighters, bound for German defence fortifications on the Brittany peninsula, which were being marked by two RAF Mosquitoes flying at full throttle at low level. We were leading the 338th BS, above and to the right of the lead squadron, 337, in the lead ship of which was Group Commander Col Robert W. Warren. Suddenly a bright-chequered P-47 formated alongside. Mickeljohn said 'That's General Earle Partridge, the new CO of the Third Division, seeing results for himself.'

In the region of Brest *Flak* was heavy. Suddenly I felt the control wheel jerk. Our starboard aileron was ragged at the tip, but lateral control seemed unaffected. Some time later everything began to feel unreal, and it took us several seconds to work out that *Suffolk Punch* was in a steep spiral dive, with the ASI needle moving past 240 mph and the altimeter unwinding past the 11,000-foot level. We had been hit, and the port outer propeller was running away.

Mickeljohn and I pulled hard and stopped the spiral, pulling out under heavy g at 9,500 feet. We recovered to level flight heading back for the smoke plume over the target, so we then made a steep 180° turn. A squadron of P-47s came alongside, their pilots waving and giving thumbs-up signs.

What had happened was that, thankfully just after our bombs had left, we had taken a flak hit in the bomb bay. It had ruptured the yellow oxygen tanks, and the supply piping, and our whole crew had gradually gone into that lethal state which thinks that everything is fine when it is actually anything but. It was sheer luck that, as we spiralled out of formation, we did not collide with anyone else. At lower level, we breathed deeply and started to come back on three engines via Ventnor and Tilbury to Snetterton. We landed late and somewhat shaken, but at least all in one piece.

Altogether, the 96th flew 8,924 sorties in 321 missions, an average of 28 aircraft per mission. It lost 239 B-17s and approximately 2,500 crew-members. It was disbanded at Camp Kilmer, New Jersey, on 21 December 1945.

Next morning at Gwydyr House Max remarked what a fine weekend it had been. Inadvisedly, I remarked that the beaches at Brest had looked nice, though the natives were hostile. A little later I reflected on the fact that, however hostile the natives, they exploded less violently than did Max – but when he had cooled down he invited me to dinner and made me tell him, Herbert Morrison and Brendan Bracken, all about it.

We sent telegrams to our Embassy in Washington to see whether a London conference could be set up for early 1945. To our surprise, on 9 September Berle announced unilaterally that a conference on civil aviation would be held in the United States before the end of 1944.

Max called this 'Roosevelt's V-Weapon'. It meant that the United States was determined to call the tune. He pressed harder for the recall of Swinton, so that he could take on the new portfolio of Civil Aviation and also our end of the conference. He saw Churchill, and came back full of glee. An invitation would be sent at once to Swinton.

Max's delight was reinforced as he read the invitation from the Government of the United States, issued on 11 September to 54 countries to attend 'an international conference on civil aviation to begin in the United States on November 1st, 1944'. It was sent to all the members of the newly formed United Nations and to European and Asiatic neutrals.

The subsequent Press Release from the US Office of War Information announced that the course of military events had already freed great areas of the world for a resumption of civil air traffic. The proposed conference would make possible arrangements for the setting up of provisional air routes for 'a transitional period'. It would also discuss the formation of 'an interim council on future civil air transport'.

On 29th September the US State Department announced unilaterally that the conference would be held in Chicago, and issued a proposed agenda:

1   **Agreements** on routes and services for a transitional period;
2   **Recommendations** on technical standards and procedures;
3   **Principles** for a multilateral Aviation Convention and an International Aeronautical Body;
4   **Consideration** of the establishment of an Interim Council.

On 6 October this agenda provoked a long Memo from George Cribbett, Assistant Under-Secretary (Civil Aviation) at the Air Ministry, addressed to the Director-General of Civil Aviation, Dick Hildred. Dick brought it round to Gwydyr House.

The Cribbett Memorandum displayed in some detail the suspicion and hostility with which the United States' ambitions in post-war civil aviation were viewed in at least some sections of the Air Ministry. The latter's objective for the United Kingdom remained an international authority 'with teeth' to control routes, rates, frequencies and everything else, and 'to safeguard air services against undue competition'.

Max read right through the verbose document. He then threw it back to me with the remark 'The Air Ministry are welcome to their views so long as I'm not associated with them.' The Air Ministry did not seem to have heard of free enterprise.

He added that, in any case, he was not going to a conference in the USA. The war might be over by Christmas, there would probably be a General Election, and, he said, 'I have to be around to support the Prime Minister.'

On 9 October 10 Downing Street announced that 'The King has been pleased to approve the appointment of the Right Hon. Viscount Swinton, GBE, CH, MC,

Minister Resident in West Africa, to become Minister of Civil Aviation. The purpose of the appointment is to enable a Minister of Cabinet Rank to devote his whole time to carrying forward the work of planning in the fields of Civil Aviation, particularly in its international and Imperial aspects.'

Max grinned as he handed it to me. 'But I want you to stay on with me. There's a lot more to do.' There was, and, despite the appointment of the new Minister, Max told me he intended to 'keep a finger in the pie'. On 12 October he had to cope with yet another of Lord Londonderry's civil-aviation debates in the Lords, and – fortunately – he continued to chair the Cabinet CAT Committee through one of its most strenuous periods, holding up the London end during the Chicago Conference.

In all of this, the appointment of a fully fledged Minister of Civil Aviation, with a Department of his own (not just a minor section of the predominantly military Air Ministry) and a seat in the Cabinet, was something for which many aviation people had long yearned, but never dared hope to see realised. It was a piece of perceptive and imaginative planning, which subsequent Governments have failed to maintain, despite the immense growth in the size and importance of international air transport.

Another area in which our national perceptions have gone downhill, despite the efforts of the Brabazon Committee, concerns the supply of airliners. On 12 October 1944 Max said in the Lords debate, '. . . It will be seen that four nations must supply the Civil Aviation requirements of the other 51 [which were to meet at Chicago]. We must take our share in that industry; we must have our share of that manufacturing output.' Today, in the 21st century, our only planemaker has deliberately removed 'aerospace' from its title!

Lord Swinton arrived in London on the 22nd, and at once met the CAT Committee (which continued under Max in spite of media reports of its disbandment). After two long talks with Max, Swinton left in a York of RAF Transport Command. Despite its marginal range the York made it by stages to Montreal, where a brief conference was held with the delegations from Canada, Australia, South Africa and India.

While they were meeting, one of the main hopes for worldwide accord at Chicago was dashed. On the 29th the USSR declined the invitation, on the grounds that invitations had been sent to three countries which were not members of the UN: Portugal, Spain and Switzerland. In the end, 52 nations sent delegates, and two (Denmark and Siam, soon to be called Thailand) sent observers. There were thus 54 nations present, with 185 delegates, 156 advisers, 43 secretaries, 105 stenographers and 36 secretariat (permanent administrators in government departments). With 158 Press representatives and numerous observers, the total came to 955!

The UK delegation, which arrived in Montreal on 31 October, was Lord Swinton (Minister of Civil Aviation); Sir Arthur Street (Permanent Under-Secretary, Air Ministry); Sir George London (of Newfoundland); J.H. Magowan (British Embassy, Washington); W.C.G. Cribbett (Assistant Under-Secretary, Air Ministry); G.C. Fitzmaurice (Legal Adviser, Foreign Office); and A.J. Walsh (Newfoundland). None of them knew much about civil aviation.

Fortunately, there were in addition, as advisers and observers, Lord Knollys, Major Ronald McCrindle and Vernon Crudge of BOAC, Air Cdre Vernon Brown, Air Chief Marshal Sir Frederick Bowhill of RAF Transport Command, Air Cdre Brackley, K.T. Spencer, Paul Gore-Booth, G.K. Boyd-Shannon, W.J. Bigg, B.StJ. Trend,

N.J.A. Cheetham, L.J. Darrell, Charles Campbell, R.D. Poland and F.A. Butters.

In London the CAT Committee held the fort, with Sir Gilbert Laithwaite of the Foreign Office and myself acting as Joint Secretaries and communications officers. Dick Hildred remained at Ariel House as an additional 'link man'. For Max, the CAT Committee and myself this was a period of hectic activity. The stream of telegrams to and from Chicago was continuous.

Max's compulsive telephoning, always with a high sense of urgency, reached a level not seen since the early days at the MAP. He called me wherever I happened to be. Possibly the climax came on a Sunday morning in mid-December, just after the Conference was over. Pat and I, with our three children, had gone for the weekend to my parents in Brentwood. At 4.10 a.m. there was an insistent ringing of the telephone in my father's study. I got out of a warm bed and stumbled sleepily to answer it.

Max's rasping voice woke me up. 'Peter! Am I calling you, or are you calling me?' I assured him that the call was his. 'Waaaal – what's new?' I racked my sleepy brains, and dared to tell him that the newest thing was that it was Sunday, with dawn some hours away. 'Ho, ho, Sunday morning, you say. And I've woken you up. Too bad. You sleep soundly. Waaal, it's a fine morning . . . Ah! Now I remember. You recall those figures about jet fighters in the Paper you sent me?'

Jets were still a secret topic, and I desperately tried to recall from the mists of sleep what figures he could have in mind. Max went on, 'They are very interesting. You have a great command of facts and logic. Ah – now I see that you have sent me a further note on them. I will call you when I have read it. Goodbye to you.' And the line went dead.

Altogether the Chicago Conference lasted through five weeks of toil among 54 nations. It closed with little resolved.

No clear account has been written of that conference, or of that in Bermuda which flowed from it, nor of what led up to them. I was the only person who went through the whole process, starting with discussions in Washington in September 1943, continuing with the Berle/Beaverbrook talks in London and Washington in 1944, and going on to the London-steering end of the Chicago Conference in 1944/5 and in Washington and Bermuda in 1945/6.

The story of the foundations of post-war air transport was not at all as it has sometimes been portrayed. It was much more complex, and more involved in human foibles, but an excellent example of the old saying:

> 'An optimist believes that he lives in the best of all possible worlds.
> Surveying it, a pessimist fears that that is true.'

19

Airliner arithmetic

A s outlined in Chapters 9 and 13, even in the middle of the war a vast amount
of thought was applied to the question of post-war air transport. Surprisingly,
among all the to-ing and fro-ing, one fundamental matter was apparently left
unexplored. Since the days of Imperial Airways, nobody had paid proper attention to
the question of the operating economics of the aircraft.

On the British side of the Atlantic this was to some degree because, in Britain at
least, air transport was hardly looked upon as a business. The state airline was there
to provide a service, principally as the carrier of His Majesty's mails, and there was
seldom any competition for the few passengers. Profitability hardly entered into the
matter. Even in the much more capitalist United States the 'mail subsidy makeweight'
was regarded as a salvation for any shortcomings in transport profitability.

This appeared to me to be a highly unsatisfactory state of affairs. I talked it over
with Max. He had no interest whatsoever in detail – especially economic detail – but
was unshakeable in his philosophy: 'As soon as possible, air transport must pay its
way.' This reminded me of Winston Churchill's famous dictum of March 1920, that
'Civil aviation must fly by itself'.

I decided that there was an urgent need to look into this basic but ignored subject.
I had done some research into the economics of airliners ten years previously, when I
was at Cambridge, so had a fair idea how to tackle the calculations. Practically nothing
of the sort was ever asked of anyone in the aircraft industry. I consulted with Lord
Knollys and George Cribbett, and they confirmed my belief that nothing had been
done to assess the economics of post-war air transport.

Accordingly, at the beginning of October 1944 I sat down with a slide rule, graph
paper, manufacturers' brochures and a wet towel. By the middle of the month I had
arrived at some preliminary conclusions concerning the economic performance of the
only long-range civil transport aircraft which could be in operational service by
the end of 1946.

I investigated six British and six American types of four-engined landplanes. I
analysed their economics on five typical routes:

1   **The North Atlantic**, by way of Prestwick and Gander;
2   **The Pacific**, the critical sector being Vancouver to Honolulu;
3   **The Empire**, the critical sector being Cairo to Karachi;
4   **The South Atlantic**, by way of Bathurst (The Gambia) to Recife (Natal);
5   **Continental** (i.e. European), with the longest sector being London to Malta.

On the basis of available information, my analyses showed the superiority of three
types of aircraft, all basically American:

1   **The Douglas DC-4C**, with four Rolls-Royce Merlin engines (later this was
    redesignated as the DC-4M, and became better known as the North Star with
    Trans-Canada Airlines and as the Argonaut with BOAC);
2   **The Douglas DC-4B**, with four Pratt & Whitney R-2800 Double Wasp engines
    (later this was to be redesignated as the DC-6, and go into service all over the
    world);
3   **The Lockheed Constellation**, with four Wright R-3350 Duplex Cyclone
    engines (this too was to be widely used).

Of the British types, the Handley Page Hermes showed a possibility of being made
competitive over shorter ranges. The Avro Lancastrian, Tudor and the projected Avro
690 (also called Type XXII) with six Merlin 100 engines all appeared to be significantly worse. Of course, the Brabazon types were still far in the future, and this was
depressing from the viewpoint of a 'fly British' policy.

To try to calculate direct operating costs (DOC) per revenue passenger mile (RPM)
I made a set of basic assumptions. These were: utilisation of 3,000 hours per annum
(in 1944 hardly any aircraft came near to this); a load factor (the proportion of the
available payload actually carried) of 62 per cent; a fuel cost of 1s 6d (7½ of today's
pence) per imperial gallon; a mean sector distance of 2,000 nautical miles
(2,303 miles = 3,706 km); and an arbitrary figure for overheads of 150 per cent of the
direct costs. On this basis, the DOCs worked out to:

	DC-4C	DC-4B	Constellation
Engines	Merlin 620	R-2800	R-3350
Block speed (kt)	210	214	235
Seats available	40	44	44
Seats occupied	25	27	27
DOC per RPM	6d	7d	8.5d

Not in the same league were:

	Lancastrian	Tudor
Engine	Merlin 24	Merlin 620
Block speed (kt)	176	180
Seats available	9	22
Seats occupied	6	14
DOC per RPM	10.5d	14d

To supplement this, and as a broad guide to the formative thinking of the airlines,
I worked out the number of each type of aircraft that would be required to carry
100,000 passengers a year over a hypothetical 2,000 nm sector (the longest in
common use, such as Prestwick–Gander or London–Cairo), assuming three stand-by
aircraft (or 10 per cent of the fleet, whichever was greater) to maintain regularity.
From this I calculated a profit/loss account, assuming a one-way passenger fare of
£70 and ignoring mail or cargo. The figures came out to:

	No. required	Operating result
DC-4C	16	£1.6 million profit
DC-4B	18	£1.1 million profit
Constellation	14	£550,000 loss
Lancastrian	69	£1.7 million loss
Tudor	30	£4.6 million loss

As noted above, for shorter ranges the Handley Page Hermes looked encouraging, but it did not show up well on longer sectors. In the event, the H.P.68 prototype crashed on its first take-off on 2 December 1945. Eventually the H.P.81 Hermes 4 re-emerged as a larger, heavier and more powerful aircraft.

In fact, it was more important to assess the potential results on a shorter sector of 1,000 nm. I did this, again making the assumptions of a hypothetical fleet of 12 aircraft, a 62 per cent load factor, and a one-way fare of half the previous, in other words £35, equating to 8.4d per mile. This time the results were:

	Block speed (kt)	Sectors per annum (10 a/c)	RPMs (millions)	Profit (loss)
DC-4C	175	5,250	131	£800,000
DC-4B	177	5,300	132	£600,000
Constellation	197	5,900	160	(£100,000)
Lancastrian	149	4,450	27	£50,000
Hermes	142	4,250	89	(£700,000)
Tudor	154	4,550	122	(£1.1m)

Again the DC-4C came out best. Surprisingly, the Lancastrian broke even. This was because, as a converted bomber, its first cost and the cost of spares were low.

History was to show that the Merlin-engined DC-4, as the North Star and Argonaut, was to give good – if very noisy – service for many years. The R-2800 derivative of the DC-4 proved to be even better, and as the DC-6B became the standard by which airliners of the early 1950s were judged. The original Constellation was a substantially less economic vehicle than the stretched Super Constellations of the 1950s. The stretched Hermes 4 gave BOAC solid service in the early 1950s, but it was only just 'in the black'. In contrast, the Lancastrian and Tudor cost BOAC dear, until they could be replaced by more suitable aircraft.

When I had dusted off my study I sent a copy to George Cribbett at the Air Ministry. On 19 October he sent a glowing acknowledgement: 'Your magnificent study will be extremely valuable at Montreal and at Chicago . . .' Among other things, the arithmetic showed the lack of realism in imposing limitations on frequency; 100 Lancastrian services would offer 600 to 900 seats, while the same number of services by a Constellation would offer at least 4,400. A little later I received a letter from Beverley Shenstone, Technical Administrator of Trans-Canada Airlines. He told me that a copy of my report had 'come to hand by devious ways'. He thought the Tudor would be faster than my estimate, or that the DC-4s would be slower, but complimented me on a 'valuable historic study'. This was the start of a lifelong friendship, and in the 1950s he was a tower of strength as Chief Engineer of BEA.

Beverley told me that back in 1943 he had worked out his own figures for a Merlin-engined DC-4, and the designation DC-4C meant 'DC-4 Canadian'. The fact that such an aircraft actually came about was due entirely to the sponsorship of TCA, but it might never have happened had I not drafted a letter for Max to send to C.D. Howe, by now (November 1944) Canadian Minister for Reconstruction, just before the Chicago Conference. It began in typical Max language: 'Go to it!! Convert Canadian industry from war to peace! Build for the air routes of the world a new aircraft which will use the engines which have won the War . . .'

This is just what happened. Barely a week after the Chicago Conference the Canadian Government organised the separation of the Cartierville (Montreal) plant of Canadian Vickers from the parent company, and renamed it Canadair Ltd. Its task was to design and build the DC-4C. Redesignated DC-4M, from its engines, the first began flight testing on 15 July 1946. Eventually 71 were built. At first they used DC-4 fuselages and went to the RCAF. Subsequently they were built entirely by Canadair with many DC-6 features including a pressurised fuselage, and they went to TCA, BOAC and Canadian Pacific. Some survived into the 1970s.

20

Aggravation at Chicago

Organised – despite all Max could do – by the United States, the Civil-Aviation Conference of November 1944 was the final stage of the wartime moves towards planning for the post-war airlines. It concluded the preparatory work, and paved the way towards a completely new era in international air transport.

The Conference venue was the Stevens Hotel, in downtown Chicago. Today the Conrad Hilton, this was in 1944 the largest hotel in the world, and the scene of many great conventions. It was being refurbished, after being derequisitioned by the US Army.

In some ways the Chicago Conference's achievements were very limited. Hardly any international commercial agreements were actually signed. Yet the conference did at last bring out into the open the fundamental issues involved, and this was to have widespread repercussions. On the one hand, Chicago revealed to the Old World the need for a practical approach, in place of academic formulae on traffic rights. On the other, it showed clearly to the New World the deep-rooted hostility which existed in Europe (and, officially, in the United Kingdom) towards 'cut-throat competition'. Strange, because Britain became Great through capitalism.

The Stevens Hotel is today the Conrad Hilton. It is on Michigan Boulevard, overlooking Grant Park.

The UK delegation set out for Chicago determined upon a cosy parcelling out of air traffic among nations in strict ratio to the amounts embarked. Commonwealth countries generally agreed, except that Australia and New Zealand (and the Labour Party in the UK) wanted to go one stage further, and set up an internationally owned and tightly controlled 'World Airways' to operate all long-haul trunk routes. They wanted to eliminate rivalry and competition entirely.

The United States delegates gathered in Chicago with a diametrically opposite view. Not only Pan American, the established US international flag-carrier, but also the major domestic airlines were 'raring to go' on overseas routes. Thanks to the war, they had donned uniform and gained worldwide operating experience under the banner of the US Air Transport Command. Unlike all other airlines, they had growing fleets of modern long-haul aircraft, and could see the Stars and Stripes being carried everywhere in the post-war era.

They demanded a 'free for all'. Indeed, right in the middle of the conference, with all the brashness of diplomatic naivety, PanAm published a long memorandum, which bore the heading:

> PAN AMERICAN'S PROGRAM for a single American flag-service across the North Atlantic will provide the finest service to the public at the lowest cost, and will best enable the United States successfully to meet foreign flag-competition on this route.

Even though the conference achieved no lasting agreements, the many and prolonged discussions did bring about a sorely needed practical grasp of the atmosphere in which such agreements would ultimately have to be negotiated. In particular, the groundwork was laid for the successful Anglo-American Bermuda meeting 14 months later.

Chicago also cleared a path towards a further foundation for international regulations, and it is one that has lasted. A direct outcome of the conference was the formation of the Provisional International Civil Aviation Organisation (PICAO), which in turn led to the permanent organisation ICAO. For more than 50 years this has been a shining example of a successful international body which sets technical standards for civil aviation everywhere. Its remit includes such diverse topics as aircraft structural strength, the size of airports, global radio networks and customs procedures.

In 1944 'Chicago-Illinois', as the US delegation invariably called it, was still redolent in European minds with the clatter of gangsters' Tommy guns, and the whole aura of the Wild West. At that time there was no international flight to the great Midwest city, and the delegations came by train, either from New York or, having crossed the Pacific, from San Francisco. As they travelled, many delegates actually discussed the possibility that they would encounter 'gangster tactics'.

Except for a few airline advisers, hardly anyone arrived by air. Under wartime regulations almost all airline seats were allocated to the military, and to Government staff, or to people on US Government business. However, though there was snow in the air as the delegates met on the last day of October, there was warmth in the welcome they received.

On that first day of checking in, Berle invited Swinton to lunch. Berle and Burden sat down in Berle's suite with Swinton and Street. It was the first time they had met – and it was a disaster. By the end of that lunch, a hostility had developed between the leaders of the two most powerful delegations, and it was to last throughout the Conference.

It was an example of what often happens when, at a meeting of leaders, 'second parties' are also present. In front of the stern and inflexible Arthur Street, Philip Swinton felt that he too must show his moral fibre and be utterly unyielding. In front of the liberal and businesslike Bill Burden, Berle felt that he must demonstrate total antipathy towards restrictions.

Had the two leaders met alone, some rapport might have been reached. Years later Swinton told me that, coming new to it from West Africa, he felt that he had to follow the party-line on which he had been carefully rehearsed by Street as they crossed the Atlantic. He would negotiate traffic matters only on the basis of a multilateral agreement signed by all. He insisted on 'an equitable division of traffic' policed by 'an international body with teeth'. He would not discuss routes, but insisted that the UK should have a half-share of North Atlantic traffic.

At the last point, Berle reared up: that would mean diverting US traffic into British aircraft. 'Is that not fair?' asked Swinton, 'If we take half of them back to the USA, clearly we must bring half of them in.' Berle launched forth on the advantages of uninhibited growth. The lunch ended with the Americans regarding Swinton as ignorant (perhaps deliberately so) of the potential of post-war aviation. The UK delegates considered Berle 'curt to the point of being surly'. Outwardly, the prospects were not good.

In a cool atmosphere (in all senses) the conference opened on Wednesday 1 November 1944. It was to last no fewer than 37 days, finishing on 7 December.

The first day was taken up with welcomes, and with the setting up of committees. Day 2 saw Adolf A. Berle elected Permanent President of the Conference. He spoke on the US Government policy of open co-operation. After him, came brief addresses by Swinton (UK), Howe (Canada), Pedro Chapa (Mexico), Sir Gurunath Bewoor (India), D.G. Sullivan (New Zealand), Max Hymans (France, who was elected V-P of the Conference), Arthur Drakeford (Australia) and W.M. de Morgenstierne (Norway).

By the end of the second day the leading protagonists had taken up inflexible postures. These were to set the paths followed by the various delegations throughout the whole five weeks.

The USA, backed by 18 Latin American countries (notably, excluding Brazil) and the Netherlands, stood for a free exchange of routes, standardised fares, a share-out of the expected fleets of war-surplus transport aircraft, the maximum of competition, and the minimum of regulation and 'worldwide equality of opportunity'. Berle called for an International Civil Aviation Assembly with advisory functions only, and an Executive Council of 15, including the USSR.

The UK, with the Commonwealth countries and most European nations (except the Netherlands), held fast for tight regulation and strict predetermination of traffic frequencies between nations. Swinton also began talking about bargaining on air bases, though we had already resolved that issue in the Beaverbrook/Berle talks the previous April.

His lordship then proposed a multilateral convention confined to the first four of the established 'freedoms' in air-transport, 'provided that there are adequate arrangements for order in the air'. The controversial Fifth Freedom – the right of aircraft of any nation to pick up loads of passengers and cargo in a second country and set them down in a third – was to be reserved for bilateral negotiation.

The UK's official view was that such a convention should:

> Offer Four-Freedom rights on a multilateral basis, subject to bilateral agreement on each route, for an interim period;

> After the war, define the international routes upon which these Four Freedoms would be granted;

> Determine frequencies in relation to the traffic embarked in each country, to eliminate 'uneconomic competition';

> Fix rates 'on a reasonable basis'; and

> Set up an international assembly with the power to enforce these provisions.

Canada's C.D. Howe aligned himself with the UK position, proposing a Civil Aeronautics Board to review rates, routes and frequencies, and a Draft Convention allowing the Four Freedoms, subject to international control. Thus three people came to dominate the conference: Berle of the USA, Swinton of the UK and Howe of Canada.

In a nutshell, while the USA hoped to gain freedom to carry the world's air traffic, the UK (as represented by the view of the Air Ministry expressed at Chicago) saw air transport as just another area of politics which should be cut and dried by regulations to ensure that nobody gained an advantage over anyone else. Inevitably, before long the aviation debate was becoming submerged within a fog of politics.

Very gradually, out of the endless detail, and the work of subcommittees, five issues emerged:

> First, was there to be an International Civil Aviation Organisation? If so, should it be given powers to regulate not only technical matters (about which there was general agreement) but also economic and commercial matters? The British, with some Europeans, wanted total control, though with a court of appeal. The USA, and some of its camp, wanted a world organisation to oversee technical standards, but vehemently opposed giving it control over economic or traffic matters.

> The second main factor was how each nation should be represented upon whatever international body was created, whatever its powers – or lack of them – might be. The United States proposed that they, the British Commonwealth and the USSR should have two votes each, while all other countries should each have one.

> The third point concerned the division of services among the nations along any particular route. Should there be predetermination or unfettered competition? Or should services be divided according to the traffic's nationality? If one country generated more traffic on a route than another, should it be allowed greater

frequency of service? Or should the UK White Paper prevail, which said that services should be divided according to the traffic leaving each country, regardless of that traffic's nationality?

Not least, how should international services be set up on a provisional basis while permanent post-war details were thrashed out? Where should temporary services begin, and with what aircraft?

From a 21st-century viewpoint all these issues, so hotly argued at the time, appear academic. They do not relate to the real world of traffic demand and economic growth. Nobody at Chicago could have had any idea how air transport would grow:

	Aircraft miles (millions)	Passengers carried (millions)	Cargo/mail (tons)	Passenger increase over 10 years (%)
1938	234	3.6	165,000	720
1948	790	24.0	600,000	580
1958	1,820	88.2	2,150,000	270
1968	3,740	262.0	10,490,000	200
1978	7,100	719.7	61,500,000	175
1988	9,091	1,072.1	145,336,000	49
1998	12,608	1,465.9	228,105,000	37

In fact, for many years, air traffic has doubled roughly every five years. Nothing like this was foreseen at Chicago, and the parsimonious doling out of frequencies would repeatedly have been overtaken by events. On the other hand, some of the concerns about over-capacity were well founded.

Everything that transpired, in an undigested and sometimes controversial form, was flashed by lengthy telegrams from the Stevens Hotel to Whitehall, arriving in the small hours. The CAT Committee met almost continuously, and cabled back its views to Swinton. As the conference wore on, Ministers in London became progressively more confused, and certainly failed to grasp the implications of what was under debate.

In Chicago a vast amount went on outside the formal meetings, in *hors concours* and off-the-floor battles. Early on, Berle sought to isolate and bypass the UK by concluding bilateral agreements with Iceland, Ireland, France, Portugal, Belgium and Sweden. Canada and Newfoundland were still problems because, in 1944, almost all transatlantic landplanes had to refuel at Gander, Goose Bay or Stephenville.

Brigadier-General Hal Harris, Chief of Staff of the US Air Transport Command (who became a close friend), was asked to survey routes to Europe which would not touch British or Commonwealth territory. All this we duly learned at Gwydyr House, where I kept a blow-by-blow account of whatever we could discover was happening.

On 8 November the conference rejected the idealistic but impractical 'Anzac' proposal, put in long and passionate pleas by Drakeford and Sullivan – supported by France and Afghanistan – for a single international long-haul airline. Despite this, Drakeford and Sullivan were accorded the greatest ovation of the entire conference, in appreciation of their wish for world co-operation. Theirs was a laudable objective, but events have since reinforced the majority view that competition is needed for economic efficiency and progress.

By the afternoon of Sunday the 12th the talks were bogged down. To break the deadlock, Berle proposed that three delegations should withdraw into secret session. Accordingly he, Burden and Pogue for the USA, Swinton, Street and Cribbett for the UK, and Howe, Symington and Escott-Reid for Canada, got down to arguing about routes, licensing of carriers, fares and schedules. There ensued a mighty wrangle, which lasted for ten days until Wednesday the 22nd. Progress was near zero.

Many possibilities were explored, including an 'escalator clause' on frequencies. Frequently, confusion existed at Gwydyr House; indeed, such was the corruption in the transmission of cables that 'pandemonium did not reign, it poured'.

On Thursday the 16th the CAT Committee scratched their collective heads at the problems. Max explained that Berle had appealed to President Roosevelt to ask Churchill to bring pressure to bear on Swinton to clear all the restrictions and regulations on which the British were insisting.

'Ah,' said Cripps, 'American Press leakage is where pressure will be put. They know the PM will not want us to be tarred with the brush of having caused a breakdown.'

'Ho, ho,' retorted Max, 'we can start our own propaganda. Two can play at that game.'

They turned to the latest telegram, in which the UK excluded reservation of Fifth Freedom rights.

'I agree,' said Sinclair, free for once from Arthur Street's advice, 'accepting F-fifth Freedom is a b-bit of a g-gamble. But the one safeguard which, Mr Chairman, you will recall the C-Cabinet approved of, is for a moratorium of four years before these rights would apply.'

'Right', said Max. 'Now, the escalator clause.'

'Highly dangerous', said Sinclair.

'Not necessary', said Cranborne.

'I don't understand it', said Leathers.

'We would lose traffic', said Sinclair, 'if all Americans insisted on f-flying in only their own aeroplanes. Our aircraft would come back empty once we had taken loads to the USA.'

'We could soon fix that', said Cripps expansively, 'We could shuttle 500 RAF men backwards and forwards to stoke up our load factors. We could even make sure we had more traffic than the USA. This makes nonsense of all these formulae.'

After much further debate, Max said, 'Let us send a telegram, then, and leave a telephone call for Swinton when he wakes. Peter, go and book a call to Swinton to be put through when he wakes, and I will speak to him.'

When I returned, Max was canvassing opinion on the escalator clause. He added, 'Efficiency attracts me to it. The better you are, the more opportunities you carve out for yourself.'

Sinclair came back with 'But if Berle gets Fifth Freedom and the escalator clause he can fly anywhere he wants any t-t-time he wants.'

'But we've also got entry anywhere', said Cripps.

After further talk, Max summed up: 'Right . . . we will prepare a telegram to Swinton. We will not reserve Fifth Freedom. We will not drop the escalator clause. And we will insist on embarked traffic as the measure.'

Betty Hogg came in, and said, 'Excuse me, Lord Beaverbrook, but Lord Swinton's on the line . . . he sounds very cross.'

Max picked up a telephone. 'Hallo, is that you, Philip?' A pause. Max guffawed. He replaced the receiver. 'He says it's six in the morning, and he went to bed at three. He says he wouldn't talk to the Lord God Almighty. He hung up on me.'

The talking resumed. Ten minutes later the telephone rang. I picked it up. Betty Hogg said, 'It's Lord Swinton. He wants to speak to the Lord.' I fetched him. 'Philip! Can't you sleep?' Noises off. 'He says he can't sleep once I've woken him . . .'

Eventually Max returned to the table. 'He was up till three talking to Berle. The US have sent in a new set of proposals. They are entirely unacceptable. Philip sounds depressed. Berle wants Fifth Freedom traffic taken into account in any calculation on frequencies. And he insists that national origin of traffic must be the measure. And he wants to be able to pick up traffic in the Colonies.'

'We must make a stand,' said Cranborne, 'the Commons will support a firm stand.'

'The way to play it', said Cripps, 'is that everyone must know that the United States put in another demand which bust the whole show.'

'Berle will, of course, appeal to the President,' said Max; 'he won't break until the President agrees. But he will leak to the Press, and try to put us in the wrong. So . . . we will send Philip the answer NO, and full support in what he suggests, except we do not reserve Fifth Freedom.'

The CAT Committee then adjourned until the morrow.

21

Reconciliation

D ay by day, we in London hoped for good cheer from Chicago. After all, we had at least expected that Fifth Freedom acceptance would prove to be a sweetener. However, Swinton took a very hard line indeed. He was absolutely adamant.

Not until the following Monday did we discover that the important telegram, which I had sent as 'We confirm that we do not wish to reserve Fifth Freedom rights', had actually arrived in Chicago with the crucial word 'not' omitted. So, for four days, Swinton had doggedly pursued a course diametrically opposite to that intended.

It was a rather childish lesson, learned the hard way. In future we resolved that in all such instances the text should either be rephrased or else repeated, such as '. . . we do not, <u>repeat not</u>, wish to . . .' In the end it made little difference, because on Wednesday 22 November the 'Three-Committee Plenary Session' was called to consider the texts of the proposals from the USA, UK and Canada.

The main question to be discussed was whether or not the conference would accept a partial agreement, chiefly on establishing uniform technical standards throughout the world, and leave the more intractable problems – such as traffic rights – for consideration at some time in the future. In short, was there any hope of solving all the problems by a last-minute effort?

Urgent appeals for continued effort were made by Fiorello H. La Guardia, Mayor of New York City and a member of the US delegation, and by H.J. Symington, President of TCA and a member of the Canadian delegation. Lord Swinton, supported by Chieh Liu of the Chinese delegation, suggested that great strides had already been made, and that further progress should be 'left to an interim council of nations'.

Berle said that it was too much to hope for that all the problems could be solved at once. He added, 'I am frank to say that we have already gone as far as I ever thought we could possibly go when the US first acceded to the British request to call the conference.' When Max heard this his laughter was loud and long.

Mayor La Guardia finished up with an impassioned speech.

> 'Freedom of the air. Without that, the meat is taken out of the convention. All the rest is sauce. There is no difficulty in the technical realm . . . Let us now establish the right of every nation to use the air in accordance with the freedoms we've heard so much about for the past three weeks. The Conference must send assurances to War-ravaged peoples that there is a place in the air for them. I appeal to you not to give up. There has never been such beautiful harmony as that which marks the War relationships of the United Nations. If we can co-operate in War, how much easier it should be to do something for the safety and happiness of the future.'

This was greeted by enthusiastic applause.

The session ended with an agreement to study the 'Three-Power Draft on an Air Convention' signed by the USA, UK and Canada on 20 November. This proposed the setting up of an International Air Administration (a working title) to foster and plan the development of international air services. It left open the thornier question of adjusting capacity to the traffic offering (broadly, the number of people wanting to travel).

On Tuesday the 21st Berle sought help from his President. The result was that, on the same day, Roosevelt telegraphed the Prime Minister to protest at 'the United Kingdom's efforts to sabotage the Conference by strangulation'.

Churchill consulted Max, and Max spoke to Swinton. Accordingly, on the following day, the 22nd, the PM sent a long reply to the President which refuted any British desire to prevent an agreement at Chicago. It made the most of the generosity of the United Kingdom in agreeing to open its bases throughout the world to foreign aircraft in transit. It suggested that valuable progress could be made on technical matters, while economic and traffic agreements were left for consideration at some future time.

Roosevelt at once bounced back objections via his Ambassador in London, John Winant. Winant was a close friend of Max. He insisted 'For the common good, these matters simply must be settled at once, and agreement achieved. Everyone in Chicago thinks that the British are wrong and unreasonable. Fifth Freedom intermediate traffic is essential to the economics of long routes.'

The President followed up this bombardment with a further curt telegram on the 24th: 'I am afraid you do not yet fully appreciate the importance of reaching a satisfactory agreement. Our people have gone as far to meet yours as I can let them go. If the Conference should end either in no agreement, or in an agreement which the American people would regard as preventing the development and use of the great air routes, the repercussions would seriously affect many other things.'

We had a hurried further meeting of the CAT Committee. On the 28th the PM cabled back, asking for an adjournment of the conference with agreement on the first two Freedoms and on technical matters.

Clearly, relations between Berle and Swinton were in a state of crisis, only thinly disguised on the surface. The talk running round the Stevens Hotel was that the prospects of a big dollar loan to the UK were in jeopardy. Swinton, egged on by the CAT Committee, did indeed press for an adjournment on the basis of achieving a multilateral agreement on the first two Freedoms, trumpeting this as no mean achievement.

In the Stevens conference rooms, between 24 November and 2 December, while the sharp exchanges between Roosevelt and Churchill were going on in the background, Berle made a final effort to get Swinton undermined by Whitehall. The conference itself played for time by considering a series of draft proposals from the USA, the UK and France. All were designed to resolve the impasse on matters of traffic. None succeeded.

Eventually, the conference decided to call it a day and make the most of what it had achieved, however thin this was in fact. So, at a Plenary Session on the 34th day, 4 December, four documents were tabled:

An agreement for the establishment of a Provisional International Civil Aviation Organisation (PICAO);

A convention to establish a permanent organisation to take over from PICAO;

An international agreement for the mutual exchange of the first two Freedoms of the Air, Innocent Passage and Technical Stop;

And an international air transport agreement for the mutual exchange of all five Freedoms.

On 6 December an election took place for the PICAO Interim Council. Those elected by majority vote were the UK, the USA, the Netherlands, Brazil, France, Mexico, Canada, India, Norway, Iraq, Peru, China, Australia, Egypt, Czechoslovakia, Turkey, El Salvador, Chile and Colombia.

Finally, on 7 December, the anniversary of Pearl Harbor, there was a wind-up session. Felicitous words were spoken, and all was sweetness and light. Indeed, once Berle had abandoned hope of achieving route and traffic agreements, and Swinton had conceded the first two Freedoms, a compromise was indeed achieved.

As its final act, the Chicago Conference accepted as open for signature five Appendices. Two of these were parallel documents, the UK-sponsored Two-Freedoms agreement and the US-brokered Five-Freedoms agreement. The line-up was as follows:

Appendix 3: **UK Two Freedoms**		Appendix 4 **USA Five Freedoms**
Afghanistan	Philippines	Afghanistan
Australia	Poland	China
Ecuador	Spain	Dominican Republic
Egypt	Sweden	Ecuador
France	Turkey	Haiti
Greece	United Kingdom	Honduras
Haiti	United States	Mexico
Honduras	Uruguay	Nicaragua
India	Venezuela	Peru
Iraq	Denmark	Sweden
Lebanon	Thailand	Turkey
Mexico		United States
Netherlands		Uruguay
New Zealand		Venezuela
Nicaragua		Denmark
Peru		Thailand

One of the surprises in the voting was that the Dominican Republic signed the Five Freedoms agreement, but not the Two Freedoms agreement which was part of it. The Chicago Conference maintained its qualities of the bizarre right to the end. In his final speech Lord Swinton referred to the obvious fact that 'What we have done here is not an end but a beginning. Chicago is the first chapter in a new work of co-operation. We shall go forward sincerely determined to write the remaining chapters.'

Berle's final speech, from the Presidential Chair, emphasised that they had dealt 'not with high diplomacy but with the quiet courtesies and mutual recognition of men of goodwill.' He claimed that Chicago had

> 'begun to put an end to the the era of anarchy in the air. When we met, the air of any country was closed to every other country. Now the free 'planes of peace-loving nations are offered peaceful passage through the air of other free nations, and the right to find free ports of call.
>
> 'By the agreement of two Freedoms – of peaceful transit and of non-traffic stop to refuel, repair or take refuge in a storm – we find a lasting tribute to the undying fairness and justice of Great Britain. She proposed and sponsored the general idea of these Freedoms. This meant to her – speaking with that frankness to which we have been accustomed here – giving up a possible stranglehold on the Atlantic crossings, which must take off and land at Newfoundland, making it possible for 'planes from North America to transit the Atlantic Ocean. I am glad to think that, on our side, acceptance means that in the Pacific – where we, accidentally, hold a like stranglehold – we have made it possible to connect the great British Commonwealths of Australia and Canada. These Freedoms are, of course, available . . . to all countries of the world who come in peace and friendship.'

Berle then referred to the United States' Five-Freedoms agreement, through which 'the outlines of the future trade of the air begin to appear'. He claimed that the Council of the Assembly of PICAO and the future ICAO would be able to remedy abuses 'through consultation and sound advice; in extreme cases, it may recommend suspension of the offending member until the grievance is cured'.

He added, 'From now on, air agreements throughout the world must be open covenants, open to all. The day of secret diplomacy in the air is long past. We met in the 17th century in the air. We close in the 20th century in the air.'

The delegations went home. The USA gained transit rights which opened a wide area of the world to through services. It gained traffic rights in a limited field which, backed by bilateral agreements, would open many places to US airlines. Canada gained widespread transit rights, and the location of the future international organisation ICAO in Montreal. The UK also gained transit rights, including staging through Europe and across the Pacific.

On the Council of PICAO the Commonwealth gained seats for the UK, Australia, Canada and India, twice the number of seats suggested in the USA's original proposal. India's place was gained by the generous withdrawal of Cuba in her favour, in order to achieve a better geographical representation. The Council ended up with 21 members: four from Europe, four from the Commonwealth, four from North and Central America, three from the Near and Middle East, and one from China. Thus, the world gained a provisional worldwide organisation with advisory powers, and the opportunity to make real progress on technical standards.

Everyone at Chicago was to some degree pleased. The UK had won progress towards 'order in the air', while the USA had achieved some 'freedom in the air'.

In fact, none of this was quite true. For example, while the United States had achieved full traffic rights through such unlikely places as Afghanistan, Chile, Haiti and Thailand, Pan American was restricted to two services a week through British or Commonwealth territory.

Indeed, the immediate aftermath of the conference was a freezing on the part of the main participants into rigid pre-Chicago attitudes. For example, the UK insisted on strict currency restrictions on the purchase of tickets by British subjects on any airline outside the Sterling area. Rates and charges were likewise strictly regulated. Just before Christmas 1945 Pan American suddenly reduced its fares on the North Atlantic, and I had the unenviable job of informing the airline that its landing rights in the UK would be withdrawn.

By that time, however, Chicago had led to a second conference in Bermuda at which, in February 1946, a full Anglo-American agreement was reached. This could not have been achieved without the preliminary exchanges at Chicago. Another big factor was that by 1946 the hardliners from Chicago – Berle, Burden, Swinton, Street and Cribbett – were no longer involved. The unsolvable issues of Chicago led to a practical approach to reality.

Most significantly, on 25 July 1947, after the required year of determination, the United States withdrew from its own Chicago Appendix 4, which called for Five Freedoms. The pipe-dream of omnibus multilaterals was replaced by a mass of liberal bilaterals.

The real significance of the Chicago Conference was that it had two important outcomes:

> First, PICAO was set up and led to ICAO, a successful and harmonious body which for more than 50 years has set world standards for civil aviation. These standards are accepted by everyone (even by the Soviet Union, which after a long wait came on board in 1970).
>
> Second, Chicago created a deeper and more realistic understanding of the needs of the world's civil air transport. Idealism, in whatever direction, had to be replaced by everyday commercial considerations.

What in the 21st century is almost impossible to recall is the atmosphere and thinking in the late-war years. Today air transport is a normal part of life, linking every part of the planet. In 1944 such a global network of routes was not even a dream.

22

What airline(s)?

February 1945 was another time for taking stock. The War in Europe was clearly in its final stage. The Chicago Conference was over, we were in the process of forming a Ministry of Civil Aviation (MCA), and our enormous aircraft industry had diverted some design teams to work on civil airliners. But who would operate these aircraft?

With the end of the war imminent, claims for a place in Britain's future air-transport industry were being staked thick and fast. The claimants all came to Gwydyr House, where Max was still in the centre of Government discussions on the future British airline or airlines, while Philip Swinton was busily engaged in setting up his MCA.

Max passed the callers on to me, to log their plans and aspirations. To Evelyn Baring and me he also gave the task of holding exploratory discussions with those who had been prominent in Britain's pre-war airlines. For three weeks we lunched, dined and talked with everyone who had been important in the field.

I dug out my 'plan' of March 1944. Since then much had happened, and we now saw the future slightly differently. I also turned up an analysis I had written for the *Sunday Times* of 14 February 1943, before I joined Lord Beaverbrook. This was based on my concern that almost all the experience being gained in air-transport operations was going to the United States.

Against the background of the Lamplugh Committee's deliberations, I had written:

> 'Questions in Parliament have evoked no statement on policy. The Government appears to be evading the issue, and afraid of offending the USA, which is not only building up a virtual monopoly of transport aircraft but is acquiring nearly all the operating experience . . .
>
> 'The question is not one of competing, but rather of sharing the opportunities and prospects . . . There appear to be two aspects, both of which require immediate planning:
>
> 1 The short-term policy for the War, which will lay the foundations . . . and build up operating experience.
> 2 The long-term policy in which such basic questions as the desirable degree of "internationalisation" and the freedom of the air must be settled.
>
> 'The United States is building up a network of routes . . . which depend largely upon the free use of British bases, which will be of inestimable value to the War effort . . . but British air and ground crews are gaining little experience on major trunk routes . . .
>
> 'After the War a single monopolistic airline would not be likely to gain the best result. Rivalry – though not cut-throat competition – is needed for efficiency . . .'

That article expressed a viewpoint which in February 1943 was gaining increasing support. However, two years on I now found myself at the action end, instead of in the more comfortable position of critic.

Evelyn and I next turned to the Lamplugh Report (see Chapter 9). As drafter of that document, I knew that its recommendations represented a broad consensus of opinions held in May 1943. On airline structures they were that:

1   Each major trunk route should be operated by a separate organisation.
2   Shipping, rail and road interests should not be debarred from tendering for mail contracts, nor from participating in or managing a chosen route.
3   Consideration should be given to operators who have no mail contracts or subsidies, particularly those who were operating at the outbreak of the war . . . but internal airlines and private operators should not be encouraged unless they could demonstrate that they could meet a public demand without cost to the taxpayer.
4   Shipping companies were in a favourable position . . . on some routes because of their long experience. Therefore due consideration should be given to their claims, especially over long-haul trunk routes.
5   Similar considerations applied to rail and road transport . . . For national and Continental work, British railways with their network of agencies should be well situated.

Thus in May 1943 there was an emphasis on existing surface operators. The background to the economic thinking was that any gap between cost and revenue should be made up by subsidy through mail contracts.

We turned next to a Memo I had written for Lord Beaverbrook on 3 December 1943, entitled 'Post-War Empire Air Routes'. It suggested that all main Empire routes should be operated by Empire-owned companies. 'Six mainline operating companies should be administered under a single joint Empire authority . . . Internal routes should be operated by, and owned by, the territories through which they operate'.

We then returned to my March 1944 'plan'. It looked forward to a number of 'British airline companies to be privately owned, limited in profits and regulated by a British Civil Aviation Commission. The BOAC Act should be replaced by an Act creating a Commonwealth Air Transport Corporation, into which BOAC should be absorbed. BOAC would continue as a public utility corporation, jointly and equally owned by the UK and the Dominions. Its function would be to operate the strategic round-the-world Commonwealth services . . . flying only from Commonwealth territory'.

That plan formed the basis for long discussions by the CAT Committee. It closely followed a major article I had written for *The Atlantic Monthly* in January 1944. That article sparked off arguments in Canada over the granting of monopoly status to Trans-Canada Airlines. On 19 February 1944 the *Montreal Gazette* wrote 'Mr Masefield's flat declaration that in Britain "monopolies are not favoured or considered efficient" is of special bearing on the situation in Canada. He says that, with their faith in chosen instruments dissipated by their experience with Imperial Airways and BOAC, the British lean towards a middle course . . . Doubt is growing of the wisdom of a single Canadian line.'

Having to prepare a speech or lecture crystallises one's thinking. With Max's agreement, I accepted an invitation from Chatham House (the Royal Institute of International Affairs) to deliver a review of 'Commonwealth Air Transport', under the Chairmanship of Lord Winster, on 25 January 1945.

My views were coloured by a year of debate in the CAT Committee, ranging from the free-enterprise views of Max to the 'single chosen instrument' line of Hugh Dalton. I was also influenced by exposure to the United States, which made a 'chosen instrument' approach seem narrow and restrictive. After much thought, at Chatham House I advocated four major British operating companies:

> Domestic, Central and South European;
> Domestic, Central and North European;
> North Atlantic, South African and Australian (BOAC); and
> South Atlantic and Caribbean.

In the ensuing discussion Lord Winster took up these points. What neither he nor I expected was that seven months later a Labour Government would be elected, which would appoint him Minister of Civil Aviation. Significantly, the White Paper (Command 6712) on *British Air Services* published by the Ministry of Aviation on 20 December 1945, set up, on very similar lines, three operating Corporations: BEA for domestic and European routes, BSAA for Central and South America, and BOAC for the remainder.

In February of that year Evelyn and I continued to examine the background, and compile lists of people and organisations which might enter the arena. We were clearly presented with a once-only chance to start from a clean sheet, and fashion a structure appropriate to the post-war world.

The existing structure merely reflected the past. BOAC, under Viscount Knollys, flew a motley assortment of aircraft: Dakota, Ensign, Liberator, Lodestar, Rapide, Lancaster, Oxford, Warwick, York and Mosquito landplanes, and C-Class, G-Class, Sunderland and Boeing 314A flying boats. The airline had a haphazard arrangement of routes: to Lisbon, Gibraltar, Africa, Turkey, Arabia, India and across the Atlantic to Canada.

In the United Kingdom, Railway Air Services (RAS), under Sir Harold Hartley, had reopened the Croydon–Liverpool–Belfast route with D.H.86s, and was preparing to renew services to Prestwick and Renfrew with D.H.89 Rapides. Scottish Airways, under Edmund Fresson, was planning to start up again on Renfrew–Inverness–Stornoway with Rapides in association with RAS.

None of this constituted any binding structure for the future, though there was much jockeying for position. For example, the Railway Companies Association, led by Hartley, proposed that, in partnership with shipping companies, RAS should operate all British internal air services, adding routes throughout Europe as soon as the war was over. John Booth of the Blue Star Line, and the Booth Steamship Co., Lamport & Holt, Pacific Steam Navigation and Royal Mail Lines, presented a proposal for British Latin American Air Lines. Eric Gandar Dower of Allied

Airways sought a licence to operate both internally and from Scotland to Scandinavia.

We kept on studying, and came to the conclusion that there could, or should, be four groups of British carriers, which might be formed around, or supported by, four groups of existing organisations. The carriers would be:

Major flag carriers on the international trunk routes;
Major domestic operators, which might also fly Continental services;
Empire airlines based in the Dominions or colonies which would need support and partnership from Britain; and
'Most-favoured nation' foreign airlines, in which the UK might take a share (Max called it 'the infiltration policy'), especially in Central and South America, Africa and the Middle and Far East.

The potentially powerful groups, around which the above carriers might be created, were:

BOAC;
The railways and short-sea shipping companies;
The major intercontinental shipping lines; and
The former independent airlines.

Evelyn and I compiled a list of names and addresses of 25 people or organisations which appeared to combine most of the expertise and financial strength which might be useful to get British civil air transport restarted after the war. Meanwhile, the stream of would-be operators who beat a path to the large downstairs room at Gwydyr House increased daily:

Sir Harold Hartley came with John Elliot from the railways; Percy Hunting came from the Hunting-Clan Line; John Booth from the Blue Funnel Line; Rolly Thornton from Alfred Holt (and the Second Brabazon Committee); Gerard d'Erlanger from the ATA and BOAC; Frederick W. Farey Jones, formerly of British Continental Air Services and the aviation insurers F.W. Jones & Partners; Arthur Lamplugh of Lloyds and British Aviation Insurance; Spry Leverton from KLM; Vagn Christensen from DDL (Danish airlines); Eric Gandar Dower and Elizabeth Bruning from Allied Airways; and Whitney Straight and George Brackley from RAF Transport Command. Their ideas ranged from uncontrolled private enterprise to statutory monopoly.

That was one of the bonuses of working at Gwydyr House: it attracted a marvellous selection of people. Three in particular stand out in my memory: Knollys, Yerex and Dodero.

Edward George William Tyrwhitt 'Edgy' Knollys, DFC, the second Viscount and Baron Caversham, was the most courtly of men, as befitted a Page of Honour to Edward VII and George V between his 9th and 16th birthdays. An Old Harrovian, and graduate of New College, Oxford, he fought in World War 1, in the 16th London Regiment and then as an RAF pilot. He then went into banking, at Barclay's in Cape Town. In 1941 he was appointed Governor and C-in-C Bermuda. In 1943 Street dispatched Hildred to see whether Edgy might suitably replace Sir Harold Howitt as BOAC's fifth Chairman in four years. Hildred thought he might.

'Edgy' Knollys.

Accordingly, on 26 May 1943 Knollys took over BOAC at the age of 48. Howitt, a chartered accountant of Peat, Marwick and Mitchell (and Chairman of the committee which in 1939 had recommended Lullingstone as London's post-war airport) stepped down to be Deputy Chairman, among a host of other good works.

Edgy was the right man in 1943, when diplomacy and goodwill were needed. Later, when the real rough-and-tumble developed, he was too much of a gentleman. Indeed Max regarded the slim and good-looking Old Harrovian with some suspicion. On 1 July 1947 he was succeeded by the vigorously 'press on' Hartley, who had previously been Chairman of BEA. Edgy became Chairman of Vickers, but died aged 71 in 1966.

Much more in Max's line was Lowell Yerex, the one-eyed buccaneering New Zealander who had challenged the dominant Pan American Grace Airways on its own ground in Central America. He came to Gwydyr House in a pearl-grey suit and broad-brimmed sombrero, and smoking a cigar of Churchillian dimensions. He proposed that the British Government should buy into his airline Transportes Aéreos Centro-Americanos (TACA), to challenge the almost total US domination of the Caribbean. Max was cautiously delighted.

Yerex had formed TACA in 1931 in Tegucigalpa, capital of Honduras, with one Ford Trimotor. By 1940 he had built up a network which spread into British Honduras (today Belize), San Salvador, Nicaragua and Costa Rica to Panama City. In 1939 he had additionally founded British West Indian Airways to fly Trinidad–Tobago–Barbados. In 1943 he had expanded further with TACA El Salvador and TACA de Mexico, which flew from Balboa on the Canal to Havana and Mexico City. US interests, including TWA, bought in, but Yerex was careful to maintain control.

This was the situation when he came to London. He proposed joining TACA and BWIA into one powerful British-owned airline, to be based in Jamaica and dominate Central America and the Caribbean, expanding through the USA and South America. Yerex knew the entire region. He had demonstrated his ability to run efficient low-cost airline operations, and to do this with mainly secondhand equipment. Here was an obvious never-to-be-missed opportunity to get a huge British toe in the Latin American door. Max was eager to act. Predictably, Berle in Washington was bitterly opposed, and regarded Latin America as a preserve of the United States.

To our utter astonishment, the Foreign Office said 'No'. Anglo-American relations were apparently too delicate. Yerex had to be sent away empty. He took it with good grace and, his sombrero still at a jaunty angle and his black patch defiant, he sold out his interests and retired from the scene. British West Indian Airways went to the Government of Trinidad and to BSAA (later taken over by BOAC), while TACA was bought by the United States, mostly by PanAm. A huge missed opportunity.

Alberto Dodero arrived at Gwydyr House soon afterwards. He was a typical Uruguayan in being short and dark; he was also always impeccably dressed. He had big shipping interests in Montevideo, but had become fascinated by flying boats. Evelyn and I took him to Rochester to talk with Arthur Gouge about Sunderland conversions for his planned airline to shuttle across the Rio de La Plata (River Plate) between Montevideo and Buenos Aires, and to serve Asunción, the capital of Paraguay, operating from the Paraguay River.

A little later Alberto backed his fancy with an order for four Sunderlands converted at Belfast into 43-passenger Sandringhams, with Pratt & Whitney Twin Wasp engines. Eventually, ten Sandringhams were delivered to the River Plate, where they operated from 1945 until 1962. Eventually Alberto sold out and retired. Like Yerex, he represented the flamboyant Latin American operator, just as Edgy had been an extreme example of the British Establishment.

Evelyn and I carried on planning. As we winnowed out the possibilities, we were left with seven, which we put forward for debate:

1   A single statutory corporation, presumably to be BOAC, which would have monopoly operating rights and a monopoly of subsidy. The capital of this 'chosen instrument' would be an interest-bearing Government loan (the Sinclair Plan);

2   More than one statutory corporation, each with a designated operating region;

3   A statutory corporation which would own all the capital of a number of operating subsidiaries;

4   A statutory holding corporation owning a controlling interest in operating subsidiaries. The remaining capital, up to 49 per cent, would be equity stock available to other transport interests and on the Stock Exchange (the Swinton Plan);

5   A statutory corporation which would own all the aircraft and maintenance bases and would lease the aircraft to licensed private companies for operations on specified routes (the Cripps Plan);

6   Licensed private operating companies set up on free-enterprise lines (the Beaverbrook Plan); and

7   Some combination of statutory corporations and private airlines.

I felt that air transport should pay its way as quickly as possible. However, it was generally agreed – especially by the Air Ministry – that direct State subsidies would be needed for many years. It was also widely concluded that indirect subsidies would have to be provided, by the assumption that no charge would be made to operators for such services as airports and ground facilities, communications and air traffic control, meteorological services, emergency services and research and development. The argument went that, if the taxpayer had to provide direct and indirect subsidies, then there had to be a measure of Government control, and that 'wasteful competition must be eliminated, as must opportunities for the speculative investor activated by the profit motive.'

Such was the official Air Ministry line. It did not suit either Max or Philip Swinton. Both looked towards a measure of private investment in a number of new airlines. An interesting clash of views developed between Ministers and leading civil servants.

George Cribbett sent me his own views:

> 'The growing recognition of State responsibility for the economic welfare of the country clearly calls for Government control of the development of our air communications . . . Forms of organisation which would dissipate money and effort on unnecessary competition or on wasteful overheads are inimical to national interests.
>
> 'I am sure that Commonwealth co-operation ought to be a cardinal feature of our policy. The possibilities of joint operating companies must be an important factor, and Government-owned or controlled "chosen instruments" – such as are contemplated by Australia, Canada and South Africa – can scarcely be blended into successful partnerships with private enterprise in the UK. Oil and water do not mix.'

Obviously intended to influence Max, it had precisely the opposite effect. His comment was, 'To Hell with that! We want efficiency, not bureaucratic bumbledom. Profits are at the root of an efficient business. Air transport will pay its way as soon as the new aircraft come along if they are any good at all, as well as the operators.'

Cribbett and I lunched on 20 February 1945, after which he came over to Gwydyr House to thrash it out. I handed him a Paper I had drafted, setting out eight objectives. Summarised they were:

1   To provide adequate air services at reasonable cost . . .

2   To operate these services safely, economically . . .

3   To provide services at rates which will achieve reasonable profits, subject to the assistance where necessary of subsidy through mail contracts.

4   To encourage and support British transport aircraft . . .

5   To make use of the experience . . . and financial support of existing transport organisations . . .

6   To contribute as appropriate to Commonwealth and foreign airlines in the form of finance, management and aircraft.

7   To institute a system of training . . .
8   To lay down a system of aerodromes . . .

I still think that these eight objectives remain a fair charter for British civil air operations. George thought so too. On the other hand, he was temperamentally a protagonist of State ownership. That was also the view of the Air Ministry and, of course, of BOAC, which was a 'chosen instrument' in being. It was not the view of Max, nor of Swinton, Baring or myself. Such a policy would throw away much experience and finance available from independent sources.

George came back with nine points of his own. All were based on the unstated premise that air transport was basically unprofitable, and that private airlines would be run by unscrupulous tycoons with no interest in the common good. Looking back at his views, after many years of actual operations, they appear academic and unrealistic in their repeated emphasis on 'exploitation of the taxpayer'.

We talked further. George believed that all his nine points would be met if BOAC were to be granted a monopoly of all overseas services. He added 'In the face of heavily subsidised foreign competition, private airlines could not serve the national interest, because they would have to have regard, first and foremost, for the interests of shareholders.'

He added, 'Shareholders are an unnecessary luxury in this business', and later argued that competition between different British airlines, all receiving subsidy, would mean that 'the State was competing against itself'. He dismissed 'the Swinton Plan' on the grounds that having subsidiaries would increase management costs. He showed himself to be dead against permitting shipping or rail companies to play any part.

He held forth for an hour upon the evils of private enterprise. He 'viewed with distaste' the introduction of private equity. The elimination of risk by Government subsidy meant that the idea of a dividend would be abhorrent. He clung steadfastly to the vision of totally centralised State control of one national airline.

Throughout this titanic pontifical statement, delivered in George's most lordly manner, Evelyn had sat with boiler pressure steadily rising. It eventually exploded. Normally the mildest of men, Evelyn burst in, 'My God, George! Never in all my life have I heard so much elevated bunkum. Don't you know that, once the war is over, a proper return on investment is the only way we can prosper? Air transport can't be different from other businesses. If air transport needs subsidy for a bit, surely "payment for services rendered" on mails is a good way to go about it?'

'Well,' said George, 'I know you are steeped in the City . . . but air transport *is* different. It's a matter of the post-war world seeing a State responsibility for the economic welfare of the country . . . Every major power regards air transport as an instrument of national policy . . . I don't see any place for private enterprise.'

There the matter rested. Two days later, Max and Swinton met and agreed to advance the prospects of 'an Internal and Continental Airline'. Hartley was at once to the fore with exuberant plans. Air Chief Marshal Sir Wilfrid Freeman, Chief Executive at the Ministry of Aircraft Production, was brought in, together with John Elliot. John was the son of Ralph D. Blumenfeld, Max's *Daily Express* Editor from 1902 to 1932, and subsequently Chairman to his death in 1948. Seeing a second war against Germany coming, Max advised John to use his second Christian name as his surname. He was said to have 'invented public relations'. In 1945 he was Deputy General Manager of the Southern Railway, a Director of Railway Air Services and a leading member of the Cavalry Club.

Evelyn canvassed others who might be interested. Many discussions went on in parallel, with the formation of British Latin American Airlines under John Booth, and a rearguard action by BOAC to keep all the strings in its own hands. In the end the proposed 'Internal and Continental' airline became BEAC (British European Airways Corporation) on 1 January 1946, initially as a Division of BOAC. The story is continued in Chapter 33.

On the same day BSAA (British South American Airways) operated its first proving flight from the bare expanse of mud called Heathrow to Buenos Aires. All this was in the totally different atmosphere of a Labour Government, elected with a big majority, which took office on 26 July 1945. As noted previously, its White Paper of 20 December 1945 set up BOAC, BEA and BSAA, just as I had recommended.

23

Jets

The story of the genesis of jet-propelled aircraft is almost beyond belief. The idea was conceived in the brain of a junior RAF officer, Frank Whittle, Service No 364365. He was a small man, a brilliant pilot, but the last kind of person supposed to invent anything. Yet in 1929 he not only invented but also worked out the mathematics of the new type of engine that was to revolutionise aviation. By October of that year he had drafted a Provisional Patent for it, and this was granted on 16 January 1930.

Amazingly, he then spent six years trying fruitlessly to find someone to show any interest. In October 1933 he was seconded to Cambridge, where I recall him as an earnest student of Peterhouse, whom I often met in the engineering laboratories and at society meetings. At last he and some friends decided to try to raise enough money to build an engine themselves, and this at last ran on 12 April 1937. Even then, there was extreme reluctance on the part of anyone in authority to recognise that this might be something of the greatest importance.

How different was the situation in Germany! Here a young student, Hans Pabst von Ohain, had had a similar idea in 1936 – six years after Whittle's Patent was published – and within weeks a vast programme was launched involving Hirth and Heinkel, followed by BMW, Junkers and many other companies. By 1944 vague glimmerings of German jet work began to emerge, partly by photo interpreters such as Babs spotting scorched lines in the grass where aircraft had been parked, and partly by crewmen of the US 8th Air Force who, on debriefing, said that they had seen German fighters with unbelievable speed.

This was in early 1944. At that time we – the Allies generally – felt we were 'on the home stretch', and that victory in Europe was just around the corner. We had fondly thought we had a great advantage in our possession of jet aircraft, and had disclosed their existence in a joint UK/US statement on 6 January 1944. Had we known that we were within a hair's breadth of being defeated in the sky and having our cities demolished by unstoppable rockets we would have been less complacent.

Max had come into the picture four years earlier. On his appointment as Minister of Aircraft Production on 14 May 1940 he had seen it as his duty to mastermind thousands of aircraft, rather than hustle in better ones. Given a choice, he would have preferred 1,000 extra Fairey Battles to having jets six months earlier. He did not even learn about jet propulsion for several weeks, and when he was introduced to the subject it was in an offhand way. His officials regarded the subject as an unimportant curiosity, and certainly not anything likely to influence the war!

Max liked to make up his own mind, and so, on 9 July 1940, he called in Whittle to see him. The interview lasted about three minutes. Max fired at the diminutive and clearly nervous young officer a few short, sharp questions. This was a time when Max was cancelling almost everything that could not bear fruit in a matter of weeks. To his credit, he blessed Whittle's efforts, and told him to 'Go away and get on with it'.

Later Max told me he thought Frank 'a little man with big ideas. I hope he'll turn out to be as difficult to the Germans as he was to my civil servants in MAP'. Thus it was that in early 1945 Max was drawn back into the story of jet propulsion. First, he talked with Cripps and then with Churchill about the future of Power Jets, the company which had been set up to exploit Whittle's by now numerous patents. Second, he participated in increasingly urgent discussions, in and outside the Cabinet, about the threat posed by the rapidly mounting operational activity of German jets, which by this time also included a rocket aircraft.

The RAF had since July 1944 had a single squadron of Gloster Meteor Mk I twin-jets (No 616), but this first version was hardly faster than piston-engined fighters and in any case production was at a snail's pace. The de Havilland company was testing a single-jet aircraft, the D.H.100 Spider Crab, later officially named the Vampire. Neither was likely to be available in numbers in the short term. In California, Lockheed was testing the XP-80 Shooting Star, again some way from operational use. Altogether the Allies had fewer than 50 jet fighters in total. In the USA there were also 66 Bell P-59A Airacomets, the first aircraft to go into production with Whittle-type engines, but these were too slow to be operational and were used as trainers.

In contrast, the *Luftwaffe* had well over 1,500 jet aircraft of three types: the Messerschmitt Me 163B *Komet* rocket interceptor, the Me 262A-1a *Schwalbe* twin-jet fighter-bomber, and the Arado Ar 234B twin-jet reconnaissance bomber, which could with impunity put heavy bombs on any target the German High Command chose. Behind these were numerous, often radical, later aircraft.

In late March 1945 I went over papers at Arlington House. Max said, 'We must get to the bottom of this jet business. Could the Germans gain an ascendancy over the US daylight bomber offensive, in spite of their escort fighters?'

Since spring 1944 the P-51 Mustang had been able to escort the bombers even on the longest missions, to Berlin or even Czechoslovakia, establishing air superiority over the Nazi homeland. Now, however, 8th AF crews were reporting increasing numbers of twin-jet Me 262s, which were so much faster than any Allied aircraft that they were able to sweep in past the escorts and blast the bombers with devastating gunfire and even with rockets.

Max said, 'It'll take a jet to catch a jet. In any case, I'm told the Meteor is a hot potato, with heavy controls and a slow climb. And they've got troubles trying to bring it into service.' Later I learned that the guns persistently jammed.

He went on, '. . . and Power Jets. It was a private company, financed by private enterprise – Tinling and Williams, I believe. Now it's been nationalised. Run by civil servants, I suspect. Find out all the facts. Archie Sinclair and Cripps say its moving along, but Harold Balfour's not so sure. Let me have a note of it all.'

On the fine sunny morning of 6 April 1945 I met Harold Roxbee Cox, the Chairman of the new State firm of Power Jets (R&D) [research and development] Ltd, which had acquired all the assets of Whittle's private firm for a little less than £136,000. We went by car to the firm's site at Lutterworth, in Leicestershire. It was a brilliant introduction to this exciting new subject, and I was brought up to date on the firm's progress and views.

On the 11th I went over the whole position with Air Marshal Sir Ralph Sorley, Controller of R&D at the MAP. Next day Hives and Sidgreaves came to Gwydyr House to put Rolls-Royce's position. They had the UK's only jet-engine production line, at Newcastle-under-Lyme, engaged in manufacturing 500 Derwent engines for the Meteor III, or F.3., which in consequence reached 465 mph over a wide band of altitudes.

On 21 April I lunched at the Athenaeum with Roxbee, and on the 24th I went to Bristol with Lord Brabazon. I then felt in a position to write a Paper for Max. I completed it on the 26th, and it was certainly the most comprehensive review of British jet development at that time. It was the day after US and Russian troops had joined up at Torgau on the Elbe.

My conclusions were that, while the *Luftwaffe* would have some 2,200 operational jets by the end of May (in fact, even if the war had lasted that long, the critical factor was shortage of fuel), the Allies would have just the 16 Meteors of 616 Sqn. A second squadron, No 504, became operational in July, two months after Germany's final collapse. No American jet fighters would be operational before 1946.

This miserable situation had arisen because of an unforgivable lethargy and lack of interest in jet aircraft in the United Kingdom prior to 1944. There was no doubt that a terrible mistake had been made in handing all Whittle's work over to the Rover Car Co., a firm with no aircraft or engine experience. The decision to do this had been largely because, despite all Whittle's pleading, the established aero-engine firms were not interested in diverting effort from the piston engines which they were making in enormous numbers.

After working with Rover from January 1940, Whittle at last became exasperated and fell out with the car company's management. This slowed the already pathetically sluggish progress considerably, and led to bitter arguments. In addition, the Air Ministry had been extraordinarily lax in framing operational requirements for jet aircraft, or in showing sufficient vision when they finally got round to doing this.

Now, in spring 1945, it could be seen that we had avoided defeat in the sky by the narrowest of margins. What was not publicised at the time was what would have happened had the German factories not been persistently bombed, and the supply of fuel to the *Luftwaffe* virtually halted. Of 1,433 Me 262s completed, only some 320 ever got into action, but their impact was tremendous. On 18 March 1945 a total of 37 got airborne. They shot down 24 USAAF heavy bombers and five of their P-51 escorts for the loss of two. On 7 April a handful from *JG7* shot down 28 B-17s for the loss of three, on a day on which escorting P-51s claimed to have shot down 133 piston-engined Bf 109s and Fw 190s. The only answer was to mount heavy bombing raids on the Me 262 bases – Oranienburg, Parchim, Borz, Brandenburg and Rechlin. This, coupled with crippling shortage of fuel, almost eliminated the threat.

There seemed to me to be an almost incomprehensible contrast between the way the dramatic new technology of jet aircraft was treated by Great Britain and by the enemy. In Germany the output of engines and aircraft was huge, despite heavy and sustained air attacks on every part of their industry. In Britain after 1941 air attack on our factories was almost non-existent, yet our output of jet aircraft could just about be counted on the fingers.

I handed over my Paper on the jet-propulsion situation to Max on 27 April. By then

Germany's final defeat was so obviously imminent that he had lost interest in the subject, and in the future of Power Jets. He skimmed through my submission and threw it back at me, saying 'History. Keep it. A great story. Write it some day.'

In fact I had written an even greater story 15 months earlier. Max had decided to inject a survey of the jet's potential for future air transport into his speech to the House of Lords of 19 January 1944. I typed out a draft on the short sheets from which he used to speak. Among other things, I typed out:

> 'But work is pressing forward. The time will come – perhaps ten years from now – when jet-propelled transport aircraft will cruise over the longest ranges at speeds far faster than any reckoned on today. And, more important still, at lower costs.
>
> 'I say to you, my Lords, that twenty years from now, in the early 1960s, when air transport is fully established throughout the world, London will be but a few short hours from New York by jet. And fares will be within the reach of all . . . for the Empire routes we shall look for a compromise: eventually a jet aeroplane to carry perhaps 50 passengers to Cairo non-stop, 2,000 miles in four hours. A challenge for the New World of the future.'

In the event, this was spot-on, but it was all too starry-eyed even for Max. In January 1944 he thought it Cloud-cuckoo-land. He did not use it.

24

Watershed

'It's all over, you know', said Max, peering at us over his spectacles at 'morning prayers'. Betty Hogg, Evelyn Baring, David Farrer, George Malcolm Thompson and I sat round his great desk. It was 27 April 1945, and I had just given him my review of 'the Jet Situation'.

He shuffled through the papers in the red Cabinet dispatch box on the little table on his left. 'Hitler's finished', he announced. 'Himmler's offered unconditional surrender.' We made appropriate noises. It was difficult to take it in, after five and a half years of war. And there were still the Japanese. I thought back through those busy, hard and exciting years. But Max's thoughts had run on:

> 'There'll be a General Election, of course. And the PM would like to keep the Coalition going until Japan is beaten. But Herbert Morrison keeps telling me that Labour won't agree. I'm bound to say, the sooner the Election the better. Of course, the country will give Winston a massive majority. But it's important to gain it before we get into all the problems of de-mobbing. I remember 1918 . . .'

Max was itching to return to the toils of Fleet Street, and the sunshine of Jamaica's Montego Bay. And the time for a decision on my own future was fast approaching. Lord Kemsley was pressing me to return to *The Sunday Times*, and not only to write. On Sunday 28 January he had invited Pat and me to lunch at his country home, Dropmore, near Beaconsfield. He offered me the position of Deputy Editor under Hadley, and alongside Denis Hamilton at Kemsley House.

Almost coincidentally, Max invited me to lunch with him at Arlington. He asked me in forceful terms to join Beaverbrook Newspapers as Air Adviser, with freedom to write on all air and defence subjects for the *Daily Express*, *Sunday Express* and *Evening Standard*. Then, with Albert hovering in the background, he stomped around and said something else:

> 'Now, Peter . . . how d'you say about going into politics? You should do it. It's the most exciting thing in the world. You know there'll be an Election shortly. And I've a seat for you in the asking, if you'll take it. Winston wants me to recommend a candidate for Carshalton. It's a new constituency carved out of Reigate and Epsom. It will be a 100-per-cent safe Tory seat for ever. What d'you say? It's yours if you'll take it . . . Politics is power, you know. And politics and journalism is power and persuasion. It's a fine combination. You can be master of both.'

Here was a watershed. On the one hand was a niche in the Beaver's fold, with a safe parliamentary seat. A unique offer to continue with Max, that mercurial

*With Lord
Beaverbrook in 1954.*

'pedlar of dreams'. Very tempting – but, deep inside, I felt it was not 'my road'.

Alternatively, there was the pressure from Lord Kemsley to stay in journalism under his banner. In the past he had been generous, and I owed him allegiance because he was still paying me a retainer of £250 a year for past work. In a confidential aside, Valentine Heywood had told me that it had been gauged that my articles on The Air War for *The Sunday Times* had substantially increased the circulation.

Two days later a third tempting opportunity appeared on the horizon. On returning from Chicago, Lord Swinton – whose Ministry of Civil Aviation was to come into being on 25 April – decided to create a new post at the British Embassy in Washington: Civil Air Attaché. The primary task would be to pave the way towards a Civil Air Agreement with the United States, as a foundation for post-war international air transport. Minutes on the subject were circulating between Washington, the Foreign Office and the embryonic MCA. Copies came to Gwydyr House.

Max kept at me: 'Before long, you might edit one of my papers. And with Aviation to the fore, once in Parliament you'd be on the front bench directly.' I think he was rather surprised that I continued to demur. What did I really want to do: talk and write, or just write, or actually do? If I were to choose Beaverbrook or Kemsley I would incur the grave displeasure of the other.

In fact this did not influence my decision to reject both. I was sad to leave Beaverbrook, whose stimulating presence had become so entwined into my affairs throughout the war. But the more I considered the position, the more convinced I became that I should take the practical job of carrying forward Anglo-American air relations in the capital of the United States.

I have naturally wondered how life would have turned out for me and my growing family if I had gone down the path of journalism, with or without politics as well. I will never know what events I might have had a hand in shaping had I stayed with Max. Nor what would have happened had I thrown in my lot with Kemsley, who in 1959 sold out to Lord Thomson and retired to the Bahamas.

The fact remains, my choice led to a very varied life in many aeronautical endeavours. I am sure that the choice I made was the right one, but I slept on it. Next morning I told Max that I felt I ought to pursue the possibilities of the attaché post in Washington. He said, 'I hope you will find that you're right. You know that I will help you, whatever you decide.'

So it was, that on 7 March 1945 I went to Ariel House and talked with Hildred. He confirmed that I would be welcomed in the post. I told him I would very much like to take it, provided that it was established at Assistant Secretary level, on a par with the Military Air Attaché and the US Civil Air Attaché in London.

On 3 May Swinton wrote to Max from his new Ministry:

> 'Hildred has written to you about the possibility of securing the services of Masefield . . . I gather that you have generously offered to make him available . . . The Treasury have now approved, as personal to Masefield, the status of Assistant Secretary with a salary of £1,000 a year, together with a USA allowance of £1,500 a year (untaxed) . . . I should be most grateful if you could see your way to releasing him soon . . .'

Max threw me the letter. 'I suppose that I must say "Yes" . . . anyway, draft me an answer . . .' I duly did so, saying that Max would release me 'with reluctance, but in the wider interests of British aviation'. The letter added that I had arranged a refresher flying course with the ATA at White Waltham 'postponed from 1943', starting in mid-May. I could take up the new appointment 'from the middle of July'.

My appointment was announced on 12 May, saying among other things: 'Mr Masefield will be responsible for all British civil aviation affairs in the United States, including the carrying forward of negotiations on a bilateral agreement and liaison on traffic and technical questions arising from the Chicago Convention . . .'

In his generous way, Max dictated a piece for the *Evening Standard* of the same date, which began: 'The appointment of Mr Peter Masefield to be Britain's first Civil Air Attaché at the Washington Embassy is first rate. Mr Masefield is 31, and adds to a keen, supple mind the enthusiasm of youth. He will carry out his duties with brilliance.' I also noticed most heart-warming comments in *Flight* and *The Sunday Times*.

I remained at Gwydyr House for a further two months, clearing up papers and doing various jobs for Max, including notes for a speech on V-weapons, notes on the future of air transport, and on aviation as an election issue. Meanwhile, I brushed up my flying.

On 15 May I went by train to Maidenhead, and then by ATA tender to White Waltham. Here I spent a quite strenuous six weeks flying the Fairchild Argus, North American Harvard and Avro Anson. The weather was warm and sunny, and the grass airfield an idyllic part of Berkshire.

The course was doubly pleasant because it afforded an opportunity to discuss plans for future airline operations with the ATA Commandant, Gerard d'Erlanger (later to run BEA and then BOAC); Philip Wills, his deputy and a famous glider pilot; Peter Mursell, in charge of flying; Bob Morgan, in charge of engineering (later to be my Chief Engineer at BEA); and Ben Bathurst, head of the instructors group.

I was allocated an enthusiastic refresher instructor, W.E. Cowan. Towards the end of the course I was able to borrow an Argus – widely used throughout the war as a taxi by ATA ferry pilots – and visit de Havilland at Hatfield, Avro at Woodford, Airspeed at Christchurch, Bristol at Filton, Vickers-Armstrongs at Wisley and Handley Page at Radlett. I brought myself up to the minute on all the British civil aircraft programmes.

At the end of my course, on 29 June, Cowan and I set off together in Anson I NK942 on a tour of Germany. We flew mostly at 800 feet. We went over Calais and Dunkerque *en route* to Brussels. Then we flew over Aachen, Cologne, Paderborn and Hannover, and landed at Celle. From there we looked at Belsen, Osnabrück, Essen, Duisburg, Munster, Dortmund and Bochem, landing at Eindhoven. Finally we returned to White Waltham by way of Bruges, Antwerp, Dunkerque, Calais, Deal and Westminster.

Seeing the utter devastation of Germany was unforgettable. I was also able to take a close look at the impressive aircraft that were in production at VE-day, especially the Me 262, He 162 and Ar 234, all scattered around at Celle.

Next I enjoyed a round of dinners, with Lord Swinton, Lord Brabazon, Dick Hildred, Lord Knollys, with Hives and Sidgreaves of Rolls-Royce, and Arthur Christensen of the *Daily Express*.

On 5 July came the General Election. To the utter astonishment of many, Labour was returned with a huge majority. Several people who had voted Labour were amazed when I told them that this meant that Churchill would not be Prime Minister. The new seat of Carshalton was indeed won by the Conservative candidate, Brigadier Anthony Head, but with the unexpectedly small majority of 1,017.

Last of all, on 9 July Pat and I dined with Max at 64 Brook Street. It was a nostalgic occasion. As we left at midnight, Max said 'After you've had a couple of years in Washington, come back and take up writing again. There'll be another seat for you in the House if you want it. Don't spend all your days in Government service. There's much more to do outside. We've had good days together. I hope there will be more.' I wished that too.

We remained in cordial but infrequent contact. After my Commonwealth and Empire Lecture to the Royal Aeronautical Society on 30 September 1948 he wrote me a congratulatory letter, and we met. He again urged me to return to writing, but at that very time Frank Pakenham persuaded me to take on the challenge of running BEA.

Then, in the midst of that job, on 6 March 1951, Max wrote to me from on board RMS *Queen Elizabeth*. Marked <u>Private and secret</u>, he referred to difficulties in the

Ministry of Supply, especially in the failure to provide modern military aircraft suddenly needed because of the Korean War. He said I might hear something, but added 'Do not take anything less than the Controllership'. In fact, I heard no more.

On 29 March 1956 Max pressed me at Arlington House to accept the Chairmanship of BOAC, on which the Prime Minister, Anthony Eden, had consulted him. As related later, I told him I felt obligated to Bristol.

I told Max that I seemed always to be turning down his generous offers. He replied, 'Ah, Peter. You have set your eyes on the stars along a path of many toils. You will not be deflected. Keep before you the words of that American psalm:

> Let us then be up and doing
> With a heart for any fate
> Still achieving, still pursuing
> Learn to labour and to wait.'

25

Aboard the Brisbane Star

arly July 1945 saw the Masefields excitedly preparing to go to America. We let our apartment furnished, for two years (that was a big mistake), and then my mother's housekeeper at Brentwood asked whether her daughter could come with us to help Pat with our family of three. Peggy, 22, was heartbroken, because her fiancé had returned from the war to say he no longer wanted to marry her. She just wanted to get away from it all. She certainly succeeded: she married an American and had six children of her own.

At last, on Wednesday 11 July six of us piled into a car hired from Brentwood's White Hart Garage, driven by old Joe Henderson who had ferried my family on many previous trips. Behind came our own Flying Standard, packed tight with the luggage. Joe was concerned to see us go, 'what with the children, and all them lethal mines . . .'

Via East Ham, Plaistow and Canning Town, we reached Connaught Road. Here, at Berth 33 of the Royal Albert Dock, we met the *Brisbane Star*, 11,100 tons, a motor vessel of the Blue Star line. She was still in wartime grey paint, weatherbeaten and flecked with rust. Her stem was a giant flat-nosed concrete plug, replacing the original bow which had been blown off by a Ju 88's torpedo on a Malta convoy in 1942. On that occasion she was one of only four vessels to reach the beleaguered island.

We were processed by Outward Customs. They confiscated my camera, and gave it to the Purser in a sealed package to be returned at the end of the voyage. Clearly, nobody had told HM Customs that, except in the Far East, the war was over. We then boarded via a steep gangplank, and watched our trunks being swung on board and the hatches battened down with slow deliberation by the blue-jerseyed crew.

After wartime austerity the cabins seemed magnificent, with outside portholes, deep carpets and bathrooms attached. We took up a quarter of the accommodation. Pat and I had a double cabin, with a cot for Richard, our youngest, bolted to the floor. Charles (now 5) shared a smaller double with Vicky (7), and Peggy had a single.

At lunch we met our fellow passengers. Only two were female: a Polish lady, who never emerged from her cabin, and Lady Baron, wife of the 43-year-old (and stone deaf) chairman of the Carreras tobacco firm. We emerged again at quarter past one – in ship time 13.15 – to see the ship slowly backing out under the pull of a tiny tug, impatiently watched from cars and buses held up before a swing bridge.

Brisbane Star, *11,100 tons, 517 feet long.*

Richard and Pat, waiting for doughnuts at the ship's galley hatch.

We eventually emerged on to the murky Thames, here called Gallions Reach. On the far side were Plumstead Marshes where, 51 years previously, Sir Hiram Maxim had briefly lifted off in his colossal biplane. That afternoon we passed many other early sites of aviation. At dinner we turned from east to south, and slowly passed the Goodwin Sands, awash with white water and littered with wrecked ships. As it grew dark we could see bright lights ashore, a strange experience after almost six years of blackout.

Next morning we set our watches an hour back. At 08.30 Start Point was just in view in the haze. At 16.30 the Scillies dropped astern, our last sight of land for 11 days. On our second day out – Friday the 13th – we awoke to rolling and lurching. At lunch the only ones present were the Captain, the doctor, Richard and me.

The theory was advanced that two-year-old Richard's normal gait was such that he did not notice the motion of the ship. He merely said 'Boat all go bouncy-bouncy,' and set about prying out the ship's cats from nooks and crannies into which they had retreated. Eventually other passengers began to appear. Richard was awed by the Captain's gold braid, and so, when he took a dislike to a meal, Pat said 'Eat up, or the Captain will put you in irons.' Next day at lunch Richard told his brother, 'Eat up, or the Captain will iron you out flat.'

One day a tarpaulin swimming pool was rigged up in the waist. On the 17th we went on a tour of the bridge, and then of the engine room. The *Brisbane Star* had been built in 1936 by Cammell Laird at Birkenhead. She had two 20-cylinder diesels turning the propellers at 108 rpm to give a speed of 17 knots. The noise and heat were almost overpowering, but Charles gloated over the gleaming machinery. We were burning about 15 gallons a mile, or nine nautical miles per ton. The ship's bunkers had been filled with 2,500 tons of oil at Panama in May, since when she had crossed the Atlantic three times, and our voyage would make the fourth. I calculated that this one bunker-load would last for four more crossings.

We came back on deck to see a shoal of flying fish and, minutes later, a school of dolphins gambolling around the ship. The morning was rounded off by another diversion: watching the seven gunners cleaning and exercising the armament, which would still be needed in the Pacific theatre. In the bow was the 3-in, or 12-pounder. There were four 20-mm cannon, and five paired 0.5-in Brownings, which I greeted like old friends. On the Malta convoy in August 1942 the ship's gunners had claimed 'five planes, for certain'.

That evening Grundy, a hearty Australian, and a Cockney friend organised a party – which, of course, was really a booze-up. There was a lot of singing, with the doctor at the piano and later playing a piano-accordion. Dr G.C. Macdiarmid had spent four years as a prisoner of the Germans, running the camp hospital. Peggy sang with gusto, while Grundy (who was 40) performed handsprings, cartwheels and somersaults.

Pat had difficulty disposing of unwanted articles. On the third day she had struggled on deck, where she collapsed into a chair. The Chief Steward advised her, 'Madam must eat, or she will never be well', and brought her a steaming bowl of greasy Irish stew. The moment he had gone, with a guilty look to left and right, she emptied the bowl over the rail into the sea (she thought) and sank back into her chair. A little later the Chief Steward came back from the deck below, wiping gravy and dumplings from his face. His only comment was, 'Madam – this is no way to get well'.

Pat had been told that, with the prospect of shopping in the USA, it made sense to bring her oldest underwear and discard it, rather than try to wash it in sea-water. So, on the 18th, she emerged on deck carrying what she termed 'a holy basket', and cast the contents over the rail into a 25-knot headwind. To the amazement of passengers and crew, the contents went *upward*, and in seconds the ship's overhead cables were bravely flying three pairs of silk panties, two brassieres and a slip.

On the 19th we saw birds. Larger than seagulls, they flew very low. They must have come at least 250 miles from Nova Scotia. At 20.50 on the 20th we had our first glimpse of America: a flashing buoy. At 22.15 we passed it, and saw another buoy ahead. At 23.00 we anchored off Cape Charles, to go into port on the tide. At

The cables which attracted Pat's cast-offs.

01.00 the pilot came aboard up a rope ladder. We could see distant shore lights.

At the last moment we were redirected to Norfolk, Virginia. On the sunny morning of Saturday 21 July the *Brisbane Star* pushed her concrete bow into Newport News, which had been the venue of the 1926 Schneider Trophy. On shore were big white houses among dense green trees. We docked at Norfolk at 09.30.

The British Consul came on board and greeted us. The Embassy had reserved for us three two-berth cabins on the river boat for Washington. The price was $24.65 for six. After a final lunch on the *Brisbane Star*, and distribution of $65 in tips, we went through the Customs shed, and straight on board the 'Showboat'-style paddle-steamer *District of Columbia*. It was lavish beyond words, and full of Saturday-night revellers.

As we chugged up Chesapeake Bay we were plied with tea in tall glasses. The children were fascinated by the stewardesses' smiling black faces. Charles asked 'Will our next baby here be black, Mummy?' Dinner of tomato juice, baked sea trout and huge helpings of ice cream cost $9.65 – just over £2 – for six.

Breakfast was again an eye-opener for my family, though I was used to such lavishness. At 08.00 we tied up to the Potomac waterfront in downtown Washington. Even though it was Sunday, we were met at that unholy hour by Gp Capt. R.L. (Dickie) Legg, our Air Attaché, and his svelte wife Pam, together with Wg Cdr Tony Greenman of the British Air Commission. Dickie had taken over on the previous day from my old sparring partner, Gp Capt. D.L. Blackford, who had left for home.

So the first UK Civil Air Attaché to be appointed anywhere in the world arrived by ancient paddle-boat. Dickie, Pam and Tony carried us off in two cars to our new home, 2918 28th St NW. We had hardly arrived when Paul and Pat Gore-Booth from the Embassy called to add their greetings. Clearly, the welcomes were going to be as warm as the torrid July weather. With the house came Gertrude. Large and black, she was a treasure, and she stayed with us after we moved later in my posting.

Our house was small, and as yet sparsely furnished, but the Embassy had had to pull all the strings to find anything at all in overcrowded wartime Washington. There were not enough beds, and on the first night Richard curled up in an eiderdown in a drawer pulled from a dressing table. Oddly, we did have bathroom scales. Everyone promptly got on these, and I wrote down (in pounds): Richard 31, Charles 50, Vicky 78, Pat 120, Peggy 135, PGM 175. About a quarter-ton, useful to remember when checking in for flights.

So, with the temperature getting near a humid 100 by day and the chirp of crickets deafening at night, we settled in to a new life. DC was a haven of bright lights, huge supermarkets (unknown in the UK), and shops stocked with things we had either forgotten or never before seen. It really felt like 3,700 miles from wartime London.

26

The Washington post

In 1945 the British Embassy in the United States, at 3100 Massachusetts Avenue, seemed to typify British solidity in both its architecture and its inmates. The approach is imposing, across a bridge over Rock Creek Park, a wooded gorge which winds down to the Potomac at Foggy Bottom and Georgetown.

The Embassy stands far back behind massive wrought-iron gates, and is gloriously situated among tall trees. The building is a formal Lutyens structure in red brick, more suited to Washington, Sussex, than to DC. Almost all the other buildings in the area are white, which together with the massive trees and blue water make the District of Columbia one of the world's most beautiful capitals.

War had resulted in a great expansion of Embassy staff, so a three-storey prefab annexe had been quickly put up in the grounds. Here was my office, next to that of the RAF Attaché Dickie Legg on the second floor, with a welcome hum coming from a window-box air conditioner. Somewhere they had preserved the ancient brass plate which proclaimed:

EMBASSY OF HIS BRITANNIC MAJESTY
Office hours: Tuesday to Friday 10 am to 4 pm
Fridays 10 am to Noon
Closed July and August

Not any more! Every part of the Embassy was a beehive of activity 365 days a year, and through most of the day and night. Discounting wives and families, the staff numbered about 65 on the Diplomatic List, made up of diplomats, serving officers, economists, engineers and businessmen. They were industrious, competent and friendly.

Over all presided the Ambassador. Lord Halifax was the American's idea of an Englishman, an amalgamation of Bertie Wooster, Lord Emsworth and the Archbishop of Canterbury. 'HE' was supported by two Scottish Ministers. Sir John 'Jock' Balfour was short and stocky, eccentric but dependable. Sir John Magowan was grey, stolid, erudite and unflappable. Next in precedence came Roger Makins, who later was to be Ambassador to the USA himself, and to become Lord Cherfield. He had a fine mind, ready wit and eight children. He was utterly removed from pomposity or assininity.

First Secretary and Head of Chancery was Donald Durt Maclean, who lived at 2710 34th St with his pretty American wife Melinda and two-month-old Fergus. He was regarded as a pillar of the Embassy, who would go far. He did indeed (see next chapter).

The Masefield family in Washington (assembling a cut-up map of the World).

Richard and Charles (helping to cut firewood).

Naval and Naval Air Attaché was Capt. E.M. Connolly Abel-Smith, who later commanded the Royal Yacht *Britannia*. His assistants were Cdrs F.G.S. Bowring RN and Ken Downey RNVR, both great characters. Tragically, in 1954 the RAF Attaché, Dickie Legg, with his wife Pam, were to be killed in a car crash in South Africa. Dickie was backed up by Sqn Ldr H.A. Roxborough, who was soon replaced by Sqn Ldr John L. Mitchell, a navigation wizard.

The Oil Attaché was the stolid Victor Butler, who had been on the non-stop Northolt-Washington flight. My 1943 friend Paul Gore-Booth was First Secretary in charge of information, and, before I arrived, also of civil aviation. He and his

Australian wife Pat lived with their twin boys just across the Avenue. Alongside Paul was William D. Clark, in charge of Press affairs. Later he was to be Anthony Eden's PRO at 'No 10'.

On my first day, after meeting all the senior staff and many others, I talked with Dickie Legg and his own team. I then had a formal meeting with Minister Balfour. I found Jock Balfour sitting on top of his desk, Gandhi-fashion, clad in a brief pair of underpants and his large moustache.

He said, 'Come in, dear boy. Excuse my undress, but this climate! Don't you feel warm?' The Embassy Chancery was like a Turkish Bath, and I was wearing an English-weight jacket over my RAF-blue shirt. Although this was my third summer in Washington, British clothes-rationing did not run to tropical kit.

Jock went on, 'In spite of this damn heat, you'll enjoy it here. Wonderful place. Terribly friendly, the Americans. Plenty of aviation problems, though. Anyway, let me know if I can help.' He scratched at a big toe, and continued, 'You know a lot already. Bill Burden, first rate, but I don't think he'll stay. Ed Warner, brilliant, but a bit professorial. Ted Wright, nice man, very competent . . . You and your wife must come and dine with Frances and me soon . . .'

I next called on the Head of Chancery. Maclean was 32, a typical product of an English public school. He stood 6 ft 4 in, in formal striped trousers cut half-way up the back and held by yellow braces, under which was an immaculate striped shirt.

He waved to vast piles of Foreign Office telegrams. 'I'm loaded with bumph . . . I'm glad to see you. Now we'll really make progress on those Civil Aviation talks. In a day or two I'll take you to meet Garrison Norton in the State Department. But at 11.30 I take you to HE.'

We walked along the long archway to the Residency. In a large, dim and blissfully cool room on the first floor Lord Halifax – tall, lean, stooping and courteous – welcomed me. We discussed the Chicago Conference. He went on, 'Let me tell you about the Americans . . . they're really quite different here in their own country. They're a sentimental nation, and the war has made them much less isolationist, and more patriotic. The extraordinary thing is the regard they've developed for Britain. And for Winston, even though they don't understand him. I'm not sure I do, either.'

We talked for half an hour before Paul Gore-Booth came in with a sheaf of telegrams, and with William Clark bore me off to the Press Club, on F Street near the Treasury and White House. Our companions at lunch were Charles Campbell of the British Information Service, René McColl of the *Daily Express*, and Malcolm Muggeridge of the *Daily Telegraph*.

My companions were in tremendous form. We got round to the antics some US airlines were getting up to. PanAm had hired Mrs Anne Archibald, a formidable 60-year-old socialite, to entertain Congressmen, especially Senators – 'and *you*, if you don't look out', said Malcolm. 'She's a real tartar. I know nothing about air agreements, but I've been practically raped on two occasions.'

Transcontinental and Western Air had engaged the services of a most personable Swede, Count Bruno Stackleburg. According to René, 'At the drop of a hat, old boy, he'll offer you untold wealth to get TWA traffic rights – say, between London and Paris.' Times were going to be interesting.

After lunch I met Abel-Smith again, followed by John Forster and Douglas

Haddow on economics; George Middleton and Michael Wright of Foreign Office affairs; Brig. T.G. Deedes, the Military Attaché, and his assistant Col Peter Molloy; Richard Miles, Third Secretary; and Miss Irene F. Boyle, in charge of hospitality. Again, all competent and friendly.

Then to the British Air Commission, at 1785 'Mass Avenue', the organisation which in six years had purchased tens of thousands of US-built aircraft. It was presided over by the urbane Henry O.R. Hindley, supported by the spry 70-year-old Sir Vivian Gabriel from the Indian Civil Service. Across the road, on the 9th Floor of the Willard Hotel, was the Treasury Delegation, with Humphrey Trevelyan and Frank Lee. From there I was taken to 1434 16th St NW, where I met Air Marshal Sir Douglas Colyer, Head of the RAF Delegation. His colleagues included Conrad Biddlescombe, a walking encyclopaedia on American aviation (and a contender for the first Atlantic flight in 1919); Gp Capt. Christopher Clarkson, an old friend from my time at Fairey and *The Aeroplane*, who had tested hundreds of US aircraft for the RAF; and 'Babs' Babington-Smith, who was now working on Japanese intelligence with the USAAF.

On the 24th Pat and I lunched with the Halifaxes, together with the Balfours, Gore-Booths, Leggs and, in a wheelchair, Richard Wood. The son of the Ambassador, Richard had lost both legs with the Eighth Army, but he was cheerful and otherwise fit. A sprinkler played on the lawn; I wished I could be under it.

After lunch, back to more introductions. My sphere encompassed the State Department, the Civil Aeronautics Administration (CAA) and Board (CAB), the Airports Administration in the Department of Commerce, the airlines and the corps of British newspaper correspondents. They were an extraordinary cross-section of people in the District of Columbia and in Alexandria, Virginia, and Baltimore, Maryland.

Our main link with the UK was the BOAC Boeing 314A flying-boat base at Baltimore, run by Ross Stainton. He was handsome and, though grossly overworked, very co-operative. One of my jobs was to allocate passenger priorities for each transatlantic flight. I could accept 80 per week, but had to turn away more.

Based at Montreal, but often in Washington, Vernon Crudge was BOAC's North American Manager. Plump and good company, he ran a shuttle service between Washington, La Guardia and Dorval, using a Lockheed Hudson III with the RAF serial FK779. Its pilot was the famed Jack Kelly Rogers, who had flown Imperial and BOAC flying boats for so long that he was alleged to have webbed feet.

On the American side, contacts with the State Department were, at least on the surface, cordial. I dealt chiefly with Garrison Norton and Stokeley Morgan. At the CAB the Chairman, Welch Pogue, was supported by Ed Warner, Harlee Branch and many other forceful characters, while the top CAB people were Bill Burden and Ted Wright.

At American Airlines I again met President C.R. Smith (as noted earlier, he had helped run the US Air Transport Command), Terry Drinkwater, and the delightful Carlene Roberts. At TWA the top man was Jack Frye, at Eastern Capt. Eddie Rickenbacker, and at Capital James H. 'Slim' Carmichael. And I was delighted to renew acquaintance with my old friend Wayne W. Parrish, Editor of *American Aviation*.

A small group of about fifty people in Washington, and a like number in London, were about to shape the whole future of international air transport. Thanks to my 20 months with Max Beaverbrook I was able to take my place in the centre of the maelstrom.

It was all most enjoyable, despite the particularly sweltering Washington summer. In the cooler fall we managed to find a much more commodious and well-furnished house at 1510 Emerson St NW, and we moved in on 1 November. At night we were able to sit out on verandahs with insect screens, and, by now used to the din of the crickets, watch the antics of the brilliant fireflies.

For Pat this new life was sheer bliss. 'Can you imagine what it was like to be able to buy any food you wanted, any clothes you needed?', she later wrote. 'After years of no fun, it went to my head to have cocktail parties (sometimes two) every evening, and all the pomp and ceremony of lunches at the Embassy. Although I was conscious of my duty I was told that any 'trouble' I might get into would be covered by diplomatic immunity. Whoopee!'

27

Maclean

On the scorching afternoon of 6 August 1945 I was telephoned by Donald Maclean. He asked me to come down to the small conference room, together with Dickie Legg and his assistant Roxborough. The three of us entered together. Donald was sitting on the table, swinging his legs and twiddling a yellow pencil. Most unusually, he appeared slightly flustered.

He said, 'It'll be in the newspapers tomorrow. I thought you'd want to know first. It's been Top Secret – a new way of making a giant explosion by splitting the atom. The Americans have just dropped what they call an "atom bomb" on the Japanese city of Hiroshima.'

Astonished, we discussed this news. I recalled the talks at Gwydyr House about 'heavy water'. Dickie asked whether any form of matter could be turned into an explosive. 'No,' said Donald, who seemed well up on the subject. 'It has to be uranium or plutonium . . . only a few pounds are needed to equal 20,000 tons of TNT.' He said the initial work had been British, and reeled off a string of famous names: Rutherford, Thompson, Appleton, Darwin, Chadwick, Cockcroft, Oliphant . . .

He gave us a complete outline of how the work had moved to the USA in 1943, and who had done what. We discussed whether, despite the new bomb, the Japanese would go on fighting fanatically. We thought they would. Eventually Donald asked us, 'Would your wife and children come to tea next Monday . . . ?' The Macleans became some of our closest friends in Washington.

In retrospect, it seems bizarre that officials in a British Embassy, one a senior RAF officer, should learn about nuclear weapons from a man who was actually a spy for the Soviet Union. There is apparently evidence that he had started to lead a double life only a very short time previously.

His background was impeccable. He was the son of a Liberal Cabinet Minister. He had been at Trinity College when I was up at Cambridge, though we had not met. He entered the Foreign Office in 1935, and married Melinda Marling from New York in Paris in 1940.

In 1948 he was transferred from Washington to Cairo, where he began drinking heavily. 'Dried out', he was brought home in November 1950, and given the key appointment of Head of the US Department at the Foreign Office. In May 1951 MI.5 for the first time suspected that a leak to Moscow was through Maclean. The renegade Kim Philby in Washington apparently learned of this, and passed the word to Maclean via Guy Burgess, who had just been recalled to London and sacked for alcoholism.

On 22 May 1951 Maclean and Burgess drove to Southampton and embarked aboard SS *Falaise* for St Malo, bound for Moscow. Melinda and the (by then three) children followed via Switzerland.

Maclean was as unlike my previous idea of a Communist as it was possible to be.

So much so, that I spent years wondering whether his 'defection' might actually have been a double-bluff. If so, to destroy a brilliant career and remain for the rest of his life vilified in his native land, whilst actually serving it courageously, would surely have been one of the most gallant gestures in history.

I was saddened when, 50 years later, all the relevant documents were released. These showed that he really had been a spy for the USSR. What remains a mystery is why he chose to do this. Did they somehow manage to blackmail him, so that he had no choice?

28

The Boeing boats

The first three months in my new post were spent in gathering staff, making contacts, seeking opinions in the aftermath of Chicago, planning the proposed future conference, and starting a weekly 'Washington News-letter' on aviation affairs for limited distribution in Whitehall and the SBAC (which then stood for Society of British Aircraft Constructors).

On Sunday 26 August I took over a six-seater Pontiac sedan. Made in 1937, it had a straight-eight engine of 4.14 litres capacity. It had had three previous owners, the most recent being Air Cdre Neville Buckle, RAF. Complete with radio and heater, he had priced it at $566. I later brought that great car home to England.

In the afternoon of that Sunday I drove the 50 miles to the Marine Terminal at Dundalk, Baltimore, to meet one of BOAC's Boeing 314A flying boats. On board were Lord Winster, the new Labour Government's Minister of Civil Aviation, and Lord Knollys, the Chairman of BOAC. Winster greeted me warmly, as a colleague of the Chatham House War Strategy Group of 1942. We dined that evening at the Belvedere Hotel in Baltimore, with Paul Patterson, publisher of *The Baltimore Sun*, for whom Winster had previously been London correspondent.

On the following day Winster, Knollys, Vernon Crudge and I boarded a VIP Dakota (KK198) of RAF No 45 Group, flown by Wg Cdr Van Der Kloot, and flew to Montreal in 3 hr 16 min. In the evening Knollys gave a dinner at the Windsor Hotel for the UK delegates to PICAO, led by my old friend Air Chief Marshal Sir Frederick

Vicky, Richard and Charles
approved of the Pontiac.

'Ginger' Bowhill. A good time was had by all, though I did manage a serious talk with Winster about the lie of the land in Washington.

Next day, after seeing off their lordships in a BOAC Liberator for Prestwick, I returned to Washington via La Guardia in Hudson FK779, this time flown by Capt. Decker, and left again the following morning for Wright Field in a USAAF Douglas C-47 with bucket seats, requiring a seat-type parachute. I had talks with Generals Hugh Kenney and Benjamin Chidlaw, together with Gp Capt. Bill Smith of the British Air Commission.

At this time, in addition to sorting things out in Washington, there was hardly a day when I was not flying in or out of National, on the bank of the Potomac just south of the Pentagon. In contrast, on 13 September I boarded a Boeing 314A for my first crossing of the Atlantic by flying boat. Between 1943 and 1976 I crossed the Atlantic almost 200 times. One crossing was by boat. Of the others, six were particularly memorable, because they were by the 314A. Each was a long, long mix of flying, yachting, eating and sleeping, in pleasant but uneconomic proportions.

In 1945 the 314A was the largest commercial aircraft in service in the world. BOAC's three examples had been bought in almost new condition from Pan American Airways in May 1941. Almost single-handedly, Ross Stainton ran the base at Baltimore, chosen because it was clear of ice in winter. The service was run by Kelly Rogers and Tommy Farnsworth.

Back in 1937 I had covered for *The Aeroplane* the first transatlantic services by Imperial Airways' Short S.23 *Caledonia* (Capt. A.S. Wilcockson) and Pan American's Sikorsky S-42B *Clipper III* (Capt. Harold E. Gray). I later flew in all three Boeing boats, *Bristol*, then *Berwick* and finally *Bangor* (whose name seemed appropriate, when starting one engine caused ear-splitting backfires).

When the boats were operating at near their 86,000 lb maximum weight the 14-cylinder Wright Cyclone GR-2600 engines, rated at 1,600 hp, ran hot unless the gills were kept open. This increased drag, and so reduced the speed, and thus also decreased the cooling airflow, a worrying vicious circle. Another problem was that flight testing showed the need for not just the original one but three fins and rudders. The heavier tail put the centre of gravity so far aft that, even with the maximum bow-compartment mail and cargo load of 2,900 lb, the boat was tail-heavy. Trimming this out again increased drag, and reduced the speed still further.

The normal Westbound fuel load was 4,200 US gal (3,497 imp. gal., 25,200 lb), which allowed a payload of 4,240 lb, typically 20 passengers each with a sleeping bunk. Endurance was 23 hours at 124 kt (143 mph), just enough to fly from Foynes in Ireland to Botwood in Newfoundland against a 25-kt headwind.

BOAC's Boeings had a crew of 11: Captain, Chief Officer, First Officer, Second Officer, Chief Radio Officer, Second Radio Officer, Chief Engineer Officer, Second Engineer Officer, Purser, Chief Steward and Second Steward. Even taxiing on the water required constant attention, because it was seldom possible to reach the 20 knots necessary for adequate lateral control. Indeed, in a crosswind it was often impossible to avoid dipping a wingtip in the water. Another hazard was that the sponsons projecting on each side, which were supposed to keep the boat upright on the water, were sometimes holed by the launches which brought passengers alongside.

I was aware of all this when, on the dark autumn evening of 13 September 1945,

Boeing 314A G-AGCA Berwick *(crew-member in nose ready to throw out anchor).*

Roger Makins, Victor Butler and I drove to Marine Terminal *en route* to London. Ross Stainton arranged for my Pontiac to be stabled in the flying-boat hangar.

We had a cup of coffee with the skipper, Capt. Craig, and then went out by launch to G-AGBZ *Bristol*. We started engines at 23.00, but for the next three-quarters of an hour we taxied around to warm them up. At last, at 23.45, we thundered off down the floating flare-path *en route* for Botwood, 1,200 nautical miles to the north-east. The whole operation was redolent of British shipping, in which an hour or two extra was of little consequence. You were in the hands of a large crew of experienced gentlemen.

BOAC stewards were what the world then expected from the British: a cross between a servant in a London Club and a ship's steward in 1st Class. As soon as we were airborne they began serving dinner, a holy ritual lasting two hours. Then, at 2 in the morning, into pyjamas and head down between clean sheets in a commodious bunk. I was awakened in time for a wash, shave and light breakfast, before *Bristol* alighted in the sunshine on Botwood Creek. We moored to a buoy. The silence was strange, after 7 hr 41 min of roar and vibration.

Ashore by launch at 08.00 to a larger breakfast of ham and eggs, presided over by Denis Bustard, BOAC's Newfoundland Station Manager. He regaled the three of us with stories of magnificent salmon fishing, and then took us in his Jeep to tour the Botwood lumber camp, deep in the endless pine forest. By the time we were back on *Bristol* at 11.20 the tanks in her wings had received 3,700 US gal (2,914 imp. gal., 22,200 lb), pumped by hand from drums on a lighter.

At 12.03 we were airborne again, for the 1,761 nautical miles to Foynes, helped by a spanking 26-kt tailwind. There followed a protracted lunch, above solid cloud at 7,500 feet, followed by an afternoon spent reading and writing, leavened by 'old-English tea', with crumpets. A snooze was followed by dinner. Then, 11 hr 22 min from take off, but at only 18.25 local time, we alighted on the Shannon and tied up at Foynes on the southern bank. The land airport, Rineanna (today Shannon Airport) is nearer to Limerick on the north bank.

Thanks to the tailwind we did not need to refuel, and were on the water a mere 1 hr 22 min. Off again at 19.47, we alighted along the flarepath in Poole Harbour at 21.44. There followed a bus to Bournemouth Central, a train to Waterloo and a taxi to 119 Piccadilly for a bed at the Royal Aero Club after midnight.

The next two weeks were packed with meetings, but I still managed to fly a Mosquito NF.30 at Hatfield, a Bristol Buckmaster with Cyril Uwins at Filton, and, with Hugh Kendall, the Miles M.7A Nighthawk (later G-AGWT) from Filton back to Woodley.

There were meetings at the Ministry of Civil Aviation, Foreign Office, Colonial Office and SBAC. I lunched with Hildred on the 17th, Cheetham on the 18th, Winster on the 19th, Baring and Dodero on the 20th, Geoffrey de Havilland on the 21st, Verdon-Smith on the 22nd, my kinsman John Masefield on Sunday the 23rd, the Beaver on the 24th, Satterthwaite on the 25th, and Cribbett on the 26th. There was a meeting of the Aircraft Recognition Journal Committee on the 18th, of the Aircraft Recognition Committee of the Ministry of Supply on the 19th, the Council of the Royal Aeronautical Society on the 20th, a visit to Hatfield on the 21st, to Filton and Woodley (Reading) on the 22nd, dinner with Brab on 24th, dinner with Bob Mayo of BOAC, Bill Lappin of Rolls and Spry Leverton of KLM on the 25th, and a meeting of the MCA Organisation Committee on the 26th. I spent nights with my parents at Brentwood and with my in-laws at Wallington.

On 27 September I caught the 08.00 train from Waterloo to Bournemouth. Then by bus to Poole and by launch to *Bristol* again, this time commanded by David Brice. We took off at 14.10, and alighted at Foynes at 16.56. Going westbound, the 294 nautical miles took 2 hr 46 min instead of 1 hr 51 min.

An hour at the Lithgoe Arms in Foynes, and then a long, long take-off, weighed down with 4,000 US gal. We settled down for the long plug into a 25-kt headwind at 4,000 ft, to avoid even stronger winds above. The flight deck was much larger than that of any modern jet, but then so was the crew. With the First Engineer I crawled along the wing to inspect the accessory gearbox on No 3 engine. The noise was indescribable.

I then spent 30 minutes flying *Bristol* among cloud tops at 7,500 feet, with 136 mph indicated and fuel burn about 201 US gal./hr. With nearly full tanks, the monster was unresponsive. Any serious attempt to manoeuvre was really hard physical effort.

Lower down, the passenger cabins were wide and high, with fabric outer walls hiding the metal hull. The large midships cabin seated 16 in pairs facing each other across tables. Behind were two smaller 8-seat cabins. This gave a total of 32 seats (55 on the shuttle to Bermuda), but on the Atlantic the weight limit was 20, which meant that each passenger could have a bunk, 10 lower and 10 upper.

Over the Atlantic we had a three-hour dinner, nine hours of reading and sleeping, and a two-hour four-course breakfast. Then, a welcome from Denis Bustard, and a high-speed refuel in 45 minutes under a cold mid-afternoon sun. Then, a seemingly endless trudge against a 30-kt headwind, giving time for lunch, tea and dinner before reaching Baltimore at 02.29 local time. On shore at 3 a.m., into the Pontiac (which seemed to be a giant, after British cars) and back to a sleeping house at 5 o'clock.

I have included a brief log of those two Atlantic crossings. They make an interesting contrast with today's timetables:

	Distance (nm)	Flying time (hr.min)	Block speed (knots)	Wind (knots)
13/15 September 1945, eastbound				
Baltimore–Botwood	1,192	7.41	138	+3
Botwood–Foynes	1,761	11.22	170	+35
Foynes–Poole	294	1.57	153	+13
27/28 September 1945, westbound				
Poole–Foynes	294	2.46	106	−34
Foynes–Botwood	1,761	15.41	105	−25
Botwood–Baltimore	1,192	9.15	106	−30

29

Planning Bermuda

Back in Washington, nine months after Chicago and with the war finally over, the cauldron of international air transport was bubbling. My principal task was to help fashion an agreement between the chief protagonists.

With a new government in London, Lord Swinton's Chicago experience had been lost, and so had his head-on collision with Adolf Berle, who now US Ambassador to Brazil. There was still the prospect of a major clash, because the UK and USA continued to pursue divergent policies.

The Freedoms of the Air (five, evolved in London in 1943, expanded to eight at Chicago) were being growled and worried over. Freedoms 6 and 7 have rarely been sought, and No 8 (cabotage) has hardly ever been granted. The real problem was No 5, the right of Airline A to pick up traffic in country B and take it to country C. The other major bone of contention was rigid regulation of service frequency. It was all complex, academic and largely unworkable, and merely a way of generating not light but heat.

After Chicago, the USA signed up as many bilateral agreements as it could. All were based on a 'free-for-all', the logical end to which was 'survival of the fittest'. The UK did the same, but based on rigid control. The result in this case was that it would bolster up the inefficient airline and deny the better carrier the extra traffic it generated. Worse, each policy attracted its own clique, to form two rigidly opposing blocs.

I spent many hours talking with Garrison Norton and Stokely Morgan at the State Department, and with Welch Pogue at the CAB. I spent even longer talking with Rex Winster, with Dick Hildred and George Cribbett at the MCA, John Cheetham at the Foreign Office and Wilfred Bigg at the Colonial Office. Gradually I began to see daylight.

I told London that the USA would welcome a fresh conference, as soon as an outline agenda could be agreed. A problem remained: the location. Obviously, it could not be Washington or London. The Canadians were likewise too involved. Geneva would embarrass the committees because of the League of Nations. But what about Bermuda? It was a pleasant location, a British Colony near to the United States, with its main airport an American base built by the Americans for their own defence.

I told Lord Halifax and Roger Makins that London would agree Bermuda, preferably in November 1945. They welcomed the idea. On 2 October 1945 I lunched with Bill Burden, Morgan and Pogue at the Metropolitan Club. They said Bermuda would be fine. From then on I was 'piggy in the middle', listening to Morgan extolling the advantages of untrammelled freedom, and reading decoded telegrams from Cribbett stressing the need for rigid controls. Street's imprint remained, though he had gone to the Allied Control Commission in Germany.

Suddenly a wider mind entered the fray. Lord (John Maynard) Keynes was 62. Tall and distinguished, and with a full drooping moustache, JMK had come to discuss the possibility of a huge US loan to Britain. I met him at an Embassy cocktail party. We talked about the civil-aviation conference. He was concerned lest a squabble should scupper the prospects of the United Kingdom receiving the enormous dollar loan.

He asked me to call on him in the Willard, where the 9th Floor had been taken over by the UK Treasury delegation under Frank Lee, with whom I had played tennis at Brentwood before the war. Lord Keynes invited me to meet him on 19 October. His grey suit and tie matched his moustache. We talked for two hours. At one point we digressed: his father and my grandfather had been 'up at Cambridge' together, in the 1870s. He went on, 'He's 93, and still lives in Cambridge . . . I do too.' Sadly, JMK was to die six months later, before his father.

He came to the problems of aviation with an open mind. He was intensely interested in the sharp divergence between the national viewpoints. He was scandalised by the Air Ministry's rigid attitude: 'Instead, let us go for regulated competition, and as much freedom as possible to build up traffic. That must always be to the greatest benefit of those who travel. The customers are the people to be considered. That is the only way to run a business.' Of course, he was right.

He asked me to see him again on the 25th, and bore me off to lunch with Makins at Apartment 22, 2009 Wyoming Avenue. He had talked with the State Department, and was almost as incensed with their 'devil take the hindmost' policy as he was with the British attitude. He also asked me to help him draft a telegram home expressing his views. He said, 'One thing is clear. We must arrange that less-committed people on both sides get round the table.'

On 1 June 1945 PanAm's monopoly on transatlantic flights had been ended when permission was given to AOA (American Overseas Airlines) and TWA to compete. On 23 October I took my place on a dais at National Airport to celebrate the naming of *Flagship America*, AOA's first DC-4. A military band, in powder blue, struck up 'I'm just wild about Harry', as Mrs Truman took her seat. After a brief speech by General Hal Harris, AOA's President, the First Lady stepped forward and, with silver scissors, cut the ribbon in AOA colours to release a bottle of California champagne. It swung against the DC-4's polished nose with a loud 'bonk' and bounced. Tess Truman was not disconcerted. She caught the bottle on the rebound, and let it swing again. She then caught the bottle by the neck and smashed it against the nose. A large dent appeared in the DC-4. At last, after a succession of devastating forehand drives, there was a splintering crash. By this time the nose was stove right in. We all cheered; it seemed appropriate.

The band struck up a familiar melody. According to the following day's *Washington Herald Tribune*,

> 'As scheduled, they burst into the strains of "America" . . . Next thing, Britain's Civil Air Attaché, hearing his own national anthem, snapped to attention. The distinguished group, including the Irish Minister, followed suit. Major Woods, AOA's Press Agent, sniffed disaster. Being of Irish descent himself, he dashed to the bandleader and whispered "For Jesus sake, play the national anthem for Eire." The reply was "We ain't got the music". Then, in a whisper that carried 100 yards, "What the Hell's the anthem for the Irish Free State?"'

'"Honest, we don't know this diplomatic stuff." With a despairing look at all the silk and brass on the platform, Woods growled "Give em 'Come back to Erin'." He stood to attention while Eire's Minister, the Hon. Robert Brennan, stood up and, with frozen fingers, the band played "Kathleen Mavourneen".'

Only later did I learn that the words include '. . . we must part . . . it may be for ever', which are hardly appropriate for a new air service! Eventually, the DC-4 was towed away to be fitted with a new nose so that it could make the very first commercial flight from Washington to England. The 14 passengers just had to wait. As for the platform VIPs, we were keeping the cold out with so much Scotch whisky and Irish whiskey that nobody any longer cared.

Despite its battering, the DC-4 made it to Hurn, by way of Gander and Rineanna, in 14 hr 5 min. It had a long career. It had been built at Douglas Santa Monica as No 27,353 and delivered to the USAAF as a DC-4E-15-DO with serial 44-9127. It was then registered as civil aircraft N90901, and on 16 May 1945 delivered to AOA. Almost ten years later it was one of a batch bought by Saudi Arabia, becoming HZ-AAW. In 1964 it appeared on the British register as G-ASRS, and in July 1964 went to Belgium as OO-FAI. It may well have gone on after that.

Amidst much toing and froing, on 10 November I went to National Airport to meet my new Prime Minister, Clement Attlee, who had arrived for talks with President Truman. He had flown non-stop from Northolt in an RAF Skymaster (C-54B), serial EW999 (Wg Cdr E.C. Fraser). I was interested to learn that it had taken 20 hr 2 min, so our Liberator record still stood. In all, the RAF received 11 Skymasters, which in 1946 had to be returned under the Lease-Lend agreement.

On the following Monday I was called for talks with the Prime Minister, the Lords Halifax and Keynes and Roger Makins. At Keynes' instigation, I expounded the value of a 'regulated competition' approach, as a more liberal British view which would

After receiving a new nose, DC-4 Flagship America *departed for Hurn, England.*

make it difficult for the USA to stick to a 'free for all'. The PM nodded. He had no views on the matter, which I gathered was quite normal.

Meanwhile, after a prolonged search, the Masefields finally found a roomier house available to rent. Well furnished, 1510 Emerson St NW belonged to a Col Mills, who had been posted to the Army Air Force complex at Dayton, Ohio. We moved in at lunchtime on 31 October 1945.

The torrid summer gave way to a beautiful and soothing fall, the trees of Washington turning red and bronze and gold in colours more vivid than I had ever seen. After early frosts in October, the city moved into a true Indian Summer in early November. The mornings were misty, as they had been 200 years previously when Indians stole in on early settlers.

By this time our proposal had been agreed in both Washington and London that a Civil Aviation Conference should be held in Bermuda in mid-January 1946. I was asked to go to Bermuda to make the necessary arrangements.

30

Bermuda

O n 20 December 1945 I drove from the Embassy to BOAC's Washington office, picked up Ross Stainton and drove to Baltimore's Marine Terminal to fly to Bermuda. On the sponson of G-AGCA *Berwick*, Ross introduced me to Capt. Denis I. Peacock, who in 1928/9 had studied Engineering at Trinity College, Cambridge. Denis said 'I need four more for the Captain's table for lunch. I select them as they board. You get a better idea than from the passenger list.' He was optimistic. His lunch companions numbered just two; all the rest were airsick.

We took off at 11.20. By the time we reached Bermuda 4½ hours later it was dark. I sat in the cockpit between the pilots, facing the mass of glowing instruments. Behind us a green curtain shut out the brightly lit flight deck, where two navigators, two radio officers and two flight engineers were busy at their desks. We circled over the lights of Hamilton, lined up along the flare path along Little Sound, and alighted in a sheet of spray. A BOAC launch brought us to the quay at Darrell's Island.

Despite the fact that night had fallen, I was entranced by the vivid colours all around us: deep blue water lapping on the pink coral shore; green foliage, purple oleanders, scarlet hibiscus, red poincianas and poinsettias, pink walls, and white roofs overhung by purple bougainvilleas. There was a soft warm breeze of tropical magic and serenity. Motor cars were forbidden. A lot of this magic came with the flying boats, and much has died with them.

Through Customs and across the lagoon, first to Eugene O'Neill's waterside house to land passengers for the Belmont Manor Hotel. Then past Hinson Island, to tie up at the Aeroplane Ferry Quay on Front Street, at Bermuda's capital, Hamilton. At the New Windsor Hotel on Queen Street I found Rex Winster, George Cribbett, Ned Dunnett and John Cheetham, engaged in inconclusive preliminary talks with the Canadian delegation. They were having a stiff drink, after a heavy afternoon during which Cribbett had proved dogmatic and inflexible.

I left them to it, and by BOAC launch returned to the Belmont Manor. Yes, they would be delighted to organise a big conference in January. They offered 60 to 70 rooms, a pool and an 18-hole golf course.

I returned to the New Windsor, and dined with the two teams. The UK team included Ronnie McCrindle of BOAC and Godfrey Boyd-Shannon of the Dominions Office. With them was the Acting Governor, Bill Addis. They were all morose, because the Canadians were being even tougher than the British. After dinner we talked until 04.00 about the problems the Anglo-American Conference must address.

Then, up early for a dawn take-off in *Berwick*, this time under Capt. Craig. We battled a north-easterly gale, and the 712 nautical miles to Baltimore took 7¼ hours. We landed at dusk, having made good an average speed of only

98 knots. I boarded an RAF Beech Expeditor (FR879) and made Washington in 25 minutes.

Then joyfully home to Emerson St, for the Masefields' first peacetime Christmas in seven years. It was like a fairytale: icy blue sky, nine inches of crisp snow, lights twinkling on Christmas trees, a magnificent snowman in the garden – sorry, 'front yard' – and a wreath on the door. The air was so dry, if you shook hands with a visitor you got an electric shock. I expect we shocked Babs Babington-Smith and Gaby Wellford (from MAP days, now at the Embassy), who spent Christmas with us.

After 'the holiday season' we got down to serious planning. Everyone rejoiced when a telegram announced that the UK delegation would be led by Sir Henry Self. He had been Director-General of the British Air Commission before he went to the MAP in 1942. He came back to Washington, serving briefly on the Combined Raw Materials Board, before returning to the Ministry of Civil Aviation.

He arrived on 8 January 1946, amazingly tall and lean, clad in a long grey cardigan, and pulling at an ancient pipe. He had a shy smile, and a flute-like voice which spoke with gentle authority. We lunched together on the 9th, and then talked with Lord Halifax and Roger Makins. At dinner he said to me, 'You and Lord Keynes' – he generously put it that way – 'made such a to-do about "no hard-liners" at the proposed meeting with our American friends that I got shot over here before I've had even one day in my new Ministry. I think you're right, rigid rationing just won't do – though we'd better play hard-to-get.'

Next day I returned to Bermuda, in *Bangor*. We had a tailwind and did it in 4½ hours. I walked up to the Belmont Manor, looked out from Room 203 over the

Sir Henry Self and Ronnie McCrindle.

Great Sound, and watched night fall as suddenly as if a gas light had been turned down. I spent next day setting up the conference, and met the UK delegation: Self, Wilfred Bigg, Cheetham, McCrindle, Crudge, and Maurice Bathurst from the Solicitor-General's office.

They had flown to Bermuda's Kindley Field in a well-worn Liberator, but times were changing. This was the swan-song, not only of such converted bombers but also of the flying boats. The Constellation was coming into service. On the 14th, the first of PanAm's new stars arrived at Kindley Field with the US delegation, together with the Press – and also with Pat, who came for a brief visit. The L-049 covered the 670 nautical miles from New York in 2 hr 22 min, a block speed of 284 kt, or 326 mph. I went by BOAC launch to the island of St George's, to meet them all and ferry them 12 miles back.

On arrival, while the Americans were simply swept through Customs, Pat – a British subject, arriving on British soil – was made to answer dozens of questions. 'My answers were carefully filled in on a long form, which I was asked to sign,' she said later, ' I took out my fountain pen. It was my first flight in a pressurised aeroplane, and when I took the cap off ink poured over their complicated form!'

Everyone repaired (on foot) to Fort Bell, the adjoining US Army base, to celebrate the arrival of the Constellation, the first commercial aeroplane to use one of the UK bases leased to the USA for 99 years. That evening the Belmont Manor laid on a cocktail party. Then the two delegations sat down for dinner, each on its own table. This highlighted the fact that the British delegation numbered 11, including Pat who acted as hostess, while the US delegation were 40 strong, plus eight wives. So, in chats over coffee, began the culmination of the work which had been started in 1943.

The 15th dawned bright and sunny, with a strong south wind blowing the huge banana bunches like soundless peals of bells. Bill Addis opened the first plenary session at 11.00 in the hotel ballroom, with ten British on the right, 40 Americans on the left, a dozen Press and the nine wives in the middle, and about a score of Bermuda high society.

Bill's welcome was followed by encouraging words from Sir Henry Self and his American counterpart, George P. Baker. Baker, 43, stocky and elegant, was later to be Dean of the Harvard Business School. I felt that, while things would be tough, Bermuda would be a conference of elaborate courtesy, unlike the brutal clash of Chicago.

At the Plenary Session, Self was elected Chairman, with Baker as Vice-Chairman. Then the Conference divided into five working groups: Traffic and Rates (Chairman, Self); Policy (Chairman, Self); routes (Chairman, Pogue); Drafting (Chairman, Morgan); and Ad hoc (Chairman, Dunnett).

The six UK delegates had to be spread thinly; Self, Hildred and Cheetham each served on two of the working committees, while Dunnett and I each served on three. Yet our lack of numbers was in fact an advantage, in that our team tended to speak with one voice, while sessions were often held up while US teams argued to resolve differences between themselves.

It was soon evident that the American hard-liners were Morgan, John Cooper, John Hickerson, Oswald Ryan, Clarence Young and James Smith. More liberal-minded

Welch Pogue; in 2001 he celebrated his 102nd birthday.

were Baker, Harold Bixby, John Leslie, General Julius Holmes, Garry Norton, Pogue and John Slater. We worked long hours, seldom finishing before 01.00, but the days were punctuated by pleasant breaks.

On the first day, at 15.30 everyone went to the opposite end of the island, to the US Navy base at King's Point. The officers were all in whites, and a good time was had by all, with the nine wives and newly arrived stenographers in great demand. Then, Cinderella's chime struck at 19.00, and it was back to dinner, and then more work.

On the next evening, the 16th, 30 horse-drawn carriages conveyed everyone to a reception in Government House in Pembroke, where Bill Addis deputised for Lord Burghley, who was home on leave. Then we clip-clopped back to the totally different world of air transport, with angry phrases such as 'cut-throat competition . . . restrictive blockage . . . Fifth Freedom' ringing in the warm air, as we sat in committee round the pool or deep in the hotel gardens.

After a week Pat returned to her family, involving six hours by flying boat, after having presided over a secretly arranged 56th birthday party for Henry Self. Next day we were disconcerted at breakfast to see a newspaper proclaiming **'AMERICAN SHOOTS SELF'**, until we read on to find that the non-fatal accident had happened to an officer at Fort Bell, who was cleaning his revolver.

We had come to Bermuda to present five points (which were in fact more severe than we were prepared to settle for), while the US stood on five points which were just the opposite. Both positions were unrealistic. Unlike Chicago, both sides knew this, and outside the conference the two teams were on excellent personal terms.

We spent time exploring the islands, which are actually the narrow tips of a mountain which rises 15,000 feet from the ocean floor, and just breaks the surface of the Atlantic. The main island is 35 miles long, but nowhere more than a mile wide. There is therefore little need for high-speed travel. One evening six US delegates climbed into a Victoria pulled by an ancient grey mare, and went to dinner in Hamilton. It is claimed that they returned with the mare *in the carriage*, being attended to by her black driver, with the six Americans led by Stokely Morgan between the shafts doing the pulling!

In the third week we were on the brink of final agreement when, on instructions from Washington, the US delegation suddenly turned intransigent, even on points which had already been agreed. By this time the tourist season was starting, and delegates began pairing up to release hotel rooms. The final heave from the Americans was met by an equally tough riposte by the British, and after 26 days the final differences were resolved on 10 February. The Agreement enshrined six fundamental points:

> Frequencies were not to be predetermined.
> Capacity provided would be related broadly to traffic demand.
> Rates would be voluntarily agreed through IATA.
> Routes were agreed for US and UK carriers to operate reciprocal services.
> Most important of all, Fifth Freedom rights would be unrestricted, the capacity being related primarily to the requirements of Third and Fourth Freedom traffic at a reasonable load factor.

The Bermuda Agreement was signed on 11 February 1946. It has stood the test of time. It finally blew away the restrictive attitude so dear to British thinking during the war, whilst setting a check on US aspirations to 'cut-throat competition'. Each side had moved far from its entrenched starting position.

I am certain that the Bermuda Conference could not have achieved more than it did. It deliberately gave freedom for manoeuvre. During the next 30 years this freedom was seized on by PanAm and TWA much more than by BOAC, with the result that the British share of Atlantic traffic declined. However, a major factor in this decline was because of inadequate capacity available to the British carrier.

Even today there are occasional rumblings of discontent, usually over fares. A few carriers have complained that their competition is swamping the route, but the Bermuda clause permitting capacity forcibly to be cut back has never been invoked.

Bermuda had, in fact, been long, intense and, on the whole, enjoyable. The conference made real progress, once the UK and US delegates had got to know each other and form lasting friendships. After the final celebratory dinner, at about 1 o'clock on the morning of the 12th, Stokely Morgan was roused from his bed by a combined US/UK team who – having borrowed nail varnish from John Leslie's pretty wife Jean – painted his toenails red. He was then, in his pyjamas, dumped in the pool, to the lusty singing of 'Oh, what a beautiful Morgan' and 'Red nails in the sunset'. He took it in thoroughly good part.

After Bermuda, the breath of fresh air which that conference brought was occasionally tainted by certain British attempts – some, to the disgust of the Americans, successful – to negotiate restrictive agreements. One wag commented, 'What could we expect, when our Self-less team was Cribbett, Cheetham and Dunnett.'

31

Constellations to the rescue

Pat had an extremely rough flight back from Bermuda to Washington, and when a steward invited her to visit the cockpit all she could say was 'Please leave me alone!' But she survived, and a few days later accompanied me to a cocktail party at The Mayflower given by Lord Halifax for Lord Burleigh. Burleigh happened to be a descendant of Henry Cecil, who had courted my great-great grandmother, the beautiful Elizabeth Masefield (née Taylor).

Pat recalls that party well:

> 'Peter and I were agog to meet Lord Burleigh, having many years earlier watched him win the hurdles in the Inter-Varsity Athletics. When I was introduced, I asked him how long he was staying in Washington. He replied that he was leaving next day for Bermuda. I excitedly told him how beautiful it was, with red pillar boxes, golden sand under palm trees, black policemen in – would you believe – British-type helmets . . . He held up a hand to stop the flow, and said, "My dear, I *know*; I'm the Governor." As we left, Peter said, "I really think that you believe a brick a day keeps the doctor away."'

My own return to Washington had been idyllic. I was sad to know that the great Boeing flying boats were about to be withdrawn. In fact, the end came on 10 March 1946. I felt that the termination of services by the Boeing 314As was premature, because BOAC had nothing with which to replace them. Though slow, they had maintained a reliable and comfortable service between the USA and Britain and Bermuda.

I was equally sad to see all our careful wartime planning being frustrated by problems which were completely unforeseen. The most endemic was a lethargy which quite quickly replaced the frantic effort of wartime Britain. Nothing like this happened in the United States, where the aircraft industry shrank to fit the reduced orders, but continued to work like beavers (and has done so ever since). With few exceptions, British companies ceased to regard delivery dates as sacrosanct, and failed to comprehend that in peacetime the need to compete is as important as in war.

One of the exceptions to this attitude was the A.V. Roe company, part of the enormous Hawker Siddeley Group. Dynamic 'Dobbie' (R.H., later Sir Roy, Dobson) and his Chief Designer Roy Chadwick maintained a US-style pace throughout the firm's factories. I really believed that the Tudor would run on schedule, providing BOAC with a true transatlantic aeroplane – albeit a small one – by the end of 1945.

In fact, though the first Tudor made its first flight only slightly behind schedule on 14 June 1945, it was found to suffer from a number of unacceptable faults, mainly of an aerodynamic nature. Whereas Chadwick was unable to say why the Lancaster bomber was so exceptionally good, he was equally unable to say why the Tudor – a close relative – was so abysmally bad. A seemingly endless succession of design changes led to a final conference between BOAC and A.V. Roe on 11 March 1946, at which a further 343 modifications were demanded. Some were trivial, but there were many which were absolutely essential.

Accordingly, by the time that I returned to Washington from Bermuda, BOAC had essentially dismissed any version of the Tudor from their plans. With hindsight, one can see that no Tudor could ever have competed successfully against the Constellation and DC-6. The final, tragic, nail in its coffin was the crash of the prototype Tudor 2 on 23 August 1947, through carelessly mis-connected control cables. This accident killed Chadwick, the mainspring of the design team. By that time, a pro-American lobby had begun to grow within BOAC. Undoubtedly justified in 1946, in the absence of anything else, it was to become an attitude of mind, maintained for far too long, to the enormous and enduring detriment of the home industry.

Back in October 1945 BOAC had applied to the new Labour Minister of Civil Aviation, Lord Winster, for permission to buy five Lockheed Constellations. When this became known, most members of the British public were outraged. Could we not supply our national airline with British aircraft?

Unfortunately for British industry, BOAC's antipathy towards British aircraft was to be reinforced by serious problems with the British aircraft they did buy, notably the Comet and Britannia. This forced the British public to become reconciled to the repeated purchase of American aircraft which did not have faults: Constellation, Stratocruiser, DC-7C, Boeing 707, Boeing 737, Boeing 747, Lockheed TriStar, Boeing 767 and Boeing 777. The pro-American attitude within Britain's national airline became so ingrained that in the 1970s, when airlines hesitatingly began to buy European-made Airbuses, British sceptics would laughingly point them out, saying 'Another airline got it wrong!'

However, in 1946 the enormous long-term implications of the failure of the British industry to deliver the goods were not appreciated. Everyone was too busy trying to solve the immediate crisis. After 10 February 1946 the only BOAC transatlantic service was the old wartime Return Ferry Service from Prestwick to Montreal, using converted Liberators. These were neither suitable nor certificatable for use as civil airliners.

Something had to be done, and quickly. I discussed with Lockheed the possibility of a British company – the preferred choice was the Bristol Aeroplane Company, which was under-employed – being invited to build the Constellation for BOAC under licence, with Bristol Centaurus engines and British instruments and radio. This promised to be an even better aircraft than the original, especially as, at that time, the Constellation was suffering from often dangerous failures of the engines, cabin blowers and electrical system.

We named the proposed Centaurus-Constellation 'Project X'. In January 1946 I wrote a Paper on this for the Cabinet. I soon received a reply from Stafford Cripps, agreeing that a British-made Constellation was a great idea, but unfortunately we could not afford the dollars for the US content.

Imagine my amazement when, three weeks later, Ivor Thomas, the Parliamentary Secretary to the Ministry of Civil Aviation, rose to his feet in the House of Commons and blandly announced that it had been decided to buy the five Constellations requested by BOAC, made by Lockheed and purchased complete with American engines! I later learned that Cripps, who by now was Sir Stafford and Chancellor of the Exchequer, had sanctioned the considerable dollar expenditure on 4 February, just as he was writing to me that we could not afford the much more modest dollar costs for British-made and British-engined Constellations!

I was dispatched to Lockheed Aircraft at Burbank to oversee the deal. The Army Air Force flew me there in a C-117A Skytrooper (DC-3). The negotiations were almost entirely with Lockheed, though the five aircraft had been built as C-69s for the Army Air Force. Their constructor's numbers, USAAF serials and UK registrations were:

049–1975	USAAF C-69-5 42-94554	G-AHEJ *Bristol II*
049–1976	USAAF C-69-5 42–94555	G-AHEK *Berwick II*
049–1977	USAAF C-69-5 42–94556	G-AHEL *Bangor II*
049–1978	USAAF C-69-5 42–94557	G-AHEM *Balmoral*
049–1980	USAAF C-69-5 42–94559	G-AHEN *Baltimore*

BOAC's first crew qualified on the Constellation.

These aircraft had been constructed in 1945 for the US Air Transport Command. Though virtually complete, and on the flight line outside the factory at VJ-Day, they were included in the huge programme of cancellations announced within hours of the end of the war. Powered by 2,200-hp Wright Cyclone R-3350-35 engines, they had military interiors with four folding four-seat benches along the left side and 11 four-seat units on the right. They were equipped for a crew of seven, and were cleared to a take-off weight of 90,000 lb.

I arranged for all five to be ferried to Lockheed Aircraft Service Inc (LASI) at New York La Guardia. Here, over a period of two months, they were stripped out, thoroughly overhauled and passed out as new aircraft with interior furnishing as specified by BOAC. The military engines were replaced by civil-certificated Wright Cyclone C-18BA-1s, with direct injection, and there were many other changes to enable all five to be certificated as civil L-049 Constellations.

In those days a pleasant custom was to give airliners individual names, as had been done with ships. Three, of course, repeated the names of the famous Boeing flying boats. I don't know who chose the other two names, but it seemed strange to over-look Birmingham, Britain's second-largest city, in favour of an American city which was no longer on BOAC's route network.

The original sponsor of the 'Connie', Howard Hughes, at that time owned the airline TWA. The war disrupted his plan to leap ahead of all competitors with this very advanced aeroplane, and in the end TWA's deliveries were interspersed between those of BOAC, and later with PanAm, KLM, AOA and Air France. Lockheed were predictably frustrated by BOAC vacillation, but at last the interiors were arranged for only 43 passengers, with freight holds in front of and behind the passenger cabin.

On 1 June 1946 the first of BOAC's aircraft was at last ready. By this time Connies

I helped Capt. Percy check out the first Constellation for BOAC.

Arrival of Balmoral, *on the first Constellation service at Heathrow on 16 June 1946.*

had been flying the Atlantic for six months with PanAm and TWA, and several other airlines were using DC-4s. I went aboard *Baltimore* with Capt. J.J. Percy, and served as co-pilot on the first handling test. On the 16th I was aboard *Balmoral* on the first passenger flight, with Capt. W.S. May in command, reaching Heathrow in 11 hours 24 minutes. The rivals using DC-4s had to refuel either once or (usually) twice, taking around 25 hours.

Westbound, even the long-legged Constellation had to refuel. On 23/4 June I returned aboard the Press Flight, operated by *Bangor II*. Even with refuellings at Shannon and Gander, the experience was swift and relaxing in comparison with the Liberator. The journalists were favourably impressed, and so was Capt. Arthur Whitten Brown, my companion on one of the twin seats, who almost exactly 27 years previously had partnered John (later Sir John) Alcock on the first non-stop Atlantic flight.

Before taking up the Washington post, I had negotiated for the provision of a personal aircraft. Actually getting it took a year, but in July I was notified that it was at last on its way. Accordingly, I went to Congressional Airport, just outside Washington in Maryland, to brush up my flying. Compared with the United Kingdom, the simplicity of the paperwork was unbelievable. I just did four dual flights in Fairchild PT-19As (British name of a close relative, Cornell), one solo flight, showed them my A-Licence and was at once issued with an updated US Pilot Licence.

Soon afterwards my Percival Proctor V arrived by sea at Baltimore. The packing case was unloaded, and the aircraft erected by BOAC in their hangar at Friendship Airport. It bore British registration G-AHGN, and proudly displayed the British civil air ensign. On 24 July I formally took delivery of the first UK-registered civil aircraft ever to be based in the United States. I got in with John Burgess, a senior BOAC Captain, and he proceeded to check me out. I then flew solo to Washington National, and saw the Proctor tucked away in the American Airlines hangar.

Having my own aircraft was not only enjoyable but it was a valuable working tool. Between 26 July and 20 September I used it 20 times. On one occasion I flew for two days to get to California. By the time I reached Denver I was almost unable to either stand up or sit down, and I bought softer seat cushions.

At Lockheed Aircraft at Burbank I had serious talks with the great Gross brothers, Robert S. (Bob) and Courtland, and with designers Hall L. Hibbard and Clarence L. 'Kelly' Johnson, and assistant sales manager Roger Lewis (who was later to run mighty General Dynamics). They naturally wanted to sell Constellations, and to this end had devoted much effort to designing installations of alternative engines, the Pratt & Whitney Double Wasp and Bristol Centaurus. They even flew a Connie with the Pratt & Whitney engines.

Of course, they did not have any examples of the British engine, but they were most impressed by the Centaurus, and they were also deeply concerned at the repeated difficulties with the still immature Wright Cyclone 18. After my return to England at the end of 1946 I invited Lockheed to try for one last time to interest Bristol, as related in the next chapter.

In August 1946 Lord Winster announced that Britain was purchasing six Boeing Stratocruisers for use by BOAC. I had been advised about this some weeks

I posed the Proctor for this photo over some famous Washington landmarks.

previously, and so had the Boeing Airplane Company. I went to Seattle to discuss this second and much bigger dollar purchase. In Britain we still had nothing remotely comparable.

The Boeing 377 Stratocruiser was a civil version of the C-97 Stratofreighter/ Stratotanker, which in turn was a transport version of the B-50 Superfortress bomber. Compared with the bomber, the main difference was the enormous whale-like fuselage. The engines were 28-cylinder Pratt & Whitney R-4360 Wasp Majors, driving Curtiss or Hamilton propellers of nearly 17 feet diameter with four square-tipped hollow steel blades. The whole aircraft was by British standards incredibly complicated. Clearly, there were huge possibilities for technical trouble, but like all the big US firms Boeing could be relied upon to 'trample the problems to death' by sheer engineering manpower.

Through all these ramifications I was astonished that BOAC had shown little interest in the Canadair DC-4M with Merlin engines. As related in Chapter 19, this promised to be a wholly competitive pressurised airliner with a dollar content of no more than $200,000 per aircraft. In the event, while Trans-Canada bought a fleet and put them into service, BOAC did nothing until 21 July 1948, when an order for 22 was announced. They were given the name Canadair Argonaut. This order could have been placed three years earlier.

With Nigel Bicknell (centre) and my *Proctor, visiting Toronto.*

My last months in the American post were most enjoyable. By this time I was fortunate enough to know most of the District of Columbia's influential people, and I even knew my way around the tortuous Washington political scene. Sir Henry Self asked me to tour the US aircraft industry and report anything that might help our own ailing planemakers. The malaise in British industry was partly an attitude of mind, possibly in reaction to the end of the war, and it did not affect everyone. I doubt that my reports achieved much. For example, if in England the waiting time for a particular kind of steel forging was two years, it hardly helped to be told that in California such an item could be provided within hours.

With the work building up, I was fortunately allocated an assistant. Nigel Bicknell was an excellent choice. I also had a piece of sheer luck. Early one morning I got into the Proctor to fly up to Maine, for a convivial lunch with members of the local aero club. I taxied out at Friendship Airport, and felt a bump. I had run over a drain cover which had foolishly been left open, and this buckled the leg of the left landing gear. Sadly, I telephoned that I would have to postpone the trip. Had I taken off, I would have run straight into a hurricane, which unexpectedly moved into my intended path.

32

Back to London

After Washington, London in December 1946 seemed drab and austere; indeed, it appeared to have much in common with Siberia. Once again, and at Sir Henry Self's behest, I found myself in a previously non-existent post: the Ministry of Civil Aviation's Director-General of Long-Term Planning.

To some degree I was carrying on the work I had done with the Beaver. The difference was that this time the planning was real, and had more or less immediate effect. There were three main tasks, none of them straightforward. One was to try to jerk the war-weary British aircraft industry into producing the aircraft that had been proposed years earlier by the Brabazon Committee. Another was to assist the Air Ministry in the closing of most of the 1,000-plus wartime airfields, whilst ensuring that major cities were provided with modern civil airports. Not least, we had to help to establish the three airline corporations, BOAC, BEA, and BSAA.

By now my parents had retired to Eastbourne, to a commodious Edwardian house in the Meads district, large enough to continue storing our furniture. With a squeeze we went to live with them, while we looked for a place of our own. We next rented a furnished house in Cholmeley Park in Highgate, but after some nine months of

Pat with the family, soon after our return to England.

Rosehill has quite a complicated layout.

searching I found a large rambling property on the edge of an old sand quarry in Reigate, in Surrey. Called Spellbrook, it was run-down, but its potential was obvious. In particular, it had six bedrooms, which meant that our family (Pat by now was about to produce No 4, Oliver) would not have to move again. Somehow, with a mortgage supplemented by borrowing from both sets of parents, we found the then-astronomic price of £7,000. Renamed Rosehill, this house has been our home ever since, with the overgrown quarry banks transformed over the years into a 2½-acre terraced garden with breathtaking variations in the vertical plane.

My London office was at the western tip of the island block of buildings at Aldwych. Before the war it had been the Gaiety Theatre. As we settled in, I went exploring with Cribbett, who by now was Sir George and the Ministry's Assistant Secretary. We came upon a secret staircase leading down from what had been the office of the managing director. We followed it down, and found it ended in the star's dressing room. This delightful evidence of past naughtiness was lost when the building was replaced by English Electric's Marconi House.

Post-war London was sprinkled with offices for new ministries. For a while we were relocated in Ariel House, not the original office block of that name in Kingsway but a faceless new office block in Theobalds Road, about half a mile to the north. After a brief spell there I was moved again, this time to Thames House South, part of the impressive head office of the chemical giant ICI, overlooking the river.

At once I was immersed in the ramifications of the British aircraft industry. This industry had done an outstanding job in the war, but now it appeared to be crippled by shortages of materials, electrical power cuts, pettifogging arguments, small-minded political manoeuvring, and a pervading air of lethargy. Even A.V. Roe appeared to have lost their way, badly hit by failure of the Tudor, and the only bright spots appeared to be de Havilland, which had so many aircraft, engine, propeller and missile projects I almost lost count, and Vickers-Armstrongs (Aircraft), which again had a profusion of dynamically managed programmes.

For the immediate future I still cherished the naive belief that Bristol could be persuaded to become a third bright spot, by going into production with 'Project X', the Centaurus Constellation. The enormous factory of the Bristol Aeroplane Company at Filton was almost empty. It was still assembling a small batch of Brigands, an attack aircraft made obsolete by jets, and civil Type 170 Freighters. Most of the design staff were trying to solve problems with the huge Brabazon, which was clearly underpowered and increasingly looked as though it should never have been started.

Just as I returned to the UK, in November 1946, a book about Bristol aircraft was published. The Introduction ended with a eulogy of the Brabazon, which concluded, 'With such enterprise and energy in our midst there is no ground to doubt the future prosperity of our island.' The book did not mention that the prospects for that aircraft, whose first-flight date had slipped by two years, were bleak, nor that in the board-room and design offices the main effort was devoted to stabbing rival staff in the back.

I became only too aware of all this, but no other British company had the spare capacity to take on 'Project X'. Bob Gross volunteered to send over a small but high-level team to try to motivate Bristol. They were led by Vice-President Courtland S. Gross, and included Hall L. Hibbard and 'Kelly' Johnson. They brought drawings of the latest Constellation, the L-749.

They came to me at Reigate, where we studied how the Centaurus 661 was installed in the Ambassador. We then managed to squeeze all the Lockheed men and drawings

G-AGRC, the first production Tudor, flew in January 1946 but never entered service.

into my Pontiac. (Against all the odds, I had managed to have the car shipped back to England, where post-1939 cars were a rarity, and American ones absolutely forbidden, except for foreign diplomats.) We then set off for Bristol to talk business.

By this time Britain was in the grip of a memorably severe winter, far removed from what the Lockheed men were used to in California. The normally pleasant journey to Bristol was a struggle through deep snow drifts. At last we arrived, and put up at the Grand Hotel, the best in Bristol. Like most households in the country that had just won the war, they had no coal. In a freezing corridor I knocked on the door of 'Kelly' Johnson, to discuss design details. I found him in bed, fully dressed and wearing an overcoat and woolly hat.

Unfortunately, and to Lockheed's astonishment, we were up against the abysmal lethargy of the Board of the Bristol Aeroplane Company. The potential first customer, BOAC, was actively hostile towards having the British engine, while the British Government was on the one hand bleating that dollars were like gold dust, and on the other making no effort to assist, or even to approve, Lockheed's plan to develop Constellations made in Britain with British engines. They kept repeating that there were no dollars available, whilst at the same time spending them on US-built aircraft, the next buy being for the Stratocruiser. This anti-British attitude was to set the pattern for the future of Britain's national airline. Had a Centaurus Constellation had a real effort put behind it, it could have become the preferred version for all non-American customers.

In fact, just as we talked, Bristol were taking on the Medium-Range Empire (Brabazon III) aircraft which we had planned in 1943. Having done nothing about it at the time, BOAC had at last recognised that, instead of simply buying American, they might show an interest in home industry, and that the MRE could be made into an outstanding aircraft. Accordingly, in January 1947 the Ministry of Supply issued Specification 2/47 and invited tenders. Eight submissions came across my desk, their evaluation made more difficult by the fact that both the airline and the competing manufacturers kept moving the goalposts.

From the start, in the absence of Project X, Bristol was the favoured company, though their sluggish progress with the Brabazon hardly filled me with confidence. In Texas, Convair were building the B-36, of Brabazon size and many times more complicated, at the rate of eight a month. In October I was one of a group which visited Filton to discuss their MRE proposal, the Type 175. It resembled a single-fin Constellation, but with a lower gross weight, less fuel, and carrying a mere 36 passengers over significantly shorter ranges.

I kept pointing out that, with four Centaurus engines, one could aim much higher. Gradually we made the Type 175 more capable, and it became obvious – not least to Whitney Straight, who had joined BOAC as Managing Director – that we ought to start considering a switch from the Centaurus, which was in the 2,500-hp class, to Bristol's own Proteus turboprop, which was intended to give some 3,500 hp.

Bristol had been almost the last British firm to get into the gas-turbine business. When it did, it concentrated on turboprops, in a style which sacrificed the gas turbine's basic simplicity in order to achieve fuel economy. Their first engine, the Theseus, even incorporated a heat exchanger. For the next, the Proteus, Chief Engineer Frank Owner went all out to achieve economy by aiming at a higher pressure ratio, with a complicated mixture of an axial compressor followed by two successive centrifugal compressors.

The root of the problem was that the Proteus had been designed to power the redesigned Brabazon 2, and also the even larger Saro Princess flying boat, which was to have ten, in the form of four Coupled Proteus and two singles. With both these monster aircraft, the designers got themselves into a ship mentality, with the engines installed in a kind of engine room in the wings, with long shafts to drive the propellers.

In turn, this led to the Proteus being designed back-to-front, with the air ducted from the leading edges of the wings to the entry to the axial compressor *near the back of the engine*. The air travelled *forwards* through this compressor, was turned through 90° *eight times* in the centrifugal compressors, and finally turned back to the rear to pass out through the combustion chambers and turbines.

The first Proteus was started on the testbed on 25 January 1947. It was intended to weight 2,600 lb and give 3,200 hp. Instead, it weighed 3,200 lb, and as for power, I will quote from *Not Much of an Engineer* (Airlife), the biography of Sir Stanley Hooker. He joined Bristol two years later, in January 1949. He recalled 'I went to see the Proteus on test and was horrified. Even at half power of 1,500 hp the outside combustion chamber casings were glowing red . . . this abysmal engine sank ever deeper in the morass, breaking its compressor blades, turbine blades, bearings and other parts, even at totally inadequate powers well below 2,000 hp.'

Even as late as 1954 the original Proteus was causing catastrophes. In February of that year the second Britannia was giving a demonstration to a delegation from the

The Proteus turboprop had a complicated reverse-flow arrangement, to suit the Brabazon and Princess.

important airline KLM. All the power to drive the propellers was transmitted through a single gearwheel. This small pinion on the starboard inner engine suddenly stripped its teeth. Relieved of any load, the turbine instantly oversped and disintegrated, causing an oil fire which could not be extinguished. Test pilot Bill Pegg was forced to put the aircraft down on mud flats on the banks of the River Severn, a mile from the Filton runway. The aircraft became a write-off.

Hooker redesigned the Proteus, to produce a reliable engine with a take-off power of more than 4,000 hp, despite being 12 inches shorter and 1,000 lb lighter. From 1955 I was to have much to do with this engine (see Chapter 35). By that time both the original applications, the Brabazon 2 and Princess, had vanished from the scene. Most unfortunately, when Hooker did his redesign, both these aircraft were still active programmes, so he had to retain the complicated reversed-flow layout.

This made the engine much clumsier than it need have been for any normal aircraft, such as the Bristol 175. Unexpectedly, it also caused a further problem which was almost to wreck the Britannia programme, as I will relate later. In 1947 nobody could predict this, and the turboprop clearly appeared to offer a better performance than the Centaurus, quite apart from replacing high-octane petrol (gasoline) by paraffin (kerosene). Accordingly, by 1948 I was urging Bristol to switch over from the Centaurus.

On 5 July 1948 the Ministry of Supply placed an order for three Bristol 175s with Centaurus engines. The second and third were to be capable of conversion to Proteus power. In October 1948 I joined the Type 175 working party a second time, to think again how this aircraft should be arranged. It was still markedly inferior to the imminent DC-6B and Super Constellation L-1049, to say nothing of the Stratocruiser.

At this series of meetings BOAC agreed to order 25 Type 175s, each with a gross weight of 118,000 lb with the Centaurus or 119,000 lb with the Proteus. By this time the maximum seating capacity had gone up to 64, and, while BOAC nitpicked over the contract, the weight went up to 130,000 lb and maximum seating to 83. At last we were in the same ballpark as our American rivals. True to form, BOAC still procrastinated, and did not sign the contract until 28 July 1949. By this time the Type 175 had been named Britannia, and I had moved from the Ministry to BEA.

Whereas it was an uphill struggle to persuade Bristol to do anything, the de Havilland enterprise was almost as dynamic as the best American companies. Unlike Bristol, they had taken the sensible step of forming separate companies to make aircraft, engines and propellers, and by 1948 the propeller company was also beginning to get interested in guided missiles. They had also purchased the Airspeed company, which had substantial factories at Portsmouth and Christchurch. Airspeed became a mere operating division and then lost its identity altogether. Thus when I needed to discuss the Ambassador airliner, a contender for the Brabazon II specification (not to be confused with the monster Brabazon 2 aircraft), I did not go to Airspeed but to Hatfield.

At that time, by far the biggest programme at Hatfield was the D.H.106 Comet. The first jet-propelled airliner in the world, this was a really bold step forward. To me it was astonishing that such competitive companies as Lockheed and Douglas, with far more design engineers than any British aircraft company, were showing no interest whatsoever in building a viable civil transport with jet engines. De Havilland already had an adequate engine, the 5,000-lb Ghost, and they proposed to fit four of these buried inside the Comet's wing roots. Almost the whole wing was to form integral tankage for the kerosene fuel. The circular-section fuselage was to seat 36 passengers. With a small stretch the Comet 1A could be a 44-seater, with 11 seat rows. With more powerful engines, the fuselage might be stretched much further.

On Wednesday 11 February 1948 I went to Hatfield to discuss this exciting programme. It was the only really 'far out' challenge posed by the wartime Brabazon Committee, and the de Havilland Board had never hesitated. What they were doing was so far ahead of the rest of the world that they were keeping the entire programme very much under wraps. Apart from the fact that they were building the Comet to meet the Brabazon IV specification, hardly anything leaked out.

On 11 February one of the subjects we discussed was whether refuelling in flight would be a viable procedure for civil airliners. It was taken for granted that, compared with existing piston-engined aircraft, the Comet would burn fuel more rapidly, and would thus tend to have a shorter range. Our general opinion was that flight refuelling should, if possible, be avoided. We had no idea that eventually jet aircraft would be able to fly airline sectors far beyond the range of any piston-engined airliner.

Another possible problem with jet airliners was that they would lack the high-speed slipstream blown back across the wing from the propellers of older aircraft. Accordingly, they appeared likely to suffer from very long take-off runs. In the USA some airliners operating from hot and high airports were already being fitted with jettisonable rockets (the Americans mis-named this development 'Jato', from jet-assisted take-off). Nobody at de Havilland liked the idea, but they were already designing a neat rocket engine, the Sprite, to boost Comet take-offs. This was to be mounted permanently between the pair of turbojets on each side. It weighed a mere 350 lb empty. It could be filled with liquid propellants, when for a weight of 975 lb it would give 5,000 lb extra thrust for about 11 seconds. For safety reasons I was not enamoured of the idea, and, in the event, it was not fitted to production Comets.

Another of the great British aircraft companies that was determined to lead the world was Vickers-Armstrongs (Aircraft). Sadly, at the start of 1948 its Chief Designer, Rex Pierson, had died. His obvious successor was 'GRE', later Sir George Edwards. He was one of the most impressive people in the entire British planemaking industry, whom I had known and admired since I was up at Cambridge. Seemingly laid back and taciturn in manner, he led a big design team as 'a happy ship' in the American style, determined to beat the competition.

At the end of the war he and Pierson had completely transformed the Wellington bomber into the VC.1 (Vickers Commercial) Viking in a matter of weeks, so that Britain at least had something in the class of the DC-3/Dakota (which had flown in 1935). He had then at once turned to designing the completely new VC.2, to our Brabazon IIB specification. Vickers named it the Viceroy.

The VC.2 prototype, the V.630, registered G-AHRF and later bearing Ministry serial VX211, was the first turboprop airliner in the world. It began its fight-test programme on 18 July 1948. By this time there was no such thing as a Viceroy in India, so the name had been changed to Viscount. Nobody could then have foreseen that the aircraft would be so good that it would find customers in the United States, where the name 'Viscount' was as inappropriate as 'Viceroy' would have been. In the 1950s Capital Airlines were to issue their staff with stickers saying 'PRONOUNCED VI-COUNT'.

Vickers had studied the use of two Centaurus or four Armstrong Siddeley Mamba, Napier Naiad or Rolls-Royce Dart turboprops. Though the Dart – named after the river – appeared to be somewhat crude and retrograde, in comparison with the more advanced Mamba and Naiad, I later decided that Pierson and Edwards had been right to have had faith in the Derby company. The V.630 had four Darts rated at 990 hp each. In 1948 we could see more powerful Darts in the future, but none of us had an idea that the Dart would be able, eventually, to offer more than 3,200 hp.

Of course, the V.630 was pressurised. It was designed for 24 passengers, with a maximum of 32, but even in 1948 Rolls-Royce had begun to test Darts at around 1,500 hp. This clearly opened the way to a stretched Viscount, with its gross weight increased from the original 38,000 lb to 50,000 lb. In turn this would give the aircraft the same 47-seat capacity as the rival Airspeed Ambassador, the other Brabazon II aircraft.

There was, however, a significant difference. Like other airliners of the day, the Ambassador had piston engines, and vibrated through the sky at 240 mph. The Viscount had turboprops, and promised to give its passengers a ride almost 100 mph faster, and so smooth that they could stand coins on their edges on the seat-back tables. However, the turboprop was still a high-risk engine, and as an insurance I concurred with the decision to order a fleet of Ambassadors. On 5 January 1948 Airspeed received an ITP (instruction to proceed) with ordering materials and signing sub-contracts prior to 'signature of the contract for 30 for BEA on 30th April'. In fact the contract was not signed until 22 September 1948, and it was for only 20 Ambassadors.

To say that this order was a blow to Vickers is an understatement. At the same time, I was impressed by the Ambassador, which was basically a fine aeroplane. Its high wing put the cabin floor only about four feet above the ground, and of course gave every passenger a perfect view, unrestricted by a wing. Sadly, it suffered from various problems, – a heavy landing which could tear out both engines, and a test wing which proved to be slightly too weak – and also from the industry's lethargy.

G-AKRD, the second prototype Ambassador, flew in August 1948.

These problems stemmed from Airspeed's puny size, and inexperience with powerful metal aircraft, exacerbated by de Havilland's takeover of the company. The Ambassador's chief designer, Arthur Hagg, quarrelled bitterly with Francis St Barbe and the de Havilland designers, led by Bishop, and retired in a huff to design and build boats at Thames Ditton. Bishop's team, busy with the Comet, showed little interest in their inherited piston-engined aircraft, and short-sightedly failed to follow up several enquiries from foreign and British independent carriers. Indeed, Sales Director Phillip Gordon-Marshall (who later worked for me in Bristol) was recalled to Hatfield just as he was on the point of selling 12 Ambassadors to Trans-Australia Airlines. Astonished, they bought Convair 240s instead. Thus, the 20 for BEA was the only batch built.

I therefore gave up studying stretched versions with four Darts or Naiads. I had no idea that I would soon join BEA and fume with impatience until the Ambassador (first flown in July 1947 and due for delivery from January 1951) first carried passengers in March 1952. For post-war Britain, this was par for the course.

When staying with my parents, I usually caught the 7.15 a.m. train from Eastbourne. At Brighton Sir Henry Self, the MCA's Permanent Secretary, would come aboard, and we would get much work done during the journey. At Waterloo I had the privilege of sharing his official car to Ariel House. I considered him the best of all the MCA officials He fought a war with Sir Cyril Musgrave, Permanent Under-Secretary in the Ministry of Supply, who insisted, 'Only I can order civil airliners'. Sir Henry proclaimed 'Airlines ought to be able to order their own aircraft', but it took until 10 January 1949 for his commonsense view to prevail. I was concerned when, in July 1947, he retired, to be succeeded by Sir Arnold Overton. In 1953, when I was with BEA, the Minister, at that time Lord Pakenham, appointed Sir Arnold to the airline's board.

De Havilland's long-overdue replacement for their Rapide was the Dove. This beautiful eight-passenger aircraft was produced with typical Hatfield urgency, and 542 were sold. However, many of these were executive or military aircraft, and in my opinion there was still a clear need for a simpler replacement for the Rapide costing about £10,000 instead of the £20,000 of the Dove. I discussed the matter with nine companies, and seven produced brochures, but nothing resulted. In my next job I had an immediate personal interest in this matter. I tried again to get a utilitarian Rapide replacement, but nobody was interested until, in the mid-1960s, John Britten and Desmond Norman built the Islander.

At the opposite end of the scale, throughout 1948 I met with the Saunders-Roe design team, both in London and on the Isle of Wight, where they were beginning to erect the colossal S.R.45 flying boat. As noted earlier, this was to be powered by ten Proteus turboprops, and was potentially a great aircraft. Fully pressurised, it had two full-length decks, and was far more capacious than the Brabazon. Unfortunately, like the Brabazon it had been ordered by a Ministry, not by any commercial or military operator. I also had to devote much attention to the disappointing Tudor, which continued to simmer, with manifold problems, in the background.

Throughout my time at the Ministry I managed to fly a varied assortment of aircraft, some of them appearing in Appendix 1. On 28 June 1948 I flew Dove G-AJLV to Woodford to discuss the possibility of converting Tudor IIs into IVBs. My co-pilot was Peter Brooks. By an extraordinary chance, he had been at Chillon College some years after me, and in 1940 had joined the staff of *The Aeroplane*. He then became a Fleet Air Arm pilot, and a very capable glider pilot. Now he was a Technical Officer in the MCA. We became great friends, and were to work happily together in different jobs for many years.

Most of my work involved discussions, many of them over lunch, preparing Cabinet papers and masses of other documents, and visiting British factories. It was a welcome change to attend two meetings of the South Pacific Air Transport Council. For the 1947 SPATC meeting I accompanied my then Minister, Lord Nathan, and his wife. While in Australia I joined him in discussions with the Government in Canberra, and the airlines TAA, Ansett and BCPA. He got me to act as his *aide-de-camp*, in the course of which I flew him to various parts of Australia and Tasmania in a Gipsy Moth. A Minister of the Crown – a huge man, incidentally – being flown by an amateur pilot in an ancient biplane on official business was probably unique!

It was at about this time that I took Ted Heath (later Sir Edward, Prime Minister 1970–74) onto my staff at the Ministry. He had recently come out of the Army as a Lieutenant-Colonel, and needed experience with the Civil Service, on his way eventually to a seat in Parliament. For our first meeting I took him out to lunch (we ate whale meat, all that was available at the restaurant), and I liked him immediately. We worked well together during my final months at the Ministry – and I'm glad to say that in later years, during my time with Beagle, we were able to share some rather more interesting menus!

In November 1948 the new Minister, Frank (later Lord) Pakenham, asked me to lead the SPATC delegation, this time to New Zealand. The meetings were held in our hotel in Wellington, the St George's. One of the first decisions was reluctantly to agree that BCPA (British Commonwealth Pacific Airlines) could order DC-6s. Spending scarce dollars on American aircraft was just what our wartime planning had tried to avoid, but more than three years after the war the British industry had failed to produce anything with equal capability. However, New Zealand's Tasman Empire Air Lines had oceanic routes, notably to Suva (Fiji), which at that time could not be operated by landplanes. Accordingly, for two years they had studied the Short Solent flying boat. This was the ultimate development of the Sunderland/Sandringham family, with a wider hull and Bristol Hercules sleeve-valve engines.

In between SPATC Policy Committee meetings, we refined the specification of the Solent 4, with 2,040 hp Hercules 733 engines and greatly increased fuel capacity. It met all TEAL's severe requirements, and eventually they purchased four, beautifully appointed for 44 passengers. They later added a fifth, bought secondhand, and these aircraft gave good service, the last not being withdrawn until 1960 at the end of the flying-boat era.

I left New Zealand on 8 December. I continued eastbound, making useful visits to Lockheed, Douglas, Boeing and de Havilland Canada. I just managed to get back to London in time for Christmas. At last I felt I had adjusted things right: having lost a Wednesday out of my life going round the planet westbound in 1946, I had now had two Fridays on successive days going eastbound.

I also found that I had been asked to take on a new job.

33

The ailing airline –
but with a sparkle lurking

Like Topsy, British airlines 'just growed'. At first, in 1919, they tried to follow Winston Churchill's premature edict, 'Civil aviation must fly by itself'. Eventually the Government thought again, and on 1 April 1924 – April Fool's day, which in 1918 had also been the birth date of the Royal Air Force – all the infant carriers were merged into the State's 'chosen instrument', named Imperial Airways Ltd. It did not fly any passengers on that day: it was grounded by a strike of its pilots.

At that time airliners were limited in safe operating range to less than 500 miles (800 km). Imperial therefore built up a network of routes throughout Europe and the Empire (except across the Atlantic, which was far too wide), with landing grounds about 300 miles apart. In the 1930s the Government allowed a rash of smaller carriers to operate. However, contrary to its attitude towards shipping, it disliked enterprise in the sky. In August 1939 it passed an Act which forcibly merged Imperial Airways with the principal private carrier British Airways, to form British Overseas Airways Corporation (BOAC).

It began operations in 1940 – also on April Fool's Day. This is where I came in, and began planning the post-war scene. By this time the longest-ranged airliners could fly sectors up to about 2,000 miles. As outlined in earlier chapters, it was finally decided that there should be an intercontinental carrier (BOAC), an airline serving Latin America, and a third airline for European and UK domestic services.

The war delayed scheduled operations in Europe until 21 September 1944. The operator was No 110 Wing of the RAF. Part of No 46 Group, they began tentative services from Croydon with Dakotas. By VE-Day, 8 May 1945, this RAF unit was operating services to Paris, Brussels, Lyon, Marseille, Naples, Prague, Athens, Warsaw, Copenhagen and Oslo. On 4 February 1946 these services were taken over by the newly created British European Airways Division of BOAC, which was formed almost entirely from 110 Wing, the personnel being rehired as civilians. On 1 August 1946 this Division became the completely separate British European Airways Corporation (BEAC).

Appointed as Chairman of BEAC was railwayman Sir Harold Hartley. His Deputy was my Cambridge friend Whitney Straight. The Chief Executive was Gerard 'Pops' d'Erlanger, the former head of the ATA (the Air Transport Auxiliary, the large wartime team of ferry pilots) and an amateur pilot himself. In March 1947 Sir Harold and Whitney were appointed Chairman and Chief Executive of BOAC, respectively. 'Pops' became Chairman of what was increasingly being called just BEA, while John Henry Keeling and John Vincent Wood (who came from BOAC) were respectively appointed Deputy Chairman and Chief Executive.

The European airline had its main base at RAF Northolt, on the north-west outskirts of London. The terminal was a sprawl of 'prefabs' on the south side, beside the Western Avenue trunk road. Though unprepossessing, they were comfortable and well carpeted. Maintenance was done in the old RAF hangars on the north side of the airfield. The airline's head office had only recently been constructed as the Bourne School. This building had been commandeered and renamed Keyline House, because the airline's slogan was 'the key to Europe' and its logo a stylised key. Today this seems faintly childish.

Between January and April 1947 BEA progressively took over all the nine private British airlines. It thus operated a rag-bag of aircraft of 11 types, including a most uneconomic fleet of ex-*Luftwaffe* Ju 52/3ms, which were called the Jupiter class. Nearly 90 per cent of the traffic was carried by Dakotas, increasingly supplemented from September 1946 by newly built Vickers Vikings. By 1949 the three-engined Junkers had gone, the airline was seeking a 'Rapide replacement' (mainly to serve the Scottish islands), and it was looking forward to receiving 20 Airspeed Ambassadors from January 1951. As already established, the Ambassador was an attractive 47/49-seat high-wing aircraft, which promised to be competitive with the latest US types such as the Convair 240.

In my Ministry job I was painfully aware that BEA was far from being the world-beating and profitable carrier it was intended to be, despite its lack of commercial experience and the effects of six years of war. In the year ending 31 March 1949 BEA suffered five serious aircraft accidents, and it was thought encouraging that it had managed to reduce its operating deficit to £2,763,085, representing *a loss of 34 pence on each pound of expenditure*.

On 15 December 1948 it was announced that Chief Executive Wood, who was an extremely nice man, was suffering from a nervous breakdown, and that he would 'take an extended rest . . . his work will be taken over by the Chairman, Mr d'Erlanger, assisted by Mr Peter Masefield, who has been released by the Minister of Civil Aviation for this purpose'. I was on my way back from New Zealand, but nevertheless received a cable from Lord Pakenham asking me if I would take on the post of Assistant to the Chairman of what was then still officially BEAC. I knew that the airline was in trouble, and without hesitation accepted the challenge. My last day at the Ministry of Civil Aviation was Friday 21 January 1949, and I started at Keyline House on the following Monday.

I was delighted to move into the stimulating world of airline operation, where I felt that I belonged, but it was obvious that we had a mountain to climb. Most of the staff came from the pre-war independent airlines or from the RAF, and their collective morale was non-existent. To make matters worse, d'Erlanger had issued a Press Statement forecasting even worse results in the years ahead! Frank Pakenham asked for my opinion. I told him there were three major problems:

> We had a poor rate structure, with many totally uneconomic services being flown at very low load factors.
> We had to operate with fleets of obsolescent aircraft flown at uneconomic rates.
> We suffered from serious overmanning.

The situation seemed to improve as soon as I began to know the new Chairman, appointed on 14 March 1949. He was Marshal of the Royal Air Force Lord Douglas of Kirtleside. Sholto Douglas was a big man in every sense of the word. Almost his first words to me were, 'Together we're going to get this collection of people into a real team, and I know I can look to you to do your stuff.' For the next six years he was a tower of strength, and we never had a cross word.

On 31 July 1949 J.V. Wood finally resigned. He took a job in South America, where in April 1952 he and his wife were tragically killed in an air crash. On his departure I was appointed Deputy Chief Executive, but doing the job of Chief Executive. On 17 October 1949 I was appointed with a seat on the Board to fill that position, which had been vacant for ten months.

Running BEA was now largely up to me. Sholto took care of the politics, while I looked after the aeroplanes, and things got better from Day 1. On that day I was visited by 'Pops' d'Erlanger, who was eager to tell me what to do. He was a charming man, and he took pains to show me an enormous book he had put together. It was the BEA operating bible. Nobody could do anything whatsoever without looking it up in this vast tome. It was difficult to lift, but I took it from him and carefully placed it on the open coal fire in the Chief Executive's office. I really shouldn't have done this, but I got the message across.

The family (minus Oliver) enjoyed the Royal Aeronautical Society Garden Party at the Handley Page airfield at Radlett on 8 May 1949.

When I joined BEA the most important aircraft was the Viking.

In 1949 BEA was just hauling itself out of its totally uneconomic early years. Almost 64 per cent of its traffic was now carried in Vikings, 42 of which were in service, with three yet to come. Though closely related to the pre-war Wellington bomber, and with higher fuel consumption and smaller capacity (27 seats) than the Dakotas, they were slightly faster, with a mean block speed of 168 mph, though this largely reflected the fact that their average stage length was 358 miles, compared with only 166 miles for the Dakotas. Viking results were profoundly affected by the type's gradual maturity, serious faults becoming less common, and the TBO (time between overhauls) of the Bristol Hercules sleeve-valve engine rising from the initial 350 hours to a reliable 1,000.

The original backbone of the airline, the Dakotas, were in use as 21- or 28-passenger aircraft (24) and as freighters (6). They carried almost all the rest of the Corporation's traffic. All were outwardly similar, and powered by the Twin Wasp R-1830-92 engine, but they differed in detail so that they actually comprised 13 different versions. One of the first decisions I took was to cycle all 30 aircraft through Scottish Aviation at Prestwick, and bring them up to a common upgraded standard.

We called this the 'Pionair' class, and named them after British aviation pioneers. Among other things we put in standarised British instruments and radio. This enabled us to eliminate the need for a radio officer, which in turn allowed the front bulkhead to be moved forward, making room for 32 seats, whilst at the same time increasing leg room.

Just 1.5 per cent of the traffic was carried by the 20 Rapides. Excellent in the mid-1930s, these biplanes were hard hit by increased costs (for example, of landing fees and fuel) and despite fitting lighter VHF radio, making possible single-crew operation, their operating costs still greatly exceeded revenue. BEA had since 1948 sought to obtain a 'Rapide replacement'.

At the same time, it had been asked by the Minister of Supply to order the Marathon (designed by the defunct Miles firm and built by Handley Page), but we were not over-eager. Eventually we agreed to take just seven of these 18-seaters, which we called the Clansman class, because they were to fly mainly in Scotland. In my opinion they were too big, fragile and complicated to replace the Rapide.

As our next main-line aircraft, we eagerly looked forward to the arrival of the 20 Airspeed Ambassadors, which, as noted in the previous chapter, the Minister of Supply had ordered for us in September 1948. In the USA the broadly similar Convair 240 was designed in winter 1946/7, first flew on 16 March 1947, and was certificated and entered service in November 1947. The Ambassador was likewise designed in 1946/7, first flew on 10 July 1947, but did not enter service until 13 March 1952!

I simply had to accept the fact that there were never going to be more than 20 Ambassadors, and no airline likes to be the only operator of a complex modern aeroplane. Moreover, I was convinced that the future lay with jets and turboprops, and though we had studied Ambassadors with four Naiad or Dart turboprops, what was the point? George Edwards, only temporarily dismayed by the Ambassador order, was pressing on with the stretched Viscount 700.

I kept in close touch with Vickers-Armstrongs (Aircraft), whom I now regarded as the only British company other than de Havilland which could be relied upon to produce aircraft that were 'world class', and developed on time. The British malaise was not confined to aircraft. In 1948 the decision had been taken to move BEA to London's new airport at Heathrow. There were obvious disadvantages in operating from prefabricated buildings at a modest RAF station, with the Vikings serviced in the open and overhauled in old RAF hangars, and the Dakotas and Rapides likewise based at another old RAF airfield, Renfrew, near Glasgow. Accordingly, plans were made for us to move to Heathrow, with all maintenance to be done at a purpose-designed engineering base, to be ready in 1950.

What actually happened was that our Report for the year ending 31 March 1951 noted with pleasure that work had started *on the foundations* of this building. It further noted that the 'new workshops at Northolt, due for completion in early 1950, were not occupied until January 1951 . . . The changes and repairs to the Renfrew Maintenance Base are more than one year late in completion.'

A few minor operations ran to time. One was the Helicopter Experimental Unit. This was set up in July 1947 at Yeovil, because that was where Westland Aircraft intended to make small Sikorsky S-51 helicopters under licence. In fact we purchased three S-51s from Sikorsky, and two Bell 47s to train pilots. In the first two months of 1948 the S-51s operated a service carrying bags of dummy mail in Dorset, moving later in the year to Peterborough, where live (i.e. real) mail was carried in East Anglia.

On 1 June 1950 BEA began the world's first scheduled helicopter passenger service, between Cardiff and Liverpool, with an occasional stop at a 'rotor station' (a hut in a field) at Wrexham. In ten months the three-seat S-51s carried 819 passengers. They logged 1,222 hours at an hourly cost of £44. We learned a lot, and looked forward to building up an enlarged network of services with later helicopters, and incidentally did much to develop the Decca Flight Log electronic navigation aid.

In a totally different field, we carried out an important programme of research into what were called clear-air gusts, using two civil-registered Mosquito PR.34 aircraft.

In 1948/9 these aircraft operated from Cranfield, flying 247 hours on complex flight profiles up to 40,000 feet. Sponsored by the Ministry of Supply, the previously unknown information on upper-air turbulence assisted the design of high-flying aircraft, including the Viscount which had become BEA's obvious future main-line aircraft.

We collaborated with Vickers in the design of the intended production Viscount. Key BEA figures were Beverley Shenstone, the airline's Chief Engineer, and Bob Morgan, the Chief Project and Development Engineer. At this point I must also mention my successive Personal Assistants, who were of course outstanding. Peter Brooks had been at Chillon College, and later was an aircraft-recognition star turn before becoming a pilot in the Fleet Air Arm. He came with me from BEA to Bristol, and thence to Beagle. Clive Adams was so good he was sent to a top job in the USA. His replacement, Edwin Whitfield, sadly caught a deadly disease in the Middle East, and he was succeeded by another excellent man, George Wharton.

In July 1950 the Ministry-owned Viscount V.700 prototype was almost complete. By that time the original, smaller, V.630 had been granted a Special Certificate of Airworthiness. On 29 July 1950 this aircraft began two months of scheduled

First service to Edinburgh by the V.630 Viscount prototype, on 15 August 1950. I am on the steps with Charles and Richard, with Lord Douglas in front and G.O. Waters (General Manager, Continental Services) beside me. Peter Brooks is on the tarmac, third from left.

passenger-carrying operations, the first in the world by a turbine-engined aircraft. The first services were flown to Paris, and later ones to Edinburgh.

Capt. R. 'Dicky' Rymer was in command, the first holder in the world of a civil pilot's licence endorsed for turbine-engined aircraft. Later he joined Vickers as a test pilot, and was tragically killed with Mike Lithgow in a 'deep-stall' accident. On the first scheduled flight to Paris (237 statute miles) the V.630 was deliberately cruised at only 10,500 feet. Carrying a payload of 6,765 lb, the aircraft was cruised at 265 mph, burning kerosene at 285 gal./hr. Block speed was 216 mph. Altogether, these experimental services carried 1,838 passengers in 88 flights in 122 hours. Passenger reaction was all we hoped it would be. Together with BOAC with the jet-engined Comet, BEA was starting a totally new era in air travel.

Heavier, more capacious and more powerful, the prototype V.700, G-AMAV, began flight testing on 28 August 1950. On the 3rd of that month Lord Douglas had signed a contract for 20 (later increased to 26) Viscounts of the V.701 type. At last, I felt that BEA was going places.

34

The flourishing airline

In my harmonious partnership with Sholto I was able to concentrate entirely on running BEA and on planning its future development, and I enjoyed every minute. *La vie en rose!* We started an excellent monthly magazine, printed on paper of a quality seldom seen in post-war Britain. The October 1949 issue announced my appointment as Chief Executive and included a brief biography, written by the Editor, Robert Cheesman, which included, 'One cannot say that one is pleased that he has come to rest with the Corporation, for he never rests. His capacity for work is enormous.' I had never before thought about this.

In the same issue I contributed a piece which began by recalling a poem I had learned at school, the opening lines of which were:

> 'In full, fair tide let information flow;
> That trouble is half-cured whose cause we know.'

I explained that from now on I was going to take two pages in each *BEA Magazine* to tell everyone how BEA was doing, no holds barred. Just before I joined there had been a damaging unofficial strike. I saw it as a major part of my job to build up a real team spirit, so that such a thing would not occur again. It so happened that in 1950/1 I was to be Chairman of the National Joint Council for Civil Air Transport, a primary function of which was to solve labour problems. Sadly, at that time BEA harboured a handful of wreckers, whose chief ambition was to cause trouble. Gradually we identified them and made sure that they found other places in which to pursue their activities.

In fact, BEA had started off with such an abysmal performance that it had not been difficult to do better. At some point a law of diminishing returns must set in, and it was my job to see that progress was maintained. For example, revenue per employee had risen from £570 in the year ending April 1948 to £1,270 in the year to April 1951. Over the same three years passengers had increased from 497,000 to 980,000, mail from 1,500 tons to 5,400 tons and cargo from 2,000 tons to 10,000 tons. (These were British 'long' tons of 2,240 lb.) All this was carried in aircraft which by today's standard were tiny.

These results had reduced the annual loss from almost £4 million to £979,000. Indeed, in my first Chief Executive's Page I noted that for July, August and September 1949 BEA had actually made a profit. The difficulty was that BEA's traffic was incredibly seasonal, and our results were dragged down by the winter months.

Our results were also significantly affected by the poor performance of the British aircraft industry. As related previously, we had incurred heavy expenditure getting ready for the Airspeed Ambassador, one of the costs being a Bristol 170 Freighter to

I periodically flew to Christchurch to check on the (slow) progress with the Ambassador.
Here Hereward de Havilland and Philip Gordon-Marshall (then Airspeed Sales Director,
later my PR and Advertising Manager at Bristol) are welcoming Vicky and Richard, who
had come with me in an Airspeed Consul.

carry the massive Centaurus engines to wherever they might be needed. These costs
built up steeply, but were not as expected offset by the increased revenue from these
aircraft, because they did not arrive in service as planned in January 1951 but in March
1952.

Even bigger costs were being incurred by the necessity of transferring our main
operating base from Northolt to Heathrow. That had to be done piecemeal, the biggest
task being the construction of an extremely large purpose-designed engineering base.
The old RAF hangars on Northolt's north side were finding it hard to cope already,
and would have been totally unable to handle either the Ambassador or the Viscount.

Hard as we tried, we were hit by many massive blows, most of them unforeseen.
Apart from late delivery of aircraft, we were hit by the Chancellor's decision to
devalue Sterling, unprecedented increases in the cost of fuel, wages and salaries, and
even the fact that the rapid increase in air traffic meant that aircraft had to fly dog-
legs and even spend long periods stacking waiting to land. In July and August 1951
we were further hit by a major nationwide industrial dispute which crippled our
services at the busiest time. As a result our 1951/2 operating loss, instead of shrinking,
increased from £979,000 to £1,423,611.

From an early age I had revelled in keeping detailed records and personal accounts,
and despite the pressures of my various jobs I continued to fill large books and ledgers
with notes, statistics and financial records. Some of this spilled over into preparing

the BEA Report and Accounts, which in my first full year grew from its previous 54 pages to 94, not including a 16-page art-paper insert for photographs and route maps. The result was a detailed yet attractive package which really showed other companies how it should be done. To break even, HM Stationery Office increased the price of the publication from 1s to 1s 6d (7½p), which from the perspective of the 21st century seems pretty good value.

On 1 June 1950 BEA ceased to serve Lisbon. This was because BOAC had to call there on various through services, and the Portuguese refused to grant traffic rights to a second British operator. It meant that our Lisbon staff had to don different uniforms, and a rumour spread like wildfire that BEA was going to be merged into BOAC. I spent much effort telling everyone that this was not so (though it did happen 17 years after I had departed).

In an earlier chapter I commented on technically illiterate Ministers who busied themselves with thinking of individual names for airliners. In fact, this is not an entirely trivial subject, and I had never been happy with the names bestowed on our Vikings. They all began with V, and (for example) included *Vibrant*, *Vortex*, *Volatile*, *Vindictive* and *Villain*. I suggested a staff competition to think of better names.

Our Magazine for September 1950 had to be typewritten (by the kindness of the Royal Aeronautical Society) because of a widespread strike of printers. In that issue I set out the results of the competition to select names for some 180 aircraft.

On another trip I flew to Christchurch by Dove; (from left) a D.H. salesman, Wing Commander A.H. Measures (BEA director), PGM, Hereward de Havilland and Capt. J.W.G. 'Jimmy' James (BEA Chief Pilot).

Among others, we decided to call the Vikings after Admirals, the Pionairs after British aviators, the promised Ambassadors after famous Elizabethans (like the Admirals, almost all of them knights or lords) and the Viscounts after explorers. Eventually the Ambassador was to become known as the de Havilland Elizabethan, to celebrate Her Majesty's ascent to the throne.

At last, after a woefully long five years of development, the Elizabethan entered service on 13 March 1952, when G-ALZS *William Shakespeare* carried fare-paying passengers on the 13.00 service to Paris. This was the start of a long climb which was to see BEA become the premier airline within Europe and one of the best in the world, with modern pressurised aircraft and – a little later in the same year, we hoped – the even more advanced turboprop Viscounts.

One of the things that worried me most about the Elizabethans was the immaturity of their engines. The 2,625-hp Centaurus 661 was still a new powerplant, lacking the essential buildup of hours which would have been possible had the Project X gone ahead. To my relief the complex new engine, carefully maintained, proved to be reliable. In contrast, the rest of the aircraft, especially its electrics, gave rise to prolonged and irritating troubles.

Despite the fact that it was, by comparison with the Centaurus, much newer basic technology, and had no background whatsoever of prior military use, I was not so apprehensive about the Dart turboprop. The magic of the Rolls-Royce name counted for a lot, and in any case the Dart was a remarkably simple and robust engine and the Viscount had four of them. Nevertheless, it was essential to do everything that we could to build up experience with the Dart, not only to accelerate the

At last, on 13 March 1952, an Elizabethan (Airspeed Ambassador) entered service! Lord Douglas has stepped onto the Le Bourget apron, with me following.

Our Dart-Dakotas had astonishing performance.

engine's maturity but also to gain experience with its servicing and maintenance.

Accordingly, we purchased two ex-RAF Dakotas which in 1951 were completely overhauled by Field Aircraft Services and re-engined by Rolls-Royce at Hucknall, each with two Dart 505 turboprops with a take-off power of 1,400 shp (shaft horsepower). As far as possible the whole installation duplicated that of the Viscount 701, including the 10-ft Rotol four-blade propeller.

This proved to be a good move, and in fact the two Dart-Dakotas were not only operated intensively but from 15 August 1951 were put on scheduled cargo services, earning revenue. Reliability was almost perfect, the main problem being that the long nacelles put the noisy propellers in line with the cockpit. Of course, in the unpressurised Dakotas the pilots wore oxygen masks, and gained some satisfaction from astonishing other traffic, such as USAF B-29 crews, by overtaking them at 30,000 ft.

Back in the war it had seemed sensible to plan new civil aircraft for the future. Now, as an operator, I felt that the British system of State Ministerial ordering of aircraft was wrong. The glaring example of resulting problems was the Miles Marathon. Powered by four 330-hp Gipsy Queen engines, this was an attractive 20-passenger aircraft first flown in May 1946 to meet our Brabazon 5A specification. Miles went bankrupt, but 40 Marathons were built by Handley Page on Ministry contract.

Unfortunately, no airline wanted the aircraft, highlighting the foolishness of the Ministerial ordering process. Meanwhile, BEA had issued its own specification

Escorting Sir Winston Churchill to a BEA flight from Heathrow to Nice.

(16/49) for a simpler and cheaper four-engined 12/20-seater to replace the Rapide. We received 16 replies, and shortlisted a Short proposal and the Blackburn B.84, both of which met our requirements fully. This was ignored, and the Minister of Supply prevailed upon the Minister of Civil Aviation to tell us that, as a lot of money had been spent on the Marathon, that was what we had to have.

Accordingly, we began negotiations for seven of the 40, and proposed to name them after Scottish Clans. At last, on 10 April 1952 a Conservative Minister of Civil Aviation informed us that our acceptance of these aircraft was 'no longer required'.

By this time we had sampled the prototype D.H.114 Heron, using it on some busy Saturdays to the Channel Islands. It carried 481 revenue passengers, who were complimentary, but it still did not meet all our economic factors. In July 1952 we decided that, except for the Ambulance Service and flights to the beach at Barra, the Rapide replacement would be the Pionair (Dakota), operated with fares cut by 20 per cent to attract a better load-factor. Remarkably, these services almost broke even.

In 1952 I did a lot of flying in Miles Geminis, which were particularly attractive light twins. One of them, with the appropriate registration G-AFLT, belonged to the magazine *Flight*. The Editor, Wing Commander Maurice Smith, let me borrow Fox Love Tare in order to fly up with Pat to an Institute of Transport dinner in Aberdeen. On the return we were still climbing away from Aberdeen when we ran into a storm that was far worse than the forecast. We lost an engine, and just managed to get down at Montrose.

By November 1952, apart from BEA, the radical new Viscount had been ordered by only Aer Lingus (4), Air France (12) and Trans-Australia (6). Then Trans-Canada Airlines ordered 15. The TCA order was for a version re-engineered for the North American market, and it promised to lead to a flurry of orders from around the world. By 1953 the number of Viscounts sold had already shot up to 75, with many more being negotiated.

This eliminated the risk of BEA being the only operator, as we were with the Elizabethan. Indeed, throughout 1952 we had been talking with Vickers about an even better Viscount. This was made possible by the astonishing growth in power of the Dart engine. With no change in size or weight, the take-off power had already improved from 990 to over 1,500-hp, and now we could see 2,000. Even with the original engine, at only 1,400 shp, or 1,547 ehp (equivalent horsepower) taking into account thrust from the jetpipe, George Edwards had been able to push up the Viscount's maximum take-off weight from 45,000 lb to 56,000 lb, enabling us to carry our maximum of 47 passengers non-stop on our longest routes, such as London to Rome.

Even our original Viscount 701 was soon cleared to 57,000 lb, and the V.801 that we were talking about would have had a fuselage stretched by 13 ft 3 in, and Dart RDa.5 engines of 1,690 ehp. In February 1953 Sholto and I signed a contract for 12, each seating 66 passengers. In the event, George Edwards and I did even better. In April 1954 we altered the order to a revised specification, the V.802.

This had even more powerful engines, Dart 510s (RDa.6) of 1,740 ehp, but a fuse-lage stretched by a mere 46 in. On the other hand, by moving the aft pressure bulkhead further back we were able to stretch the cabin by 9 ft 3 in, to seat 65 (other airlines packed in a lot more). Moreover, such was the unstoppable growth in the Dart that one of my last big jobs with BEA was to sew up the specification for an even better version.

Originally called Viscount Major, but later called just the V.806, this looked exactly like a V.802, but with Dart 520 (RDa.7) engines, potentially of 2,000 shp but specially derated to 1,700 shp, or 1,990 ehp, they were to carry their maximum payload at 365 mph over ranges up to 1,725 miles, approximately double that of the original 700. This version brought our total Viscount fleet by 1958 up to 77. Altogether, Vickers built 445, but without BEA the Viscount might never have gone into production.

The first Viscount service was flown on 18 April 1953, on the route London–Rome–Athens–Nicosia. By this time both the aircraft and its revolutionary engines were already mature and reliable, and we had no hesitation in entering it in the air race to Christchurch, organised for October 1953 by the New Zealand city to celebrate its centenary. The race was organised in a speed section and a handicap section. The former would obviously be won by a jet; we naturally thought jet bombers would be up against D.H. Comet jet airliners.

Astonishingly, no Comet was entered, and entries from the USAF and by an RAF Valiant also failed to materialise, so the winner, in a time of just under 24 hr, was an RAF Canberra. The handicap section took into account the payload carried. There was no way our Viscount could win, because we could carry either payload or fuel, whereas long-range airliners could do both. We still felt we could put the Viscount 'on the map' and publicise both BEA and its radical new airliner. I felt ashamed to see that no other British civil aircraft was entered.

I acted as BEA Team Manager. We elected to carry fuel, and arranged for passenger seats to be replaced by four rather crude tanks in the cabin, increasing capacity to 2,900 gallons, giving us an estimated range of some 3,500 miles. What we did not expect was that by October 1953 the few V.701s that we had were so intensively utilised that none could be spared. We were forced to ask the Ministry whether we could borrow G-AMAV, the V.700 prototype.

Christened *Endeavour*, and fitted with Dart 510 engines, we had it cleared to take off, even in the tropics, at 65,000 lb, instead of its originally certificated weight of 48,000 lb. Apart from the extra tanks, the fuel system was modified to permit extra-rapid refuelling. We assembled a crew of 12 in brilliant white BEA flight overalls, including Capt. W. Ballie in command, Capts A.S. Johnson and S.E. Jones and myself acting as First Officers, I.A. Dalgleish and E.H.S. Bristow as radio officers, R.H. Chadwick as navigating officer and S.R. Jones, R. Shaw and E.W. Walker as flight engineers (they had little to do). J.D. Profumo MP (Parliamentary Secretary to the owners, the MCA), whom we soon christened Philip Harben (a famous chef of the day) because of his prowess in the galley, was with us, and Raymond Baxter came along as BBC Air Correspondent.

Before the start all competitors were lined up on Heathrow's Central Area, which was a vast area of concrete and a small forest of steel girders of buildings in an early stage of construction. Next to us was a DC-6A of KLM, which appeared likely to win the Handicap Section as it carried a full payload of 64 young emigrants.

G-AMAV all ready for the Christchurch race.

At Heathrow ready for the start of the race to New Zealand (details, see Appendix).

In the event we did brilliantly. The race log (all times GMT) went:

> 8/9 October, 16.40 depart London (Heathrow) 02.52 arrive Bahrain (Muharraq), 3,240 miles, 10 hr 10 min, 2,788 gal.
>
> 9 October, 03.06 depart Bahrein 11.07 arrive Colombo (Negombo), 2,350 miles, 8 hr 3 min, 2,470 gal.
>
> 9 October, 11.26 depart Colombo 17.50 arrive Cocos (West Island), 1,790 miles, 6 hr 25 min, 2,009 gal.
>
> 9/10 October, 18.12 depart Cocos 04.28 arrive Melbourne (Essendon), 3,530 miles, 10 hr 16 min, 2,810 gal.
>
> 10 October, 04.40 depart Melbourne 09.23 arrive Christchurch (Harewood), 1,580 miles, 4 hr 42 min, 1,540 gal.
>
> Overall, 12,490 miles in a flight time of 39 hr 36 min and total elapsed time of 40 hr 43 min, equating to an overall average speed of 316 mph and fuel consumption of 290 gal./hr.

Of course the DC-6A won on handicap, even though it arrived more than nine hours after us. Apart from that, nobody could fail to be impressed by the leg from Cocos to Melbourne, 3,530 miles in 10 hr 16 min. And we all arrived feeling fresh as daisies.

After all the festivities we took *Endeavour* on a demonstration tour, visiting 31 places. After that, the world's airlines no longer regarded turboprops as a quaint curiosity, and they scrambled to buy Viscounts. Thanks mainly to that aircraft, our year to 31 March 1955 turned in BEA's first clear profit.

Turboprops could give any power needed, and I could see that soon the Viscount – BEA's heaviest and most powerful aircraft – would appear to be a mere tiddler. On 9 April 1953 I began talks with George Edwards about something much bigger. These led to the Vanguard, a superb 135-seat turboprop airliner which cruised at 422 mph with outstanding economics.

Had this been produced quickly it should have repeated the success of the Viscount, but what actually happened was that – after my departure – the specification kept changing. Rolls-Royce (perhaps predictably) increased the power of the engine from the promised 2,750 shp to 4,500 shp, and the Vanguard did not carry passengers until 1961.

To the surprise of some, aviation is severely prone to the whims of fashion. By 1961 the world's airlines were being bowled over by short-haul jets. Things with propellers were almost unsaleable, and only 43 Vanguards were built. Some 20 years later reason returned, and the turboprop came strongly back into fashion, but by this time the Vanguards had been scrapped.

On 2 June 1953 Pat and I dressed in extraordinary garb (mine included mandatory knee-breeches), avoided drinking anything, and by 09.30 took our places in Westminster Abbey, next to Sir Miles and Lady Thomas, my opposite number in BOAC. For the next eight hours we witnessed the Coronation of a small and beautiful girl. I had forgotten my white gloves, and when I wrapped my hands in handkerchiefs Pat hissed 'They look like amputated stumps'. She also commented that the Dukes and Duchesses in the benches opposite looked just like battery hens! It was nevertheless unforgettable.

Until well into 1953 our relatively tiny and ancient aerodrome at Northolt handled more traffic than mighty Heathrow. Keyline House was right under the flight path, and during an important meeting in my office a Pionair landed with its trailing radio aerial still extended. The lead bob-weight smashed in through the window, crashed across my desk and embedded itself in the opposite wall. It hit nobody – it could easily have killed one of us – but Capt. J.W.G. James, BEA Flight Operations Director, exclaimed 'I'll have him on the carpet!'

By 1953 I had built up a superb technical team. Chief Engineer Beverley Shenstone had a distinguished record of aircraft design (he had worked on the Heinkel He 70, various Junkers aircraft and the wing of the Spitfire). Chief Project Engineer R.C. 'Bob' Morgan was also outstanding, and a practising pilot like myself. It was soon evident that faltering BOAC coveted our expertise, but with Sholto at our head we were always able to repel boarders!

By 1953 our annual total of passengers had exceeded 1,600,000, which in turn made possible very competitive fares. For example, we offered London–Glasgow at £8 return, or 2.67d (in modern currency, one penny) per mile. At the other end of the scale, we had three Bristol 171 Sycamore helicopters. These four-passenger machines, the first all-British helicopters to go into passenger service, began operating in July 1953 on the route Gatwick–Heathrow–Birmingham.

My personal staff at BEA in 1955: (middle at back): Ron Davies and Bill Thomas. (Seated, left to right): Peter Brooks, Margaret Lawrence, PGM, Eileen Keefe and John Guy.

As the cost per mile of the Sycamore was roughly the same as that of the 32-seat Pionair, we hardly expected this service to make money. We embarked on it mainly to provide experience to underpin what we were certain would be future operations with real helicopter airliners. As the next stage we purchased two Westland-Sikorsky WS.55s, each seating eight passengers. From 25 July 1955 we operated these between Heathrow and the South Bank heliport in central London, following the curves of the Thames.

Again, we did not expect to make money, and in the event we were restricted to five passengers by the need to fit a heavy silencer and floats. The Port of London Conservancy Board told us that we had to carry an anchor, in case of a forced landing on the river. Rather desperate, we made ours of balsa wood. We were then asked to demonstrate it, when it promptly floated off in the strong current.

We looked forward to the introduction of what became popularly called 'the Bealine Bus', a big helicopter airliner. In the October/November 1953 *BEA Magazine* (uniquely, production problems forced us to merge two issues) I forecast the BEA of 1963. Cruising at 180 mph, the Bealine Bus would load its 50 passengers from the 'rotor station' above Waterloo Station and in 75 minutes – just time for lunch – take them to Les Invalides Heliport in the heart of Paris. Meanwhile, the 'Victory class' airliner assigned to the 10 a.m. Silver Wing service to Rome, Athens and Cairo would have four 4,000-hp turboprops and load 80 passengers. They would have arrived at Heathrow either by Underground or by a special super-fast surface train.

I got it wrong. Airliners grew even bigger and faster, but the Bealine Bus failed to appear. And, for no good reason, Heathrow had to wait an extra 30 years for the new rail link.

35

Go West, young man

In 1910 Bristol had possibly the best system of tramways and taxicabs of any city in the world. It had been created by the farsighted Sir George White Bt, followed by his less-ambitious son George Stanley White (GSW), his brother Samuel White, and his nephews Henry White Smith and Sydney Smith. The shareholders were shocked when, at the Annual Meeting in February 1910, Sir George announced that they were going to make aeroplanes. They were mollified when he added 'We won't use a penny of shareholders' money'.

Trading as The British & Colonial Aircraft Co., the company prospered in World War 1: how could it do otherwise? In 1920, to avoid massive tax bills, it was started again as The Bristol Aeroplane Co. In World War 2 it became huge, masking the fact that the family Board – which now included Sir William G. Verdon Smith as Chairman, GSW (by now likewise knighted as Sir Stanley) as Managing Director and his son W. Reginald Verdon Smith (VS) – were becoming increasingly out of their depth. However, they did have one go-ahead and hard-working employee.

In 1920 the Board had purchased a small Bristol company run by the brilliant engineer Roy Fedden, who pioneered air-cooled radial aircraft engines. Between the wars these sold by the thousand, and they accounted for more than 80 per cent of Bristol's profits. Unfortunately, Fedden was such a forceful character that, always pursuing clear objectives which the Board did not understand, he was perpetually at loggerheads with the Whites and Smiths. Thus, instead of recognising his enormous value, the family Board's attitude was that he had to be 'kept down'. His knighthood in January 1942 was the last straw. Instead of being offered a seat on the Board, which he should have had from the start, he was fired.

Predictably, the Bristol engines subsequently staggered from one crisis to another. I have already described how the company's entry into the field of gas turbines turned out to be a complete mess. By the 1950s there was little money coming in, and the extensive factories contained the last few Bristol 170 Freighters, a few three-seat Sycamore helicopters and the incomplete second Brabazon.

The one hope for the future was the Britannia, originally conceived as the Bristol 175 to the MRE Specification, as outlined earlier. The design had been laid down by the gifted and astute Chief Designer Leslie Frise, but the Bristol Board thought he was 'getting too big for his boots'. In 1948 he resigned, to go to Percival Aircraft. At last the first Britannia prototype, G-ALBO, flew on 16 August 1952, after five years of development. It still had unacceptable Proteus 625 engines, but Frise's basic design was outstanding. Had Bristol proceeded with American – or Fedden – speed, the engines would swiftly have been redesigned and several hundred Britannias would have been sold. Unfortunately, in the real world things were different. The Bristol company was run entirely from ivy-clad Filton House by a family clique

At Bristol, Sir Reginald Verdon Smith had a virtual monopoly on decision-taking.

of non-engineers, which for all practical purposes comprised just VS and GSW.

The second Britannia did not fly until 23 December 1953. Just over a month later the aircraft was written off after a disastrous engine failure resulted in a forced landing on the muddy bank of the River Severn. By this time the Whites and Smiths had reluctantly begun to admit non-family people on to the Board, but in no way were they permitted to take any decisions. Outwardly impressive, the whole edifice was out of control.

Among the Whites and Smiths, one member of the family stood out, VS who had been up at Oxford, reading Law, a year or so before I was at Cambridge. He had gained the coveted Vinerian Prize. Immaculate, and with film-star looks, the family had appointed him to succeed his father as Chairman, and also to be Joint Managing Director. In 1949 he had invited Stanley Hooker – a graduate of his Oxford college – to join Bristol and endeavour to make the Proteus turboprop work properly, as noted earlier and related in Hooker's autobiography. In 1954, by which time VS was Sir Reginald, recognising at last that the company was floundering, he began looking for further help.

As told in his biography (*Fedden*, Rolls-Royce Heritage Trust), back in 1939 Roy Fedden has caused a storm at the Bristol company by daring to make the eminently sensible suggestion that there ought to be separate Bristol aircraft and engine companies. The very fact that he had made this suggestion ensured that such a thing would not happen. Not until 1954 did the Bristol Board feel that they could actually embrace such an idea, as if it was their own.

Accordingly, whilst retaining The Bristol Aeroplane Co. as parent, three subsidiary companies were formed: Bristol Aircraft, Bristol Aero-Engines and Bristol Cars. They begin trading on 1 January 1956.

VS invited Air Chief Marshal Sir Alec Coryton, a distinguished officer who had been Controller of Supplies (Air) and Director-General of Guided Weapons at the Ministry of Supply, to be Managing Director of Bristol Aero-Engines. Then, out of the blue, in March 1955 VS offered me the job of Managing Director of Bristol Aircraft.

We had met, but only briefly. When I reflected that VS could have picked almost anyone in the British aircraft industry for such an appointment I felt somewhat encouraged, the more so as he proposed an annual salary of £10,000, *almost three times* what I felt able to pay myself at BEA. While the airline was still in the red I had not felt justified in taking what most leaders of industry might have considered to be a fair salary (it was, in fact, less than J.V. Wood had received back in the late 1940s). Now we were moving towards a year-round profit, but I would never have considered hiking my salary to the level VS offered. I enjoyed BEA, and told him that I needed time to consider the offer.

We had several further meetings, at which VS also offered me a new Bristol 405 car. This was one of the outstanding 2-litre high-performance saloons derived from a BMW design, and the indirect creation of my former Cambridge colleague George White. To cap it all, in due course VS offered me a personal light aeroplane, invaluable as my own executive tool. It was exceedingly persuasive, and certainly too good to turn down without much further thought. Bristol was a famous firm, and what could go wrong?

I was given the second Bristol 405 car; in the background, engines running, G-ALBO, the first Britannia.

VS repeatedly emphasised that Bristol needed someone capable of driving through the Britannia programme, which had for eight years proceeded at a snail's pace. In the summer of 1955 Boeing was already testing the 707 jet airliner, and Douglas had announced the DC-8. It seemed to me probable that these aircraft, carrying more passengers than the Britannia, and cruising at least 150 mph faster, would prove daunting competition for the Bristol turboprop. On the other hand, the Britannia would be quieter, and promised to burn much less fuel. I warmed to the enormous challenge.

In late 1952 Bristol had hired Barry Bailey-Watson – Bill Gunston's predecessor as Technical Editor of the magazine *Flight* – as Public Relations Manager. He saw it as his first duty to proclaim that the future American big jets could not equal the range of the Britannia. Indeed, with the full backing of the Bristol company, he was telling the Press they could not fly the North Atlantic non-stop until they were *redesigned with six engines*. This was perhaps gallant, but unwise. I knew Boeing and Douglas better than this. They had a reputation for delivering what they promised, and on time. The chief uncertainty was the precise economics of the large jetliners.

Clearly, the Britannia was running a race which, unless its development was accelerated, it would probably lose. This was a formidable challenge which appealed to me. British European Airways had turned the corner and was almost unique among the world's airlines in making a true, unsubsidised, profit. I did not want to leave BEA, but I was hard-pressed to find the rapidly escalating school fees of my four children. It was the salary, and Bristol's reputation, that clinched it.

Of course, my discussions with VS were confidential, but I did mention the fact that I was being wooed by him to an old friend, Capt. J. Laurence Pritchard, the wise and experienced Secretary of the Royal Aeronautical Society. To my astonishment, he begged me to reject VS's blandishments and stay at the helm at BEA. He assured me that I would regret throwing up my happy relationship with Sholto to go to Bristol.

Instead, on 29 August 1955 I foolishly wrote to the Minister of Transport and Civil Aviation (at that time John Boyd-Carpenter) telling him of the great challenge from Bristol, which I felt I had to accept. There was an urgent need to do everything possible to make a success of the Britannia. Thus, in November 1955 I found myself walking into Filton House with high hopes for the future.

I was installed in a sumptuous suite of offices on the ground floor of the recently built headquarters block, New Filton House. Having got used to the bleak austerity of the converted school which had been BEA's head office at Northolt, I took some time to become acclimatised to the lavish attitudes at Bristol. I was made to understand that it was a place for gentlemen, who were above such things as balance sheets.

About three weeks later Sir Miles Thomas came to see me. He told me, out of the blue, that he had decided to resign his position as Chairman of BOAC, with effect from 31 March 1956, in order to take up the far better-paid Chairmanship of the chemical giant Monsanto. He told me that he had the authority of the Minister of Transport and Civil Aviation to invite me to be his successor. I ought at once to have discussed this unexpected turn of events with both VS and with Sholto. Stupidly, I did neither.

Soon afterwards I was telephoned by the Minister (who now was Harold Watkinson) and pressed to take on the top job at BOAC. In British aviation there could hardly be a more plum job than the Chairmanship of the nation's worldwide airline. The Minister had even said 'Don't turn this down . . . you are the obvious choice.'

When the Minister telephoned me at Bristol I was busy with final preparations to depart on a sales tour of Scandinavia with the first fully furnished BOAC Britannia 102, G-ANBJ (Baker Jig, but about to become Bravo Juliet in the new phonetic alphabet). To my astonishment the special BOAC flight and cabin crews picked for this sales tour told me how delighted they were that I was being tipped as the airline's next Chairman. To cap it all, as we were about to take off, I took a call from Sir Arnold Overton, by now Permanent Secretary at the Ministry. Could he – backed up by Sir George Cribbett, who now was BOAC's Deputy Chairman – make me change my mind? I could only reply that, as I had only just walked in the door at Filton House, I could hardly walk out again. I put the phone down, and we took off for Oslo.

Many times since then I have ruminated on the fact that to have run BOAC, along-side Sholto at BEA, would have been the most enviable post in British aviation, if not in the world. Indeed, other eminent people told me I was making a serious mistake in going to Bristol. Marshal of the Royal Air Force Lord Trenchard, the 'father of the RAF', asked me to visit him in his office in Unilever House, on London's Embankment. I was delighted to meet him, and I had not realised that by this time – he was 83 – he was almost completely blind, but still very much 'on the ball'. He told me that he had enjoyed my articles in *The Aeroplane*. He went on, 'You ought to be warned about Bristol. The people they have relied upon, such as Frank Barnwell, Leslie Frise and Roy Fedden, never received support from the family Board, but instead much hostility.' I was also telephoned by the great Lord Hives. He said, 'I am disturbed that you have gone to Bristol. You should have come here, to Rolls-Royce. I urge you still to consider it.' That, too, would have been agreeable, as Whitney Straight had just left BOAC to be the engine company's Executive Vice-Chairman. We had been friends since schooldays, and got on well together.

I was naturally much disturbed by all of this. But I felt that I had given my word to VS, and could not go back on it. Moreover, I felt that I really could not, in all fair-ness, walk out of a job which now so urgently needed doing, within a few weeks of starting on it.

Then on 28 March 1956 Max Beaverbrook asked me to lunch with him on the following day. When we met, at Arlington House, he told me that the Prime Minister, briefed by Harold Watkinson, had asked him to try to persuade me to move to BOAC. I still felt, by now doggedly, that my loyalty lay with Bristol. Accordingly, I told Max that the tempting offer of running BOAC had unfortunately arrived too late. Later Watkinson called me. He said he might have an alternative Chairman for BOAC. I asked who, and he replied 'An old friend of yours, Gerard d'Erlanger. What do you think of him?' Though I had serious misgivings, out of loyalty to 'Pops' I had to say blandly that I wished him every success. He succeeded Sir Miles on 1 May 1956. The airline was soon in difficulties.

Very quickly, as I learned more about Bristol and VS, I came to realise that my loyalty to the company had been a serious mistake. At BEA everyone had pulled together, with 'all the facts on the table'. At Bristol I was surrounded by enormous problems everywhere I looked, but it was soon made abundantly clear to me that, while my role was to manage Bristol Aircraft, and solve all these problems, I had to do so without membership of the Board and without ever daring to take any significant decision. Such decisions were the strict prerogative of the family.

On reflection, and taking the longer view, going to Bristol was possibly not an entirely bad move. For the next 18 years, at Bristol and then at Beagle, I had important and varied experience back in the world of manufacturing, before I returned to a less-opulent position in the airline operating industry.

Overall, the new Bristol companies were working on an impressive range of products. Bristol Aircraft's main programmes were the 170 Freighter, the 175 Britannia, the 188 supersonic research aircraft, the Types 171 Sycamore, 173, 191 and 192 helicopters, and a big surface-to-air guided-missile project under the code name Red Duster. Bristol Aero-Engines was working, with varying degrees of success, on the Proteus and Orion turboprops, the Olympus and Orpheus turbojets, and the Thor supersonic ramjet. Altogether, it was a daunting range of products, which required the highest possible standard of leadership.

In addition to all this, Bristol was working on the Type 187 so-called Super Britannia, the 189 ocean-patrol derivative of the Britannia with the complicated Napier Nomad compound engines, the 194 winged helicopter airliner, and the 195 giant turboprop freighter. It was about to start work on the 198 supersonic airliner with six Bristol Olympus engines, the 199 tilt-wing convertiplane with four RR Tyne engines, and the 200 and 201 jetliners with engines at the tail.

This was all very exciting, but it was far too much and totally unrealistic. The immediate trouble was that the only things being delivered to customers were the Type 170 Freighter and 171 helicopter. These brought in relatively trivial sums, and were obsolescent products about to go out of production.

Nevertheless, full of hope and enthusiasm, I called a Press conference, attended by virtually all the air correspondents. My news was, 'There is new life here, we have new Bristol companies, we are going to solve the problems, watch this space, we look for your support, such as I have enjoyed at BEA' – without revealing anything whatsoever of either company private or military classified activities.

Immediately there was an explosion of cataclysmic proportions in the Bristol Boardroom. I was told, 'How *dare* you tell people what we are doing?!' I was told sharply that I was never again to invite the Press to anything.

When I referred to the outstanding *BEA Magazine*, and suggested that Bristol should produce something similar, I instantly fell further foul of VS and his ex-Oxford cronies on the Board, with – as a non-Bristolian – the extraordinary and implacable opposition of GSW. The fact was made plain to me that all decisions were to be taken by VS and (on the Board of the parent Bristol Aeroplane Co.) by GSW. I was to understand that the role of the other directors was to nod approvingly.

I was additionally made to understand that, in stark contrast to BEA, nothing of significance should ever be brought into the open. This applied with particular force to anything of a financial nature. To add to the frustration, there was no way I could endeavour to brief VS/GSW to help them take the big decisions. It could not have been a more extraordinary reversal of the welcome I had received on my first day.

All that gave me an opportunity to resign immediately, and indeed I felt inclined to do so. Unfortunately, I judged that I had left it just too late to reverse my earlier refusals, and to take up one of the other tempting opportunities. I had to bite the bullet, and do all I could (which didn't seem to be very much) to try to make a success of all that Bristol Aircraft had in hand.

Included in VS's blandishments had been the promise that, 'when I had settled in', I would be appointed to the Board of the Bristol Aeroplane Company. After all, in industry generally it is normal for managing directors of subsidiary companies to have a seat on the Main Board. When I reminded VS of this he dodged the issue, saying that he wanted me to concentrate on the vital main task, the Britannia. Being on the Main Board would, he said, distract me with engines and missiles. Not until much later did I understand that GSW – having had the experience of Fedden – was determined to prevent further watering down of the family dominance. He thought I would be 'difficult', and try to speak my mind.

To my surprise and relief there were a few people at Bristol who were prepared to speak their minds. Robert S. Brown, the Works Director, and Ken Hayward, who was not a director but General Manager, found life utterly soul-destroying. So did Dr W.J. 'Bill' Strang, the Aircraft Company's Chief Designer (Fixed-Wing). Like most of the technical staff, Strang was completely repressed by Dr A.E. Russell, the Chief Engineer. Russ was an intensely political animal, who despised any non-Bristolian. More to the point, unlike me, he had a seat on the Main Board. He could, and did, make my life a misery, and he resented having to report to me as his Managing Director.

Brown, Hayward and many others perked up a little when they discovered that I was prepared to stand up to VS/GSW. They were the only people of standing who did not object when I set up regular weekday meetings at 8.30 a.m. Previously, staff had drifted in at 10, and spent an hour opening the mail. I also caused trouble by setting up a chart room with progress and cost charts on the walls in an effort to distil and present information in the way that had proved so valuable at BEA. I persuaded Bill Thomas to leave BEA's chart room and set up a similar presentation of facts and

The Britannia (in this case Mk 312 G-AOVB) was a beautiful aircraft.

trends at Bristol. Almost all the information I requested was refused, and to my astonishment VS insisted that I must keep that room securely locked.

Naturally, when I accepted the job at Bristol I expected to move from Reigate to the Bristol area. Fortunately I had taken no action towards seeking a new home when the reality of my situation made me decide to stay put, allowing the children to continue at their schools. During each of the first few weeks I usually stayed, not very comfortably, in Bristol's Grand Hotel. At weekends I would drive back to Reigate, leaving Filton at about 8 p.m. on the Friday. Later I commuted almost daily.

Though I was shocked by the violent response to my daring to call an early Press conference, it still took me some weeks to realise the hostility that existed in the hierarchy in Filton House. Even more seriously, because I was refused even the most basic information, it took me still longer to discover how completely at sea the whole top management of the company actually was. The overwhelmingly important immediate product was the Britannia. When I was at BEA I had known that it was approximately two years late. Now I could see that the Filton works was quite unfitted to complete the development of such an advanced and complicated aircraft.

Back in 1943 the big US aircraft companies had had in place administrative structures and supporting departments, fully equipped with all manner of special equipment, which in 1956 the Filton works seemingly had never heard of. In my

Driving almost daily from Redhill to Bristol and back, I spent hours dictating en route.

innocence I suggested that we should get together with the customer, BOAC, which did have a strong engineering department, to try to solve the problems of the Britannia and its engines. VS was outraged by this proposal, which he appeared to consider an insult to the company.

The contract to supply 25 Britannias to BOAC called for entry into passenger-carrying service in 1954, with all 25 delivered before the end of 1955. In fact, no aircraft were delivered in 1954. For political reasons the Air Registration Board decided to grant the Certificate of Airworthiness before the end of 1955 (in my view prematurely), so that two aircraft could be delivered on 30 December. These were the third and fourth Britannia 102, G-ANBC/ANBD. They were formally handed over by VS at Heathrow at a ceremony to which I was not invited (nor even informed of), and then went to Hurn where BOAC had set up a Britannia training school.

I did not breathe any sigh of relief. As we entered 1956, and I took up my duties at Bristol, I could see a future full of problems. These would emerge from the fog of secrecy only at a stage when finding solutions would be doubly difficult.

36

Bristol fashion

At Bristol I did my best to get things moving energetically in the right directions. But at almost every stage I found myself blocked by Verdon Smith, who continued to insist on complete control and to disapprove of most of my endeavours.

I need hardly say that I became increasingly frustrated and miserable. I had no intention of moving my house, and so tended to do a lot of travelling. Fortunately, one thing at Bristol brought me pleasure, and kept me sane and optimistic for the future. It was a small aeroplane, a Chipmunk.

Powered by a 145-hp Gipsy Major 8, this trim all-metal two-seater had been designed by de Havilland Canada but built by de Havilland in England as one of 735 Chipmunks to train pilots of the RAF. Originally WP988, in July 1956 it came on to the civil market, registered G-AOTM, and I got the company to buy it.

I was to fly Tango Mike throughout my time at Bristol, commuting between my house (using Croydon, Gatwick or occasionally Redhill) and the vast Brabazon

With Charles in my Chipmunk 'Tango Mike'.

How the Chipmunk looked after all the modifications.

runway at Filton. I had a few close calls, and on one flight from Gatwick I really pushed my luck, arriving at Filton after dark in dense fog. Filton tower talked me down, but after I had come to a stop I had an exceedingly long wait while a car tried to locate me on the runway.

Gradually I got better avionics, including excellent VHF (very high frequency radio), a Grimes rotating beacon and even ILS (instrument landing system). Later, the Filton workshops made a Mustang-style clear-view bubble canopy. They also made a pair of wheel spats, which reduced drag, and increased fuel capacity from 24 gal. to 34 gal. By this time Tango Mike was the best Chipmunk in the world, and when I left Bristol I bought it.

Life at Filton did not, of course, centre around Tango Mike but around the Britannias. These were really beautiful aircraft, totally sound in design despite some unusual features. From the start the main landing gears had four-wheel bogies (trucks), which saved bulk and weight and spread the load better on weak airport pavements. Equally unusual were the flight controls, which were operated entirely by aerodynamic forces on narrow servo tabs along the trailing edges. And, of course, the engines were the world's first high-power turboprops, with the propellers driven by mechanically independent free turbines. One wag said, 'I understand that the Britannia is like other aircraft, except that the engines are not connected to the propellers and the pilot is not connected to the flight-control surfaces.'

All that this great aeroplane needed was engineering manpower. From the start it had suffered from a total absence of the American spirit, which simply trampled problems to death, usually in hours. At Bristol problems simmered for months. The one encouraging factor was that the engines had been redesigned by Hooker to give more power for 30 per cent less weight.

The improved Proteus 755 had enabled the design staff under Russell and Strang to produce the Britannia 300 series, with the fuselage stretched by 10 ft 3 in (3.12 m), and the 310 series, which added integral tanks in the outer wings to increase fuel capacity from 6,670 gal. to 8,486 gal. These modifications made the Britannia a much more competitive aircraft. From the start its radical new engines (if they could be made reliable) and fuselage diameter of 12 ft had given it a big edge over the rival DC-6/-7 and Super Constellation. Now it had more capacity and greater range.

Back in 1952 BOAC had requested that the last 10 of its order for 25 should be of a proposed cargo version. Different variants started to proliferate, so that Bristol began churning out brochures but not aircraft. So hopeless did the situation look that the decision was taken to set up a second production line at Short & Harland's factory at Belfast. The cargo version was replaced by a mixed cargo/passenger sub-family starting with the Series 250. Meanwhile, BOAC signed for a version called Series 305, with the longer fuselage. The plan was to send these to Belfast to be fitted with outer-wing bag-type fuel tanks, but in the event they had to be limited to 165,000 lb by their 102-type landing gear.

To confuse matters further, by the time I became involved BOAC was saying it preferred the definitive long-range 312 to the 102. It already had 11 of these on order, and eventually the BOAC fleet numbered 33, comprising the 15 Series 102s and 18 substantially different 312s.

I had much to do with the second-source firm in Belfast, whose Chairman and Managing Director, Rear-Admiral Sir Matthew Slattery, was later to join Bristol and later still to be Chairman of BOAC. While Bristol struggled to do development and produce versions for BOAC, Belfast produced the Series 252 for the RAF and some export versions.

Thus, as we moved into 1956 there were plans for many kinds of Britannia. At last production aircraft were trickling off the line at Filton and going to the BOAC training unit, while orders had been taken for three Series 313s, with an option for a further 10, for Israel's El Al, and we were discussing the Britannia with five other airlines, three of them in North America. At last we seemed to be getting somewhere.

I devoted some time to looking at Bristol Aircraft's many other programmes. For example, on 10 January 1956 I had a meeting with Air Commodore Chacksfield, the Ministry of Supply's Director of Guided-Weapon Trials. Bristol Aircraft and the Ferranti electronics giant were joint prime contractors for the RAF's principal SAM (surface-to-air missile) system. This had been developed under the code name Red Duster, and was now, in 1956, about to go into production at a new Bristol factory at Cardiff.

Bristol had begun by firing test vehicles for the 16-in-diameter Thor ramjet. Called Bobbin, dozens of these vehicles had been fired from the test range at Aberporth. The SAM itself was launched by four rocket motors made by Bristol-Aerojet Ltd. In approximately one second these accelerated the 25-ft missile to over Mach 2, where-upon the two Thors took over to provide cruise propulsion. Range was about thirty miles, which was being approximately doubled in an improved Mk 2 version. Guidance was by semi-active homing radar.

The production missile was called Bloodhound. It was to go into service not only with the RAF but also the Royal Australian Air Force and Sweden. Sweden and Switzerland were to buy the upgraded Bloodhound 2. It was ironic that this programme, the most high-tech. thing Bristol was doing, should also be the most successful.

Bloodhound, the most advanced Bristol Aircraft product, was the most trouble-free.

In contrast, another big Bristol Aircraft responsibility was helicopters. Knowing nothing about the subject, Bristol had started in June 1944 by hiring Austrian-born helicopter pioneer Raoul Hafner. What eventually resulted was the little Type 171 Sycamore. After prolonged development problems, a total of 178 of these were built. Most were military, but two had been sold to BEA.

The next step seemed logical enough. The Bristol 173 essentially comprised a Sycamore front end joined to a new tail end with a second engine and rotor. Linking the two was a tubular cabin for 13 passengers. First flown on 3 January 1952, with civil registration G-ALBN (immediately preceding the first Britannia G-ALBO), this machine was subsequently subjected to over 180 modifications, some of them (especially to the tail end) visibly obvious.

In 1953 a second Bristol 173 began flying, initially with two sets of wings to unload the rotors in cruising flight and thus enable speed to be increased. Three more 173s followed, like their predecessors all powered by 850-hp Alvis Leonides Major piston engines at front and rear. Some had Service markings and others BEA livery, but none ever went into service. The programme lost sight of the fact that it was meant to lead to a commercial product.

By 1954 the emphasis had shifted to purely military and naval machines. These began with the Type 191, a derivative of the 173 for the Royal Navy. Intended for ship-based ASW (anti-submarine warfare), anti-ship attack and general rescue and communications roles, it differed from the 173 in that the fuselage, which had fewer windows, was raised higher, especially at the front, to facilitate loading torpedoes, depth charges and other large stores underneath.

During the war a big production factory had been established at Old Mixon, about 20 miles from Filton near Weston-super-Mare, to make Beaufighters. With growing orders for Sycamores the production of that helicopter was transferred there just before I joined the company, and in 1956 all Bristol helicopter design and development was moved there as well.

In April 1956 I was pleased to oversee contracts for the three 191 prototypes already built with Leonides Major engines, 65 production 191s with two 1,465-shp Napier Gazelle turboshaft engines, 22 Bristol 192s for the RAF, and an initial four 193s for the Royal Canadian Air Force with Lycoming T55 turboshaft engines. This was the basis for a really big programme, and we greatly expanded the Old Mixon design and production strength.

Through 1956 the helicopter teams toiled round the clock to solve problems, such as avoiding ground resonance on pitching ship decks. Their reward was to see the 191 and 193 cancelled. This left only the RAF's 192. As the naval order had been much larger, this had dictated the design, so the RAF was left with a helicopter with an inconvenient door high above the ground, totally unsuited to loading troops, cargo or casualties. Among other nonsenses, instead of putting the Gazelle engines above the fuselage, as in the Sea King, or outside it as in the Chinook, they were put inside it, where they occupied a great deal of space and blocked access between the cabin and cockpit. The noise can be imagined. For the RAF version this was a great handicap.

In 1952, to meet BEA's Bealine Bus specification, Bristol had proposed the 181, an 80-seater with two Proteus turboshaft engines. Among several projects in my time were the 194, a 48-seater with four 1,175-shp Gnome engines, and the exciting 199 tilting-wing convertiplane with four RR Tyne turboprops giving a speed of 400 mph. All looked like being potential world-beating machines, but the management in Filton House seemed to have lost interest. Nothing got off the drawing board. After I left Bristol the company was broken up, the helicopter remnants going to Westland.

The little Car Division had become Bristol Cars Ltd. Their products were beautifully made and outstanding in every way. Having previously used the mighty Pontiac, followed by an SS Jaguar, I was used to impressive cars, but those made at Bristol were quite exceptional. I did over 250,000 miles in my 405. My co-director Air Cdre Rod Banks used a 407, and said it looked absolutely new after 300,000 miles.

In March 1956 the Britannia 102, the original production version for BOAC, was fully certificated and on the point of entering scheduled service. I felt that at last, after years of effort, the Britannia was coming 'out of the wood'. One day in that month a Britannia on one of the last tropical clearance trials, near Entebbe in Uganda, suffered a strange problem.

Suddenly, one of the engines gave a kind of hiccough and stopped. The other three engines quickly followed suit. There was plenty of fuel, and the captain was puzzled. He let the aircraft drift gently on as a glider. After a while he tried restarting the engines – he had to press the starter buttons, because the windmilling propellers drove only the free turbines – and in a minute or two he had all four running again.

The problem had been encountered while flying in cloud at about 20,000 feet. We

The reverse-flow layout of the Proteus engine almost killed the Britannia.

began looking for similar conditions, and soon found that in regions with a ground temperature around 40 °C (104 °F) the sky at 20,000 ft was full of ice crystals at about freezing point. Prolonged flight in these conditions led to a build-up of ice in the 180° bend of the Proteus's unique inlet ducts. Chunks could break off and either stall the compressor or extinguish the combustion or both. There was never the slightest danger, and a captain could avoid the problem by selecting a different cruise altitude.

The problem thus appeared to be trivial. Though the Air Registration Board was within its rights in revoking the Britannia's Certificate of Airworthiness, I – and, indeed, the Board – thought that Bristol Aero-Engines would find a cure very quickly. I saw no reason for BOAC to be unduly concerned.

To our dismay BOAC trumpeted the problem to the world as if it was a deadly hazard, which it emphatically was not. It was suddenly obvious that many of the top BOAC people had become so used to American aircraft that they were determined to stop the Britannia. Had BOAC shown a positive attitude, the problem could indeed have been solved in weeks. Instead the customer, more than the ARB, forced Bristol to carry out tests in all kinds of conditions, especially over the North Atlantic, where it was simple to prove that the ice-accretion problem *could not possibly be encountered*.

With Bristol Aero-Engines, we fitted the engines with a host of unnecessary palliatives, including Napier Spraymat electric de-icer surfaces, hot-air jets in the inlet elbows and platinum glowplugs which, energised continuously, relit the engine the moment the flame was extinguished. I never received any answer to my question, 'Why are you turning such an unimportant molehill into a huge mountain?'

A more detailed account will be found in Sir Stanley Hooker's *Not Much of an Engineer*. We continued making unnecessary modifications for *two years*. It delayed the Britannia's entry into service from March 1955 until February 1957. The ARB was only doing its job in demanding a cure to the problem, but what upset me was BOAC's determination to rubbish in the most public way what might have been a world-beating all-British airliner. One Fleet Street reporter said 'If it blows a fuse we hold the front page.' The ultimate result was that the Britannia's acceptance by BOAC was repeatedly postponed until the American big jets were also on the point of entering service. It destroyed the Britannia's widespread market appeal, and the cash-flow crisis came within an ace of driving the Bristol company bankrupt.

Through all of this there was little I could do. I sometimes even wondered if it had been a mistake to switch from the Centaurus piston engine, which would have resulted in a not greatly inferior Britannia and would probably have saved five harrowing years.

With each succeeding month VS and GSW became increasingly and more openly hostile to me, while at the same time subverting my efforts to heal the personal breach between us, and between the company and BOAC. Meanwhile, Bristol Aircraft's Chairman (VS held that role in the parent company), Cyril Uwins, the former Chief Test Pilot, radiated bonhomie and sat on the fence, never daring to say anything that would incense VS and GSW.

The root cause of all the problems had been the Proteus's maddening reverse-flow layout. Back in 1952 Stanley Hooker had seen the obvious need for a completely new-generation turboprop, with a sensible straight-through layout. He launched this as the BE.25, and it was soon named Orion and supported by the Ministry.

It was similar to the Proteus in size and weight, but twice as powerful. However, to absorb 9,000 hp would have called for enormous reduction gears and propellers, so Hooker hit on the neat idea of making the Orion give a power at take-off limited to 5,150 ehp, and holding this constant to 20,000 ft. Whereas, at 400 mph at 36,000 ft, a Proteus would give some 900 hp, the Orion still put out 3,300 hp.

Thus, while looking much like an installed Proteus, the Orion would enable a Super

G-ALBO, the original Britannia prototype, tested the superb Orion engine.

Britannia to be built, carrying over 200 passengers in a 'double-bubble' fuselage. With a thinner wing and slim nacelles making full use of the high Orion jet thrust, this aircraft would cruise at about 470 mph for ranges at least as great as the Britannia. The Orion began bench testing in October 1955, and in August 1956 flight testing began with an Orion in the No 1 (port outer) position on the Britannia prototype G-ALBO, with outstanding results. It was obvious that we could compete with the 707 and DC-8.

In 1953 the exciting prospect of a four-Orion aircraft took shape on the drawing board as the Bristol 187. Sixty Orions were ordered by BOAC, either for the 187 or for retrofitting to existing Britannias. However, the immediate task was to get something we could sell. In August 1956 I organised a sales tour with G-ANBJ, the tenth 102 for BOAC. Though less impressive than the Britannia 312, it could be shown to the growing number of people who had begun to show interest.

One of the latter was Capt. Eddie Rickenbacker, the World War 1 ace who had for many years run the huge Eastern Air Lines. I had visited him at his offices in New York's Rockefeller Plaza, but now he came to see us. We flew him around England, and he was so impressed we got to the stage of detailed negotiations. These foundered on Bristol's inability to produce. Eddie went off and bought DC-8s, and launched the slightly smaller Lockheed Electra turboprop.

Our sales tour began in Montreal. Here I naturally renewed acquaintance with TCA, who had put the Viscount firmly on the map. They were talking with Douglas about a DC-8 with Rolls-Royce engines. Our main discussions were with Canadair. Supremely capable, they were just finishing high-rate production of 1,815 Sabres and 656 T-33AN Silver Stars. To replace these huge programmes, the top men, John Jay Hopkins and J. Geoffrey Notman, had in 1954 signed a deal to build new versions of the Britannia for the RCAF.

One was the CL-28 Argus, a long-range ocean patrol and ASW (anti-submarine warfare) aircraft. It was powered by 3,700-hp Wright Turbo-Compound piston engines, which were more economical at the very low altitudes at which ASW aircraft fly. The fuselage was unpressurised, and provided with stations for a crew of 15 and a large weapons bay.

Apart from the complete redesign, every drawing was redrawn to US standards, and North American equivalents were established for all materials and parts. Despite this, the first CL-28 flew on 28 March 1957 and the 33rd and last was completed in July 1960.

The second derivative was the CL-44 transport. This was to be powered by the Orion, enabling take-off weight to be increased to 205,000 lb. In turn, this enabled the fuselage to be stretched by more than 12 ft. After I had left Bristol this aircraft went into production with Rolls-Royce Tyne engines, and the same engine was fitted to a high-wing cargo derivative of the Britannia which began life as the Bristol 195, became the Short SC.5 Britannic and was eventually produced as the Short Belfast.

Another potential customer was Howard Hughes, who ran TWA. We carried out detailed negotiations by telephone with Mr Hughes in his office in Culver City, Los Angeles. We sent him the massive Britannia 310-Series engineering and pilot manuals. A day or two later, in the middle of the night, Mr H said, 'I'd like to fly the

Britannia. I'll meet you in the lobby.' All the time, he and his aides had been in our hotel, in rooms just below us.

We drove out to the airport. Mr H got in the left-hand seat and removed his shoes, saying 'This gives me a better feel for the airplane.' He then proceeded to do everything unaided. Despite the Britannia's complexity, he had absorbed every detail, and our test pilot Walter Gibb was as amazed as I was.

We flew for the rest of the night. On return, he opened a cheque book and asked for a discount on the first 12, deliveries to start in November 1957. We just couldn't produce in time, and this perfectly genuine deal was never clinched.

From Montreal we went to Vancouver, where Canadian Pacific wanted a demonstration. President Grant McConachie led a CPA team on board, and we headed for Honolulu. Half-way there, oil pressure on No 4 engine fell to zero, and the propeller resisted all Walter Gibb's efforts to feather it. We diverted to Los Angeles. On the way we lost No 3 engine. We kept going, and landed on the two engines on the port wing.

To our relief, the Canadians were so impressed by the way the Britannia flew on Nos 1 and 2, and Gibb's outward unconcern, that they bought six Britannias, and at once set records from Vancouver to Amsterdam and Tokyo.

A brief respite from the problems came when Gordon Wansbrough-White (left), Technical Secretary (Britannia), organised a major TV programme on aviation in Bristol. Here I am explaining things on camera to two young air cadets.

Incidentally, the Britannia maintained the company's tradition of making quiet aircraft. The Japanese called the Beaufighter 'Whispering death', and the popular name for the Britannia was 'Whispering giant'.

Our main business in California was with Convair, in San Diego. Like Canadair, they were a Division of General Dynamics, and Hopkins was Chairman of both. They were keen to co-produce an Americanised Bristol 187 with Orion engines. We made good progress until in 1957 the British Government decided in its wisdom to terminate its support of the Orion. With Bristol's desperate cash-flow problems there was no way we could continue developing this superb engine. In turn, that killed the Bristol–Convair Super Britannia stone dead.

Looking ahead, while the factories at Filton and Belfast strove to build what eventually turned out to be a total of 85 Britannias, the design offices had almost nothing to do. I managed to get VS and GSW to permit Bristol Aircraft to start working on a jet airliner. By October 1956 this had firmed up as the 200 for BEA and the 201, with additional fuel, for BOAC. But would these ever get off the drawing board?

37

Decline and fall

In April 1957 Duncan Sandys had become the Minister of Defence. Having commanded a wartime rocket battery appeared to have gone to his head. He thought it would be nice to save money by replacing all British warplanes with rockets, and, with little discussion with Service chiefs (who could hardly argue) and none at all with the aircraft industry, he then actually put this ill-considered policy into effect. It was to have a devastating effect on everything from RAF recruitment – there was to be no further need for pilots – to British planemakers and advanced technology generally.

A dramatic side-issue was that – again without discussion – the Government also decided that there were too many aircraft companies. In its wisdom, it announced that there would henceforth be Government orders only for groups of firms which collaborated or, better still, proceeded to merge into single entities. That there were too many individual companies was probably true, but enforced mergers – at the time likened to shotgun weddings – were obviously a foolish proposition.

When these damaging policies hit the already struggling British industry, Bristol Aircraft was at last churning out Britannias in modest numbers. Having run out of reasons for not doing so, BOAC put the long-range Britannia 312 into London to New York service on 19 December 1957, two years later than planned.

However, on the same day the headlines were grabbed by a more enthusiastic customer. Israel's El Al flew their first proving flight from New York. Everyone waited to see where they would refuel. They did not refuel at all, but went on non-stop to Tel Aviv, 6,100 miles at 401 mph. On the 20th the airline placed an advertisement in the world's Press featuring larger and smaller terrestrial globes, saying, 'From the 23rd the Atlantic becomes 20 per cent smaller'. What a pity that we couldn't have had such support from our own airline. Two weeks later El Al flew NY to London at a block speed of 445 mph. They put the Britannia right back on the map, but by now it was too late. The world's airlines were queueing up to buy 707s and DC-8s.

By this time I was increasingly unhappy about the way VS was directing affairs at Filton, without any consultation with me. Besides the Britannia, which was coming off the line at dramatically reduced constructional man-hours, there was one other significant aeroplane contract: for the Bristol 188 supersonic research aircraft. I had long since ceased to be excited by the 188. Built to meet a Government specification of 1952, its main purpose was to investigate stainless-steel construction (for which one does not need to design a costly supersonic aeroplane and build six). By the late 1950s it was obvious that any programme relating to the 188 had become meaningless, and in fact the first of just two Bristol 188s did not fly until 14 April 1962. Designed for Mach 2.6, it actually achieved only Mach 1.8.

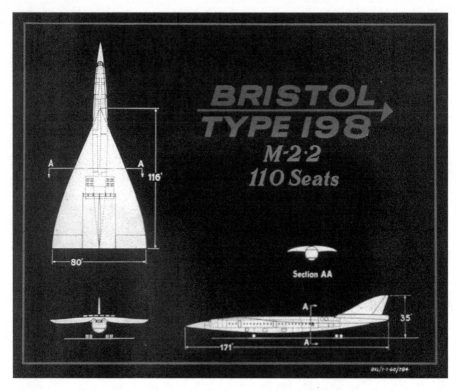

Bristol Aircraft never had the faintest chance of actually creating the Type 198.

The 188 had been expected to underpin the Type 198 six-engined SST, but by 1957 it was clear that the notion that Bristol Aircraft could make such a challenging aircraft was a pipe-dream. Indeed, I was increasingly aware that the whole situation of the company was perilous, and I could do nothing about it.

By 1957, while the Boeing and Douglas long-range jet airliners were coming into production on a massive scale, we could see the parts of the last Britannia to be built at Bristol coming onto the assembly line. We had nothing with which to follow it, and the cash-flow crisis was getting worse week by week. The attractive Bristol 200 small jet for BEA was still nothing but a series of drawings and brochures.

Without products a company is in a hopeless shape, and without the Type 200 I could see no future for Bristol Aircraft. Bill Strang did a masterly job in laying out this aft-engined jet. The only intractable problem was lack of a suitable engine. All we could do was hang four Bristol Orpheus on the back, but this turbojet in the 5,000-lb class had not been designed for such use. It had a short time between over-hauls, and its specific fuel consumption was unacceptably uneconomic.

As an alternative, we schemed the Bristol 200 with two 13,550-lb Olympus 551 turbojets. Sir Alec Coryton then persuaded his engine designers to come up with the much more suitable BE.47 turbofan, which used the low-pressure spool of the Orion. By spring 1957 the Type 200 had three engines. A year later Boeing began to firm up the design of the 727, and it looked almost precisely the same as our Bristol 200.

Thanks to Government (i.e. Sandys) policy, we were entering a long period of Cloud-cuckoo-land in which virtually the entire energy of the Boards of the British aircraft companies was devoted to organising partnerships, and in a few cases discussing genuine mergers. At Filton House, collaborating with another company, even on the Brabazon, had previously been unheard of, but the Government had said 'You'll get no work without it'. The Supply Minister, Aubrey Jones, even made it clear that consortia would have to finance aircraft development. In effect, the world-class British aircraft industry was being deliberately destroyed.

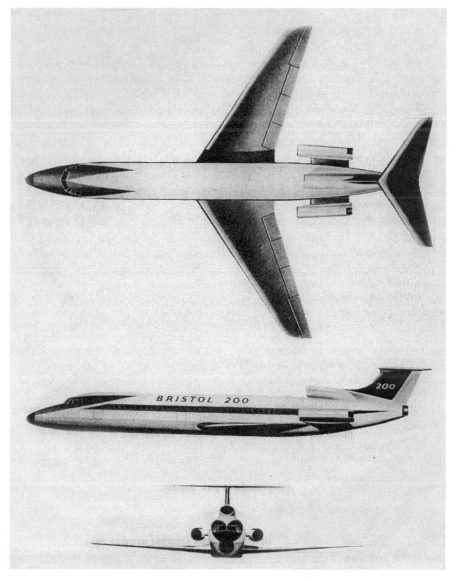

I even doubted Bristol's ability to finance and build the 200.

In September 1957 VS and Cyril Uwins attended a meeting at the Ministry of Supply at which leaders of major aircraft companies were told that there might, after all, be a new RAF aircraft. Beyond that, apart from possible civil aircraft, there was nothing. This was to be the crunch, to force through mergers. Bristol Aircraft was not invited to compete in the RAF project, which became the TSR.2.

I did all that I could to interest BEA in the Type 200 and derived versions, but found that Lord Douglas and Managing Director Tony Milward strongly favoured a de Havilland proposal, with Rolls-Royce engines. The airline was convinced of the merits of this partnership, and had already decided to buy the Comet 4B as an interim aircraft (the order was placed in March 1958). Proposals for the future BEA jet, to follow the Comet, were being offered with two, three or four engines, mounted on the rear fuselage or under the wings.

To my dismay, in September 1957 de Havilland offered to build BEA a three-jet aeroplane designated the D.H.121. for which Bristol Aircraft would be responsible for the wings. This was news to me! By that time VS was talking not with de Havilland but instead with Hawker Siddeley. Bristol had always been rivals of the giant Hawker Siddeley Group, but now VS was discussing collaboration.

By this time we had refined the design of the Bristol 200, while Hawker Siddeley were offering a rival project, the Avro 740. However, the Hawker Siddeley Board succumbed to VS's blandishments, and on 22 December 1957 I went to the Ministry of Supply to make a joint proposal with Hawker Siddeley for the BEA order.

What we proposed was the formation of a joint company, owned 65 per cent by Hawker Siddeley and 35 per cent by Bristol, to produce an enlarged Bristol 200 powered by three 14,000-lb Rolls-Royce RB.141 engines. Hawker Siddeley would handle the structure, stressing, flight controls and tankage, while Bristol would take care of the other systems. At once the media publicised a comparison of our supposedly inferior proposal with the supposedly preferable D.H.121.

On 8 January 1958 Hawker Siddeley held their Annual General Meeting. Its famous and genuinely furious Chairman, Sir Thomas Sopwith, said

'The combination of the most recent civil airlines experience enjoyed by Bristol with their great Britannia and by Hawker Siddeley with its outstanding record of flight in the Mach 0.9 speed regime is an unbeatable combination.

'To our astonishment, we now find that suggestions have been raised into the technical superiority of one of the paper designs submitted to BEA . . . This . . . is nonsense. The designs submitted to the BEA specification are almost exactly alike . . . this talk of technical superiority at this stage is simply a smokescreen.

'The eventual quality of the product is determined by the quality and strength of resources in terms of knowledge, experience and facilities which are placed behind the project . . . Let there be an end to this ill-founded gossip that the project we are offering is technically inferior . . .'

By this time, without consulting me, VS had offered the Chairmanship of Bristol Aircraft to Sir Matthew Slattery. He was an old friend of mine. He urged the Government to hold off the decision on the BEA jet, to see which rival was first to secure export orders. We soon announced that Pan American was interested in the

Bristol 205, with various engine options including Pratt & Whitney JT3s. Lord Douglas retorted that BEA would buy the D.H.121.

There wasn't much more we could do. Eventually, having failed in their team effort with us, Hawker Siddeley simply purchased the de Havilland company. Thus, the aircraft which BEA sponsored became known as the Hawker Siddeley 121, later named the Trident. What Hawker Siddeley had not counted on was that BEA would take leave of their senses and order the Trident to be made smaller, with engines of only 9,850 lb thrust. This absolutely destroyed its market potential, and handed the world market to the Boeing 727, which was exactly like Bill Strang's original Bristol 200.

Loss of the BEA order thus proved to be a blessing in disguise, but at the time it knocked out the little stuffing that the Bristol company had left. For the first time in the proud firm's existence, it was reduced to drawing things that it knew it had almost no chance of actually building. I did at least consider this potentially more useful than bickering over politics and mergers.

We produced drawings of the Type 211 twin-jet wing-pod transport, and of the Type 212 four-jet strategic freighter (which would have been rather better in most respects than the multinational A400M turboprop which by 2010 might start fulfilling the same task). We went on with the Type 214 twin-turboshaft helicopter, and the Type 216 car freighter derived from the Bristol 170 and powered by two 3,000-hp RR Dart turboprops. Unfortunately, nobody had the slightest expectation of seeing any of these projects built.

To put it bluntly, Bristol was flat broke. My own view was that there could still be a future for Bristol Aircraft, but in a totally unexplored field: light aeroplanes, otherwise known as General Aviation. I could not help wistfully recalling my youth. In 1935 British factories had delivered over 400 lightplanes. Now, in 1958, there was essentially no light-aircraft manufacturer in Britain, apart from Auster, whose designs were basically obsolete. I believed we might attack that market. It meant producing aircraft to attractive new designs.

A fundamental problem was that light aircraft are crucially sensitive to selling price, and the overheads at Bristol were among the highest in the industry. Short of forming a new 'back yard' subsidiary company which could build light aircraft at a competitive cost, all we could do for the moment was produce drawings and brochures. We started with the Type 218, an attractive light twin with four seats. This was the first Bristol lightplane since the Type 110A, a five-seater of 1928.

Hardly had we begun to work on this when, later in 1958, we learned that a new OR (Operational Requirement) had been issued for a light communications aircraft for the RAF. The particular requirement was to replace the venerable Avro Anson, 11,020 of which had been built since 1936. The OR specified a smaller twin-engined aircraft, with five seats.

We decided to compete, but almost at once had to put the idea on one side because of increased pressure on the impressive Type 198 SST. This pressure eased in late 1959, and Bill Strang managed to sidestep the dead hand of Russell, who was immersed in supersonic projects, and get the Chief Project Engineer, W.W. Morgan, to do the layouts for the Types 219 and 220. The former was a neat single-engined five-seater, and the 220 a twin-engined version of the same machine to meet the RAF

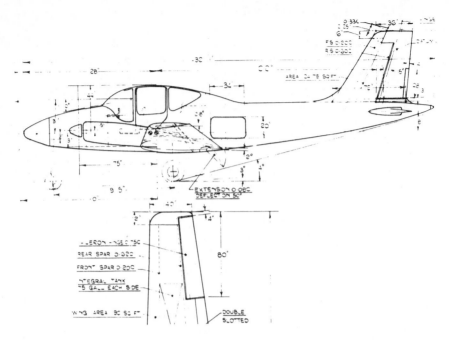

All we could produce of the 220 were drawings.

requirement. Little did we know that the 220 would be the last project ever drawn at Bristol (the 221 was a modified Fairey F.D.2).

Both projects were to have an all-metal airframe, tricycle landing gear and accommodation for a pilot and up to four passengers. As de Havilland had failed to produce a new engine to succeed the famous Gipsy family, the engines were to be two 260-hp six-cylinder Continental IO-470s. A key factor in this choice was that, after I had talked with Lord Hives, Rolls-Royce planned to back the Type 220 by making the American company's engines under licence. I met with John P. Herriot, who had managed Rolls-Royce's construction of their first Whittle jet engine. He agreed that, if I could launch a British General Aviation industry, Rolls would make Continental engines at their Motor Car division at Crewe.

I kept tweaking the 220, locally called the 'Masefield Twin'. We calculated the gross weight could be 5,000 lb, and cruising speed 230 mph. One day my son Charles came home from Cambridge University and found drawings on top of the piano. He criticised what he said was an unattractive vertical tail. I invited him to do better. He came up with a swept fin and rudder, scaled from that of the Vulcan. We adopted it.

Rather to my relief, VS and GSW showed not the slightest interest, because they knew Bristol did not have the cash needed to build a prototype. As each day went by, I became less interested in what was to all intents and purposes a defunct Bristol Aircraft, in which VS ruled the roost as an absolute monarch. I began to search for ways of turning the lightplane drawings, especially the 220, into actual aircraft. We even began costings for 100 Type 219s and 150 Type 220s. Meanwhile, in order to keep my Chief Test Pilot, Godfrey Auty, occupied I got him to evaluate the competition. In February 1960 he carefully tested a Cessna 310 and a Piper Apache.

While I did so, VS and GSW began talking with other companies about possible mergers. VS had come to realise that that was the only way for Bristol Aircraft to have any future. The fortunate result was that in February 1960 the powerful British Aircraft Corporation was set up, with the parent Bristol Aeroplane Company allocated a 20 per cent share. English Electric Aviation and Vickers-Armstrongs (Aircraft) each received 40 per cent. I had already left for pastures new.

38

Beagling

It is a reflection on the situation in the British aircraft industry at the end of the 1950s that, despite strenuous efforts, the only new aircraft work at Bristol Aircraft was the conversion of half a dozen Chipmunks up to the standard of Tango Mike. Called the Chipmunk Touring Conversion, this small batch found eager buyers. We wished we had built more, converting ex-RAF Chipmunks by arrangement with de Havilland Aircraft at Hatfield.

The entry for these aircraft in the Bristol pages of *Jane's All the World's Aircraft* seemed out of place alongside the Britannia and the supersonic Bristol 188, neither of which was actually being marketed. To keep as much of the Filton workforce occupied as possible, we assembled five Britannias from airframe sections shipped from Belfast. Having put on ice our plans for a short-haul jet, all we at Bristol Aircraft then had left were plans for a supersonic airliner, the mighty Type 198, which in 1962 were to bear fruit in partnership with the French as Concorde, a contract for 26 Belvedere helicopters for the RAF, and various helicopter projects.

The Belvederes had been designed mainly at Filton, but they were being made at the company's Old Mixon factory. Without consulting me, VS and GSW handed over that efficient helicopter factory to Westland, lock, stock and barrel, together with plans for the Bristol 181 helicopter airliner. The 181 would have carried 60 passengers at 200 mph, which no helicopter can do even today. I think it was foolish to give it to Westland, and even more foolish of Westland to do nothing with it, simply because it was 'NIH' (not invented here).

Since the RAF had been told by Duncan Sandys that it was to replace its aeroplanes with missiles – Bristol had nothing we could sell to airlines, the Company Board had got rid of its helicopters, and showed no interest in supporting my proposals for light aircraft – I had time on my hands for the first time in my life.

This was fortunate, because in 1959 I had been elected President of the Royal Aeronautical Society, and if properly fulfilled that eminent yet onerous position could take over one's waking hours entirely. I received no support from the Board whatsoever. Indeed, VS and GSW coldly resented my daring to take time off my work at Bristol in order to undertake my duties as President. However, by this time their opposition no longer bothered me. I used the Dove, and later Tango Mike, to visit branches of the society all over the United Kingdom, which no President had done previously. I attended a succession of Branch Dinners, and failed to attend just one: I arrived over Dublin in the Dove, in the dark, and found fog right down to the ground. I had no option but to return to Filton, and I managed to get back in there entirely because of a brilliant talk-down by the company's GCA (ground-controlled approach) team.

A little later in 1959 I was again airborne one morning, when the weather unexpectedly clamped in a way that brooked no argument. I was forced to land just north of Oxford at what had been RAF Kidlington, and was now a civil aerodrome. Over lunch, in near darkness and torrential rain, I found myself chatting with an impressive and pleasant character named Mike Bellhouse. It was potentially a meeting 'arranged in Heaven'.

Before the War Mike had been *in statu pupillari* at Magdalen College, Oxford. He had also become a Lloyds underwriter. During the war he had served in the RAF, but not as a pilot. Now he was learning to fly at the Oxford Aeroplane Club. He was most interested to hear about Tango Mike, which was parked outside, and wished he had bought one of the Chipmunk Tourers.

He casually told me that he was Deputy Chairman and Chief Executive of the great Oxford-based Pressed Steel Company. Its main business was bodies for road vehicles: in fact, they made about 40 per cent of all the bodies for British car manufacturers. They also made such things as railway rolling stock, Prestcold refrigerators, and aerospace hardware, notably rear fuselages and tails for Hawker Hunters.

I told him of our light-aircraft designs which we were just toying with at Bristol. To my astonishment and delight he replied, 'I've always wanted to get into light aviation. We're not short of a bob or two. Perhaps we ought to talk seriously.'

To get the ball rolling, on 15 July 1959 Mike Bellhouse wrote me a formal letter merely expressing interest in purchasing a Bristol Chipmunk Tourer, and inviting me to advise Pressed Steel upon the possible development of Kidlington. The company had production factories not only at Cowley (the head office, just outside Oxford) but also at Swindon, Swansea and at Linwood outside Glasgow. They were increasingly using aircraft (made in the USA, of course) to link all these big plants. They had just leased 580 acres at Kidlington, of which 123 were on the aerodrome.

Then began a cordial correspondence between us, as I made plans to disengage from Bristol Aircraft. I made my final formal proposal regarding General Aviation aircraft to the Bristol Board in November 1959, but the result was a foregone conclusion. As part of the forthcoming British Aircraft Corporation, they had no interest whatsoever.

At last, on 6 May 1960 – a fine morning, utterly unlike my first visit – I flew to Kidlington in Tango Mike and lunched with Mike and with his Managing Director, Joe E. Edwards. At that lunch we decided to form what we called British Executive & General Aviation Ltd. BEAGAL instantly suggested the name Beagle. This was to be a wholly owned subsidiary of Pressed Steel. Mike was to be Chairman and Joe Deputy Chairman. I was to be Managing Director, once I was free of Bristol.

Thus, from that chance meeting came a rebirth of the British General Aviation (GA) industry. At Pressed Steel's request, to get a better handle on the problem, I wrote a detailed Memorandum outlining the prospects for a new British company to build light aircraft. One of its first acts would be to acquire, for £1,000, the rights to the Bristol 219 and 220. It would also consider purchasing existing companies working in this field of activity. The document was dated 2 June 1960.

I have already related how in the 1930s the skies were filled with light aircraft produced by many famous British companies. Some, such as Avro and de Havilland, moved up to bigger aircraft. With others, either their leaders died, or they were taken over by big companies, or for many other reasons, by 1959 they ceased to exist.

Yet if anything the market was bigger than ever. In the USA sales of light aircraft had risen from 6,100 in 1957 to 6,400 in 1958 and to 7,700 in 1959. A similar firm growth could be seen in Canada, Australia and France. In the United Kingdom the position was somewhat different.

Before 1939 in the United Kingdom a light aircraft which had been made in a foreign factory and imported was a strange curiosity. Then came the war. From that time onwards there was no such thing as a British civil lightplane industry, and imports of such aircraft were strictly prohibited. Then in 1959 the ban on imports had at last been lifted, and there was a huge pent-up demand.

In 1960 almost every light aircraft now coming on to the British register had to be imported. With one exception, the famous British light-aircraft firms had disappeared, or were vanishing into the huge groups BAC and Hawker Siddeley, which had no interest in such lowly products. There had been a few tiny groups that did not give up without a struggle – such as Thruxton/Paragon, Rollason and Phoenix – but these all eventually had to call it a day. It left only one British company still producing light aeroplanes: Auster Aircraft.

This had started in 1938 as Taylorcraft Aeroplanes (England), building under licence the American Taylorcraft designs. These were simple high-wing monoplanes made of welded steel tube covered with fabric. At the outbreak of war some were impressed into the RAF and given the name Taylorcraft Auster. The RAF started ordering Austers, and wartime production of the Auster Mks 1 to 6 amounted to almost 2,000. They gave excellent service, often in harsh conditions.

Rearsby, about eight miles north-east of Leicester, was the home of Auster.

In 1946 the Leicester-based company changed its name to Auster Aircraft. It set about marketing a civilian version of the wartime three-seat Auster 5, called the Autocrat and priced at £815. Soon different versions proliferated, and in the 1950s Auster turned out about 1,050 new civil aircraft, apart from hundreds of 'civilised' ex-RAF machines. By 1960, for all practical purposes the British General Aviation industry *was* Auster, and it was dying on its feet.

We lost no time in talking with Auster Aircraft, who quickly became enthusiastic about our suggestion that we should simply buy them. The Chairman, and founder of the original firm, was Frank Bates. He was not a pilot, but he was a keen businessman. He recognised that Auster designs were becoming outdated, but was reluctant to spend large sums developing new technology. This situation, so common in British industry, could have only one conclusion.

On 7 October 1960, funded by Pressed Steel, Beagle was formed. A month later it purchased the Auster share capital for £525,000. We then formed Beagle-Auster Aircraft, and appointed Frank Bates Deputy Chairman of this subsidiary.

This was a good move, and from then on new Beagle-Austers continued to proliferate. They had not only names but also numeric designations with the prefix A, notably the A.61 Terrier, A.109 Airedale and A.113 Husky. All were derived from earlier Austers, retaining the high-wing layout and steel tube/fabric construction.

At the same time we began talking with Miles. Fred Miles had begun designing aircraft in 1930, soon assisted by his beautiful and talented wife Maxine, widely known as 'Blossom'. He was also joined by his younger brother George, and as Phillips & Powis Aircraft they produced trainers (see page 313) and target tugs for the RAF throughout the war, changing the company name in October 1943 to Miles Aircraft.

After the war they became too ambitious, producing a profusion of new prototypes, and went bankrupt in November 1947. Their largest product, the four-engined Marathon (as related earlier, this was almost foisted on BEA) was taken over by Handley Page.

In 1951 F.G. Miles Ltd was formed, to undertake aircraft and plastics work at Shoreham, later building actuators and even flight simulators. In May 1957 Miles flew the M.100 Student, an attractive light jet trainer, but this failed to find a customer. As before, Fred was Chairman and Managing Director and George was Chief Designer, though Blossom did at least as much of the designing without receiving the credit. The director in charge of production was Jack Angell. He never let a fondness for strong liquor interfere with his work.

By 1960 Miles had expanded into making significant airframe parts under subcontract, such as installations of the jet engines for the Comet, Caravelle and Conway-707. They also carried out most of the design work for Bill Lear's SAAC-23, which became the original Learjet. George, in particular, was a talented designer/pilot. They were worth talking with.

On their drawing boards were two versions of the same four-seat design, the M.114 Martlet, intended to replace the Messenger, and the M.115 Merlin, to replace the twin-engined Gemini. A bold feature was that these aircraft were to have airframes made mainly of GFRP (glass-fibre reinforced plastics), though such structure had not gained Air Registration Board approval.

Beagle offered the brothers an excellent deal. Secretly, they were delighted, but they thought it a good ploy to reject our offer – at least for the time being. By October 1960, however, the writing was on the wall. The British aircraft industry was suffering from merger-mania, and the Government hinted that Miles might receive no further work unless they toed the merger line.

We arranged 'a technical and manufacturing liaison' with Miles, and on 16 February 1961 the aviation work at Shoreham became Beagle-Miles Aircraft. The brothers banked a hefty cheque, and began drawing developed versions of the M.114 and M.115. These were designated the M.117 and M.218, respectively. (The 218, with twin engines, was to become a junior partner of our Bristol 220, replacing the Bristol 219.)

We also talked with Wing Commander Ken Wallis, who had developed the Bensen light autogyro to the point where it could be flown 'hands and feet off'. We took him under the Beagle wing, and encouraged him to keep making Beagle-Wallis 'WA' autogyros. In the years that followed, he pressed ahead with a succession of record-breaking designs. Beagle-Wallis was the least of our problems!

To tie everything together, we opened a small corporate head office at Sceptre House in London's Regent Street. Here the management set up shop, together with, to my delight, my long-time colleague Peter Brooks. The outgoings each month were awesome, but with Pressed Steel behind us and careful management I had no fears. In any case, we intended soon to be selling lots of aircraft.

By far the biggest programme became dubbed the 'Masefield Twin', which I had originally schemed as the Bristol 220. Pressed Steel bought the rights to this design for £1,000, and we then renamed it the Beagle B.206. Top of the Beagle range, this aircraft was targeted squarely at the RAF's need to replace the venerable Avro Anson in various transport and crew-training roles. We hardly expected to equal the Anson's production run of 11,020, but felt confident that the RAF total would get well into three figures. I received hints that the initial batch would be for 80 aircraft.

Perhaps predictably, the customer kept 'moving the goalposts', by adding to the range, payload or equipment, to incorporate the latest RAF thinking. Among other things, we switched from electric to hydraulic actuation for the flaps and landing gear. Without increasing the aircraft's size or power, the ever-increasing demands made the gross weight go up from our starry-eyed 5,000 lb to more than 6,300 lb. The Beagle Board agreed that the prototype, called the B.206X, should be constructed by Beagle-Miles at Shoreham. At that time this was the only Beagle factory with stressed-skin capability.

During 1961 I spent much time trying to rationalise the diverse parts of our scattered company. I was delighted to find that our owner, Pressed Steel, was in all respects absolutely straightforward. On the other hand, I soon received warning signs in our relationship with the Miles brothers. George Miles, a capable and experienced man, had been appointed Beagle Technical Director and Chief Designer. I began to regret having assigned Beagle-Miles the crucial job of undertaking the detail design and construction of the B.206X. Getting this into the air as quickly as possible was the top priority, but I soon considered it prudent to set up a purely Beagle design team at Shoreham, headed by my former Bristol colleague Ron Woodhams.

This was largely because time was of the essence. While the Miles team worked long hours to get the B.206X ready for the 1961 Farnborough airshow, the Woodhams team liaised with potential customers, especially the RAF, in order to define and then create the production aircraft. Inevitably, this soon began to diverge from the smaller B.206X.

There were dangers in such a procedure. One was that it offended the Miles brothers, whose attitude from the start had been totally self-centred. It did not occur to me at the time, but I now realise that in setting up Beagle I was also offending the political establishment. On the one hand they were intent on merging and shutting down British aircraft companies, while, with Pressed Steel, I was daring to start one (in fact, I was merging two into what I hoped could be a harmonious whole).

This is a good point at which to mention that for many years my problems were eased by a supremely capable personal assistant. Margaret Lawrence had joined me at BEA. She learned to fly and became an aviation authority herself. She came with me to Bristol, where, for example, she played a key role in a long non-stop Britannia flight to Canadian Pacific at Vancouver. At Beagle she not only managed my office but also flew as co-pilot with our diminutive but brilliant test pilot 'Pee Wee' Judge on many Royal Aero Club competitive events.

I subsequently received abundant evidence that the RAF had adopted a vehemently anti-Beagle attitude, losing no opportunity to rubbish the B.206 even before the B.206X had flown. I was repeatedly told that the choice of the Service was the Dove 8, a version of an aircraft first flown in 1945. Again, it was only later that I realised that much of this was due to intensive lobbying by de Havilland's long-time Sales Director, Francis St Barbe.

He was said to oppose anyone seeking to compete against de Havilland, even though that company was in any case vanishing into the giant Hawker Siddeley Group. I am sure that, had I known the personality and political problems which would confront the Beagle enterprise, I would never have ventured to start it!

39

Trying to please the RAF

As they were simple derivative designs, the Beagle-Austers appeared first. They brought detail improvements to the existing Auster range, and also introduced two new types first flown shortly before Pressed Steel took over the Leicestershire company.

In March 1960 Ranald Porteous, the famous Auster test pilot at Rearsby, had begun testing the D.5/160 Husky, a multirole utility machine with a 160-hp Lycoming and balloon tyres. It flew well, with an exhilarating performance. Renamed the A.113, Beagle-Auster managed to sell a handful, upgraded with the 180-hp Lycoming. However, we failed to find a buyer for the A.115, previously known as the AOP.11, or Mk Eleven. Powered by a 260-hp Continental, this was a much more powerful derivative of the AOP.9. An outstanding multirole machine, able to take off in not much over 100 metres, it ran into a brick-wall attitude with the British Army, who emphasised that they wanted nothing but helicopters, which were much more costly both to buy and to maintain.

We were astonished that the Army did not want the Mk Eleven.

The B.206X.

First of the Beagle-Austers, the three-seat Terrier flew on 13 April 1961. Based on the military Auster 6B, this had improved furnishings, glassfibre spats, a Fairey-Reed metal propeller, long exhaust pipe and silencer (muffler), and other changes. It was priced at £1,995, and we lost heavily on each Terrier sold.

On 16 April 1961 Ranald Porteous began testing the four-seat Airedale. This was a new design, with a 180-hp Lycoming O-360, tricycle landing gear and my son Charles's sweptback vertical tail. Priced at £4,750, it looked attractive, and was the type of traditional aeroplane the Rearsby factory was used to. The down side was that it was seriously underpowered. The venerable D.H. Gipsy Queen family were all much too heavy, and we had to make do with an engine of not much more than half the power the Airedale really needed. The second Airedale was bought by *Flight International*, whose Mark Lambert once famously said to a colleague 'Let's take the Airedale, we can have breakfast during take-off'.

By far the biggest project was the Beagle B.206. After a round-the-clock effort at Shoreham the B.206X flew on 15 August 1961, in good time for the Farnborough airshow where it made an excellent impression. From the handling point of view, the B.206X was almost perfect from the start.

Had we been able to go straight into production all would probably have been well. The B.206X, powered by two 260-hp Continental IO-470 engines and derived directly from the projected Bristol 220, came out at a gross weight of 6,194 lb. The beautifully furnished interior, schemed by Pressed Steel Ltd, could be arranged for a pilot and four passengers. The media liked the fact that the instrument panel was 'wider than that of a Viscount', and that leg room was 'better than in airliners'. With maximum payload, the range was about 1,150 miles at 170 mph. Not least, it looked beautiful, its appearance being enhanced by the Beagle house colours of cream and bronze.

We were later to discover that the specially mixed bronze paint was not only expensive but also not colour-fast. In the course of a few months it changed from shiny bronze to a dirty brown. We didn't need such pinpricks, because, by the time the B.206X flew, the ever-increasing demands made by the constantly changing RAF requirement had almost forced Beagle to start all over again with the larger B.206Y.

Had we simply tooled up to manufacture the original aircraft I have no doubt we would have sold a considerable number. Though less capable than the B.206 which was eventually developed, it nevertheless did a fine job, and, apart from the superficial problem of the bronze paint, had no shortcomings. However, the prospect of a significant RAF order – we were led to believe it might be for an initial 79, almost certainly followed by further orders for derived versions – offered not only a good foundation but also a valuable sales cachet.

Optimistically, I built up the Shoreham design office until it numbered almost 100. I regarded it as essential to concentrate on the swiftest possible production of a B.206 to meet the RAF's ever more severe requirements, and this demanded a design

Here flown by 'Pee Wee' Judge, the M.218 was flawed by its unproven glassfibre structure.

organisation matched to the job. It was quite distinct from the adjacent Beagle-Miles design office, which was in any case heavily committed to the previous Miles programmes, and to the M.117. This pre-existing Miles design for a four-seater to follow their M.28 and M.38 was notable for its bold use of GFRP for control surfaces, fuselage decking and canopy, and wing leading and trailing edges.

As soon as the original B.206X design load eased, the Miles brothers switched the effort to the M.218, a twin-engined version of the M.117. This four-seat prototype flew on 19 August 1962. Powered by 145-hp Continental O-300s, it had a design range of nearly 600 miles at 160 mph. It looked attractive, and would have sold well, but unfortunately the Air Registration Board said, 'We have no experience of GFRP, so we will impose a 100-per-cent strength reserve on these parts.' This was an almost crippling imposition, which had greatly increased the empty weight over that of a traditional metal aircraft, and over GFRP aircraft without such a penalty.

In 1962/3 the Rearsby factory was in production with the Airedale. This was almost the only product Beagle was selling, and, because of its inadequate performance, there were few customers. I stopped production at No 44. From the start, we had recognised that this aircraft needed at least 220 hp, but had to make do with only 180 hp. Apart from 'lack of poke', the Airedale was a nice aircraft, with no vices. My son Charles and David (Lord) Trefgarne flew the second production Airedale to Australia, where it immediately found a buyer.

Sadly, it took us more than two years to sell the remaining 43, and we did not build any more. This was 524 aircraft short of our break-even point, which itself was almost certainly optimistic. Life is full of 'if onlys', but if only Rolls-Royce had gone into production with six-cylinder Continentals, starting with an engine rated at 220 hp, the Airedale might be in production at Rearsby to this day. Perhaps I should have tried harder with Rolls-Royce, but at the time my thoughts were concentrated entirely on the B.206, at Shoreham.

That left only the Terrier to bring in a trivial income, while the main force of Beagle's engineers strove to meet the RAF's demands for the B.206. Nearly all the technical staff had come to Beagle from other companies in the once-great British aircraft industry. One day I was presented with A PETITION TO MR. P.G. MASEFIELD. It deplored 'rumoured changes in the Beagle organisation', and proclaimed that 'we do not wish to work for a Miles company in any shape or form'. It was signed by 41 names, each with the previous employer added. The latter included almost every one of the famous British planemakers, led by 16 who were ex-Vickers-Armstrongs.

I was able to assure the signatories that the 'Miles' rumour was without foundation. Indeed, I was able to tell them that F.G. Miles had been fired. Apart from other problems, he had used Beagle staff to build a swimming pool at his house near Shoreham. His brother George could have been a valued member of the team, but, influenced by his brother, he was highly critical of almost everything we did, always put his own company first, and spent his time organising subcontract work, such as making nacelles for the One-Eleven, and trying to sell the Miles Student to the South African Air Force. I was relieved when he finally resigned in July 1963.

My only relief from these early problems was the unwavering support of Mike and Joe at Pressed Steel, even though our results for 1962 showed the disappointing net loss of £2.1 million. By the spring of 1963 the production B.206 for the RAF still seemed as far away as ever, with the requirement still being changed month by month. By this time the demands included conveying the pilot, plus a five-man V-bomber crew in full flying clothing with parachutes, plus a ground-crewman, non-stop between the UK and Malta, whilst burdened with more than 400 lb of additional communications and navigation electronics. An alternative requirement was to provide a comfortable ride for an Air Marshal in full-dress uniform complete with a sword in its scabbard.

All the time, we were receiving dismal reports of apparent disparagement of Beagle by influential uniformed RAF and civilian officials. Ranald Porteous made a practice of getting into conversation with civil servants and RAF offices around the world, and learned that their opinion of the B.206 (before any had flown) was that it was 'second-rate rubbish'. The primary choice of the RAF continued to be the less-capable D.H. Dove 8, while the Ministry of Aviation (MoA) lobbied for the much more expensive Beech Queen Air, to support Short Brothers' Light Aircraft Division (which was developing the HDM.105 transport after purchasing the rights from Miles!).

Throughout this disappointing and stressful period, as well as frequently meeting with the RAF and MoA, I spent a great deal of time endeavouring to hold the various parts of Beagle together. On a typical day I would be out of the house early in the morning, drive to Redhill or Gatwick and fly Gemini G-AIRS to Shoreham. After discussions there I would fly to Rearsby and back. I soon felt that I knew every tree on the route, just as I had along the track to Filton.

The prototype B.206Y.

After a heroic round-the-clock effort, on 12 August 1962 the first of the stretched – and, I hoped, definitive – B.206 prototypes began flight testing at Shoreham. Designated B.206Y, and registered G-ARXM, it had 310-hp Continental GIO-470A engines, which, regrettably but understandably, Rolls-Royce still showed no inclination to make under licence. Span was increased from 38 ft to 43 ft, and it was later extended to 45 ft 9½ in. Other changes included largely redesigned flight-control surfaces, and a cabin which maintained its full width one frame further aft to provide for a triple seat in the third row. Lockheed (no relation to the American company) provided a hydraulic power pack which operated the landing gear, flaps and inbuilt airstairs.

In late 1962 we received the first order for the B.206, but it was merely for two aircraft ordered by the Ministry of Aviation 'for evaluation'. We designated these the B.206Z. Aircraft Z1 was completed at Shoreham, and flown there by 'Pee Wee' Judge on 24 January 1964. Z2 was completed on the intended future assembly line at Rearsby, and began flight testing, also by Pee Wee on 20 February 1964. Both were close to the standard of the intended RAF aircraft. They were the first to incorporate wings made by Boulton Paul Aircraft at Wolverhampton, to which company, led since 1934 by Dr J.D. North, we had subcontracted all production wings.

Tired of the sniping, and to bring matters to a head, in February 1963 I managed to set up a direct comparison between the B.206Z and a Dove 8. Flown at Northolt, this was to be a 'gladiatorial contest' between the aircraft, each loaded to its maximum weight. It was flown off before an audience of Ministry officials, de Havilland observers led by Francis St Barbe, and my Beagle team.

The result was even more one-sided than I had expected. The B.206 took off in a shorter distance, climbed faster and demonstrated a better single-engine performance, turning against the live engine. In addition, it showed an impressive slow-flying ability, and ended the contest with a landing run barely half as long as that of the Dove. At that point Stewart Scott-Hall, Principal Director of Technical Development at the Ministry of Supply, shook my hand whilst smiling broadly, though of course he made no comment. I believe that the capabilities shown by the Beagle contender came as a surprise to the officials, and to our competitor.

At last, on 6 May 1963 the Minister of Aviation (at that time Julian Amery) announced that the RAF would indeed buy the B.206, *but a mere twenty*. With the Pressed Steel Board, I did some rapid arithmetic which suggested that we would lose money on the deal. The basic price of the RAF aircraft had been pegged at £30,000, whereas the minimum price for an unequipped civil B.206 was £35,000 and the price with full airways equipment could hardly be less than £57,000. All our calculations had been based on a run of at least 250, of which not less than 79 would be for the RAF. By the narrowest of margins, and after full consultation with Pressed Steel, we decided not to cut our losses but to go on.

Our outgoings were already several times greater than our optimistic original guesstimates. Even more serious, the British motor-car industry was no longer riding the crest of a wave but was sinking deeply into recession. The last thing Pressed Steel now wanted was to find a way of spending the dwindling store of excess profits!

My only consolation was that in the B.206Y we had created a beautiful and refined aircraft which could compete against anything else in its class. On 7 March 1963 Pee

Wee, I and others climbed aboard X-ray Mike to give a payload of 900 lb, took off from Shoreham, overflew Wick, at the tip of Scotland, and flew back. We calculated we had covered 1,130 miles non-stop in 5 hr 44 min at an average ground speed of 197 mph against an average headwind of 24 mph, and landed with fuel for a further 530 miles. Taking into account a mild centre-of-gravity problem at full load when the maximum possible weight was loaded into the aft baggage compartment, I felt that all we had to do now was to go into full production.

40

The dream fades

By 1965 the rosy future for Beagle had appeared harder to achieve. The underlying reason was a severe and prolonged downturn in the motor industry. That had been Pressed Steel's main business. To make things worse, their substantial production of Prestcold refrigerators was now making losses instead of profits. So far Beagle had achieved little for Pressed Steel, other than spending a lot of its money. Ever an optimist, I believed that in the B.206 and B.242 we had two world-class products which from now on would begin to repay their investment.

The key factor had been the carrot of an RAF order. When this at last came I was dismayed to be informed that 20 was indeed to be the overall total. The aircraft the B.206 was intended to replace had been bought to the tune of 11,020. Moreover, I continued to receive evidence of sustained hostility by the RAF towards the Beagle aircraft, which had been designated Basset CC.1. We had been faced with an almost impossible task in trying to meet performance standards which had been agreed at a time before the RAF had added a heavy burden of extra equipment.

We managed to start flight testing the first B.206C civil production aircraft on 17 July 1964, followed on Christmas Eve 1964 by the first Basset CC.1 for the RAF. Both aircraft were as enjoyable to fly as the 206Y, though the mass of equipment finally specified for the Basset had a severe effect on the practical range. This burden included comprehensive duplicated radios and navigation systems, including a Decca Flight Log and SP.2 autopilot, a large dinghy and survival gear, engine fire detectors and extinguishers and airways-standard de-icing.

To replace 11,020 Ansons (left) the RAF bought 20 Bassets.

These were not wide-bodies but small aircraft, and more than 1,000 lb of equipment meant an equal weight cut off either the payload or the fuel. Though it is a matter
of simple arithmetic, the RAF wanted it both ways, and did all it could to put poor
figures into the Boscombe Down report. It publicly rubbished the Basset, because its
engine-out climb gradient did not meet British Civil Airworthiness Requirements
minima, overlooking the fact that no other RAF aircraft were operated to civil
standards.

We did our best, and delivered all 20 Bassets very quickly. At the start there were
several problems, affecting the landing gear, exhaust augmentor tubes and, when
operating at maximum weight on bumpy grass airfields, the tips of the propeller
blades could hit the ground. These difficulties were soon overcome, and – perhaps to
the chagrin of its detractors – the Basset settled down to give good service. The fact
that in 1969 one was allocated to the Queen's Flight, where among other things it was
used for the multi-engine conversion flying of Prince Charles, says it all.

To this day I harbour a suspicion that the RAF was prejudiced against any aircraft
made by us. Every air force needs a versatile light transport, and the RAF needed to
replace not only 11,020 Ansons but also 40 Devons (the RAF name for the Dove) and
52 Pembrokes. Instead of replacing these, the RAF required the Basset *to carry
V-bomber crews with full equipment non-stop to Malta and Gibraltar.*

Seen off Beachy Head, the second B.206C went to the United States as N163.

This was such an unlikely requirement, I am not surprised the order was for a mere 20 aircraft. Once in service, the Bassets were just used for odd jobs in the UK. I felt that we had suffered all the worst features of a protracted procurement process and, having been almost broken financially by the process, received a scant reward.

The only comfort was that we had produced what was by any standard a superb aeroplane. Indeed, with still more power it could be made even better. Recognising this, we purchased a pair of 340-hp Continental GTSIO-520C turbocharged engines to power a new prototype which we called the B.206S or Series II. Meanwhile, we followed up leads all over the world, many of them triggered by Ranald Porteous, who had moved from being Auster's famous test pilot to Beagle Export Sales Manager. One hot prospect was the Royal Flying Doctor Service in Australia, and my son Charles, who by 1964 was a sales and demonstration pilot for Beagle, argued that we should take a B.206 'down under'.

The first production civil B.206 aircraft, G-ASMK, had flown very successfully on 17 July 1964. The second, G-ASOF, followed on 22 October. While No .01, Mike Kilo, completed performance trials, I sat with a team at Pressed Steel's office in Cowley and planned a sales tour through the Near and Far East and Australia. We readied the second B.206C, Oscar Foxtrot, and in November 1964 this aircraft left Shoreham crewed by my son Charles as pilot and Harold W. Dawes. I was deep in discussions with the BAA (see Chapter 42) at the Ministry of Civil Aviation, but followed by BOAC, and caught up with them on 20 November in Singapore. We were at once engaged in serious talks, particularly involving our projected single-engined B.121 (later named Pup) for the Singapore Flying Club.

Our route to Australia had to give Indonesia the widest possible berth, because of the state of 'confrontation' which had broken out there. We had no option but to plan a route by way of the Philippines and the Palau islands. These are mere dots in the Pacific, about 500 miles east of the Philippines and 900 north of New Guinea.

I was not encouraged by the fact that this was where, 27 years previously, Amelia Earhart and Cart. Noonan had disappeared without trace. From Davao on the southern tip of the Philippines a 1,400-mile detour was required, with absolutely no alternate and the prospect of only a very short-range radio contact. Charles and I left Davao and held an accurate course, but were unable to raise Palau until we were less than 100 miles away. We hit Palau on the nail with just an hour's fuel to spare!

Just like pioneer flights of the 1930s, we refuelled from barrels of Shell. Then, from Palau we set course due south for Wewak, in North-East New Guinea. Nearly five hours later we arrived at dusk, to be welcomed by a missionary who told us that he had come to replace his predecessor who had been eaten by a local tribe! We had dinner outside a hut. Then they started a generator set and set up the cinema. As the film started I was concerned to notice a horde of humans emerging from the jungle. I was told, 'They're Jap army. They never surrendered. When we have a film they creep out of the jungle and watch, and then creep back. There are about 300 of them.'

In Australia we found intense interest in the 206. We plugged on through fierce heat to Sydney, where, after demonstrations at Broken Hill, the Royal Flying Doctor Service of New South Wales bought two. What clinched the deal was that extensive experience of operations in high temperatures had rammed home what we had long believed: that we had to offer a supercharged 206. Accordingly, the Australians signed for the B.206S, the first of which, G-AVHO, began flight testing on 23 June 1965. Apart from GTSIO-520 engines it had further improvements, the most important of which was to extend the cabin aft with a large (43 × 37 in) door on the left. All subsequent 206s were to this standard, apart from the Series III mentioned later.

It was soon clear that most customers wanted the B.206S. With pilot and six passengers, and full airways radio, autopilot and other equipment, the range was 915 miles at 219 mph, or 1,210 miles at 191 mph. With four passengers and very generous baggage and refreshment allowances the range was 1,605 miles. We priced the bare aircraft at £39,000 or around £49,000 with avionics. The customer list grew rapidly.

Meanwhile, on 27 August 1964, we had flown the first B.242. Constructed at Shoreham, this was basically a much-improved B.218, in which the plastics parts had been replaced by metal. Powered by two 195-hp Continental IO-360A engines – which Rolls-Royce intended to make, but never did – the B.242 was a most attractive four-seater, with hydraulic flaps and inwards-retracting main landing gear, the only unusual feature being the 'slab' tailplanes, each with a large trim and anti-balance tab. Able to cruise at up to 205 mph, it was a delight to fly, and before long orders came in like the proverbial hot cakes, against a quoted price for the basic aircraft of £14,000.

Unfortunately, our total concentration on what we saw as the primary task of getting the B.206 fully developed and into production caused us to postpone production of the smaller twin, until its development became economically possible. On the

While Beagle's world was collapsing, we built the fuselage mock-up for the B.222 (piston engines) and B.224 (PT6A-17 turboprops).

Bassets on the assembly line at Rearsby.

other hand, by 1964 the fact that our business had been built on the foundation of small Auster aircraft, for which we had no replacement, caused a swift rethink and a quick decision to get cracking on our single-engined projects.

The result was that, when we staged a big sales presentation at Shoreham in early 1965 one of the disclosures was the B.121, a two/three-seater derived from the B.242. Powered by a 100-hp Rolls-Royce Continental O-200A, it looked attractive, despite having fixed tricycle landing gear. Another disclosure was the B.222, a bigger pressurised derivative of the B.206. We had a wealth of attractive projects, in most cases fully costed. Sadly, we were never to build any of them.

What was to prove a bombshell smote us in July 1965. For several years the recession in the motor industry had hit Pressed Steel particularly hard, and in that month its Board accepted a takeover bid by the giant British Motor Corporation, which had a single-minded fixation on road vehicles, particularly cars. I had seen this coming, and prepared to do battle. At one Board meeting BMC chief Sir George Harrison expressed the thought that our aeroplanes might be a useful adjunct to quality cars, but this turned out to be 'pie in the sky'.

In the real world, even mighty BMC were struggling as badly as Pressed Steel were. Indeed, it came about that, at the instigation of the Industrial Reorganization Corporation, BMC in turn was taken over by the even more single-minded Leyland Motors, to form British Leyland. The upshot was that Pressed Steel, the prosperous, versatile and positive-thinking foundation on which Beagle had been built, was brutally dismantled and sold off, mainly to Ford and Rootes. This left Beagle as an orphaned lamb looking for a buyer.

Throughout 1965 one of a succession of Government committees, this time under

Lord Plowden, had been investigating British aviation and deciding what should be done with this problem child. At last, in December 1965, the committee issued its Report. To my great relief it said that Government support should be given to the manufacture of light aircraft. There was only Beagle Aircraft Ltd.

In the end, after tortuous and difficult negotiations, the Government – in the form of the Ministry of Aviation, initially under Roy Jenkins and then under Fred Mulley – agreed with my forecast that Beagle had a useful range of aircraft in development. It also agreed that the business could be expected to break even five years hence, in 1972/3, and then go on to make substantial profits, especially in the export market. On 13 December 1965 the Government agreed to offer us the necessary backing. The sum needed was put at £3.75 million, though I must admit that I never expected to get it.

At 31 December 1965 Beagle had already received from Pressed Steel a total of £5,435,667. We had delivered two Bassets to the Ministry and 13 to the RAF, with the remaining seven awaiting collection. We had also delivered six B.206C civil aircraft, the first going to Rolls-Royce. We had delivered 322 other aircraft, 166 of them for export, all of these being of basically Auster design. We had a further 102 aircraft awaiting buyers or under negotiation. Most importantly, the B.206 was a proven product, and the first supercharged B.206S, a superb aircraft in all respects, was ready for delivery. What did the future hold?

41

End of the dream

From August 1966 we beavered away at Shoreham on our single-engined aircraft, the design team now led by the excellent ex-Bristol Director of Engineering John Larroucau. Almost inevitably, after a most amicable consultation with the creator of an earlier aircraft of that name, Sir Thomas Sopwith, we named the B.121 the Pup. In parallel, we planned the B.121T military version. With a more powerful engine, this eventually went into production as the B.125 Bulldog.

The first Pup, G-AVDF, began to be flight-tested by Pee Wee Judge on 8 April 1967. From the outset, everyone who had a go at it, including Prince Philip, the legendary Capt. O.P. Jones and of course myself, raved about its flawless handling. They heaped praise on the panel, the use of two sticks instead of control wheels, the all-round view, and the steerable nosewheel. Most of all, they enjoyed flying the Pup, including trying its exemplary spinning characteristics. The all-metal structure was stressed to +4.5g/–1.5g. Almost the only change we had to make was to add small fillets ahead of the tailplanes – which, unlike the B.242, were fixed – to make spin recovery even more prompt and positive.

We also planned to offer the Pup with the 150-hp Lycoming O-320 (by this time we had reluctantly abandoned the hope of Rolls-Royce ever making a Continental engine of this power). The resulting Pup 150 flew on 17 January 1968. We gave it a larger rudder, which then became standard on all Pups. We also optimistically planned a 180-hp four-seater called the Pup Major, and various Twin Pups as a possible adjunct to the B.242.

We priced the basic Pup 100 at £3,495 and the Pup 150 at £4,250, and as word got around the order book passed the 250 mark within the first year. We expected to produce 200 aircraft during 1969, rising to 400 in 1972. We naturally concentrated the first deliveries on local customers so that any problems could be quickly overcome and, where necessary, modifications introduced. Almost the only enduring problem concerned the big doors, which people grabbed when climbing out, either distorting the door or buckling the stay, which was inadequately stressed. That problem was soon sorted out.

More serious was the fact that the Pup was not sufficiently economical to produce. Despite later increasing the basic price to £4,350/5,200 for the two versions, we found we were still losing money on every sale. From then on we strove to increase production, thereby cutting the cost of manufacture.

In these circumstances, in July 1968 Beagle was formally taken over as a Government-owned company. It was to be administered by the Ministry of Technology. The Minister, Anthony Wedgwood Benn, began by showing a benevolent, helpful and understanding attitude, saying that he hoped we would become profitable during 1972. He backed my choice of Nicholas Myer as Managing

Shoreham built the B.121T mock-up to launch what became the Bulldog.

Director, while I took on the job of Chairman. I handed over most of the executive power. Most of my time had to be devoted to setting up a completely new State-owned business, the British Airports Authority, to take control of five major airports (see next chapter).

With such an outstanding basic design at the Pup, the obvious next development was to press ahead with all speed with the military derivative, and the first B.125 Bulldog flew on 19 May 1969. 'Pee Wee' Judge was delighted with it. The main differences, compared with the Pup, were that it was cleared for +8g aerobatics, had a 200-hp Lycoming IO-360 driving a Hartzell constant-speed propeller, 34 imp. gal. of fuel instead of 24, and an excellent aft-sliding canopy.

The Bulldog got rave reviews everywhere, even from Boscombe Down. Within weeks it had won an order from Sweden for 58, with a further 45 on option, plus other significant export sales. The RAF took much longer to decide that the Bulldog was the obvious replacement for the Chipmunk.

At Rearsby the Beagle factory did its best to produce the fully developed B.206, while at Shoreham we tested a Series III, with ten seats. In the end we were able to complete just one production Series III, for a Brazilian customer, before the Rearsby line had to be halted at the 85th aircraft.

With hindsight, Beagle should have started by concentrating on the singles – which became the Pup and Bulldog. Unfortunately, we had been mesmerised by the obvious RAF need for an all-new twin to replace the Anson, Dove and Pembroke. It was the RAF's written requirement for an initial 120 such aircraft that was the carrot Pressed Steel had needed. Had I gone to Mike Bellhouse and Joe Edwards and said, 'Let's build little single-engined aircraft', I do not think that they would have been interested. I still do not know why the RAF should have taken so many years to write the specification for the Basset, and then order only 20.

As it was, 1968 saw us taking orders for the Pup and Bulldog hand-over-fist, whilst urgently needing an investment of £6 million spread over five years to plan for a solid production rate of 1,200 aircraft per year, and install the necessary tooling. It so happened that, just at this time, Upper Clyde Shipbuilders also needed a big rescue package, and it came to exactly the same amount.

I had a long meeting with Wedgwood Benn at which I pleaded that we should not be cut off without a penny. I said 'For God's sake, here we are on the brink of success, with proven products selling like the proverbial hot cakes. Please let our 1,000 employees get cracking making them.' At first he agreed, and he called meetings of the workforce at Rearsby and Shoreham at which he held out encouraging prospects of full support. Indeed, he waxed enthusiastic over the future of the British light-aircraft industry.

It has been said that politicians are not moved by the success or failure of industries but by votes. There were not many Labour votes in southern England, and in November 1969 Wedgwood Benn refused to help Beagle. In his view, anyone out of work in southern England could soon find other employment, which was not the case in Glasgow. So he handed the required £6 million to Upper Clyde Shipbuilders, and lost the lot six months later when the company shut down.

The Bulldog was simply handed to Scottish Aviation to build in quantity.

After the demise of Pressed Steel, there was nothing more we could do. In December 1969 Beagle was placed in the hands of the Receiver. He was Kenneth Cork, a pleasant man of many talents, including a sympathetic understanding of troubled companies, who was quite used to presiding over collapsed British plane-makers.

In our search for a buyer we had many 'near misses', but none came to anything. Tragically, our fine team was gradually dispersed, and the 152nd and last Pup made its maiden flight on 12 January 1970. A further 250 were on order, but could not be built for lack of funds.

Then, unexpectedly, after discussions with the Ministry, in June 1970 Scottish Aviation at Prestwick announced that they would take over production of the Bulldog for the RAF. Unlike Beagle, which had to take awesome risks, they took over a fully proven product with a healthy order book. Not long after they took on the Bulldog, the RAF confirmed their long-expected order for 130.

Altogether 320 Bulldogs were built, many of them after Scottish Aviation had itself been nationalised into British Aerospace. Since then the United Kingdom has had a General Aviation industry composed of tiny struggling teams, which Cessna and the rest of the world's GA companies would hardly notice.

42

BAA

On Monday 25 October 1965, in the midst of Beagle's problems, I was invited to lunch at London's Café Royal by an old friend from BEA days, Lord Wilfred Brown. Formerly Chairman and Managing Director of Glacier Metals, he was an expert in management, and had moved on to become Minister of State at the Board of Trade. When we got to the coffee stage he told me that he had instructions from the Prime Minister, then Harold Wilson, to offer me a pressing invitation to be elevated to the House of Lords.

The deal was that I could take as title Baron Masefield of whatever location I wished, but that it all had to be done quickly, in order for my name to appear in the New Year Honours List. He added that, of course, I would be expected to take the Labour Whip, that being the party in power. I would become the chief Government spokesman on aviation in the House of Lords.

I replied that I felt greatly honoured, but that I had never taken part in party politics, and would be reluctant to start. My host immediately said that the need to take the Labour Whip might not be essential, but the upshot was that, on the following Saturday morning, I telephoned Wilfred and declined the offer.

As I explained to him, this was because Mr Wilson's Minister of Aviation, Roy Jenkins, had recently asked me to become the Chairman of the new British Airports Authority. The BAA had been formed to run London's three main airports – Heathrow, Gatwick and Stansted – and Prestwick in Scotland. Even though it was a part-time appointment, paying just £6,000 a year, it was an important duty and I had accepted. As Chairman-elect, I considered that I ought to remain free from political involvement.

On the following morning I chaired the very first BAA Board Meeting, at Prestwick. It might have been nice to be a lord, but I have never regretted my decision.

Until 1965, though I had never had anything to do with the running of airports, I had naturally taken a keen interest in the subject. Even at the time, it appeared that the planning of the country's main international airport at London could hardly have been worse. In 1919 the country's first airport was opened on Hounslow Heath. Only a few months later, in March 1920, this was abandoned when it was decided that the airport should be at Croydon. By the late 1930s houses had encroached, hemming in a grass field offering a maximum run of 3,450 feet, while in other countries airports were being given long runways. In 1939 it was accepted that a new site had to be sought. More than fifty were investigated, and the choice narrowed down to Cliffe, Fairlop, Heston, Gatwick and Lullingstone. The war put a stop to these plans.

In 1943 Fairey's Great West Aerodrome, also known as Heath Row, was requisitioned for use by heavy bombers and transport aircraft to support Tiger Force, the

British force for the war against Japan. It had been one of the sites rejected in 1939, but in December 1943, at a meeting lasting just 45 minutes, a Cabinet Committee took the decision that after the war this should be London's future airport. Indeed, in 1946 Lord Winster, then Minister of Civil Aviation, said 'It was the *only possible site* [my italics] on which a great airport for London could be built.'

As related in Chapter 3, even at that time much of the area surrounding the site consisted of farms and apple orchards. Nobody appeared to realise that, once the war was over, the builders would move in and cover the rest of Middlesex with new suburbs. Heathrow is a mere 15 miles from Piccadilly Circus. Of course, many of the houses that have been built around the airport are occupied by the people who work there (40,000 in 1966, just over 80,000 in 2000), but in my opinion it was a strategic error to say 'the only possible site' was one that would soon be swallowed up by London itself.

RAF airfields generally had three runways in a triangular pattern, and in 1944 three reasonably long, wide and thick concrete runways were laid down, obliterating Fairey's original aerodrome. With the war ending, in 1945 the newly formed Ministry of Civil Aviation formed a committee to study the problem (a member of which was future Prime Minister Edward Heath). This recommended, amazingly, three sets of parallel runways, but later changed this to three parallel east–west runways, including a pattern of runways north of the Bath Road. They were needed in order to meet a perceived future requirement for 'up to 160 aircraft movements per hour'. Eventually this complex pattern disappeared, being replaced by just two parallel runways aligned

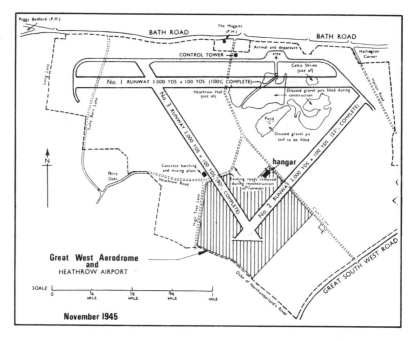

Fairey's Heath Row aerodrome looked insignificant on the 1945 plan of Heathrow.

10/28. Unfortunately, in 1953 the then Minister, Alan Lennox-Boyd, decreed that the development north of the Bath Road was 'politically inexpedient' – he did not explain what that meant – and cancelled it. Over the years, this area was of course built over, as was the entire area surrounding the airport. Therefore, the airport's 2,718 acres can never be extended, limiting its capacity to much less than that possible at other international airports, and certainly not 160 movements an hour.

On 1 January 1946, the desolate new airport, by then named Heathrow (written as one word), dispatched an Avro Lancastrian of BSAA on a proving flight to Buenos Aires. BOAC began to transfer its services from Hurn (can you imagine London's airport being at Bournemouth?), and regular services started on 31 May 1946. Incoming travellers entered Great Britain via a mass of tents in a sea of mud.

The control tower was the only brick building on the airport. It was on the north side, and beside it there grew up, first, a village of tents and marquees, then a town of prefabs, and then a growing number of somewhat better buildings. Because of the triangle of runways, the long-term decision was taken to construct the permanent buildings in the centre of the airport. Having adopted a site that could never be extended, the planners then selected the worst possible place for the supporting infrastructure. This was done even though by this time it was at last understood that modern airports do not have runways laid down in a wartime triangular pattern. Her Majesty opened Heathrow's Central Area on 16 December 1955.

Hardly anyone appeared to notice the folly of putting all the buildings in the centre, where there is limited room for expansion, and where the entire area has to be accessed by tunnels. Of course, these tunnels were planned for the traffic of the 1950s, and so provide just two lanes in each direction – and one of my major headaches in 1970 was the need to *close one tunnel for seven months* for major repairs.

The result can be imagined. By the end of the century the central area has for years been seriously overcrowded. Terminal 4 was built far away on the south side, a desperately needed Terminal 5 has been held up for years by opponents, in the most costly public inquiry of all time, and it is now seen what folly it was not to build the extension north of the Bath Road when this was still possible. Foresight was conspicuously absent.

Moreover, when BAA was formed, the four airports handed over to its control had suffered years of poor management. Their history had been an appalling catalogue of costly and time-consuming public inquiries, decisions deferred, decisions overturned, decisions that were obviously mistaken (and seen to be so at the time) and golden opportunities missed.

We British have a history of dragging out decisions for as long as possible, as if time and money were unimportant. It was in 1959 that the Government decided to hand at least the airports of London over to an independent body, and this decision was published two years later, in June 1961. The Airports Authority Bill was presented to Parliament on 6 November 1964, and, as I have noted, the first BAA meeting took place just a year after that. Vesting Day, when the BAA actually began to run the airports, was in April 1966 – on April Fool's Day, of course. Hardly a breakneck pace. I may add that an army of opponents of the very idea of an independent authority tried to block every move, and they were outraged when it was announced that I would be the new body's first Chairman. I was perceived as 'pro-aviation', which was considered a bad thing. Back in the 1830s a vociferous minority tried to stop the railways.

Almost the only bright area in a generally bleak scene was that I was able to assemble a Board of outstanding people. My Deputy was a splendid Scot, Robin MacLellan, Chairman of a rubber-products company in Edinburgh. As Chief Executive I had wanted Ross Stainton, of BOAC, and the man eventually appointed, George Hole, proved rather too much a civil servant for my style of management. Financial Controller was John C. McGrath, and other Members were Prof. Alan Day, Sir John Elliott, Mrs Diana Self, and Charles Delacourt Smith. Secretary and Solicitor was V.P. Harries.

The Departmental heads were Sir John Briscoe (Operations), Eric Hewitt (Admin and Personnel), Graham Hill (Research and Projects), Keith McLeod (Finance), Norman Payne (Planning), A.R. Macrae (Engineering), P.E.R. Bailey (Personnel) and Geoffrey Pitt (Commerce and Public Relations). The airport General Managers were Leslie Green (Gatwick), Harry Johnston (Stansted), David Livingston (Prestwick) and Denis Waldron (Heathrow).

They were generally a first-class team, but we had a vast amount of leeway to make up. The only directive handed down by the Government was that we should run the airports properly, consulting with local residents but not interfering with navigation services.

I have commented on the leisurely pace at which the Authority came into being, but in fact its first eight months, from 2 August 1965 until Vesting Day, were hectic. Whilst carrying out the Ministry of Aviation's responsibility for the airports, we had to become totally familiar with the airports and their many problems, evolve new operating procedures appropriate to a harsh new commercial environment, find and equip offices, recruit staff, and decide countless details of future policy.

One far from trivial aspect of future policy concerned signs put up to warn or guide the public. At Gatwick I found an amazing number, informing people of activities that were prohibited. I consumed rolls of film photographing them. BAA was able to dispense with almost all of them, and from the start our attitude was positive.

Of course, like any commercial organisation, the new BAA had to produce an annual *Report and Accounts*. When I was at BEA I took a special pride in making this publication as informative, clear and attractive as possible, and I was determined at BAA to do even better. My objective had been never to leave a reader searching in vain for anything. Several commentators hailed our first report, for 1966/7 as 'the best to be produced by any Government organisation'. I was particularly pleased about this, because I wrote it myself. It comprised 100 pages of text, tables, histograms, pie charts, organisational trees, airport plans, and four pages of monochrome photographs on art paper.

At that time the number of passengers to and from the United Kingdom by air had only recently exceeded the total passenger movements by sea. The international total at all UK airports was, in fact, slightly over 13 million. Including just over 3 million domestic passengers, the overall total at the four BAA airports was 14,379,361, a 13 per cent increase over the previous year. Of this seemingly impressive total, 12,208,259 were handled by Heathrow. When one plotted the figures on a graph, Heathrow was out on its own, sloping steeply upwards, while the other three were almost horizontal lines near the bottom.

By 1966 Heathrow had established its position as No 1 in the world in terms of international passengers, international aircraft movements, and average number of passengers per aircraft. This led many quizmasters to state that it was the busiest airport in the world. In fact, in 1966 it ranked No 4 in terms of passengers, No 7 in terms of scheduled air-transport movements, but only No 51 in terms of total aircraft movements. In terms of air-transport movements, of the top 12 airports, all the other 11 were in the USA. Those busier than Heathrow, in order, were Chicago O'Hare, New York JFK, Los Angeles International, San Francisco, Atlanta Municipal, and Washington National.

Though very much 'the jewel in the BAA crown', Heathrow's position at No 51 in terms of total movements appeared to astonish many who read our first report. For the record, Nos 47 to 50 were all in the USA: Newark, Detroit, Kansas City, and Philadelphia. When I looked at the mass of American airports which were busier than

Prince Philip opened Heathrow's new travelators for the first 'Jumbo Jets'.

Heathrow I discovered that all of them had more runways in use at the same time, all accepted substantial peak-hour delays in queuing for take-off and stacking for landing, all operated primarily to VFR (visual flight rules), and they imposed no restriction on movements on the grounds of noise.

On the vexed question of noise, in 1966 piston-engined aircraft, though still important, had dramatically declined in importance. Most movements, and a much higher proportion of passengers, travelled in turbine-engined aircraft. The turboprops, used chiefly on short-haul services, were relatively unobtrusive. The first-generation jets, however, were deafeningly noisy, and many, especially those made in the USA, which were numerically dominant, left sooty trails. These, though visible, were harmless, but there were invisible emissions which were not. These were then just being recognised as carbon dioxide and oxides of nitrogen. Emissions therefore became an important issue, and one with which we had to deal immediately.

This was just one of many problems. Air traffic was likely to keep on rising at about 13 per cent per year; in other words, every five or six years it would double. A big spur to air travel was going to follow the introduction of the Boeing 747 'Jumbo Jet' in 1969. This would more than double the number of passengers per movement, and

At the opening of the Heathrow cargo tunnel. Beside me is BAA Board Member Mrs Diana Self.

while it would bring welcome relief in terms of noise, its promised ability to move traffic cheaply would if anything cause traffic growth to accelerate. We put in hand an urgent programme of extending the capacity of lounges, putting in improved docking facilities with more room and extra apron-drive bridges (passenger jetties), and such extra services as underground fuel tanks and high-capacity hydrant re-fuelling connections. Over the years, it was also essential to expand facilities for animals in quarantine, and increase the specialist staff.

In many ways BAA took over at a pivotal time, when the old order was changing. One factor was the imminent doubling in the size of aircraft, as noted above. Another was the fact that air cargo, previously trivial in comparison with sea traffic, was growing even faster than passenger traffic. While passenger numbers were doubling every 5½ years, cargo was doubling every 4¼. Already, in terms of cargo value, Heathrow was the UK's No 3 port. What we did not expect was that London's docks, then Britain's No 1 port by an enormous margin, would soon suffer labour disputes which would result in the entire port closing down and vanishing from the landscape!

When BAA took over, a big Air Cargo Terminal was already being built on the south side of Heathrow. It was costing £23 million, of which the Authority's share was £8 million. This terminal seemed impressive, but today there are two, each far larger than the original. Unlike passenger traffic, which has always been significantly greater in the British summer than in the winter, cargo is almost constant throughout the year.

Another turning point was the question of how passengers travelled to or from the airport. In 1946 air travellers were an exotic species, and there was no problem. By 1966 Heathrow was handling 12 million. Roughly half used the airline coaches, and the rest used taxis or their own cars. But what about the future, when the total would reach, say, 100 million? It was self-evident that high-capacity rail links would have to be provided.

By sheer chance, the Piccadilly Line of what is now London Underground Ltd had in 1933 reached Hounslow West on a long branch line pointing at the airport. This was an ideal basis, and we began talks straight away to hasten the construction of the short extension needed to reach the airport's central area. This was one of the easier solutions, and by 1974 the Piccadilly Line had been extended to Hatton Cross to serve the by now enormous airline maintenance area in the south-east region of the airport.

Just over a year later, Heathrow Central station was opened in the overcrowded central area. After another 11 years, in 1986, BAA and British Airways were to open a large new Terminal 4, specially for long-haul passengers. This was constructed far from the central area, but directly over this underground rail link, and it was there-fore a straightforward task to provide it with its own station. Since then an army of protesters have tried to stop Terminal 5, which likewise would be built over the Piccadilly Line airport loop. I refer to this at the end of this chapter.

Our 1966 talks envisaged a second rail link being opened to the British Rail Southern Region at nearby Feltham. This would provide a speedy electric-train link to Waterloo or Victoria. Compared with the Piccadilly Line, the trains would be faster and could run non-stop, putting central London only 23–25 minutes away. By 1967 BAA was in discussion with the Ministry of Transport, British Rail, London Transport and the Greater London Council, with a view to this rail link going to an enormous multi-modal interchange between all transport systems at Victoria.

It is sadly typical of Britain today that these carefully considered plans came to nothing. The great interchange at Victoria was never built, nor the seemingly obvious spur to what was then the Southern Region railway at Feltham. Instead, long after my departure, a completely new high-speed rail line was constructed to Paddington.

In 1966 there were still many people, especially in Government and the media, who repeatedly called Heathrow 'London Airport', or LAP. From the start, I prohibited this usage by BAA staff, and over the years I am glad to say the name has all but disappeared. At the same time, when BAA took over, Heathrow pretty much *was* 'London Airport', because it handled more than seven times as many passengers as Gatwick and Stansted combined. In fact, Stansted (35 miles by road to the north-east of central London) had hardly any traffic at all, and was being held in reserve as the future Third London Airport.

Looking around the world, there were several cities where traffic much greater than London's was handled by a single airport. If Heathrow had been properly designed it could have coped with London's needs by itself well into the 21st century, though there are obvious advantages in having more than one airport. The problems were that nobody had had sufficient foresight, and while Heathrow had limited size and a crazy layout, Gatwick had only one runway. Obviously, with each passing year it became more difficult to build a second one.

The British are perhaps the world's greatest protesters. Residents near Gatwick are well equipped with huge placards saying 'NO SECOND RUNWAY'. Having just one runway makes it difficult when that runway needs repair. It also ensures that, at

How Gatwick looked when it was opened on 6 June 1936.

By 1984 it looked like this, but even in 2001 the essential parallel runway is still absent.

some time in the future, that airport will be unable to cope with the traffic, and a totally different site will have to be found for yet another airport. The protesters might think that even worse than having the obvious second runway at Gatwick, which is now unbelievably overdue, to enable that otherwise excellent airport to handle the traffic safely.

In May 1968 I read a paper before the Royal Society of Arts entitled *The Modern Airport – and its Future*. In it I pictured future airports with two pairs of parallel runways. The runways of each pair were 3,000 feet apart, and the pairs were 9,000 feet apart laterally. Today better electronic guidance may enable the pairs to be closer than 3,000 feet, but 9,000 feet is still the kind of space needed in which to put down the terminals required to handle 100 or 200 million passengers a year.

Cities around the world are finding such airports an enormous and essential investment for the future. One has only to look at the airports of most great cities to see how an international airport should be designed. Alternatively, if you get it wrong, as we have repeatedly at London, it is difficult to put things right.

One of the few things about aviation that is absolutely predictable is that, if you fail to take decisions in good time, you will regret it later. For BAA's first Report I wrote, in 1966, 'A second runway was included in the plans put forward at the Public Inquiry before the development [of Gatwick] was started.' By failing to construct *at least* a second parallel runway at Gatwick, as soon as it was selected as a major airport for London in 1953, we have simply stored up trouble for the future.

That the problem has not already become acute in 2001 results from the fact that millions of passengers who in 1966 had first to go from distant parts of Britain to London, in order to fly to foreign countries, can now fly direct from a provincial airport. A further major factor in postponing the future crises at Heathrow and Gatwick has been the rapid growth of traffic at Stansted and Luton (which is not run by the BAA), and the opening and more gradual growth of London City Airport.

An ongoing problem with Gatwick has always been the strongly seasonal nature of its traffic. In BAA's first year it handled around 60,000 passengers a month between November and March; then the total zoomed to 300,000 in July. Obviously, most holidays are taken in the summer, but the peaky nature of air travel is less pronounced today, with a general rise in business travel and the rapid increase in vacations in the winter.

In 1966 Stansted was barely operational; it was officially being 'held in reserve'. Prestwick, however, remained an important gateway for transatlantic traffic. It was unusual in that, for most of the airport's previous life, almost all its passengers were merely passing through, for example on their way between London and New York. By 1966, however, the airlines were increasingly using aircraft which could fly a route such as London–New York non-stop, and ever since then most of Prestwick's passengers have been people who want to go there.

In our first year BAA made an operating profit of some £5.4 million. Even after paying £2.8 million interest on the Authority's capital debt, and almost £1 million in

On 3 February 1967 I had discussions with the Port of New York Authority; on the left is Executive Director, Austin J. Tobin, and on the right Neal R. Montanus, PATH Director of Rail Transportation, John E. Wiley, PNYA Director of Aviation, and Matthias E. Lukens, PNYA Deputy Executive Director.

taxation, we still cleared a net surplus of £1,697,798. Such a thing had never happened before.

In the second year we retained £1.83 million, despite a massive increase in taxation to over £1.55 million. This helped the Authority to maintain a strong programme of capital works to fit the airports for the future. I was delighted when in May 1967, following a long and costly review of all the issues, the Government published its White Paper, *The Third London Airport*. It said that the airport would be Stansted.

There was an immediate outcry, *as there would be no matter what site was chosen*. Nobody appeared to comprehend that if the Third London Airport were to be in the Outer Hebrides, it would eventually become surrounded by a city.

It is not difficult to guesstimate how many people are needed in order to send 80,000 adults to work at Heathrow each day. On top of that, major airports attract factories, offices, hotels, courier companies, warehouses, schools and everything else people need. Unlike a French Government, ours lost its nerve, and said there would be a new inquiry!

This was set up under Mr Justice Roskill in May 1968. It was 'to inquire into the timing of the need for a four-runway airport . . .' At a cost of millions of pounds, this inquiry finally reported on 21 January 1971. It stated that the Third London Airport would be Cublington, near the aptly named village of Wing in Buckinghamshire. One wondered why this massive and protracted inquiry had bothered, because three months later, on 26 April, Her Majesty's Government said that the airport would not be built at Cublington at all, but off the Essex coast at Foulness!

Despite this pathetic succession of nonsenses, we at BAA soldiered on. On the one hand we wanted traffic to continue to increase, as an indication of success, and on the other we were reduced to hoping that it would not, because of the unbelievable way the Government refused to take decisions for the future. Unusually, Heathrow's traffic in 1967 exceeded that for 1966 by a mere 5.6 per cent. The increase for the world's other 'top 12' airports averaged higher than 20 per cent. In Britain the only big increase was in days lost from industrial disputes, which partly explained the poor figure of 5.6 per cent.

In 1968, even though traffic at Stansted was minuscule, we considered it prudent to design a new terminal building for that airport, which was opened in 1969. We also began discussions with bus companies regarding a special service linking the airport with Bishop's Stortford railway station, and with British Rail to see whether they would consider building a station at the airport and linking it via a spur to the main line.

In our third year, ending on 31 March 1969, I reported 'solid progress'. We even put coloured pictures in the Report. Only in one respect was the situation unsatisfactory. It would have been simple not to rock the boat, and Britain is a country which hates to face facts, but I felt bound to put my job on the line by pointing out the increasing need to do something about a site for a Third London Airport.

Even worse, I continued to recommend Stansted, but I was forced to describe this as an interim answer. Rather spinelessly, I considered it prudent to reaffirm the Authority's 'support for whatever fresh site might be chosen'.

Our fourth Report, for the year ended March 1970, noted the opening of the first hotel actually on Heathrow airport, and outline permission for a hotel on Gatwick airport. There had previously been a growing number of large hotels close to both, but in fact the growth in hotel accommodation has not stopped to this day.

Heathrow's Runway 28R was extended from 9,300 to 12,800 ft, enabling long-haul aircraft to use it for take-offs and then turn right without crossing other traffic. Other major works continued on terminals, 747-compatible jetties and gates, and underground hydrant fuelling, and for the first time the profit from traffic operations was outstripped by that from concessions.

The Authority's fifth year, 1970/1, should have been my last, but I accepted an invitation to stay for one further year. I felt we had achieved much in those first five years. When we began, not one airport ran profitably, whereas in 1970/1 all four did. This was not at the expense of our standards, and in 1969 BAA had won the Royal Society of Arts Presidential Award for design management. We also gained a fifth airport: after four years of dithering, Edinburgh Turnhouse was transferred to BAA on the first day of the Authority's sixth year. We undertook to provide a new terminal complex and runway.

One of my last acts was to introduce a sliding scale of landing fees to try to spread traffic more evenly. Every airline wants to land during peak hours on peak days and peak months. Typically, what I called Golden Hours were, and still are, 9 a.m. to 1 p.m. from May to October. Whereas the landing fee for a 707 at Heathrow or Gatwick

Outside Buckingham Palace on 22 February 1972. The new Sir *Peter and* Lady *Masefield were supported by Vicky and Charles.*

With Henry Marking (far left), who followed me (much later, in 1964) as Chief Executive of BEA, escorting Her Majesty to her aircraft at Heathrow in October 1971.

remained US$625, we raised it to $780 during Golden Hours. I also planned a differential scale based on the number of passengers actually on board.

However, the main news in 1971 was the decision, announced in April just after our fifth Report was published, to develop Foulness as the future main airport for London. My colleagues did not dissent from my often expressed belief that this decision was an unfortunate one. Later called Maplin, because it was to be built on the treacherous Maplin offshore sands, it was selected on no sensible ground whatsoever, but simply because it seemed far away from people (not a very good idea for an airport). An all-party motion in the Commons strongly recommending it was signed by a massive number of MPs (excluding the MP for that part of Essex).

Fortunately, I have lived to see that ill-considered decision overturned and forgotten, like all the others, but the problem can never do what the politicians would like and simply go away. Every year more people, and more loads of cargo, want to fly. It is a poor answer to try to frustrate this growth by imposing penalties or extra costs, or by siting the nasty airport as far away as possible.

Before I left BAA we had drawn up plans for Heathrow's Terminal 5, which would obviously be needed by about 1990. The biggest of all, and the last major new structure possible at Heathrow, this would be built on the redeveloped site of the Perry Oaks sludge works on the western side between the runways. Everything has followed

BAA gave me a portrait in oils by Michael Noakes, unveiled on 17 July 1972.

the same procedure as all the previous plans. Terminal 5 was designed at great cost, a public inquiry was held at great cost, and a decision has been repeatedly deferred. As this was written, in 2001, a decision has still to be taken. Eventually, a decision *must* be taken. So far, all that the most costly public inquiry in the history of the human race has accomplished is to delay a decision to the point where, when it is finally opened to traffic, Terminal 5 will be inadequate. Meanwhile, Heathrow is seriously overcrowded, passengers scream at overworked staff, and Britain is seen by 'arrivals' as a Third-World country.*

---

* As this book goes to press, it has been announced that Terminal 5 at Heathrow is to be built.

43

London Transport

It has been my good fortune to be invited to take part in a remarkable succession of interesting jobs. Thanks to enjoying the company of Sir John Elliott and Sir Kenneth Robinson on the Committee of the Institute of Transport and the Society of Road Transport Engineers, in 1973 I was invited to become a part-time Member of the Board of the London Transport Executive. There are easier jobs than running the public transport system of one of the world's biggest cities. Even in 1973, much of London Transport's infrastructure was more than 100 years old.

It followed that being on the LT Board was no sinecure. We met weekly, in the offices above St James's Park station. London Transport ran the city's Underground system, one of the world's largest, with nearly 600 trains and 273 stations (today there are rather more). London Transport also had a monopoly of the entire bus network, which was considerably more complicated than the rail system, and required 5,000 buses. Altogether LT had 59,000 staff, and carried seven million passengers each day.

When I came on the Board I was busy with several other responsibilities, including commitments to BAA. I took on this additional task because I had always been interested in railway operations, and in the Underground in particular. Moreover, I liked the people concerned, and knew that among the professional personnel were skilled and devoted long-term members who were almost impossible to replace. On the other hand, LT's economics were bad, and getting worse.

There were many causes. One root cause was that, while the Underground had a strong professional corps of railway engineers, the enormous infrastructure was suffering from decades of underinvestment. Government funding had been static for years. In comparison with such cities as Paris or New York, London's transport was underfunded to an unbelievable degree. Thus, instead of being something in which every employee felt a sense of pride, as it once had been, LT had become a vast edifice cracking at the seams, propped up by ever-rising fares, and with the morale of its employees sinking rapidly.

I had already formed a high regard for the Chairman, Sir Kenneth Robinson. A Labour MP, he had been Minister of Health, yet he chain-smoked without a break. He was moderate politically, and worked hard at everything he did, and we got on well while I assimilated the multitude of problems which LT faced. The obvious megaproblem was trying to stay within the impossibly small budget. Regrettably, because of his wife's ill health, Robinson soon decided to retire.

The next most senior person on the Board was a long-time LT man, Ralph Bennett. Pleasant and easygoing, he was in no sense a ball of fire, and, in the absence of the strong leadership so urgently needed, we tottered from one crisis to the next. Soon LT's top management was floundering in a morass of positive disregard for tight financial control, and a stubborn refusal to tackle the problems. The individual

Board Members could see that this must not be allowed to go on indefinitely.

Matters came to a head in early 1980 when Sir Horace Cutler, the ultra-right-wing, and fearsomely autocratic, Chairman of the Greater London Council, summoned poor Bennett and fired him on the spot. Cutler then called me in and asked, 'Will you take on the Chairmanship, and put some spirit into the business?'

Although I must admit that I enjoy challenges, at the age of 66 this was more than I really needed. I had to think fast. What I said was, 'No less than six months, no more than a year. I don't want to spend the rest of my life in LT. I just hope that, at the end of that time, London's transport will be in better shape than I found it in.' I followed my usual practice in setting up detailed wall charts showing all aspects of LT's operations, especially the finance, and arranged to go to County Hall each week to meet with Cutler and report on progress.

Soon after being appointed I was interviewed by the weekly *The Accountant*, which then wrote:

> 'With the gold clock on the mantlepiece already gathering dust, most ageing company chairmen relish the prospect of tending their overgrown cabbage-patch . . . Not so, Sir Peter Masefield! He has taken over the hottest seat in world transportation . . . Without his even seeking or expecting it, he was asked to take over the Chairmanship of an authority that has had so much *flak* over the previous six months that a public hanging of the Board might have been less gruesome.'

When Sir John Elliott retired I handed him a bound volume of his memorabilia. Pat's smile reflects the affection he inspired.

I had a good middle-level professional team, and I built up an even better one. Among the Board Members was the vastly experienced Sir John Elliott. An old railwayman, he was outstandingly capable, and I worked with him not only at LT but also in many other activities. Among other outstanding directors, I recruited from Hong Kong Dr Tony Ridley, who later went to the University of London; Dr David Quarmby, who later had a go at running the Dome; Ian Phillips, who went on to the BBC; Eric Ellen, who had already had a long career on the Underground; Patrick Elliott; and John Cameron, who was Director of Personnel. We had an outstanding medical doctor, Dr Andrew Raffle, and an excellent Press Officer, Barry LeJeune.

For years LT had been seriously underfunded by the GLC, and its programme of capital works was woefully inadequate. It was obvious that we were only storing up trouble for the future. Trying to avoid spending money on essential works is one of the most obvious examples of false economy I can think of. Sir Horace Cutler began with an inclination in this direction, and he was not the easiest person to get on with. I went to see him every Thursday, to get down to fundamental issues. When he saw that I was not to be bullied, and could show him detailed achievements each week, our relationship improved, and so did LT's finances.

I have strong views about the impossibility of politicians attempting to run business affairs, but over the months we managed to bring about a 'tight and happy ship'. I was fortunate in that the Permanent Secretary at the Department of Transport was the outstanding Sir Peter Baldwin. Ably supported by his Deputy, Peter Lazarus, he appreciated that LT should never take a short-term view.

Perhaps against all the odds, we gradually managed to put in place the foundation of strategic improvements to both bus and train systems. I was equally fortunate in the Secretary of State, David Howell MP. Not all Ministers are as capable as he was, and without such a man in that key position our task would have been impossible.

I had meant to occupy the Chair for no more than a few months, in order to attempt to straighten out what had become a serious mess. In the end, I stayed for three years, and might have gone on a bit longer had not Ken Livingstone managed to superannuate Cutler and find his own way into the administration from County Hall.

It was soon abundantly clear that 'Red Ken' and I could never work happily together. Livingstone himself said, 'We don't get on well', so in due course I packed it in. I handed over to Keith Bright, the Chairman of Weston Biscuits, and departed with few regrets. I left in the nicest way, with a dinner from the great LT team at the RAF Club on 19 August 1982. Throughout my time on the LT Board I had not taken any pay, so I was to be rewarded with a modest Golden Handshake. 'Red Ken' said he didn't agree with Golden Handshakes, and vetoed it.

Unexpectedly, just over a year later a subsequent administration awarded me a small pension. But one does not take on a job like London Transport with any thought of one's own finances!

44

A full life

R eaders who have reached this point will appreciate that I have been fortunate to have had a most unusual diversity of careers. Many people like to collect directorships, but in my case my aeronautical job kept changing, and in an increasingly interesting way. There is, however, even more to the story. Over the years I have become involved with so many other organisations that I find difficulty in arranging them all in chronological order.

I must give pride of place to the **Royal Aeronautical Society**. Founded in 1866, it is the longest-established aeronautical organisation in the world, and it is certainly the first that I visited. The date was 6 October 1927, and I was taken to the society by my father in order to hear a lecture – more an extended talk – by Frederick Handley Page on 'The future of civil air transport'. At that time, many of the Society's important lectures were delivered at the premises of other organisations which had large lecture theatres, such as the Royal Society of Arts. On this occasion, however, we entered the rather cramped first-floor conference room at 7 Albemarle Street, from the ceiling of which 'Claude the condor' – a famous stuffed bird with a wing span of 9 feet – hung by a wire. I took notes as Mr (later Sir Frederick) Handley Page showed us his vision of the future, which including projecting a slide showing drawings of his 40-passenger H.P.42, which was to be built for Imperial Airways.

I little thought then that I would fly in these great aircraft, and still less that I would join the society and become the friend of the gallant unpaid Secretary, Capt. J. Laurence Pritchard. I joined in 1932 as a Student member, moved up to be a Graduate, became Chairman of the Graduates and Students section, and was then elected as an Associate Fellow, and ultimately reached the highest normal grade of membership, Fellow.

Indeed, I did even better: In due course, I was elected an Honorary Fellow, and also to be the Society's President, an office I held in 1959/60. I cannot imagine what I would have thought, had I been told in 1926 that I would have a son, Sir Charles, who would also be elected the society's President!

Next there came the **Aircraft Recognition Society**. This was formed in 1943, with members drawn from all interested parties (see Chapter 6) including the fighting Services. It originally held its meetings on the third floor of what had been Thomas Cook's offices in Berkeley Street. The ARS flourished for many years, among other things holding a major annual contest, before finally being wound up in the peaceful year 1969/70. Throughout its life I was its President.

In 1949, after I had become Chief Executive of BEA, I found myself elected to the **Scottish Advisory Council**. They were a great bunch, who saw it as their bounden duty to get as much out of BEA as they could. We met at Northolt each month and in

Glasgow every three months. Even in terrible weather, I invariably managed to get myself there by Gemini.

In the same year, 1949, I was elected to membership of GAPAN, the **Guild of Air Pilots and Air Navigators**. This is one of the City livery companies, and is far more than a trade union for Britain's professional civil aircrew. It does a great deal to advise successive Ministers and generally educate all British civilians who fly profession-ally, promote safety, and in many cases help dependants. I was elected a Liveryman in 1953 and an Upper Freeman in 1962, but I asked to be excused from nomination as Chairman because I had too many other commitments. I could not have done the honourable role justice.

In 1950 I was elected to serve on the **National Joint Council for Civil Air Transport**. This comprised about twenty representatives of the national airline corpo-rations (at that time BOAC and BEA), and of all the independent airlines, and the relevant trades unions. The Council's remit was to sort out any problem brought to it, almost all of them involving labour relations, real or imagined grievances and conditions of service. The Council met about four times a year, either at the HQ of BOAC or BEA or at the RAeS. I could not help being struck by the contrast between those who wanted solutions and those whose objective was to frustrate any solution. There was just as sharp a distinction between the sheep (the powerful corporations) and the goats (the poor little independents).

In 1955, as I was leaving BEA to join Bristol, I was appointed President of the **Chartered Institute of Transport**. The Institute is a professional body to which eminent transport people can be elected. Probably the largest single group are rail-waymen, but all modes of transport are represented. I am still a member, and it was against my advice that the name has unfortunately been changed to the Institute of Logistics and Transport.

The next thing to come my way, in 1956, was to be asked to serve on the **Cambridge University Appointments Board**. Its task is to co-ordinate the interests of all the colleges in deciding who should fill posts within the university. I would drive to Cambridge every two months, and found it enjoyable revisiting the haunts of my youth. We would have lunch, hold our deliberations in one of the colleges, and stay for dinner. I served on the CUAB until 1969.

In 1957 I renewed a link with my youth when I formed and accepted the Presidency of **The Croydon Airport Society**. We used to meet monthly under the old airport control tower. Despite the pressures at Bristol and all my other commitments I was glad to become deeply involved. The airport finally closed on 30 September 1959, but the CAS still exists, in alliance with the renovated Airport House at Croydon.

In 1958 I was delighted to be invited to become a member of the **Aeronautical Research Council**. This is the most senior British aeronautical research organisation. It comprises equal numbers of official and independent members, all with many letters after their names. We usually met at the National Physical Laboratory, at Teddington. I served on the ARC for four years.

In February 1959 I was appointed a Member of the Council of **The Air League of the British Empire**. Founded in 1909, this was a body dedicated to furthering every aspect of aviation throughout the Commonwealth, and air-mindedness in the young. On the same occasion Sir Miles Thomas accepted an invitation to become

Vice-President, the President being His Grace the Duke of Hamilton. The Air League then had its headquarters in Sloane Street, and the monthly *Air Pictorial* was its organ. The League still exists, stronger than ever, but no longer with any reference to the Empire. So does the magazine, but without any connection with the League.

In 1960 I was elected to the Council of the **Royal Aero Club**. Founded in 1901, this again is the most august organisation of its type. I had been a member for many years previously, and enjoyed the daily pre-lunch scrum in the overcrowded bar at No 119 Piccadilly, which was a marvellous centre of aviation chit-chat, politics and intrigue. Quite different in atmosphere was the grandeur of the club's later home, Londonderry House, on Park Lane. Over all presided Secretary Rupert L. 'Mossie' (pronounced Mozzy) Preston, whose immaculate turnout and bearing bespoke his background of the Coldstream Guards. I chaired the club's Aviation Committee in 1960–65, and was the club's Chairman until 1970. Sadly, after my departure the club ceased to operate as a club, but as a valuable mailing address in Leicester. Beautiful Londonderry House was demolished, and No 119 now has nothing to do with aviation.

Another committee to which I was appointed in 1960 was the **Cairns Committee on Aircraft Accidents**. I was having a hectic time getting Beagle launched, but this committee was too important for me to decline the invitation. It met at the Royal Aeronautical Society every week for nearly four months, thrashing out in the greatest detail how civil air accidents should be investigated. Its massive Report established all the standards by which investigations are carried out today. As Mr Justice (later Lord) Cairns was frequently indisposed I often took his place.

In 1961 the **Business Aircraft Users' Association** was formed, with the declared objective of ensuring that such users in the United Kingdom should in no way be disadvantaged in comparison with any airline, military Service or other official user of airspace. From the start I was a Council Member.

In 1967 my old friend Sir John Elliott hijacked me on to the Board of the **Institute of Travel Managers**. I had hardly accepted this directorship before I was appointed Chairman, and I served until the end of 1970. The ITM is mainly a social organisation, dedicated to organising lunches and dinners, though it does have two business meetings each year. These are yet another function held at the Berkeley Street offices of Thomas Cook. Ministers are frequently invited to take part in the discussion of travel requirements and problems.

Sir John Elliott also played a central role in getting me on the Board of Trustees of the **Imperial War Museum**, in 1969. Under its Chief Executive, Dr Noble Frankland, a gallant ex-member of RAF Bomber Command, this famous museum, in central London, was working on literally hundreds of activities, of which three stood out: the purchase of the hallowed RAF airfield at Duxford, the establishment of the famous cruiser HMS *Belfast* on the Thames in London, and (though hardly warlike) the preservation of Concorde 01. In 1976 the Chairman sadly died, and I was co-opted as his successor. Many of our meetings were on board HMS *Belfast*. I served as Chairman until 1978, when I handed over to MRAF Sir John Grandy.

My involvement with the IWM led in 1970 to my election as President of the **Duxford Aviation Society**. I am very proud to have assisted this excellent society, and have never relinquished my association with it. It meets at the famous museum whose title is The Imperial War Museum, Duxford.

I was surprised and delighted to hear that my name was to appear in the New Year's Honours List for 1972 under the heading **Knights Batchelor**. One often has no idea how such honours are bestowed; the recipient is merely asked whether he or she will accept it. The investiture took place at Buckingham Palace, and I was pleased that it was carried out by Her Majesty The Queen Mother, a magnificent rock in a shifting sea of public life.

In 1972 the dynamic Ken Joyner, then of BOAC, asked me to join him to help run two small but very profitable companies he had started. He learned his trade as Property Manager of BOAC, and the companies he asked me to join were **Worldwide Estates** and **Project Management**. Ken was an expert at buying, developing and then selling property, concentrating on flats (apartments) and factories in the south of England. Each company had a three-man Board, and in each case I stayed from 1972 until 1989.

Another invitation that came my way in 1972 was to the Presidency of the **British Association of Aviation Consultants**. The BAAC jealously guards its right to represent professional consultants, and admits only engineers, economists, lawyers and pilots with a proven track record. The association has its own offices in central London, but we used to meet at the Royal Aeronautical Society.

In 1973 I was invited to join the Board of the **Nationwide Building Society**. I knew this to be a wholly reputable company, unlike some in recent years, and was pleased when Robin MacLellen – an absolutely super Scot who had been my Deputy at the BAA Scottish Advisory Council – said he would be happy to 'add weight'. I was impressed that Nationwide thought it could use more engineering expertise. Indeed, quite soon the Chairman, Sir Herbert Ashworth, said that he was retiring and offered me the Chair. I am sure I was right to reply that I was not really the man for that job, and the post was occupied by the experienced Leonard Williams. I stayed until 1986, and as well as quite hard work enjoyed various NBS overseas trips, for example to California.

When I was running BEA I had been impressed by one of my Captains as a man who would literally go far. A very capable Scot, Adam Thompson did just that. In 1975 he invited me to lunch at Gatwick, and asked 'Will you join the Board of my airline?' Caledonian Airways had begun at Prestwick with charters flown by a single DC-7C. It had progressed through fleets of Britannias and 707s, and in 1970 had merged with British United to form **British Caledonian**. It set the highest standards, and the cabin service provided by its tartan-clad stewardesses was justly famous.

In the world of air transport BCal was thus a force to be reckoned with, and I was delighted to come on board. By 1975 the merged airline was operating scheduled services on the North Atlantic on routes opened up by the so-called Bermuda 2 agreement. Thus, eventually BCal was to operate to New York, Chicago, Houston, Atlanta, Dallas and Los Angeles. We went from strength to strength. In 1978 I was appointed Deputy Chairman, while another whose career had in many ways paralleled my own, Alastair Pugh (who is a neighbour of mine) became Managing Director. By this time I had flown the entire route network, often in Adam's company (he maintained his Air Line Transport Pilot's licence). At the start of 1979 I went with Pat by BCal to

Long Beach to take delivery of the first of eight DC-10s, all named after famous Scots. We were a happy ship, and an object lesson of how a global airline should be run. I remained Deputy Chairman until BCal was expensively swallowed up by British Airways in 1987.

Several interesting things came my way in 1977. Particularly enjoyable was the Chairmanship of the Council of the **Royal Society of Arts**. In fact, the RSA is a sum of many parts, by no means concerned only with huge canvases in gilded frames, but with 'arts, manufactures and commerce'. It has a magnificent property on John Adam Street, where one day the lecture theatre was packed to attend a film of the life of Lord Louis Mountbatten. 'Dicky' to his friends, he sat next to Pat, who found the epic film so uncaptivating that she went to sleep on his shoulder. Of course, Her Majesty and the entire Royal Family were present, and afterwards the queue of eminent people waiting to meet Mountbatten was most impressive.

I took over as Chairman of the RSA from Lord Nathan (see Chapter 32). Chairmen are appointed for two years, and in 1979 I handed over to my successor. There had never been a lady Chairman, but I was delighted to be able to propose that my successor should be Dame Diana Reader-Harris, and she was outstanding in that role. Ex-Chairmen continue as a Vice-President, and I am now a Vice-President Emeritus.

Other happy events of 1977 were the awards of honorary degrees from two of the country's most important technical seats of learning, **Cranfield University** and **Loughborough University**. Accordingly, I am now able to write after my name 'Hon. DSc (Cranfield)' and 'Hon. DTech (Loughborough)'.

In 1979 I received two additional invitations which were most welcome. One was to become the President of the **Institute of Road Transport Engineers**. The IRTE is an excellent body,with real executive power. Based at Solihull in the Midlands, at one time the hub of an enormous road-vehicle industry, it not only meets to talk shop, and to put on a very impressive exhibition each year, but it also serves as a good and effective force in the bus, coach and trucking industry. During my time as President, which lasted until 1983, the IRTE Secretary was the industrious Tony Fletcher.

Right on my own doorstep, **Reigate Grammar School** invited me in 1979 to chair a meeting of people who were concerned about the school's future. Since 1640 RGS had been one of the best schools in the country, and the parents were very worried by the fact that the Minister of Education, then Shirley Williams, was opposed to grammar schools and was determined to do away with them. Accordingly, I invited concerned parents to a meeting at Rosehill, as a result of which we eventually raised enough money to pay the fees of boys whose parents could not afford them as a private school. Since then the school has gone from strength to strength under outstanding Headmasters, Howard Ballance and subsequently John Hamlin and John Dixon. I was Chairman of the Board of Governors from 1979 until 1991. I am sad that, as this is written in 2001, I could not attend the opening by the Duke of Gloucester of the school's new Peter Masefield Hall, but Pat went and tells me it is magnificent.

In 1980 I was elected President of the **International Federation of Airworthiness**. This is a distinguished body which exists to co-ordinate international airworthiness standards. Its members meet quarterly all over the world, and I had the good fortune to preside over many of these assemblies in places as far apart as Australia and Canada. At every one of these gatherings there was a packed agenda responding to an unforeseen problem or the emergence of new technology. I remained the IFA's President until 1983, and was then elected Patron for five years after that.

In 1981 I was appointed Governor of **Ashridge Management College**. Once a famous naval college, it is a residential college for outstanding men and women sponsored by their employers. Under its dynamic Chief Executive, Philip Sadler, it was prospering, and I considered the long drive to the quarterly Board Meetings well worth while. I held the post for 11 years, to 1991.

In 1982 I was invited to join the Board of **London Regional Transport International**. This had been created to run a variety of London Transport's associated companies, and met in the familiar LT premises above St James's Park station. I had little to do, and I considered this a sinecure which I continued until 1991.

In between whiles, I had been researching and writing a tale of high drama which had affected me emotionally all my adult life. This was the story of the great airship R.101, and also of Air Minister Lord Thomson (who died in the airship). Especially moving was his impossible and virtually unspoken lifelong love for the beautiful Princess Marthe Bibesco. In 1982 my efforts emerged as a substantial volume, *To Ride the Storm*, published by William Kimber.

In 1986 I was appointed to the **CAA Flight Time Limitations Board**. This official body of the Civil Aviation Authority had teeth, which were needed to establish standards of employment for all civil aircrew. Often junior aircrew were only too happy to work excessive hours in order to earn more money and, in particular, to ensure that customers went away satisfied. There was much to be done, and I served until 1991. Most of the Board's meetings were held not at the dramatic CAA House in Kingsway but at the Royal Aeronautical Society.

In 1987 I was invited to become Chairman of the **Brooklands Museum Trust**. I had known from boyhood that Brooklands is a very special place, for aviation as much as for motor racing. I have been appalled at the carelessly brutal way in which its famous race track has been built over or left to rot, and the hallowed airfield covered with buildings, most of which have subsequently been demolished and replaced by others.

I was delighted to do what little I could to help the Trust , which is an entirely voluntary organisation reconstituted largely by ex-Vickers staff, led by Norman Barfield and the splendid Mrs Morag Barton. The Trust is devoted to creating and then caring for a most necessary museum. This has got ever better, and has assembled a unique collection of famous Vickers aircraft and historic cars.

In 1993 I stepped down from the Chairmanship, and was elected President, an office I am still delighted to hold. I was succeeded as Chairman by the Lord Tombs of Brailes. A tireless worker for the Museum, he led a most successful money-raising series of appeals, before being in turn succeeded in 2001 by my old friend Lord Trefgarne.

In 1991 I was surprised and gratified to be presented with the Golden Eagle Award by the **American Society of Senior Aerospace Engineers**. This award is for 'sustained leadership'. It takes the form of an impressive plaque for mounting on the wall. I was delighted to go to the Smithsonian in Washington to receive the presentation, and to address a distinguished gathering on the subject of Anglo-American collaboration.

What surely must be my final appointment, dating from 1993, was as a Director of **Air Bristol**. This charter airline operated daily services for staff seconded by British Aerospace to Airbus, the usual route being Chester–Filton–Toulouse. It maintained these services with several One-Elevens, painted in a distinctive purple livery. I remained a Director until 1996.

I should add that it is the men and women I have had the good fortune to work with, throughout the world, who have made all this so congenial for me – and so worthwhile.

45

Envoi

With the above title I rounded off the special Centenary Number of the Journal of the Royal Aeronautical Society in 1966, and I think it is appropriate now. Reviewing what Bill and I have put into this book, I am astonished at its length, and many parts – such as the Beagle story – could have been much longer.

As this is written, in October 2001, I feel fortunate to have been one of the few people to have celebrated a 65th Wedding Anniversary. At our Diamond Wedding in 1996 we received very kind and thoughtful congratulations from Her Majesty the Queen and from the then Prime Minister, John Major. We held a great party in a marquee at my son Richard's farm in Sussex. I spoke of my first sight of the 'girl in the stunning blue frock'. I had brought with me my favourite photo of her as a girl, and passed it along the tables with the comment that she looked very much the same as she did then.

Pat and I are immensely proud of our large and expanding family – of our four children and eleven grandchildren, with all their husbands and wives – and of our (so far) twelve great-grandchildren. They are all much loved.

Our eldest, Vicky, who arrived smiling in 1938, trained after school in Switzerland (close to my own college near Chillon) and at a domestic science college in Eastbourne, working in the catering business until her marriage – to a wonderful husband, Jeremy Burt. Widowed at the age of thirty-six, with four young children to bring up, she has since managed alone, and managed splendidly, training herself to become an accountant for Jeremy's family business, sitting on every local committee in sight, and eventually finding a new career for herself in the world of fashion. She has eight grandchildren.

Charles (knighted Sir Charles in 1997) learned to fly before his 17th birthday. He followed me to Jesus College, and flew with Cambridge University Air Squadron. He then sold and helped test Beagles, before being appointed Chief Test Pilot at Manchester for Hawker Siddeley, and subsequently British Aerospace. He became Production Director, Divisional Director and General Manager, and then Deputy MD for BAe at Hatfield, Manchester and Prestwick. In 1992 he was appointed President, BAe Commercial Aircraft, followed by the same post for Avro International and, in 1994 – the year in which he uniquely followed me as President of the Royal Aeronautical Society – Commercial Director of Airbus. He was knighted when he was Head of the UK Defence Export Services Organization. Since then he has been Vice-President of GEC, and Marketing Director of BAE Systems. He and his wife, Fiona, have two sons.

Our second son, Richard, is more interested in living things, and in conservation, than in the world of aviation. After experimenting with repertory acting, he became Associate Director of an international advertising agency, subsequently buying his own farm to produce milk and beef. Retaining the farm, he has written three successful novels, and won a literary award, working for the past twelve years at a school for severely disabled children. He currently spends a good deal of his time ensuring that Pat and I retain as much independence as possible in our own home – with the indispensable help of our wonderful live-in carer, Mimi Chibanda. Richard and his Australian wife, Lee, have three children and four grandchildren.

Our third son, Oliver, did inherit the aeronautical gene. After training at Loughborough University, he made his name in Switzerland as Chief Engineer and Engineering Director of Pilatus. He returned to Loughborough to receive his Ph.D – and, as Dr Oliver Masefield, he could not resist the chance to cross the Atlantic to create a brilliant little 'bizjet', as Vice-President Engineering of the American Eclipse Aviation. Formed in 1999 with the backing of jet-engine maker Williams, this company is based in Albuquerque, New Mexico, where the Eclipse 500 is to fly in mid-2002. Thanks partly to joining the metallic components using the revolutionary friction stir-welding technology, it is hoped to price this shapely six-seater at a scarcely believable US$837,500 – and I'm glad to say that initial orders for the 'plane have been enormously encouraging. Oliver and his Swiss wife, Irma, have two sons.

I myself kept busy until 9 November 1998. On that day I rose as usual before 5 a.m., and soon afterwards ascended the steep staircase bearing a tray with two hot cups of tea. I overbalanced and, not wishing to let go of the tray, crashed all the way back. To say the resulting broken hip has slowed me up is an understatement, though I can still walk with help from a frame. I find it frustrating to spend much of my time telling people where to find the countless documents that fill Rosehill.

I would rather leave the reader in 1994, when my 80th birthday was celebrated in grand style at Brooklands. I said then that life is rather like setting out on a lake in one of those time-limited rowing boats. Having contributed dozens of obituaries to *The Times*, I know that one will eventually hear 'Come in No 6, your time is up!' I like to think I am still No 8, but in any case it has all been fun, because in the end one remembers only the good times.

Oliver, at our Diamond Wedding celebration.

Appendix

Selected flights

7 April 1930 (Monday), first flight: Imperial Airways Armstrong Whitworth Argosy G-EBLF *City of Glasgow*, Paris (Le Bourget)–London (Croydon), 2 hr 50 min.

19 June 1930, Imperial Airways Handley Page H.P.42W G-AAXD *Horatius*, Le Bourget–Croydon, 2 hr 20 min.

14 March 1931, Imperial Airways Armstrong Whitworth Argosy G-AACJ *City of Manchester*, Le Bourget–Croydon, 2 hr 40 min.

19 June 1931, Imperial Airways Armstrong Whitworth Argosy G-AAEJ *City of Coventry*, Le Bourget–Croydon, 2 hr 15 min.

22 July 1931, RAF Mount Batten, Blackburn Iris III S1263, Captain Sqn Ldr J.H.O. Jones, flight along South Coast, 16 SOB (souls on board), 1 hr 20 min.

2 October 1931, Imperial Airways Armstrong Whitworth Argosy G-AAEJ *City of Coventry*, Croydon–Le Bourget, 2 hr 40 min (1 hr at night).

8 April 1932, Imperial Airways Handley Page H.P.42W: G-AAXE *Hengist*, Le Bourget–Croydon, 2 hr 30 min.

24 April 1932, Hillman's Airways D.H.80A Puss Moth G-ABVX *Gilford*, local flying at Maylands, price five shillings (25p).

G-EBLF City of Glasgow.

S1263, the Blackburn Iris III.

23 October 1932, D.H.82 Tiger Moth prototype G-ABRC (ex-E.6), pilot C.A. Pike, familiarisation at Hatfield, 10 min.

5 November 1932, first lesson, D.H.60 Moth G-AASL, pilot R.W. Reeve, 25 min. Followed by three lessons on subsequent two days.

December 1932, Hillman's Airways D.H.84 Dragon G-ACAN *Maylands*, at Maylands, local flying, 15 min.

20 December 1932, Hillman's Airways, D.H.80A Puss Moth G-ABSB *Sonny*, Capt. Sam Morton, first flight with Pat, Croydon–Maylands, 25 min.

17 April 1933 Whitney Straight's D.H.60G Moth G-ABYV, Cambridge–Brooklands and return.

9 July 1933, Imperial Airways Ltd, Handley Page H.P.42W G-AAXC *Heracles*, Capt. A.S. Wilcockson, air test after major overhaul.

August 1933, General Aircraft Ltd, test-flying Monospar ST.6 G-ACGI, pilot H.M. Schofield.

27 June 1934, Airwork School of Flying, Heston, Avro Club Cadets G-ACHO/ACHP/ACTX, nine flights at Heston with instructor Brian Davey.

August 1934, Wrightson & Pearse D.H.84 Dragon G-ACHX, three flights (pilot Bill Rimmer or Jack Duggan), Heston local, Heston–Le Bourget, Le Bourget–Heston.

April 1935, Wrightways Ltd D.H.84 Dragon G-ACHX and D.H.86A G-AEJM, in each case a round trip Croydon–Le Bourget.

September 1935, Fairey Hendon modified prototype K1695, pilot Flt Lt C.S. Staniland.

1935/36, Various flights in Fairey aircraft, notably the Seal and prototype Swordfish.

1936, several dates, D.H.87B Hornet Moth, local flying at Hatfield.

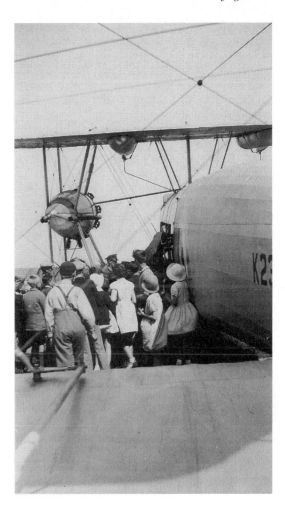

Boarding the Vickers Valentia.

7 April 1937, Miles M.11B Whitney Straight G-AERC, testbed for 135-hp Villiers Maya engine, assisted on 1 hr 45 min test from Heston.

29 May 1937, RAF Hendon, Vickers Valentia, visited Northolt, Farnborough, Odiham, Worthy Down, Hamble, Lee-on-Solent, Thorney Island, Tangmere, Upper Heyford, Wyton and Halton, 4 hr 40 min on Empire Air Day.

6 August 1937, KLM Douglas DC-3-194 PH-ALI, Croydon–Amsterdam, Capt. J.J. Moll in command, first DC-3 in Europe.

7 August 1937, *Deutsche Luft Hansa*, Junkers Ju 52/3m, Amsterdam–Dusseldorf–Cologne.

1937, RAF Finningley, 20-min flight in Vickers-Armstrongs Wellesley bomber.

Same date in 1937, RAF Finningley, 35-min flight in Armstrong Whitworth Whitley I bomber.

1 September 1937, London Air Park Flying Club, Hanworth, D.H.60 Moth I G-ASSY, dual with J. Kirwan, first of 48 flights with the Civil Air Guard. The first 19 were on various D.H.60 Moths (see below).

23 February 1938, Imperial Airways Short S.23 Empire flying-boat G-AEUC
Corinna, Capt. A.J. 'Taffy' Powell, flight from Rochester to observe Mayo
Composite aircraft.

25 April 1938, Olley Air Service D.H.89 Dragon Rapide, Capt. Sam Morton,
Croydon–Soesterberg. On the same day, Dornier Do 17 development aircraft
D-APAL, test pilot Hoffman, Soesterberg–Amsterdam. On the same day, the
same Olley Dragon Rapide Amsterdam–Croydon.

17 July 1938, Cambridge University Air Squadron Avro Tutor, local flying at
Duxford.

24 July 1938, Koolhoven F.K.52 two-seat fighter, PH-ASW, company test pilot Dick
Asjes, demonstration flight at Heston.

The year 1939 began well! My first 19 CAG flights included my *first solo* on G-AAET
on 3 January 1939. At this time I had logged 12 hr 55 min over seven years; at
Hanworth I had flown 6 hr 20 min in four months with five instructors. From
21 February 1939 all my CAG flying was on B.A. Swallows.

14 February 1939, Railway Air Services de Havilland D.H.86B G-AEFH, Glasgow
(Abbotsinch)–Belfast (Newtownards). On same day return Belfast–Liverpool
(Speke)–London (Croydon). Total flight time 3 hr 20 min.

3 March 1939, Percival Vega Gull G-AELW, owner O.F. Maclaren,
Heston–Cambridge, returning on following day.

10 May 1939, RAF Hawker Hart Trainer K6427, pilot Mike Collins, aerobatics and
circuits at Hanworth.

23 May 1939, G.A.L. Cygnet G-AEMA, modified with nosewheel undercarriage, test
pilot D.L. Hollis Williams, at Hanworth.

20 June 1939, Messerschmitt Bf 108B Taifun, G-AFRN, imported by AFN Ltd., pilot
Otto Brindlinger, vertical turns, stalls, at Heston.

27 June 1939, Stinson SR-10C Reliant G-AFRS, pilot in command Brian Allen, flown
with H.A. 'Tony' Taylor of *Flight* at Hanworth.

8 July 1939, British Airways Lockheed 10 Electra G-AEPN, Heston–Brussels
(Evère).

9 July 1939, SABENA Savoia-Marchetti S.M.73 OO-AGL, Brussels–Croydon.

13 July 1939, Tipsy B G-AFGF, first British-built example, pilot Mike Collins, at
Hanworth.

6 November 1939, de Havilland D.H.86 Express G-ACZO, ex-Jersey Airways,
impressed for National Air Communications, later RAF AX841, Heston–Reims,
2 hr 20 min.

10 November 1939, Fokker F.XII G-AEOS, ex-British Airways, impressed for
National Air Communications, Reims–Heston, 2 hr 30 min.

April 1940, KLM Douglas DC-3 PH-ALU, Shoreham–Amsterdam, 2 hr 00 min.

April 1940, KLM Douglas DC-3 PH-ALM, Amsterdam–Shoreham, 1 hr 35 min.

20 November 1940, G.A.L. Owlet G-AGBK, pilot Charles Hughesdon, at Hanworth.

26 February 1941, Miles Aircraft Ltd., Master II AX247, pilot Tommy Rose, at Woodley.

4 March 1941, RAF Miles Magister, Northolt–Hawkinge, 40 min.

5 March 1941, RAF Bristol Blenheim IV, Manston–Northolt, 30 min.

26 June 1941, RAF Douglas Boston II (later converted to Havoc), Hendon–Boscombe
Down, 20 min. Same day, RAF de Havilland Mosquito II, Boscombe
Down–Exeter and return, total 50 min. Same day, RAF Bristol Beaufort I,
Boscombe Down–Hendon, 30 min.

1941, A.W. Whitley V, used as propeller testbed by Rotol Ltd, at Staverton, 30 min.

1942, A.V. Roe Ltd, Lancaster I, air test at Woodford, 20 min.

I enjoyed wartime flying in (from the nearest) Miles Magister, Miles Master III and Airspeed Oxford.

17 August 1942, USAAF Boeing B-17E 41-9023, 97th BG, at Bovingdon, 1 hr 15 min.

19 May 1943, D.H.82A Tiger Moth T5491, pilot C.A. Pike, refresher at Hatfield.

22 May 1943, Avro Tutor L6120, pilot T.G.A. Gale, checkout at White Waltham for ATA.

17 June 1943, USAAF 92BG, 326BS, B-17E 41-9119 JK-F, 4 hr 00 min.

6 July 1943, USAAF Beech AT-7 42-2429, Bovingdon–Honington–Snetterton Heath.

6–29 July 1943, five practice missions and five combat missions in Boeing B-17F Fortress aircraft of the USAAF 96th BG, based at Snetterton Heath.

8 August 1943, USAAF Douglas C-47, Heston–Prestwick, 2 hr 25 min.

9 August 1943, USAAF Douglas C-54 42-32948, Prestwick–Meeks Field (Keflavik, Iceland), 5 hr 12 min. On same day, on to Presque Isle, Maine, 11 hr 46 min.

10 August 1943, USAAF Douglas C-53 41-90095, Presque Isle–NY La Guardia, 3 hr 27 min. Then on to Washington National, 1 hr 49 min. Both legs at night.

13–22 August 1943, USAAF AT-7 42-2449, Washington–NY (La Guardia)–Cleveland–Detroit (Willow Run)–Cleveland–NY. Transferred to USAAF C-56D 42-57223 to Cleveland–Chicago (Midway)–Minneapolis–Bismarck–Billings–Spokane–Seattle (Boeing Field)–Portland–San Francisco (Mills Field)–Burbank, Maj. J.T. Fitzwalter in command, total 30 hr 19 min.

*With the Boeing
(Stearman) PT-13B
Kaydet of Cal-Aero in
August 1943.*

23 August 1943, USAAF Douglas C-54A, Santa Monica (Clover Field)–Long Beach,
22 min; then return to Santa Monica, 30 min; test flights of a new aircraft, Col
Stith in command, self as co-pilot.

25 August–28 September 1943, C-56D 42-57223, 41 further flights, total 67 hr
48 min. This period also included two flights as co-pilot to Capt. Al Carl in
similar Lockheed C-60 and also the following:

Undated, USAAF (formerly on British account) Lockheed RP-322 (Lightning)
AF118, with rear passenger seat, total 30 min.

27 August, California Aero Flight Academy, Boeing-Stearman PT-13B 40-1716, solo
with loop, spin and roll, 35 min.

28 August, USAAF Curtiss AT-9 Jeep 41-11955, dual with Capt. F.H. Scott from
Williams Field, Phoenix, Arizona.

17 September, USAAF Sikorsky YR-4 helicopter 42-107236, pilot Col Cooper, self
as co-pilot, at Wright Field, Dayton, Ohio, 15 min.

20 September, USAAF Curtiss-Wright C-46 Commando 41-24713, served as co-pilot
on first flight of new aircraft at Buffalo, NY, 1 hr 20 min.

28/29 September 1943, USAAF Douglas C-54, NY (La Guardia)–Stephenville
(Newfoundland)–Prestwick–Northolt, total 17 hr 12 min.

20/21 July 1944, RAF Consolidated Liberator II (demilitarised, long-range) AL578

Marco Polo, Capt. G.J. Evans, 1st Officer K. Abbott, navigator Flt Lt H. Farley, record non-stop Northolt–Washington, 19 hr 46 min.

29 July 1944, American Airlines DC-3 NC21949, Washington–NY (La Guardia), 1 hr 20 min. Return on the following day in NC18142, 1 hr 28 min.

4 August 1944, USAAF impressed DC-3, Washington–NY (La Guardia), 1 hr 25 min.

13 August 1944, RAF Consolidated Liberator II (mod) AL504 *Commando*, Wg Cdr W.H. Biddell, Flt Lt F. Donaldson, Flt Lt H. Farley, record inter-city NY (La Guardia)–London (Northolt), 17 hr 34 min.

18 August 1944, USAAF Beech C-45F, co-pilot to Lt Robinson, Heston–Meir (Staffordshire).

3 September 1944, USAAF 96th BG, Boeing B-17G 43-377603, combat mission Snetterton Heath to Brest (96th dropped 927 US tons), 7 hr 31 min.

5 September 1944, second combat mission in same aircraft.

In May 1945 I began flying with the ATA. Between 16 May and 29 June I made 38 flights in Fairchild Argus Is, one in an Argus II, four in an Argus III, two in N.A. Harvard IIBs and four in Avro Anson Is. Total 46 hr 50 min, just over half being solo ferrying. Also in this period, 20 min as passenger Aldermaston–White Waltham in Airspeed Oxford.

In July 1945 my family went by ship to the USA.

26 July 1945, American Airlines DC-3 NC33317, Washington–Nashville, first flight of Vicky, Charles and Richard and *au pair* Peggy, 3 hr 20 min.

28 July 1945, American Airlines DC-3, Nashville–Washington.

13 August 1945, American Airlines DC-3, Washington–NY.

14 August 1945, RAF Lockheed Hudson IIIA FK779, NY–Washington, 1 hr 15 min, then on to Montreal (Dorval), 3 hr 05 min.

17 August 1945, RAF Lockheed Hudson IIIA FK779, Montreal–NY, 2 hr 10 min, then on to Washington, 1 hr 17 min.

27 August 1945, RAF Douglas Dakota, Baltimore–Montreal, 3 hr 16 min.

28 August 1945, RAF Lockheed Hudson IIIA FK779, Montreal–NY, 1 hr 48 min, then on to Washington, 1 hr 15 min.

29 August 1945, USAAF Douglas C-47, Washington–Wright Field, Dayton, Ohio, 2 hr 28 min.

31 August 1945, USAAF Douglas C-47 43-30695, Wright Field–Washington.

11/12 September 1945, four flights by American Airlines Douglas DC-3A, NC45383 (2) and NC17686 (2).

14/15 September 1945, BOAC Boeing 314A G-AGBZ *Bristol*, Capt. Craig, Baltimore–Botwood, then Capt. John H. Austin, Botwood–Foynes–Poole, total 21 hr 00 min.

21 September 1945, de Havilland Mosquito NF.30 NT250, test flight at Hatfield, 30 min.

22 September 1945, Bristol Aeroplane Co., Buckmaster T.1 TJ714, dual with chief test pilot Cyril Uwins, 30 min.

22 September 1945, Miles Aircraft Ltd, Nighthawk U0225 (later G-AGWT), Filton–Woodley, 30 min.

27/28 September 1945, BOAC Boeing 314A G-AGBZ, Poole–Foynes–Botwood–Baltimore, 27 hr 49 min.

Between 20 December 1945 and 15 February 1946 I made four further flights in BOAC Boeing 314As, three between Baltimore and Darrell's Island and one from Bermuda (Kindley Field) to Washington.

Then 42 passenger flights, various, plus:

19–26 February 1946, two flights in USAAF Douglas C-117A Skytrooper as co-pilot to Maj. Kohn, flying Washington–Birmingham (Alabama)–Kansas City–Albuquerque, followed by two as co-pilot to Capt. Gilley flying Albuquerque–Burbank–San Francisco–San Diego.

On arrival at San Diego, Stinson 150 NC82950 solo with passenger, 15 min.

I then made a round-the-world flight by scheduled airlines:

7/8 April 1946, United Airlines Douglas DC-3A NC16068, Washington–Toledo–Chicago–Omaha–Cheyenne–Salt Lake City–Elko–Oakland–San Francisco.

9–13 April, BCPA/ANA Douglas DC-4 VH-ANC San Francisco–Honolulu–Canton Island (John Rogers Field)–Fiji (Nandi)–Melbourne (Essendon).

14 April, TAA Douglas DC-3, Melbourne–Sydney (Mascot).

17–19 April, BOAC Avro Lancastrian G-AGME *Newhaven*, Sydney–Darwin–Singapore (Changi)–Karachi (Mauripur)–Lydda–Hurn.

4 May, BOAC Douglas Dakota 3A G-AGHU, Northolt-Prestwick, where I went on by BOAC Consolidated Liberator II freighter G-AGJP to Shannon, and then on the following day to Montreal (Dorval).

5 May, Colonial Airlines Douglas DC-3, Montreal–Syracuse–Washington.

The circumnavigation comprised 23 sectors, 26,759 miles, in 128 hr 45 min flight time.

1 June 1946, BOAC Lockheed L-049 Constellation G-AHEN *Baltimore*, co-pilot to Capt. J.J. Percy on handling test of new aircraft.

16 June 1946, BOAC Lockheed L-049 Constellation G-AHEM *Balmoral*, NY–Heathrow, Capt. W.S. May, first passenger flight by BOAC Constellation, 11 hr 24 min.

23/24 June 1946, BOAC Lockheed L-049 Constellation G-AHEZ *Bangor II*, westbound Press flight with Capt. Arthur Whitten Brown (1919 Atlantic flyer) on board, Heathrow–Shannon–Gander–NY (La Guardia). I then went on to Washington.

11–17 July 1946, four dual flights in Fairchild PT-19As (NC58305 and 46357) at Congressional Airport, Maryland, followed by solo flight, to clear me for US solo flying. There followed a period of intensive flying by US domestic operators.

24 July 1946, I took delivery of my assigned Percival Proctor V G-AHGN, and was checked out by John Burgess. From 26 July until 20 September I flew this aircraft 20 times on my Attaché duties, also flying Taylorcraft B-12B three times on 14 August and on August 31 a DHC-1 Chipmunk prototype CF-DJF-X, with test pilot Pat Fillingham as co-pilot.

4 December 1946, back in England, at the Bristol Aeroplane Co., I flew the 170 Wayfarer IIA G-AHJC with former chief test pilot Cyril Uwins.

23 December 1946, John Belson checked me out in Auster V G-AGLK.

By 1947 my pilot's (as distinct from passenger) log book was filling up rapidly. In May of that year I flew (solo or dual) 12 aircraft of 10 types, notably Miles Gemini light twins. On 13 May I flew the first Ercoupe in Europe, Belgian demonstrator OO-ERU, finding no problems with its unusual flight-control system. Later, after this aircraft had been re-registered G-AKFC, I flew it 17 times. Other 1947 types sampled included the N.A. Navion, Danish KZ.VII, various Austers, the Avro Lancastrian, Canada C-4 (DC-4M), Douglas C-54A G-AJPM, Miles M.28, Newbury Eon, D.H. Moth Minor coupé, Portsmouth Aerocar and Cunliffe-Owen Concordia. Airline flying was equally varied.

In 1948 Geminis still predominated, but de Havilland Doves began to appear frequently, among such rare species as the Fairey Junior, Avro Avian, Saab Scandia, a Tiger Moth Coupé (cabin conversion, done in New Zealand), the Zaunkönig (which took 1 hr 20 min to fly from Hendon to Gatwick), G-AKPK the civil-registered Gloster Meteor 7 prototype (which with Bill Waterton flying went rather faster), and the prototype Vickers-Armstrongs Viscount V.630, which was to lead to great things in my later life. Airline flying included my second circumnavigation, in 1948/9.

New types in 1949 included the Avro 19, D.H. Puss Moth, Percival Prince, Miles Aerovan VI, and the second Airspeed Ambassador G-AKRD. The Ambassador was to be important to me after I joined BEA, and so was the Vickers Viking which I first flew in 1950. In the same year I managed to persuade BEA to purchase a D.H.84 Dragon, G-ACIT. First registered in July 1933, it was flown intensively by Capt. E.E. Fresson throughout World War 2, mainly in terrible weather in northern Scotland and to the Hebrides and Shetlands. I first flew it on 22 August 1950, and on the following day I took my entire family and cousin Denis Lloyd-Owen on a 1 hr 30 min tour from Shoreham.

The year 1951 was dominated by flying G-ALZL, the prototype D.H.114 Heron, another type we bought for BEA. On 23 May I did dual with Jock Bryce on G-AMAV, the first Viscount V.700. On 15 July I gave my 10-year old son Charles four trips in Argus G-AKIZ, on one occasion visiting the BEA helicopter base at Birmingham Elmdon. On 21 August I accompanied Airspeed chief test pilot George Errington doing stalls and single-engine flying in our first 'Elizabethan' Ambassador G-ALZN, with Vicky, Charles, Richard and cousin Lloyd-Owen on board. At the end of the year I flew DHC-2 Beaver G-ALOW and Handley Page (Miles) Marathon G-ALUB.

With Beverley Shenstone and the prototype Heron, on 29 June 1950.

Dominant in 1952 were Geminis, but on 20 July I flew the Miles Aries (Gemini development), cruising effortlessly at 155 mph. I also put Auster Aiglet Trainer G-AMTD through its aerobatic repertoire.

The big event in 1953 was the race from London to Christchurch to celebrate the centenary of the city on the South Island of New Zealand, described in detail in Chapter 34. During this race I spent 13 hours at the controls, the rest of the time serving as crew member in charge of cruise control. We went on to fly 14 demonstration flights in New Zealand and Australia before returning to London via Singapore, Colombo, Delhi, Bahrain, Cyprus and Rome.

Back on 10 April 1953 I had done 'circuits and bumps' in G-ALWE *Discovery*, our first BEA Viscount 701, and on 22/23 September I had served as co-pilot to Capt. Ballie on a proving flight in G-AMAV to Bahrain–Basra (Shaibah)–Beirut and back to London, to assist planning for the race. Other 1953 flying included two 1-hr trips in Bristol 171 Sycamore helicopter G-AMWG with J.A. 'Jock' Cameron giving me dual from Northolt to Bristol, returning the following day.

The most interesting trip in 1954 was a 30-min check by Max Fieschl at Shoreham on the Hurel-Dubois H.D.31 F-WFKU. Powered by two 800-hp Wright Cyclone 7s, it had an amazing wing with an aspect ratio of 20.2. I did an overshoot on one engine.

In 1955 the same French company returned to Shoreham with their H.D.32 F-WGVG, powered by two 1,200-hp Twin Wasps. We did steep turns and stalls with 13 passengers, but these ultra-high aspect ratio aircraft never really 'took off'. Another interesting type in 1955 was the Convair YC-131C 53-7996, a regular USAF Convair re-engined to serve as a testbed for the 3,750-hp Allison YT56-A-3 turbo-prop. I flew as co-pilot to Col S.T. Smith at Boeing Field, Seattle. Another oddball was G-AIYX, a Piper L-4H Cub fitted with the 55-hp Coventry Victor Flying Neptune engine. The year ended with 40 min as co-pilot to c.t.p. Bill Pegg on G-ANBA, the first of BOAC's Bristol Britannia 102s.

By 1956 I was based in Bristol and flying mainly from Filton, initially using Auster J.5B Autocar G-AMNC, and on 6 November switching to Chipmunk G-AOTM (Tango Mike). On 1 May I twice flew F-PHFR, a VW-engined Druine Turbulent.

In 1957 I flew Chipmunk Tango Mike 173 times (a total of 174 hr 50 min), often in very poor weather. The highlight came on 5 April when I enjoyed 30 min solo on D8096, the only airworthy Bristol F.2B Fighter. I was surprised to find this famous 1917 aircraft, designed for close combat, heavy on the controls and directionally unstable. Easier to fly was F-PHZH, the first two-seat Jodel with a 90-hp Continental, with me accompanying the Homebuilt's designer.

In 1958 I flew Tango Mike 148 times, the last flight of that year (8th December) having Bristol test pilot Walter Gibb in the front seat.

In 1959 included a Percival Prentice, dual with Alfredo Gasperi at Villanova d'Albenga (Italy) on the Piaggio P.148 and (nosewheel) P.149, a 15-min evaluation of the first Garland-Bianchi Linnet with John Fricker as co-pilot (brilliant ailerons but noisy and poor brakes), and 1 hr as co-pilot on Max Karant's Bonanza from Wings Field (Philadelphia) to Washington. On 4 September I flew Tango Mike from Croydon to Filton (a trip I had now done well over 100 times), then on to Kidlington where I flew Piper Tri-Pacer EI-AKP (blind in turns), Piper Comanche EI-AKV and Piper Apache G-APLJ (landing at Woodley), then retrieved Tango Mike and flew to Fair Oaks to demonstrate it to glider champion Philip Wills, and finally flew to Croydon. A major milestone came on 9 May 1959 when I passed the 1,000-hr mark as pilot-in-command. On 1 April 1960 I left Bristol Aircraft and purchased Tango Mike. In that year I flew nothing but Chipmunks, Tango Mike being replaced by

G-ARFW on three occasions at the beginning of June. On 3 June Tango Mike averaged 145.28 mph in a London–Cardiff (Rhoose) race, and on the following day I averaged 136 mph in a closed-circuit race at Cardiff.

In 1961 I flew a variety of Beagle and pre-Beagle types, together with competitor aircraft. I did a lot of flying on G-ARKE, the prototype Beagle Airedale, and all the other Beagles including the B.206X (noting 'stall 38 kt IAS'). I flew G-APUT, Pressed Steel's Tri-Pacer, 29 times. Among the competition I flew the Piper Colt, Cherokee and Aztec, Cessna 175A, 185 and 210, and the Riley 65 Twin. On 22 August

About to board a BEA Sycamore.

I flew twice as co-pilot in the back of Tango Mike, with my son Charles in front. In December I achieved a long-felt ambition in purchasing the venerable Dragon G-ACIT from the Air Navigation and Trading Co. I had it overhauled and painted in Beagle colours. I flew it a great deal, my only regret being that, as there could be only one seat in the tiny cockpit, I could not let Charles fly. That Dragon was later stored in the Science Museum's facility at Wroughton, and in 1983 it was restored to the active register.

In 1962 I also used Tango Mike a great deal, and also tested the Terrier 2 and sound-proofed Airedale. While landing the 10th Airedale at Thame the nose leg collapsed. In September, in the B.206X, I took Henry Tiarks and 14 large pieces of baggage from Gatwick to Leuchars (Scotland) in 2 hr 10 min, and then returned to Shoreham.

The year 1963 was dominated by the Airedale, the B.206X prototype and the B.206Y pre-production aircraft. Whenever I could, I flew as co-pilot with Beagle test pilots W.C. 'Pee Wee' Judge and V. Mitchell, and was often accompanied by Charles.

By 1964 I did a lot of flying in Tango Mike, achieving a 3rd Place in the King's Cup on 1 August, at an average of 144.25 mph. In April I took a week's holiday, and with Sir John Elliott flew the B.206X (which was becoming surplus to Beagle's requirements) on a tour of the battlefields of northern France. Ignoring such niceties as French Customs, we would fly from Gatwick to old wartime airfields, having arranged for a car to meet us. We did a lot of air-to-ground photography. Most of the sites we visited were World War 1. The terrible gassed area which I had visited in 1939 (Chapter 5) had not changed.

At that time I had logged over 4,000 hr, including about 1,250 hr in command and a further 249 hr as co-pilot.

Index

Aeroplane, The, 29, 34
Aeroplane Spotter, The, 54
Aero Research Snark, 37
aircraft recognition, 50
airliners, post-war, 128, 154
airlines, British, 156
airships (from R.100), 104, 305
Airspeed
  Ambassador (de Havilland Elizabethan),
    83, 213, 226
  Consul, 224
Air Transport Auxiliary, 41, 170
Aitken, The Hon. Max, 8, 95
Armstrong Whitworth, 101
  Argosy, 11, 21
  Whitley, 36
Arnold, General Henry H., 35, 61, 69, 70
Attlee, Clement, 190
Auster, 264, 268
Avro, 198
  Anson, 259, 275
  Lancaster, 102
  Lancastrian, 103
  Tudor, 99, 198, 208
  York, 82, 98, 102

Babington-Smith, Constance, 37, 119, 120,
  179, 193
B.A. Swallow, 38
BEA, 216 *et seq*
Beagle, 263
  B.206X, 266
  B.206Y, 273
  B.206 to Australia, 277
  Bassett, 275
  Bulldog, 282
  M.218, 270
  Pup, 281
Beaverbrook, Lord, 78, 85, 89, 106, 108,
  168
Beech AT-7, 70
Bellhouse, Michael, 263
Berle, Dr Adolf, 109, 114, 144
Bermuda, 192
Bicknell, Nigel, 206

Blackburn Iris, 12
BOAC, 216
  Chairmanship offered, 238
Boeing, 71
  299 B-17 Fortress, 61, 73, 134
  314A, 86, 179, 184
  377 Stratocruiser, 204
  PT-13B Kaydet, 75
Brabazon, Lord, 79, 81
  Committee, 82–3, 97
Brentwood Mental Hospital 6
Brisbane Star, 172
Bristol, 101, 209, 235
  171 Sycamore, 232
  173, 248
  175 Britannia, 83, 211, 235
  188, 255
  198, 256
  200, 256 *et seq*
  220, 260
  405 car, 237, 242
  Bloodhound, 246
  Chipmunk Touring Conversion, 262
  Orion, 250
  Proteus, 209,
    icing, 249
British Airports Authority, 285
British Caledonian, 305
Brooklands Museum Trust, 307
Brooks, Peter, 59, 221

Cabotage, 127
Canadair
  DC-4M Argonaut, 204
  CL-28, 252
  CL-44, 252
Cheetham, John, 93, 188, 192
Cherwell, Lord, 91, 94, 117
Chicago, 142
Chillon College, 9
Christchurch, NZ, 229
Churchill, Sir Winston, 80, 95
Civil Air Guard, 37
Consolidated B-24 Liberator, 76, 81, 128,
  131

Coronation. 232
Cranborne, Viscount, 94
Cribbett, Sir George. 93, 135, 160, 192, 207
Cripps, Sir Stafford. 81, 101, 147
Croydon Airport, 19, 29, 303

de Havilland, Maj. Hereward, 224, 225
de Havilland
  D.H.84 Dragon, 23
  D.H.89 Dragon Rapide, 219
  D.H.98 Mosquito, 220
  D.H.104 Dove, 84, 214
  D.H.106 Comet, 84, 211
  D.H.114 Heron, 218
de Havilland Canada DHC-1 Chipmunk,
  244
Dodero, Alberto, 159
Dornier Do 17, 47, 314
Douglas, Donald, 75
Douglas
  DC-1/C-47 Dakota, 69, 219,
  (Dart-engined), 227
  DC-4/C-54, 69, 75, 189
  Long Beach 74
Douglas, Sir Sholto, 9 (not mentioned by
  name), 218, 258

Edwards, Sir George, 212, 220
El Al, 255
Elliott, Sir John, 299, 300, 304
d'Erlanger, Gerard, 216, 218, 239

Fairey Aviation 25
  Battle, 31, 44
  Hendon, 27
  Swordfish, 28
Farrar, David, 90
Fedden, Sir Roy, 79, 236
flying instruction, 16, 23

GAPAN, 303
Gatwick, 32, 288, 292
General Aircraft, 19, 21
Grey, Charles Grey (CGG), 33, 38

Gross, Courtland S., 73, 203
Gross, Robert E., 72, 203
Gwydyr House, 89
Handley Page, 100
  H.P.42, 20
  H.P.70, Halton 104
  H.P.68/81 Hermes, 101, 104
Hawker Hurricane, 46

Hearkers' Club, 53
Heath Row, 26
Heathrow, 113, 285
  cargo, 291
  rail link, 291
  Terminal 5, 297
Hildred, Sir William, 82, 93, 112, 135, 169
Hillman's Airways, 17
Hogg, Betty, 89, 90
Hughes, Howard, 201, 252

Imperial War Museum, 304
Inter-Services Journal, 58

Japanese aircraft, 57
Jesus College, 15
jet aircraft, 163
Junkers Ju 88, 86

Keynes, Lord, 188
Knollys, Viscount, 157

Leathers, Lord, 91
Le Rougetel, John, 93
Lloyd-Owen family, 1, 319
Lockheed
  10 Electra, 38, 80
  18 Lodestar, 71
  P-38 Lightning, 73, 77
  Constellation, 199, 208
London Transport, 299

Maclean, Donald, 176, 181
Masefield
  Sir Charles, 172, 244, 296, 309
  David, 4
  Sir John, 1, 186
  Oliver, 309
  Lady Patricia, 14, 17, 24, 173, 180, 194,
    206
  Sir Peter
    marriage, 29
    first solo, 38
    tries to join RAF, 41
    War Correspondent, 42
    at Ministry, 206
    house, 207
    rejects peerage, 285
    knighted, 296, 305
  Richard, 172, 173, 224, 309
  Victoria (Vicky), 40, 172, 224, 296, 309
Messerschmitt Me 262, 165
Miles brothers, 265

Miles
  Gemini, 229, 318
  (Handley Page) Marathon, 84, 219, 227
Monospar, 22
Montreal, 136, 183
Morgan, Stokely, 188, 196

Nathan, Lord, 215
North American Aviation, 75
Northolt, 217, 224
North Weald, 86

Observer Corps (later Royal), 52
Oslo parcel, 118

Pakenham, Lord, 215
Percival Proctor V, 202
PICAO, 152
Pogue, Welch, 130, 179, 188, 195
Pontiac car, 183
Pressed Steel, 263, 279
Prestwick, 294

RAF in France, 43
Reigate Grammar School, 306
Rolls-Royce Continental, 260, 273, 278
Royal Aero Club, 304
Royal Aeronautical Society, 79, 262, 302
Royal Society of Arts, 306
Russell, Sir Archibald, 241

Sandys, Duncan (later Lord Duncansandys),
    117, 262
Satterthwaite, Livingston, 112
Saunders-Roe SR.45 Princess, 83
Scottish Aviation, 284

Self, Sir Henry, 82, 193, 195, 214
Shenstone, Beverley, 221, 319
Short Brothers, 101
  Solent, 215
  Stirling, 36
Sikorsky S-51, 220
Sinclair, Sir Archibald, 91, 93, 94, 147
Smith, C. R., 130, 179
Stansted, 292
Straight, Whitney, 18, 209, 216
Sunday Times, The, 70, 85, 87, 168
Swinton, Lord, 133, 135

Thompson, George M., 90, 127
Trenchard, Lord, 127, 239

UK bases leased to USA, 114
USAAF 8th AF, 58, 60
  96th BG, 62, 134

Verdon Smith, Sir Reginald, 236
Vickers-Armstrongs, 101
  Viking, 217, 219
  Viscount, 83, 212, 220
V-weapons, 117

Wallis, Wg Cdr Kenneth, 266
Warner, Edward P., 109, 115
Washington, DC, 70, 175
Westminster School, 7
Whittle, Sir Frank, 16, 163
Winster, Lord, 203
Wood, John V., 216
Wren, Flt Lt E. A. 'Chris', 58

Yerex, Lowell, 158